SLAVERY AND ANTISLAVERY IN SPAIN'S ATLANTIC EMPIRE

EUROPEAN EXPANSION & GLOBAL INTERACTION

General Editor: Seymour Drescher, *University Professor, Department of History, University of Pittsburgh*
Editor Emeritus: Pieter Emmer, *Institute for the History of European Expansion, Leiden University*

It may be said that the question of how the technology, languages, institutions, and even pastimes of Western Europe came to dominate global civilization—even came to create that civilization—is the greatest historical question of modern times. Yet scholars have paid relatively little attention to this veritable monumental phenomenon. This new series is designed to offer a forum for debate and bring new research to light.

VOLUME 1
The Language Encounter in the Americas, 1492–1800
Edited by Edward G. Gray and Norman Fiering

VOLUME 2
The Jews and the Expansion of Europe to the West, 1400–1800
Edited by Paolo Bernardini and Norman Fiering

VOLUME 3
The Dutch-Munsee Encounter in America: The Struggle for Sovereignty in the Hudson Valley
Paul Otto

VOLUME 4
The Sounds of Silence: Nineteenth-Century Portugal and the Abolition of the Slave Trade
João Pedro Marques

VOLUME 5
The Dutch Slave Trade, 1500–1850
Pieter Emmer

VOLUME 6
Possessing the World: Taking the Measurements of Colonisation from the 18th to the 20th Century
Bouda Etemad

VOLUME 7
Pious Pursuits: German Moravians in the Atlantic World
Edited by Michelle Gillespie and Robert Beachy

VOLUME 8
Who Abolished Slavery? Slave Revolts and Abolitionism: A Debate with João Pedro Marques
Edited by Seymour Drescher and Pieter Emmer

VOLUME 9
Slavery and Antislavery in Spain's Atlantic Empire
Edited by Josep M. Fradera and Christopher Schmidt-Nowara

SLAVERY AND ANTISLAVERY IN SPAIN'S ATLANTIC EMPIRE

※

Edited by
Josep M. Fradera
and
Christopher Schmidt-Nowara

berghahn
NEW YORK • OXFORD
www.berghahnbooks.com

First published in 2013 by
Berghahn Books
www.berghahnbooks.com

©2013, 2016 Josep M. Fradera and Christopher Schmidt-Nowara
First paperback edition published in 2016

All rights reserved. Except for the quotation of short passages
for the purposes of criticism and review, no part of this book
may be reproduced in any form or by any means, electronic or
mechanical, including photocopying, recording, or any information
storage and retrieval system now known or to be invented,
without written permission of the publisher.

Library of Congress Cataloging-in-Publication Data

Slavery and antislavery in Spain's Atlantic empire / edited by Josep M. Fradera and Christopher Schmidt-Nowara.
   p. cm. — (European expansion & global interaction ; v. 9)
Includes bibliographical references and index.
ISBN 978-0-85745-933-6 (hardback) — ISBN 978-1-78533-026-1 (paperback)
ISBN 978-0-85745-934-3 (ebook)
   1. Slave trade—Caribbean Area—History. 2. Slave trade—Latin America—History. 3. Slavery—Caribbean Area—History. 4. Slavery—Latin America—History. 5. Antislavery movements—Caribbean Area—History. 6. Antislavery movements—Latin America—History. 7. Spain—Colonies—America—History. I. Fradera, Josep Maria. II. Schmidt-Nowara, Christopher, 1966–
   HT1052.5.S58 2013
   306.3'6209729—dc23

2012037871

British Library Cataloguing in Publication Data

A catalogue record for this book is available from the British Library

ISBN 978-0-85745-933-6 hardback
ISBN 978-1-78533-026-1 paperback
ISBN 978-0-85745-934-3 ebook

To Althea and Pere

In Memoriam
Christopher Schmidt-Nowara

My colleague and friend Chris died unexpectedly in Paris on June 27, 2015. He had been the heart and soul behind the publication of this book, which now has reached its paperback edition. Having originated in a gathering of historians at Barcelona's Pompeu Fabra University, from the very beginning both he and the local hosts had thought of publishing the papers as a collective book. Our aim was to make available a broad-ranging and up-to-date history of slavery and emancipation in the Hispanic world, and we looked to colleagues from a wide range of backgrounds for help. That this task was a shared one would not anyone surprise anyone who knew Chris. His dedication and enthusiasm had long served as a bridge between Catalan, Spanish, and American historians interested in slavery, popular politics, and empires. That he is no longer with us is a loss we all feel, along with the warmth of remembrance. In the name of all the authors, I dedicate this second edition to the scholar who did the most to inspire this collective work.

Josep M. Fradera

Contents

List of Illustrations — ix

Acknowledgments — xi

Introduction. Colonial Pioneer and Plantation Latecomer — 1
  Josep M. Fradera and Christopher Schmidt-Nowara

Chapter 1. The Slave Trade in the Spanish Empire (1501–1808): The Shift from Periphery to Center — 13
  Josep M. Delgado Ribas

Chapter 2. Portuguese Missionaries and Early Modern Antislavery and Proslavery Thought — 43
  Luiz Felipe de Alencastro

Chapter 3. The Economic Role of Slavery in a Non-Slave Society: The River Plate, 1750–1860 — 74
  Juan Carlos Garavaglia

Chapter 4. Slaves and the Creation of Legal Rights in Cuba: *Coartación* and *Papel* — 101
  Alejandro de la Fuente

Chapter 5. Cuban Slavery and Atlantic Antislavery — 134
  Ada Ferrer

Chapter 6. Wilberforce Spanished: Joseph Blanco White and Spanish Antislavery, 1808–1814 — 158
  Christopher Schmidt-Nowara

Chapter 7. Spanish Merchants and the Slave Trade: From Legality to Illegality, 1814–1870 — 176
  Martín Rodrigo y Alharilla

Chapter 8. La *Amistad*: Ramón Ferrer in Cuba and
the Transatlantic Dimensions of Slaving and Contraband Trade   200
  Michael Zeuske and Orlando García Martínez

Chapter 9. Antislavery before Abolitionism: Networks and
Motives in Early Liberal Barcelona, 1833–1844   229
  Albert Garcia Balañà

Chapter 10. Moments in a Postponed Abolition   256
  Josep M. Fradera

Chapter 11. From Empires of Slavery to Empires of Antislavery   291
  Seymour Drescher

Selected Bibliography   317

Notes on Contributors   322

Index   324

Illustrations

Figures

8.1	Death of Capt. Ferrer	210

Tables

1.1	Slave Population in the Caribbean (1770)	30
3.1	Buenos Aires, 1813–1815, Dependent Workforce by Zones	79
3.2	Distribution of the Masculine Nondomestic Workforce in the Countryside	79
3.3	Distribution of Slaves (Male and Female) by the Zones of the Countryside	81
3.4	Workforce: Domestic Workforce, Slaves and Peons, San Isidro, 1815	83
3.5	Capital Goods, 1754–1815	84
3.6	Slaves and Levels of Capitalization in the Diverse UP, 1754–1815	84
3.7	Capital Goods and the Slaves on the Estancia Laguna de Barragán	85
3.8	Slaves and Peons in the UP with Greatest Number of Individuals, 1813–1815	86
3.9	Rivero's Estancias in 1805	87

3.10 Population of Mendoza, 1777–1812   89

3.11 Mendoza, Means of Production, 1750–1821   92

7.1 Estimate of Direct Profits Obtained from African Slave Sales
     in Cuba, 1820–1867   178

Graphs

3.1 Population Pyramid of Slaves in rural Buenos Aires, 1813–1815   77

3.2 Population Pyramid in Rural Buenos Aires, 1813–1815   78

3.3 Slaves in San Isidro, 1815   82

3.4 Slaves in Areco Arriba, 1815   82

Maps

3.1 Two Slaveholding Regions in the Río de la Plata   75

3.2 Environs of Buenos Aires   80

8.1 Atlantic Itinerary of the Schooner Amistad   208

8.2 Map of Cuba Showing Guanaja ("Cuba 1850")   212

8.3 Map of the Sugar Regions of Cuba   214

Acknowledgments

Our most grateful acknowledgments go to our friend and colleague Stephen Jacobson, who diligently laid the groundwork for our meeting at the Universitat Pompeu Fabra (Barcelona) in June 2009. He was ably assisted by Teresa Segura. Thanks also to Rebecca Scott and Jean Hébrard for their contributions to our conversations in Barcelona. The necessary financial support for our meeting, writing, and revising was provided by the Departament d'Humanitats of the Universitat Pompeu Fabra, the Institut Universitari d'Historia Jaume Vicens Vives, Fordham University's Office of Research, the Prince of Asturias Chair in Spanish Culture & Civilization at Tufts University, and several grants from Spain's Ministerio de Ciencia e Innovación: HAR 2008-04960-E, HAR2009-07103, and Proyecto I+D+I HAR 2009-C02-C01. Thanks also to the three readers for the press who provided constructive feedback. Mary Ellen Kerans, Mary Savage, and Ailish Maher made the careful translations of the articles by Josep M. Delgado, Juan Carlos Garavaglia, Martín Rodrigo, Albert Garcia Balañà, and Josep M. Fradera. Our thanks to them.

INTRODUCTION
Colonial Pioneer and Plantation Latecomer

Josep M. Fradera and Christopher Schmidt-Nowara

The history of slavery and antislavery in the Spanish Empire fits uneasily into the narrative of Atlantic history. Spain was the first Atlantic empire to establish sugar plantations in its American colonies, but it was also the last to engage directly in the transatlantic slave trade. Just as antislavery ideals seemed to gain the upper hand in the British and French Empires, pro-slave trade and pro-slavery policies were on the ascent in Spain and its colonies. As most of Spanish America achieved independence in the 1820s and the new republics abolished the slave trade to their shores and took gradual steps against slavery, too, Spain retained Cuba, the single largest plantation society in Spanish colonial history. This apparent discord with the Atlantic currents of slave trading, plantation slavery, and abolitionism has often made the Spanish Empire seem a case apart in the study of slavery and abolition. Our view, however, is that this apparently singular case is in reality part of the very historical trends it would seem to defy.

This historiographical isolation has a clear explanation. For the Portuguese, Dutch, French, English, and Danish, the enslavement of people of African descent was a central institution in their colonial systems. Such was not the case until a quite late date in the Spanish domains when the overseas empire was already entering a period of crisis. This difference, which is often ignored in the historiography of Atlantic-world slavery, suggests the urgency of reconsidering the Spanish Empire in dialogue with the international scholarship on the slave trade, slavery, and abolitionism. This reconsideration is the purpose of this collection, the result of a meeting in Barcelona that was the culmination of contacts for more than a decade among a small international academic community interested in these issues.

African slavery was already a well-established institution in the fifteenth-century Iberian Peninsula because of the increasingly frequent contacts of its inhabitants with the African coasts. As in so many other things, the Portuguese were far in advance of their Iberian neighbors and competitors, which Luiz Felipe de Alencastro's essay shows us in great detail. Castile was a rising power, but it remained inward-looking until very late. The domains of the Crown of Aragon in the Mediterranean did not develop the forms of enslavement that the Portuguese were forging on the West African coast and the islands of the Eastern Atlantic. The pioneering works of Charles Verlinden still explain these processes very well.[1] When the Crown of Castile (and by extension the Spanish monarchy) did embark upon expansion in the Eastern Atlantic, it confronted the challenge of how to support its endeavors. The slave traffic from Africa and the formation of pockets of slave labor in distant possessions were crucial aspects of the dilemma that Castile confronted, i.e., expansion into the Atlantic or retreat to Europe and North Africa. The conquest of the Canaries sharpened this dilemma but without providing a definitive solution. The Castilian conquerors enslaved and decimated the archipelago's population so that the islands had to be repopulated by migrants from the Spanish dominions and southern Portugal.[2]

The same problem but on a far greater scale, reemerged with the conquest and colonization of the West Indies, which, as in the Canary Islands, destroyed the indigenous population. This time, however, because of the development of Portuguese networks of slave trading in the Eastern Atlantic, the Spanish monarchy turned to African captives, carried by Portuguese slavers, as an alternative to the forced labor of the indigenous population. As is well known, even Bartolomé de las Casas briefly advocated this solution, though he came to regret it when he learned more about the conduct of the Portuguese slavers in Africa.[3] This was the beginning of the forced displacement of Africans to the Spanish Empire, a tragic story that lasted for centuries, from the conquest until the second half of the nineteenth century.

The demographic crisis in the mainland colonies again put the question of African slavery on the table, as well as the possibility of enslaving the conquered Indians. The Spanish crown discarded the latter option after agonizing debate, though the enslavement of Indians on the edges of Spanish settlement remained a key feature of the new empire.[4] In the end, however, the societies that took shape in the mid sixteenth century relied on complex forms of forced indigenous labor as the foundation of the colonial order, sometimes on a massive scale, as in the mining sector of Upper Peru. At the margins of the systems of forced indigenous labor, the colonizers introduced flexible and varied forms of African slavery, both in the towns and the countryside, a division of labor that would persist until the collapse of the empire in the early nineteenth century.[5] What would distinguish these colonial societies from the other Atlantic empires was the very late appearance of large-scale plantation slavery, with its great productive capacity and social disorder.

The long duration of slave trafficking and slavery, and their comparatively small role in the construction of Spain's Atlantic empire, raises questions that are still unresolved. The first concerns the institutional mechanisms of forced migration from Africa to the territories of the Spanish monarchy in America. The second corresponds to its quantitative aspects, arising from the data gathered by David Eltis and David Richardson and their colleagues.[6] Josep M. Delgado Ribas's essay shows some of the peculiarities of the Spanish experience. Unlike other European colonial systems in the Atlantic, the Spanish never developed a direct connection between their American dominions and the African coast until very late, almost at the end of empire. The causes were not technical: Spanish explorers were the first to circumnavigate the globe, and there was continuous maritime contact between the two sides of the Atlantic, as well as across the Pacific. The reasons for Spain's absence from Africa lay in the specialization in slave trading developed, debated, and refined by Spain's Portuguese neighbors (see Alencastro's essay), the main carriers of slaves to the Spanish Indies, a dependency enhanced when the two monarchies were combined in 1580 through dynastic maneuvering.

For Spain's rulers, the most important consideration was the security of its Caribbean and continental colonies. Security came to the fore almost from the beginning of colonization because French and northern European piracy and privateering against Spanish shipping had major effects on shipments of precious metals and tobacco to Seville. Protecting the Indies became the central concern of the state in a context of increased hostilities and became the fundamental motive for institutional adjustments that would turn the empire into a mercantilist power. Because of this desire for security and religious unity, Spain forged its peculiar economic system. Imperial policy, which was not in the least arbitrary, integrated military and fiscal issues as a whole into a strong protectionist regime. In other words, the religious and political conflicts of the era, more than precise ideas about how to organize the imperial economy, dictated Spanish involvement (or rather, lack of involvement) with the slave trade. The *asiento* system, the contracts between the Crown and foreign companies, which persisted until the late eighteenth century, guaranteed a strict control of the traffic and the Crown's proprietary interests, the highest priorities for the governing bodies of the empire.

Moreover, this arm's-length relation to the slave trade jived with the concerns of sixteenth-century Spanish clerics and jurists such as Tomás de Mercado, Bartolomé de las Casas, and Bartolomé de Albornoz, who, although recognizing the legitimacy of slavery, attacked the Portuguese slave traffic as a form of plunder that violated Christian norms. Their dismay at Portuguese raiding and duplicity in Africa, criticisms of the mechanics of the slave trade that resembled those made more than two hundred years later by British abolitionists such as William Wilberforce and Thomas Clarkson, led them to question whether Spaniards could be justified in purchasing African slaves from the Portuguese traffic. Thus, in contrast to the Portuguese missionaries in Africa and Brazil, who elaborated pragmatic yet sophisticated defenses of the traffic between Angola and Brazil, the topic closely examined in Alencastro's essay, Spanish clerics abhorred the traffic, contributing to the factors shaping Spain's indirect connection to the slave trade until the end of the eighteenth century. When the Spanish Crown did sanction direct trading with Africa and other American colonies for slaves in 1789, Spanish criticisms of this reform harkened back to the earlier system of slavery without slave trading, as Christopher Schmidt-Nowara shows in his study of Spanish antislavery in the early nineteenth century.[7]

The asiento system served its purpose because African slavery had a relatively small role in a social system whose foundation was Indian labor. The union of the crowns of Portugal and Castile between 1580 and 1640 produced a surge in the Portuguese traffic to Spanish America but without leading to the consolidation of large-scale plantation agriculture.[8] Slaves worked throughout the colonial economies, on plantations and small farms, as skilled artisans, and as soldiers; they gathered in religious brotherhoods and other associations, and some found routes to freedom sanctioned by Spanish law and colonial customs (the subject of Alejandro de la Fuente's article). Others sought escape and freedom through flight (a phenomenon, marronage, that did cut across the different colonial regimes).[9] The plantation was not absent from the Spanish realms—sugar planting in the early Hispanic Caribbean and in Central Mexico in the sixteenth and seventeenth centuries, for example, relied on enslaved labor—but it did not occupy the central place that it would in other Atlantic empires beginning in the seventeenth century.[10]

The particular development of slavery in the Spanish Indies is made clear when we contrast it to the massive flow of African captives to the plantation zones of Northeastern Brazil and, beginning with Barbados in the mid seventeenth century, to the Caribbean settlements of imperial rivals. For the Spaniards, slavery was complementary to the exploitation of the indigenous workers, whereas for their European competitors (including the Portuguese), slavery gradually became the central labor system.[11] This contrast, which came into sharp relief by the early eighteenth century, is at the core of the major questions for scholars studying the era of European colonization because Spain's divergence was the starting point of the different paths taken by the European colonial regimes.

European expansion in the New World unfolded in diverse social landscapes: areas for fishing, ranching, hunting and trade with native peoples in North America and in frontier areas across the Americas; the *sui generis* reproduction of the European agricultural landscape in New England and several frontier zones in the Spanish and Portuguese Empires; genuinely multiethnic societies in the Spanish Empire, organized since the mid sixteenth century for the production of precious metals; extensive slave economies in the settlements of the Portuguese, Dutch, British, and French in Northeastern Brazil (and Minas Gerais in the eighteenth century), the Caribbean, and the southern part of North America. This topography of societies, articulated on diverse foundations, should be considered as a whole, integrating the economic, demographic, environmental, and political factors. Politics most clearly determined what was viable and what was not. In other words, once the competition among empires reached a certain degree of intensity in the Atlantic world, the logic of imperial rule as a whole became the determining factor.

Viewed from this perspective, two models of production and social organization allowed the maintenance of overseas empires by generating sufficient revenues: the mining of precious metals in the Spanish case and plantation slavery in the others. The other models of colonial economy that we mentioned above were on the margins of the main sources of wealth that ensured the reproduction of empire. Both possibilities, mining in the Spanish Empire and the slave plantation in the others, developed from well-known impulses and rationales. Moreover, once they reached a certain level of development, they became the driving forces behind these societies. In the medium term, the distinctive economies of the colonial settlements took shape in response to long-term imperial dynamics and the whole chain of decision making regarding the free and forced labor of Indians, the organization of chartered companies for the slave trade, the emergence of the plantation as an economic and social unit, and the military imperatives of organizing transatlantic territorial rule.

In the eighteenth century, slavery in Spanish America began to change, partly in response to demands by colonial planters and miners, partly because of the fiscal needs of Spain's Bourbon monarchy, which found itself involved in almost constant wars in Europe and the Americas.[12] As it expanded spatially, slave labor was projected onto an imperial structure that bound together very different societies and economies. Nonetheless, even though slavery spread in this period it still differed from the massive plantation slavery characteristic of Brazil and the non-Hispanic Caribbean. This gradual change allowed for continuity in the legal and institutional frameworks that had governed the forms of slavery and emancipation since the sixteenth century, as shown by Alejandro de la Fuente in his essay, a structure that contrasted sharply with that of other countries.

In describing this difference, we are not seeking to revive Frank Tannenbaum's theses about slavery, freedom, and race in the Americas.[13] Rather, we are emphasizing that slavery in the Americas was far from uniform because it developed in distinct institutional, political, ideological, and economic situations. The development of a large-scale plantation economy came very late to the Spanish colonies and did so precisely when abolitionism and the condemnation of slave labor and slave trafficking were gaining ground in the Atlantic world. What triggered the demand for more slave labor in the Spanish colonies was the gradual emergence of plantation production and easing of restrictions on the slave trade to different corners of the empire. Colonial planters began lobbying the empire's governing bodies, such as the Council of the Indies, for a complete deregulation of the slave trade. Economic changes, geopolitical considerations, and the demands from the colonies led to a rethinking of the role of slavery by the monarchy's top officials. The most dramatic outcome of this process was the liberalization of trade with Africa and other American colonies and the liquidation of the asiento system in 1789. These radical changes put Spain in a delicate position because it became more vulnerable to British pressure, especially after slave-trade abolition in the British Empire, a situation that would remain unchanged until the late nineteenth century, as David Murray has shown.[14] At the same time, paradoxically, many Spaniards demanded the suppression of the odious commerce because they believed that abolition would be Spain's passport for entry into the modern world.

The transformation of slavery in the Spanish world was not only an economic phenomenon nor did it take place in isolation from other imperial regimes. On the contrary, it happened during the most severe crisis of the European Atlantic empires. The eighteenth-century wars destabilized most of the colonial systems in the Atlantic, despite the great differences in their political structures. The high cost of war and its negative impact on the finances of European governments led to unusual pressures on the overseas possessions, undermining the stability of the metropole-colony connection. During the crisis of the Atlantic empires, slavery was destroyed in some parts of the Americas but then emerged more vigorous than ever in others.¹⁵ The Haitian Revolution was the pivotal event, but it was not the only one: the suppression of the slave trade to the British West Indies in 1807; U.S. abolition of the slave trade shortly thereafter; the Luso-British treaty of 1810 to abolish the traffic from certain African ports (but not from Angola); and, finally, the weakening or collapse of slavery in most of the Spanish Empire during the wars of separation in the 1810s and 1820s were also transformative.

While abolition was gaining ground, so too was a new phase of mass enslavement and the spectacular growth of the plantation economy in Cuba, Brazil, and the southern United States, what one scholar has called the "second slavery" of the Atlantic world, new in its productive capacity, market conditions, technological sophistication, and voracious appetite for enslaved and other unfree workers.¹⁶ That slavery could expand so dramatically in Spain's last colonies, Cuba and to a lesser degree Puerto Rico, is a further demonstration of the plasticity and flexibility of the institution and the enormous power of entrenched interests. Yet, slavery thrived in Spanish America only under Spanish rule; in the rest of the old continental empire it entered into decline despite the resistance of slave owners. Such was true even in those areas with the potential for growth in plantation slavery in the late eighteenth century, such as Venezuela and parts of New Granada/Colombia. Juan Carlos Garavaglia shows conclusively the strange vitality of an institution deeply rooted in colonial life in the Río de la Plata and its steady decline in the decades following the collapse of the empire. Two factors shaped this process of decline and abolition. First, the wars of national liberation mobilized huge numbers of slaves and former slaves, in both the royalist and independence armies, undermining the institution's stability and legitimacy. Independence and abolition, even if gradual, went hand-in-hand in Spanish America. The same would be true in the greatest Spanish-American slave society, Cuba, later in the nineteenth century.¹⁷ Second, Britain used its diplomatic, naval, and economic leverage over the new Spanish-American republics to force them to suppress the slave traffic to their shores.¹⁸

The challenge for historians is to comprehend the paradoxes at work during the revolutionary cycle that came to a close in the 1820s. Attitudes toward the peculiar institution in the Hispanic world were changing, but slaves were flowing into the last Spanish colonies at the greatest rate in Spain's history of rule in the Americas. Thus, these years witness a complex relationship between the increase in the number of slaves and the opposition to slavery expressed by people throughout the empire.¹⁹ Ada Ferrer and Christopher Schmidt-Nowara's essays, for example, show the variety of sources from which antislavery sentiments could arise. In some cases, networks established in the colonies between slaves and former slaves produced attacks on slavery; in others, the belief held by intellectual and political elites that slavery was neither a reasonable nor a viable alternative for the imperial economy led to an engagement with British and French abolitionism. Nonetheless, at this critical political and ideological juncture, Cuban planters, headed by Francisco Arango y Parreño, forged persuasive arguments about the necessity, even the inevitability, of slave trafficking and the sugar plantation.[20] They decisively shaped metropolitan policies that protected the slave trade and slavery in Cuba, despite the growth of antislavery sentiment and widespread concern over the Haitian Revolution and its influence in the Spanish colonies.

The changes that occurred in the late eighteenth century placed colonial slavery at the center of contemporary discussions. For this reason, we cannot explain changes to slavery in terms of the Hispanic world's inertia, traditionalism, or political, cultural, and religious continuities. Readings of this kind are not only insufficient but also entirely wrong because they ignore the traumatic revolutionary cycle that shook the Spanish Empire between 1780 and 1830. At the beginning of that cycle it was still an empire based upon a foundation of indigenous forced labor; by the end, the reduced imperial system had plantation slavery as its core. The political transformations of the era were also far-reaching, as Josep M. Fradera shows in his essay. Spanish liberals had to overcome their instinctive distaste for the expansion of slavery because of the demands of colonial planters, especially in Cuba. During the Cortes of Cadiz in 1811, the extraordinary power of the Cuban planter class was manifested when it successfully torpedoed liberal attempts to ban the slave traffic and thus satisfy the demands of Spain's principal ally against Napoleon, Great Britain. In the 1810s and 1820s, during the denouement of imperial conflict, Havana's pro-planter institutions and the rising trade with Cuba, now the indispensable foundation of the Spanish presence in America, compelled the Spanish government to ignore its 1817 treaty for the abolition of trade with Britain (the same happened again in 1845). African captives continued to flow to Cuba, reaching historic heights in the 1820s and 1830s.

When metropolitan liberals returned to power in 1836, they had practically renounced abolitionism altogether, an ideological and political commitment to slavery and other forms of forced labor that Fradera explores in depth. From then until 1868, abolitionism was marginal in Spain and did little to affect the great interests on either side of the Atlantic. It was most visible in the literary world and among economic reformers in mid-nineteenth-century Madrid.[21] However, expressions of antislavery continued to surface both in the colonies and in the metropole. Albert Garcia Balañà's essay reconstructs radical abolitionist currents at work in reformist (and sometimes Protestant) circles in Barcelona, where industrial conflict and the close connection with the colonies made slavery a more immediate issue. Studies of Cuban and Puerto Rican slave society show that rebellions and conspiracies to end slavery, as well as everyday use of the law and custom to secure individual freedom and autonomy, recurred throughout the century.[22] Nonetheless, the sporadic antislavery agitation from the 1830s onward attracted little metropolitan support because the defense of the Cuban status quo mattered more to Spaniards.[23] Martín Rodrigo y Alharilla's essay explains why this was so: economic linkages with the Caribbean colonies were a major source of wealth in the metropole and motivated fierce defense of Cuban slavery in moments of crisis. The well-known story of the *Amistad* and its captain, the Catalan Ramón Ferrer, the subject treated by Michael Zeuske and Orlando García Martínez, offers a concrete example of the intense relationship between different regions of Spain and the Caribbean slave colonies. Thus, the weakness of abolitionism was not the result of a failure of liberalism but because of the broad support for Antillean slavery in Spanish society and the metropolitan state. However, explaining why humanitarianism never gained ground in Catholic circles is a question still in need of explanation, especially since, as we have seen, prominent clerics and theologians in the sixteenth century had attacked the transatlantic slave trade in terms that bore some similarity to eighteenth- and nineteenth-century British antislavery.

The persistence of various abolitionist currents in Spain and in the colonies must be kept in mind when explaining the vigor of the attacks on slavery stimulated by the outbreak of rebellions in Cuba and Puerto Rico in 1868 and the overthrow of the Bourbon monarchy in Spain in the same year. Seymour Drescher's essay and his extensive work on these questions shows convincingly that the circumstances that gave British abolitionism its mass appeal rarely pertained elsewhere, an observation that frames Fradera's exploration of Spanish abolitionism and its historical weakness. In Spain, without the intervention of outside factors—the U.S. Civil War and its impact on Caribbean geopolitics, the suppression of the Cuban slave trade in 1867 in response to British pressure, and the emergence of an independence movement in Cuba—it would be difficult to imagine the radicalization of abolitionism in 1868 or the state effort's to abolish slavery in the 1870s and 1880s. The mobilization of free people of color and of slaves in support of the Cuban insurgency represented a point of no return, as Spanish abolitionists acknowledged at the time.[24] After abolition in Puerto Rico (1873) and Cuba (1886), Spain for the first time in four centuries of colonialism governed an American empire without slaves, a new phase of empire that was the briefest of all.

Notes

1. *The Beginnings of Modern Colonization: Eleven Essays with an Introduction* trans. Yvonne Freccero (Ithaca, 1970).
2. On the colonial and plantation complex in the Eastern Atlantic, see William D. Phillips, *Slavery from Roman Times to the Early Tranatlantic Trade* (Minneapolis, 1985); Felipe Fernández-Armesto, *Before Columbus: Exploration and Colonization from the Mediterranean to the Atlantic, 1229–1492* (Philadephia, 1987); and John K. Thornton, *Africa and Africans in the Making of the Atlantic World, 1400–1800* 2nd ed. (Cambridge, 1998). See also Philip D. Curtin, *The Rise and Fall of the Plantation Complex: Essays in Atlantic History* (Cambridge, 1990).
3. Rolena Adorno, *The Polemics of Possession in Spanish American Narrative* (New Haven, 2007), chap. 3; and Lawrence A. Clayton, *Bartolomé de las Casas and the Conquest of the Americas* (Chichester, UK, 2011), chap. 6.
4. Anthony Pagden, *The Fall of Natural Man: The American Indian and the Origins of Comparative Ethnography* (Cambridge, 1982); and David Weber, *Bárbaros: Spaniards and Their Savages in the Age of Enlightenment* (New Haven, 2005).
5. Invaluable works on slavery in early colonial Spanish America include Fredrick P. Bowser, *The African Slave in Colonial Peru, 1524–1650* (Stanford, 1974); and Colin A. Palmer, *Slaves of the White God: Blacks in Mexico, 1570–1650* (Cambridge, MA, 1976). For an overview of urban slavery, see Carmen Bernard, *Negros esclavos y libres en las ciudades hispanoamericanas* (Madrid, 2001). On slaves and early mining economies, see Kris Lane, *Quito 1599: City and Colony in Transition* (Albuquerque, 2002).
6. *Extending the Frontiers: Essays on the New Transatlantic Slave Trade Database* (New Haven, 2008); and *Atlas of the Transatlantic Slave Trade* (New Haven, 2010). See also Herbert S. Klein, *The Atlantic Slave Trade* 2nd ed. (Cambridge, 2010).
7. On Spanish qualms about the Portuguese slave trade in the sixteenth century, see Antonio Domínguez Ortiz, "La esclavitud en Castilla en la Edad Moderna," *Estudios de historia social de España* II (1952): 406–418; David Brion Davis, *The Problem of Slavery in Western Culture* (New York, 1966), chap. 6; A.J.R. Russell-Wood, "Iberian Expansion and the Issue of Black Slavery: Changing Portuguese Attitudes, 1440–1770," *American Historical Review* 83 (February 1978): 16–42; Adorno, *Polemics of Possession*; and Clayton, *Bartolomé de las Casas*.
8. On the Portuguese traffic to Spanish America, see Linda A. Newsom and Susie Minchin, *From Capture to Sale: The Portuguese Slave Trade to Spanish South America in the Early Seventeenth Century* (Leiden, 2007).
9. Of the many works that treat religious and associational life in the colonies, see María Elena Díaz, *The Virgin, the King, and the Royal Slaves of El Cobre: Negotiating Freedom in Colonial Cuba, 1670–1780* (Stanford, 2000); Herman L. Bennett, *Africans in Colonial Mexico: Absolutism, Christianity, and Afro-Creole Consciousness* (Bloomington, 2003); Matt Childs, *The 1812 Aponte Rebellion in Cuba and the Struggle against Atlantic Slavery* (Chapel Hill, 2006); and Nicole von Germeten, *Black Blood Brothers: Confraternities and Social Mobility for Afro-Mexicans* (Gainesville, 2006). On Brazil, see João José Reis, *Death is a Festival: Funeral Rites and Rebellion in Nineteenth-Century Brazil* trans. H. Sabrina Gledhill (Chapel Hill, 2003). For an introduction to the large literature on manumission, see Lyman Johnson, "Manumission in Colonial Buenos Aires, 1776–1810," *Hispanic American Historical Review* 59 (May 1979): 258–279. Manumission and self-purchase were also important practices in Brazil. See for example Júnia Ferreira Furtado, *Chica da Silva: A Brazilian Slave of the Eighteenth Century* (Cambridge, 2009). On marronage, see the classic volume edited by Richard Price: *Maroon Societies: Rebel Slave Communities in the Americas* 3rd ed. (Baltimore, 1996).
10. On the slow and uneven development of the American sugar plantation, see Stuart B.

Schwartz, ed., *Tropical Babylons: Sugar and the Making of the Atlantic World, 1450–1680* (Chapel Hill, 2004).
11. On the transition from enslaved indigenous labor to enslaved African labor in Brazil, see Stuart B. Schwartz, *Sugar Plantations in the Formation of Brazilian Society: Bahia, 1550–1835* (Cambridge, 1985): 3–72; and from indentured labor to slavery in the English and French Caribbean, see John J. McCusker and Russell R. Menard, "The Sugar Industry in the Seventeenth Century: A New Perspective on the Barbadian 'Sugar Revolution,'" in *Tropical Babylons*, 289–330; and John D. Garrigus, *Before Haiti: Race and Citizenship in French Saint-Domingue* (New York, 2006).
12. This is a rich vein of scholarship, but among the many works see Manuel Moreno Fraginals, *El ingenio: complejo económico social cubano del azúcar* 3 vols. (Havana, 1978); Miquel Izard, *El miedo a la revolución: la lucha por la libertad en Venezuela (1777–1830)* (Madrid, 1979); Francisco Scarano, *Sugar and Slavery in Puerto Rico: The Plantation Economy of Ponce, 1800–1850* (Madison, 1984); P. Michael McKinley, *Pre-Revolutionary Caracas: Politics, Economy, and Society, 1777-1811* (Cambridge, 1985); John Robert Fisher, Allan J. Kuethe, and Anthony McFarlane, eds., *Reform and Insurrection in Bourbon New Granada and Peru* (Baton Rouge, 1990); Josep M. Fradera, *Colonias para después de un imperio* (Barcelona, 2005); and Josep M. Delgado Ribas, *Dinámicas imperiales: España, América y Europa en el cambio institucional del sistema colonial español, 1650–1796* (Barcelona, 2007).
13. Frank Tannebaum, *Slave and Citizen: The Negro in the Americas* (New York, 1946). For recent discussions of Tannenbaum's influence and relevance, see Frederick Cooper, Thomas C. Holt, and Rebecca Scott, *Beyond Slavery: Explorations of Race, Labor, and Citizenship in Postemancipation Societies* (Chapel Hill, 2000); and Alejandro de la Fuente, María Elena Díaz, and Christopher Schmidt-Nowara, "Forum: What Can Frank Tannenbaum Still Teach Us about the Law of Slavery?" *Law and History Review* 22 (Summer 2004): 339–388.
14. *Odious Commerce: Britain, Spain and the Abolition of the Cuban Slave Trade* (Cambridge, 1980). See also Arthur S. Corwin, *Spain and the Abolition of Cuban Slavery, 1817–1886* (Austin, 1967).
15. The tension at work in this period between abolitionism and mass enslavement are explored in Robin Blackburn, *The Overthrow of Colonial Slavery, 1776–1848* (London, 1988); Dale Tomich, *Through the Prism of Slavery: Labor, Capital, and World Economy* (Lanham, MD, 2004); Márcia Berbel, Rafael Marquese, and Tâmis Parron, *Escravidão e política: Brasil e Cuba, 1790–1850* (São Paulo, 2010); David Geggus, "The Caribbean in the Age of Revolution," in David Armitage and Sanjay Subrahmanyam, eds., *The Age of Revolutions in Global Context, c. 1760–1840* (New York, 2010), 83–100; Miranda Frances Spieler, "The Destruction of Liberty in French Guiana: Law, Identity, and the Making of Legal Space, 1794–1830," *Social History* 36 (August 2011): 260–279; idem., *Empire and Underworld: Captivity in French Guiana* (Cambridge, Mass., 2012); Rebecca J. Scott, "Paper Thin: Freedom and Re-enslavement in the Diaspora of the Haitian Revolution," *Law and History Review* 29 (November 2011): 1061–1087; and Christopher Schmidt-Nowara, *Slavery, Freedom, and Abolition in Latin America and the Atlantic World* (Albuquerque, 2011), chaps. 3 and 4.
16. See Tomich, "The 'Second Slavery': Bonded Labor and the Transformation of the Nineteenth-Century World Economy," in *Through the Prism of Slavery*, 56–71. Specifically on the growth of the plantation complex in nineteenth-century Cuba, see Moreno Fraginals, *El ingenio*; Franklin Knight, *Slave Society in Cuba during the Nineteenth Century* (Madison, 1970); Laird Bergad, *Cuban Rural Society in the Nineteenth Century: The Social and Economic History of Monoculture in Matanzas* (Princeton, 1990); and Laird Bergad, Fe Iglesias García, and María del Carmen Barcia, *The Cuban Slave Market, 1790–1880* (New York, 1995). On Puerto Rico, see Scarano, *Sugar and Slavery in Puerto Rico*; and Andrés Ramos Mattei, *La hacienda azucarera: su crecimiento y crisis en Puerto Rico (siglo XIX)* (San Juan, 1981).

17. See George Reid Andrews, *Afro-Latin America, 1800–2000* (New York, 2004); and Peter Blanchard, *Under the Flags of Freedom: Slave Soldiers and the Wars of Independence in Spanish South America* (Pittsburgh, 2008) for overviews of slavery and the independence struggles of the 1810s and 1820s in Spanish America. On the Cuban independence wars later in the century, see Aline Helg, *Our Rightful Share: The Afro-Cuban Struggle for Equality, 1886–1912* (Chapel Hill, 1995); Ada Ferrer, *Insurgent Cuba: Race, Nation, and Revolution, 1868–1898* (Chapel Hill, 1999); and Rebecca J. Scott, *Degrees of Freedom: Louisiana and Cuba after Slavery* (Cambridge, MA, 2005).
18. James Ferguson King, "The Latin-American Republics and the Suppression of the Slave Trade," *Hispanic American Historical Review* 24 (August 1944): 387–411.
19. For example, the organizers of the Aponte Rebellion responded to the dramatic changes overtaking Cuban slave society, as Matt Childs shows convincingly in *The 1812 Aponte Rebellion in Cuba*.
20. See Moreno Fraginals, *El ingenio*; Dale Tomich, "The Wealth of Empire: Francisco Arango y Parreño, Political Economy, and the Second Slavery in Cuba," in Christopher Schmidt-Nowara and John Nieto-Phillips, eds., *Interpreting Spanish Colonialism: Empires, Nations, and Legends* (Albuquerque, 2005), 55–85; and Ma. Dolores González-Ripoll and Izaskun Álvarez Cuartero, eds., *Francisco Arango y la invención de la Cuba azucarera* (Salamanca, 2010).
21. On literary expressions of antislavery, see Lisa Surwillo, "Representing the Slave Trader: Haley and the Slave Ship; or, Uncle Tom's Cabin," *PMLA* 120 (May 2005): 768–782. On the Madrid reformist milieu where abolitionism took hold in the 1860s, see Christopher Schmidt-Nowara, *Empire and Antislavery: Spain, Cuba, and Puerto Rico, 1833–1874* (Pittsburgh, 1999), chaps. 3–5.
22. See Childs, *The 1812 Aponte Rebellion*; Pedro Deschamps Chapeaux, *El negro en la economía habanera en el siglo XIX* (Havana, 1971); Robert L. Paquette, *Sugar Is Made with Blood: The Conspiracy of La Escalera and the Conflict between Empires over Slavery in Cuba* (Middletown, CT, 1988); Ma. Dolores González-Ripoll Navarro et al., *El rumor de Haití en Cuba: temor, raza y rebeldía, 1789–1844* (Madrid, 2004); Luis A. Figueroa, *Sugar, Slavery, and Freedom in Nineteenth-Century Puerto Rico* (Chapel Hill, 2005); Guillermo Baralt, *Esclavos rebeldes: conspiraciónes y sublevaciónes de esclavos en Puerto Rico (1795–1873)* 6th ed. (Río Piedras, 2006); Manuel Barcia, *Seeds of Insurrection: Domination and Resistance on Western Cuban Plantations, 1808–1848* (Baton Rouge, 2008); Michele Reid-Vazquez, *The Year of the Lash: Free People of Color in Cuba and the Nineteenth-Century Atlantic World* (Athens, 2011); Astrid Cubano-Iguina, "Freedom in the Making: The Slaves of Hacienda La Esperanza, Manatí, Puerto Rico, on the Eve of Abolition, 1868–1876," *Social History* 36 (August 2011): 280–293; and Camillia Cowling, "'As a Slave and as a Mother': Women and the Abolition of Slavery in Havana and Rio de Janeiro," *Social History* 36 (August 2011): 294–311.
23. Jordi Maluquer de Motes, "La burguesia catalana i l'esclavitud colonial: modes de producció i pràctica política," *Recerques*, no. 3 (1974): 83–136.
24. Rebecca J. Scott, *Slave Emancipation in Cuba, 1860–1899* (Princeton, 1985).

– *Chapter 1* –

THE SLAVE TRADE IN THE SPANISH EMPIRE (1501–1808)
The Shift from Periphery to Center

Josep M. Delgado Ribas

This article was inspired by my reading of *Extending the Frontiers*,[1] a collection of essays, edited by David Eltis and David Richardson, that draw on new data from the Trans-Atlantic Slave Trade Data Base (TSTD2), first published on CD-ROM[2] and for which an updated version is now available online at www.slavevoyages.org. The main objective of this monumental collective research work was to provide a detailed reconstruction of the slaving expeditions that transported across the Atlantic more than 12.5 million human beings who had been forcibly uprooted from their continent to provide labor in the European colonies of the New World. To this end, the project's research team devised a rigorous methodology that aimed to standardize information from the archives of all slave-trading countries by removing duplicated documentary records and combining complementary sources in an attempt to fill existing gaps. As a result of the efforts to compile these data, we are now able to provide aggregate figures, make comparisons, and trace the rhythms and trends of the slave trade plied by the European and United States maritime powers and also provide details of the names, tonnages, and crews of slave ships, their ports of embarkation and destination, voyage duration, the sex and survival rates of slaves, etc. As Eltis and Richardson point out in their introduction to the TSTD2, one of the improvements in the extended database is the new information gathered from searches in Spanish and Portuguese archives on both sides of the Atlantic, which enables us more accurately to estimate the true magnitude of the slave trade carried out by Spain and Portugal.

However, the desire to measure and compare should not distract us from the specific characteristics of the slave trade in the various European colonial systems, particularly in the modern era, or from making distinctions between, on the one hand, slave trading as an essential means of Atlantic expansion and of constructing a colonial structure based on plantations and the preference for slave labor and, on the other hand, slave trading at the periphery of the system as an alternative that only took shape when its secular foundations began to crumble in the last decade of the eighteenth century.[3] What follows is the result of reflections inspired by Antonio de Almeida Mendes' thought-provoking essay "The Foundations of the System: A Reassessment of the Slave Trade to the Spanish Americas in the Sixteenth and Seventeenth Centuries,"[4] published in the above-mentioned collection of essays.

Almeida's work, which makes a key contribution to our understanding of the history of the Spanish Empire in the early modern period, includes aggregated data on the trafficking of slaves to Spanish America during the sixteenth and seventeenth centuries, gleaned from the sparse and scattered Spanish literature on the subject and from new evidence from Portuguese and Spanish archives; he also found documentary evidence of 1,213 voyages, that is, more than double the number given in the first database in 1999. However, Almeida tells us little about how the slave trade fit within the Spanish imperial system. With hindsight, and given the pioneering role of the Christian kingdoms of Spain and Portugal in the enslavement of Africans, it is somewhat surprising that the slave trade did not become integrated in the colonial trading activities of the Spanish merchant class until a very late date.

In the Castilian expansionary period, seizures of slaves, linked to pillage and conquest in the Canary Islands, first occurred in the second half of the fourteenth century[5] and continued through much of the following century, with occasional forays on the coast of West Africa. The Castilians' direct access to the slave supply areas of West Africa was greatly hindered by the Treaty of Alcáçovas (1479) with Portugal, which ousted Spanish vessels from the coasts of Guinea and Cape Verde; it was conclusively terminated at the beginning of the sixteenth century on the orders of Charles V, who prohibited any raids and incursions on the African coasts near the Canary archipelago and banned the transport of Africans from Islamized regions to America. From the 1480s onward, Guinean slaves arriving at ports such as Sanlúcar de Barrameda, Cadiz, or Seville were brought from

Portugal, where they were acquired by Genoese, Portuguese, Florentine, and English traders for sale to aristocrats, agricultural landowners, and manufacturers in Lower Andalusia or land concession holders in the Canary archipelago. Gustav Ungerer does not dismiss the possibility that English traders like William de la Founte, Thomas Malliard, or Robert Thorne, who had settled in the south of Spain at that time and who were active in the slave trade, may also have brought the first black slaves into England through the port of Bristol.[6] After 1520, the capture and transport of Islamized Africans to America was prohibited once and for all, bringing to an end any opportunities for the Spanish to acquire slaves on the African coast directly, at a time when the rapid decline of the Amerindian population in Hispaniola and Cuba and the incipient conquest of the Aztec Empire intensified demand for forced labor to work in the American mines.

From the beginnings of colonization, the introduction of Africans into America was differentiated from ordinary trade in goods and, as such, was subject to heavy restrictions. To prevent the circuit of precious metal imports from being infiltrated by foreigners, the Crown kept slave trading controlled by Portuguese intermediaries away from the route to the Indies. Thus a dichotomy that would be legally upheld until 1789 arose in the Spanish monarchy's Atlantic relations, which distanced Spanish traders from any Atlantic activity involving African ports of call. Although responsibility for the inspection and control of all operations fell to the Casa de Contratación (House of Trade), the issue of licenses to deliver Africans to America became a royal prerogative, or favor, granted at the discretion of the reigning monarch. A royal license authorizing the crossing to the Indies was not only required for slaves, but also for servants of Spanish settlers and even the crews of the ships for which captains and ship owners were obliged to pay high securities.[7]

During the early decades of Charles V's reign, licenses were granted to subjects who had provided outstanding services to the monarchy—such as Cortés, Pizarro, and María Cortés, the widow of Diego Colón (son of Christopher Columbus), royal functionaries, and members of the monarch's entourage—who received the license in exchange for a payment of between two and seven ducats per head and who then renegotiated the licenses with (usually Portuguese) slave traders who performed the operation.[8] Perhaps the most representative examples of this type of royal favor were the monopoly licenses granted to Laurent de Gouvenot, governor of Bresa and a close friend of Charles V. The license allowed this Flemish nobleman to transport four thousand slaves directly from the coasts of Africa to America without putting in at Seville, an exclusive privilege he enjoyed until 1527. Gouvenot resold the license for twenty-five thousand ducats to a consortium of Genovese traders established in Seville,[9] who, in turn, sold on the license but broken down into smaller units. In 1528, in similar conditions and also on payment of twenty-five thousand ducats, a new license to take a further four thousand slaves was granted to the agents of the Welser bankers in Seville, Ehinger and Sayller, to remain in effect until 1533. From that year on, exclusivity was abandoned and licenses were granted, at the request of individuals and corporations, in exchange for a stipulated amount per slave that rose steadily to peak at thirty ducats by the end of the 1570s.

The shift from the license system to the system of *asientos*—contracts negotiated by the Crown with *rendeiros*, important Portuguese suppliers from the judeoconverso diaspora[10]—was officially marked by the contract signed with Pedro Gómez Reynel in 1595. The shift, however, was actually the consequence of the slow transformation of the role of the slave trade in the Spanish colonial system in response to the growing financial needs of the imperial treasury and resistance from the Casa de Contratación in Seville, which for two decades had tried to prevent the lucrative slave trade from permanently slipping out of its hands.[11] The process began during the five-year period of affliction (1552–1556), when Charles V, with all his revenues pledged and on the point of bankruptcy, was forced to take extraordinary measures to finance his vigorous European policies, including delayed payments for fairs, the disposal of military and ecclesiastical jurisdictions, the sale of offices and titles and authorizations to extract money from the Crown's creditors.[12] These emergency measures also included maximizing profits from the emperor's royal slave-trade prerogative. In Monzón in August 1552, the future Philip II, following instructions from his father, who was in Metz at that time, negotiated an asiento contract with Hernando de Ochoa.[13] The terms of the contract stipulated that, on payment of 184,000 ducats, Ochoa would be granted an exclusive license, valid until the end of 1559, to deliver twenty-three thousand slaves, 75 percent of whom would be male, to "the Islands and Tierra Firme" for sale "at a moderate and set price." In addition to this monopoly of the trade, Ochoa would enjoy other exceptional advantages: the asiento ships could leave port without waiting for the fleet, they would not be subject to Casa de Contratación ordinances governing arms and fitting out, and, despite regulations prohibiting any foreigner from traveling to the Indies, foreign partners from allied countries could form part of the asiento administration.[14] In May 1553, complaints from merchants registered in Seville, who considered the contract to be illegal and highly damaging to their interests, forced Prince Philip to call an assembly of theologians to pronounce on the legality of the asiento. Despite minor differences of opinion, all the theologians without exception judged the king's decision to be illegal, considering, moreover, that it might constitute an act of tyranny, and so recommended rescission of the asiento granted to Hernando de Ochoa. The lengthiest and most reasoned opinion came from the prestigious Franciscan jurist Fray Alonso de Castro,[15] who put forward an argument against the royal authority to negotiate licenses for the export of slaves, which could potentially jeopardize the financial plans of the emperor and his heir:

> The sending of slaves to the Indies was not of itself an unjust or illicit act, but is only thus by the King's law prohibiting the transport of slaves to the Indies without his express licence. And since this is the case, it is necessary to examine the purpose for which this law was made. Because if this law were established for the sole advantage of the King, that he might sell those licences and thereby derive money for himself, that law would be unjust.... to make the law for the sole advantage of the King and not for the utility of the Kingdom would be the work of a tyrant and not of a true king.[16]

The arguments of Fray Alonso de Castro and the resistance of the Sevillian oligopolists foiled Prince Philip's aspirations and, on 26 June 1553, he revoked the agreement with Ochoa and returned the 140,000 ducats paid.

Although the license system remained in force until 1595, the monarchy could not ignore the grievances expressed by the viceroys, captains general, and American *audiencias* (high courts) to the effect that the shortage of forced labor was threatening the king's revenues by preventing full exploitation of American mineral resources;[17] their reports were added to others from Spanish plantation owners and settlers who, in addition, insisted that slave prices were being pushed up by inadequate supply, caused by the speculative practices of the license beneficiaries. Moreover, the deterioration of the Crown's financial affairs caused the concessions to be increasingly tied up with the negotiation and renegotiation of loans solicited by Philip II, with those that failed to generate tangible profits for the royal treasury coffers being disregarded.[18] One example of the contracts authorized during the transition period was that agreed in 1556 with the Portuguese banker Manuel Caldeira. *Cavaleiro fidalgo da Casa Real*, Caldeira had been the most important moneylender to King John III of Portugal, who recommended his services to Philip II. Consequently, in 1556 he was already one of the Spanish monarchy's largest creditors, together with Antonio Fugger and Nicolás de Giraldo.[19] This position of strength enabled him to obtain a license, in the same year, to deliver two thousand slaves to the Spanish colonies in exchange for a *servicio* tax payment of fifty-five thousand ducados;[20] the agreement, however, would be systematically hindered by corporate interests associated with the Casa de

Contratación.[21] The case of Caldeira demonstrates that the Portuguese judeoconverso diaspora was involved in the lucrative slave trade before the unification of the two Iberian Crowns, although it acted in open competition with registered traders from the Consulado of Seville who were also trying to gain a foothold in the trade. But the experience of the Sevillian merchant Hernán Vázquez illustrates how this Portuguese network's privileged connections with the slave supply areas and their financial solvency proved difficult obstacles for their competitors to overcome. Vázquez, one of the most active Sevillian merchants on the route to the Indies, had been granted authorization by Royal Cedula, dated 24 September 1561, to deliver one thousand slaves to New Spain.[22] From the biographical data known to us,[23] it does not appear that he had actively participated in the slave trade beforehand. Rather, his main activity consisted of exporting wines from Andalusia and the Canary Islands, principally to New Spain, where he would settle in 1562 to manage his enterprise personally. Until then his business had revolved around Seville and the Canary archipelago; he regularly used the islands as a port of call to benefit from the tax advantages they afforded the Atlantic trade. Vázquez entrusted the Portuguese trader Duarte Rodríguez, well known to the Casa de la Contratación, to act as contract factor in Cape Verde and take charge of slave purchases. As planned, in December 1561 the two vessels chartered by Vázquez set sail from Sanlúcar de Barrameda to take the human cargo, previously procured by Duarte, to New Spain. However, it seems that Duarte's supplier was only able to supply 411 of the 1,000 slaves initially envisaged. Two years later, Luís de Mercado, Vázquez's partner in New Spain, was still trying to obtain royal authorization to use the remainder of the concession.[24] Added to the problems caused by their lack of privileges and only indirect access to the Portuguese *feitores* in Guinea, Cape Verde, and Angola, Spanish traders had to contend with another no less important obstacle, of which Hernán Vázquez had firsthand experience. In 1563, in response to Philip II's plan to put the trade in the hands of a (presumably Portuguese) company, Vázquez approached the monarch with a proposal to create a joint venture devoted to the slave trade and quicksilver exports, with the undertaking to deliver one thousand hundredweight of mercury and one thousand slaves to America each year. The proposal was rejected, probably because it had little in it to attract the Crown. By personally contributing 114,000 ducats, Vázquez hoped to obtain funding amounting to 130,000 ducats from the royal purse—but this was inconceivable to a monarch who regarded the slave trade as a source of quick revenue and not as a long-term commercial investment.[25]

Perhaps the exception to this relentless advance of Portuguese control over slave transport to the Spanish colonies was the license—the first fully fledged asiento, according to the widely endorsed opinion of Rafael Antúnez y Acevedo,[26] — granted by Royal Cedula on 8 November 1579 to the Seville merchant Gaspar de Peralta, probably a converted Jew in origins. According to terms stipulated in a contract that was the immediate precedent for subsequent Portuguese asientos, Peralta received a *merced*, or favor, to deliver 221 slaves to New Spain at a cost of thirty escudos for each license, in this way acquiring an amount equivalent to the capital and interests that he held in *juros* (bonds) in the Casa de la Contratación.[27] In this case, the Crown used the license to repay a debt, shortly after the 1576 bankruptcy. The terms agreed were fairly favorable to Peralta. If he agreed to forgo the fee payment of two ducats per license, he would be exempt from paying customs tariffs and other duties and would be permitted to take slaves on board in Seville, Lisbon, Cape Verde, and "the coasts of Africa." The contract also specified that the slave ships must set sail "under convoy" of the fleet, but entirely separate from it. Finally, the initially established destination restrictions would be lifted in 1580 with the authorization to land slaves in Honduras, Guatemala, Cartagena de Indias, and the New Kingdom of Granada. However, certain features of this contract suggest that what Peralta had obtained was actually a special license for a relatively small number of slaves with no concession for a monopoly over supply. Conversely, although Peralta had previously acted as an intermediary in transactions for some individual licenses,[28] slave trading was not his main business. Gaspar de Peralta, his son Alonso, his brother Agustín, and his nephews Agustín and Gaspar achieved much greater notoriety as *señores de canoas* (pearl traders), extracting pearls from the waters around Nuestra Señora de los Remedios de Riohacha.[29] All the evidence seems to suggest that the slaves delivered under this contract were destined to replace the Guajiro divers that had practically monopolized all pearl extraction activities until 1570.[30]

The final stage in the transfer of slave trade control to the Portuguese — in which neither the Council of the Indies nor the Casa de Contratación played a direct role — took place within the framework of the unified Spanish and Portuguese kingdoms. From 1583 onward, the Spanish Philip II, crowned King of Portugal at the Cortes of Tomar (1582), took over management of the redemptions and revenues of Portuguese establishments on the west coast of Africa; as a further incentive to improve bidding for tenders, he incorporated additional licenses for the direct sale of slaves in Spanish America. In the case of Cape Verde, we know that the first contract was signed, in 1583, between the Crown and the rendeiros Antonio Mendes de Castro and Pedro de Sevilla. One of the conditions agreed was the concession of a license to deliver three thousand slaves to the Indies over a period of seven years in exchange for a payment of one quarter of the sale price. In September 1589, now with the direct participation of the Council of Portugal, the exploitation of Cape Verde resources was leased, on the same terms, to Simón Ferreira, Ambrosio de Taide, Pedro Freire, and Diego Enríquez.[31] When this lease expired, the new contractor, Diego Núñez Caldera, was allowed to retain the concession, even though the first official asiento had been agreed with Reynel. Similar clauses also appeared in leases for Angola and Sao Tomé, at least in the last two decades of the sixteenth century.[32] The incorporation of contractors from Angola, Cape Verde, and São Tomé in the slave trade was, in the eyes of the Crown, an ideal alternative that would replace the licensing system, make the slave trade profitable and find an alternative that would guarantee sufficient supplies of slaves to the Spanish colonies, although the continuing complaints from America show that this final target was never fully met.

The asiento contract signed with Pedro Gómez Reynel in 1595 embodied all the characteristics of the contracts that would follow in subsequent decades. With the guarantee of a nine-year monopoly for himself or whoever assumed responsibility for the contract, a total of 38,250 slaves would be supplied at a rate of 4,250 per year, with at least 3,500 to be delivered alive. They were to be transported in ships unconnected to the fleet, with Portuguese or Castilian crews, in exchange for a payment of 100,000 ducats per year and the obligation "not to trade in the Indies." Reynel was obliged to give up the asiento in 1601 after acknowledging that he had committed numerous irregularities. The contract was managed until it expired in 1609 by Juan Rodríguez Coutiño, governor of Angola, and his nephew Gonzalo Báez Coutiño. Following a final attempt, between 1611 and 1615, by the Consulado of Seville to regain control of the slave trade,[33] a new asiento contract, valid until 1621, was signed in 1615 with Antonio Fernández Delvás. He agreed to transport five thousand Africans a year to Cartagena de Indias and Veracruz in exchange for an annual sum of 115,000 ducats.

This system functioned on the basis of similar contracts until 1641, when the breakout of the Portuguese Restoration War forced suspension of the asientos. In fact, the war interrupted the negotiations initiated in 1638 by the asiento beneficiaries since 1631, Melchor Gómez and Cristóbal Méndez Sousa, to extend the contract by a further eight years, with highly advantageous conditions for the Spanish treasury: in addition to offering an annual sum of ninety-five thousand ducats, they were prepared to write off a Crown debt that amounted to a further four hundred thousand ducats.[34] Reprisals against Portuguese settlers in Lower Andalusia and America, mainly carried out by the Inquisition, prompted the Portuguese to flee Cadiz and Seville; the interlocutors involved in the asiento transaction were among those who left.[35] As Enriqueta Vila notes, the regulation of the slave trade through asientos lasted for four decades because of the additional resources generated to finance the Crown's European wars and despite the *asentistas'* systematic flouting of restrictions designed to prevent the importation of slaves becoming what it actually was: a front for large-scale contraband activities by Portuguese agents in American ports, an activity that justified the sums paid by the asentistas and even the many diverse problems and uncertainties—bankruptcy, lawsuits and prison—they had to deal with in their relationships with the Crown, the Council of the Indies, and the Casa de Contratación.[36]

During the 1640s, the supply of slave labor to the Spanish colonies was apparently uninterrupted, at a time when recourse to supply through fraudulent contraband was impractical, because neither the French nor the English had begun colonial expansion in the Caribbean and the Dutch were just beginning to transport slaves to supply their sugar companies in the north of Brazil. Almeida Mendes states that the end of the asientos caused Atlantic slave traffic to fall sharply to around two thousand slaves a year and adds that the 1641–1663 period constituted one of the most obscure stages in the Spanish Empire's involvement with the trade.[37]

The Portuguese exit from slave trading to the Spanish colonies left the way open for intermediaries from other nations to vie for their place. Even before relations between Philip IV and the United Provinces of the Netherlands had stabilized, enclaves recently acquired by the Dutch in Angola and Congo provided alternatives that would guarantee supply. In 1642, the English traders Burchett and Philips offered to transport two thousand slaves a year from West India Company trading posts in Angola in a proposal that, like others from similar traders, the Spanish refused.[38] From 1648 onward, agents from the West India Company itself would try in vain to obtain asiento contracts from the Spanish Crown, despite the fact that their control over the areas of capture had been reduced by the Portuguese counteroffensive in Angola. Although in 1649 a formal proposal along these lines was also rejected by Spanish authorities,[39] thanks to Wim Klooster we know that at least thirty-eight hundred slaves were sent to the Spanish Caribbean from the island of Curaçao between 1648 and 1657.[40]

The clandestine nature of these imports and the collaboration of authorities in the Spanish American ports allow us to posit that the volume of traffic was greater than estimates to date would indicate. Although officially, and according to agreements made in Munster and The Hague (1648–1650), Dutch vessels were prohibited from trading with the Spanish colonies, they were given access to ports of distress and permission to load provisions and water. These circumstances provided them with the perfect excuse to land human cargo, aided by the permissiveness of the governors and viceroys. Hence, in 1652 the ships *El Sol* and *El Ángel* left the port of Amsterdam fitted out for trade and privateering against the Portuguese and English. The ships made a port of call on the Mina coast to board slaves and, in theory, transport them to Curaçao, although they were forced to dock in Santo Domingo to carry out repairs. According to accounts by the island's inhabitants, when the nature of the cargo was discovered, they brought pressure on the audiencia to negotiate the sale of some of the slaves and undertake to send the money and the fruits of the transaction to Spain registered in Spanish ships for the payment of the corresponding duties. The entire cargo from the two vessels was finally sold in Santo Domingo, and the audiencia authorized the Dutch merchants then to sail to Cadiz on the condition that they first collaborated in the expedition to take Tortuga Island. Once the Dutch had fulfilled their side of the bargain, the audiencia refused to grant the permit, believing, perhaps, that the decision had been taken too lightly.

But protests from the Dutch consul in Cadiz led the Council of the Indies, in a ruling of February 1655, to oblige the tribunal to keep its side of the agreement.[41] This and other even more interesting examples appear to suggest that the connection between Dutch trade and the Spanish colonies was not restricted to cabotage around the Caribbean. In November 1658 the Viceroy of New Spain, the Duke of Alburquerque, informed Madrid that the governor of Campeche had captured a Dutch ship that had landed goods worth forty thousand pesos fuertes "of contraband from Portugal, France and England." An inspection of the vessel revealed that all the cargo belonged to Cadiz merchants and that the two agents traveling on board were also from Cadiz.[42] The perplexity of the New Spain authorities would indicate that this must have been a relatively novel kind of contraband operation, almost certainly linked to the speed with which the Dutch colony in Cadiz had reestablished its connections with the merchant class in the city after 1648.[43] However this was not an isolated case. In the same year, the governor of Campeche, Francisco Bazán, reported to the Council of the Indies that the Keeper of Papal Bulls of Obispado had been caught buying the entire cargo of a Dutch merchant ship anchored within sight of the city, in exchange for gold, silver, seeds, and dye wood. He managed to flee to Spain with the intention of negotiating a pardon from the Council of the Indies. Bazán advised the metropolitan authorities that if they acceded to the offender's petition, in light of the volume of contraband trading involved they should demand a payment of no less than fifty thousand pesos fuertes for the pardon.[44] The problem not only affected Campeche. Again in 1658, Viceroy Alburquerque saw fit to send precise instructions to royal officials in the port of Veracruz on how to deal with Dutch vessels visiting the port and also instructed them regarding the need to avoid any conflict that might upset Spanish-Dutch relations because this would only benefit the French and British. If possible, Dutch vessels should be prevented from putting into port with the excuse that authorization from the viceroy was required. If heavy seas forced a vessel to take refuge, it should dock below the castle of San Juan de Ulúa to ensure that "not so much as a cantlet" be landed and to prevent residents of Veracruz "in any capacity whatsoever" from making contact with the crew.[45]

The frenzied activity of Dutch merchants around Spanish ports in the Caribbean coincided with the beginning of the rise of Curaçao as a major slave distribution hub, of particular interest to the West India Company, which could now only sell to Spanish landowners due to increasingly rigorous mercantilist policies in the French and British colonies.[46] In 1657, the director of the West India Company in Curaçao informed the parent company in Amsterdam that a Spanish merchant had journeyed to the island to establish regular links with Venezuela; these links were consolidated within two years and showed a promising future.[47]

However, the speed with which the mercantile connections that enabled continuity of the slave trade were rebuilt cannot be explained without considering the role played by the Jewish merchant diaspora in Atlantic trade, which found, in the New Jerusalem of Amsterdam, a climate of tolerance favorable to their activities. Sephardic Jews who had emigrated to the capital of the United Provinces from Spanish Crown territories played an important role in reconstructing the international Atlantic traffic network by reestablishing contact with their converso counterparts in Seville and Cadiz during the Twelve-Year Truce (1609–1621). Growing persecution of the Sephardic Jews remaining in Lower Andalusia subsequently forced many to emigrate to Amsterdam, taking with them all the information they had gathered on the workings of Spain's trade monopoly. There they came into contact with distinguished members of the Sephardic community who, from the outset, backed the West India Company project. According to Friedman, in 1658 at least 6.5 percent of West India Company capital was in Jewish hands.[48] One of the most interesting aspects of the period of Dutch predominance in the slave trade, which would continue until the end of the seventeenth century, was the inextricable link between slave trading and goods smuggling. The illegal nature of the two activities meant that the Jewish merchant network in Curaçao did not need to conceal earnings from products sold in Spanish America using the subterfuges that had been customary during the time of the Portuguese *asientos*. For the first time in many years, trade in slaves and goods went hand in hand.

A report prepared in 1661 by the audiencia of Santo Domingo alerted the Spanish authorities to the magnitude of this clandestine trade, carried out with in collusion with merchants and landowners in the Spanish Caribbean. According to the audiencia, three procedures were used to bring goods and slaves into Venezuela, Santa Fe, and Santo Domingo from West India Company warehouses in Curaçao and Aruba. The first consisted of direct purchases by Spanish cabotage traders, who arrived in ships carrying silver, gold, Barinas tobacco, and other goods from the tropics to acquire textiles, arms, munitions, and slaves. Another procedure was for a Dutch firm to be concealed under the name of three or four Spanish front men working for a commission and promoting the distribution of contraband goods in Spanish territory. The third and most sophisticated method consisted of passing off foreign cargoes as seized goods and selling them on as legal by paying a token sum to the royal treasury.[49] According to P. C. Emmer's estimates, 100,000 slaves were landed in the Spanish colonies from Curaçao by one or other of these three means between 1658 and 1730.[50]

The system worked to the satisfaction of everyone except the Spanish monarchs, who, more anxious than ever due to lack of resources, resorted once again to the asiento system in 1664 and thereafter. Probably the most reasonable course of action at that moment would have been to turn directly to the Dutch and English, who were the most competitive slave distributors. But moral obstacles to direct negotiation with the Protestant powers led the Crown to draw up a new contract with two Genoese traders, Domingo Grillo and Ambrosio Lomelin. These men agreed to transport thirty-five hundred slaves per year over a seven-year period, to begin effectively in 1668, in exchange for a payment of 100 ducats per license.[51] To ensure supply, the Genovese contractors first attempted to subcontract the entire asiento to the Company of Royal Adventurers Trading to Africa, but lack of resources prevented the company from fulfilling this commitment. The company's resources were further seriously depleted by the negative impact of the second Anglo-Dutch war (1665–1667), which brought the firm to the brink of bankruptcy.[52] These difficulties of the British suppliers shifted most purchases toward Curaçao. Between 1663 and 1667, agents of the Grillo-Lomelin asiento had transported an average of seven hundred slaves per year to Cartagena de Indias, Portobelo, and Veracruz; however, from 1667 to 1673 the volume of shipments grew considerably. Dutch hegemony over legal trading was consolidated after 1670, when the Genoese titleholders transferred the asiento in force to the Portuguese trader Antonio García, who entered into an exclusive contract with the West India Company to meet the requirements of the asiento. According to J. Postma's estimates, between 1668 and 1674, when the Dutch company went bankrupt, an average of forty-two hundred slaves left Curaçao for the Spanish colonies each year, taking into account both legal and clandestine operations.[53]

The last quarter of the seventeenth century was a turbulent time in asiento negotiations. Antonio García and Sebastián Silíceo began operating under a five-year contract in 1675 but were forced to withdraw the same year, partly due to financial difficulties and partly because of the Crown's failure to meet its commitments. This debacle was followed by a Spanish proposal to the West India Company made through the Spanish trade attaché in Amsterdam, Manuel Belmonte, asking the company to take responsibility for direct legal provision of slaves to the Spanish colonies. An agreement appeared to have been reached in September of that year, but was broken off when the Dutch company refused to accept the condition of transporting slaves directly from trading posts on the African coast without putting in at Curaçao, as this obligation would have precluded any contraband activity out of the Caribbean island. Two fiascos in the same year opened the doors for the Consulado y Comercio in Seville finally to take charge of the monopoly in February 1676 in exchange for 1,125,000 escudos and a voluntary donation of a further 200,000 escudos. The return of the slave trade to Spanish hands, apparently strengthened with the concession to the Cadiz traders Juan Barroso del Pozo and Nicolás Porcio in 1682, was no more than an illusion, however. Just as in previous years of trading, Spanish traders acted as mere front men, on this occasion for the Royal African Company and the West India Company, which cornered the trade from their trading posts in Barbados, Jamaica, and Curaçao. Although the asiento gave this traffic an appearance of legality, it was no more than a cover-up for much more far-reaching operations combining legal and illegal slave trading and large-scale goods smuggling, with the Dutch banker Baltasar Coymans as the main beneficiary. After 1683, efficient management of the asiento was encumbered by a conflict over its control following the death of Barroso. His successor, Nicolás Porcio, was arrested in Cartagena de Indias on suspicion of conspiracy and was unable to return to Cadiz for three years. Coymans took advantage of the situation and took up the asiento, which he held until 1692 despite denouncements of his Protestantism to Charles II by the Spanish partners and the papal nuncio in Madrid.[54]

The appearance of Bernardo Marín de Guzmán in the name of the Real Compañía Portuguesa de África and the return of the slave supply monopoly to the Portuguese in 1692 had little impact on the Anglo-Dutch domination of Atlantic trade; this agreement, together with the one signed with Manuel Ferreira Carvalho immediately before breakout of the War of Succession, made the Spanish authorities more tolerant of the parallel commercial activities of the Real Compañía de África and its collaborators. While clause 17 of the Marín asiento opened up direct routes to ports in Chile and Peru, clause 21 of the Carvalho contract permitted an annual cargo of three hundred tons to be transported from the Canary Islands to America in a ship expressly authorized for inter-American trading and with the right to call at ports in Trinidad, Cumaná, Caracas, Campeche, and Veracruz.[55] This clause may be regarded as a direct precedent of the special permission called the *navío de permiso* granted to the English at Utrecht.

Old Problems, New Solutions: Slave Trade Inclusion in Spanish Atlantic Commerce (1701–1808)

A change in asiento title holding was the first sign of growing French influence on the decisions of Philip V and the main cause of the War of Succession.[56] The concession granted to the Compagnie de Guinée, by virtue of a Royal Cedula of 27 August 1701, put an end to a century of Portuguese-Dutch domination of the slave trade[57] and transferred to the French full control over the supply of slaves to the Spanish colonies.[58] The Compagnie de Guinée was commissioned to transport an average of forty-eight hundred negroes per year under terms that few asentistas had previously enjoyed: expeditions were authorized to sail from French ports to the Barlovento Islands, Cumaná, Maracaibo, New Spain, and Tierra Firme and to deliver between seven hundred and eight hundred negroes to Buenos Aires. Peru would be supplied from Tierra Firme and, to this end, the asentistas were authorized to construct two four-hundred-ton vessels for the distribution of slaves on the Pacific coast. The interests of the Compagnie de Guinée, defended in America by their own *jueces conservadores* (charged with protecting the company's privileges) and factors, also enjoyed royal protection. Their ships were entitled to load, gold, silver, and fruit, free of taxes, in ports where they had sold slaves and to land goods such as food and rough cloth, destined in principle to cover the needs of slaves during the crossing. In addition, article 14 of the contract prevented the viceregal authorities from detaining asiento vessels "under any pretext." In exchange, for every slave transported to America, the Spanish treasury would receive 33 1/3 escudos and an advance of 200,000 escudos against the first remittances.[59]

Despite all expectations, the profits from the enterprise were at best paltry. The French had pinned their hopes on clauses unrelated to the asiento that would allow them legally to cover up contraband practices, but they were greatly frustrated by the breakout of war against England. According to Malamud,[60] the profitability of the Compagnie de Guinée was undermined by insufficient initial capital, a lack of collaboration from the Portuguese authorities in Brazil, the war, and unfair competition from compatriots who carried out direct trade without any restrictions and protected by corrupt bureaucrats.[61]

The signing of the treaties of Utrecht and Madrid represented major diplomatic victories for Great Britain, particularly with regard to trade concessions. The agreement signed in Madrid on 6 March 1713 gave England control over the asiento contract for the supply of slaves for the first time in its history, under conditions that were even more advantageous than those secured by the French in 1701.[62] The basic terms agreed for delivering slaves to the Spanish colonies were similar to those established with the Compagnie de Guinée in 1701, namely forty-eight hundred slaves per year, for each of which the king of Spain would receive 33 1/3 silver escudos and an advance of 200,000 escudos; they were also similar in stipulations regarding the payment of duties, navigation in America, factors, and jueces conservadores. However, a clear difference in favor of Great Britain was the length of the agreement (thirty years) and the inclusion of an additional clause allowing an annual shipment with a cargo of five hundred tons to the asiento titleholders, the South Sea Company, as compensation for losses it might incur in the slave trade.

The annual navío de permiso constituted, in particular, a breakdown of the principles of exclusivity that had traditionally obtained in the route to the Indies, in that legal foreign competition was admitted within the monopoly. The concession, however, was made with certain conditions. The arrival of the English vessel to an American port was to coincide with the arrival of the Spanish fleet or galleons. If the English vessel docked first, its cargo was to be stored in a customs depot until the expedition from the metropolis arrived. Of the profits obtained by the English traders, a quarter would be handed over to the Spanish Crown along with a further 4 percent of the remaining profits. The goods unloaded and taken on board by the English were otherwise free of duties.[63] The Spanish government's inability to ensure that its fleet and galleons arrived on an annual basis led to complaints from the English and the terms of the contract had to be renegotiated in 1716.[64] The new agreement stipulated that the navío de permiso would leave for the Spanish colonies each year in the month of June and would wait in America for up to four months until the Spanish convoy arrived. If the convoy failed to appear, the English were entitled to sell their goods without further delay. The new agreement recognized that the conditions of the license had not been met in the first three years; this proved advantageous to Great Britain because it laid to rest the contentious issues that had arisen with the first two navíos de permiso, the *Elizabeth* and the *Bedford,* sent under the 1713 agreement. The fifteen hundred tons of cargo that the English should have profited from in this period was therefore spread over the following ten years, giving the English traders a concession of 650 tons per year.

Advantages directly linked to colonial trade contained in the treaty of trade and friendship signed in Utrecht on 9 December 1713 and ratified in Madrid the following January[65] provided a strong foundation for the 1713 and 1716 treaties of Madrid. This bilateral treaty of trade and friendship was in reality an endorsement of that signed in 1667 between the two countries, but with express recognition of the *convenio de Eminente*, the *gracia del pie de fardo* (reduction of duties that varied according to goods) and all the tariff reductions that would favor the introduction of imported goods through the customs posts of Lower Andalusia.

The South Sea Company took advantage of a new renegotiation of the asiento in the Treaty of Madrid of 1721 successfully to request authorization to land four hundred slaves per year in Upper Peru and Chile from its trading post in Buenos Aires.[66] The asiento's trading posts in Buenos Aires and Portobelo played the dual role of supplying slaves and harboring European goods from Jamaica and other Caribbean islands that arrived, camouflaged in slave ships, as general cargo assigned to feed and clothe the slaves.[67] These goods were left in stores at the trading post to await the arrival of a cargo vessel, the galleons or the *navío de permiso*, which would enable the goods to be dispatched discreetly. In 1722, the asiento agents in Buenos Aires used the arrival of two cargo vessels from Cadiz to flood the south of Peru and Chile with contraband goods, while stores in Panama and Cartagena de Indias provided cover for the open fair held in the Bay of Leonés by twenty-one ships, mostly proceeding from Jamaica; meanwhile, the *Royal George* (that is, the navío de permiso) and galleons of General Guevara disputed the legal preferences of the Peruvian purchasers in neighboring Portobelo, with the advantage held by the former, which was selling its cargo at two thirds of the price.[68]

In the mid 1720s, in response to English contraband trading, José Patiño gave precise instructions to the royal officials in America to keep a close watch on the activities of the South Sea Company's agents and ships. In October 1724, the Spanish government wanted to prohibit entry of asiento ships coming from Jamaica and Barbados, with the excuse that the slaves they carried were contaminated and would not accept conversion to Catholicism. Protests from the English, who considered that such a measure would violate the agreements of 1713 and 1716, obliged Spain to moderate its position and readmit slaves from the West Indies provided they had not been in these islands for longer than four months. But this did not prevent the controls over the South Sea Company from becoming increasingly onerous from 1726 onward. In December of that year, a Royal Order declared the isthmus of Panama to be an imperial holding and the city's trading post was closed. The English ambassador in Madrid, Benjamin Keene, intervened, and reopening was authorized, with the final decision on whether it would continue left in the hands of the local authorities. Other measures were devised to stop the contraband activities undertaken by South Sea Company slave ships. In 1732, port governors in the Indies were ordered not to authorize entry to vessels with fewer than four slaves for every five tons of cargo; the idea was to prevent slave ships from arriving in Spanish ports in America with few slaves but heavily laden with other goods.[69] Undoubtedly, the effectiveness of the measure depended on the honesty of the functionaries charged with implementing it; yet significant changes must have taken place because the asiento agents added to their long list of complaints the growing disloyalty of the jueces conservadores, who were less willing to accept bribes. Around 1733, this stringency was applied to the inspection of provisions transported in slave ships, which had to be deposited in stores locked with three keys, one to be kept by the South Sea Company's factor and the other two in the hands of Crown officials. All these controls harmed the South Sea Company's interests; twelve of its vessels were detained for contraband activities between 1730 and 1734.[70]

These measures, which forced the South Sea Company to limit its activity to strict compliance with the terms of the asiento, were designed to strengthen the Spanish position in negotiations over pending claims by the government and by the directors of the company. Philip V was demanding payment of duties owed by slave ships and navíos de permiso that had entered American ports under the terms agreed in Utrecht, namely 33 1/3 escudos per imported slave, 25 percent of the total profits from the sale of goods transported in the navíos de permiso, and 4 percent of the rest of the profits. The English, meanwhile, alleged that the South Sea Company had suffered losses estimated at two hundred thousand pounds and that there were no profits to be distributed—although they allowed the accounts from only one expedition to be inspected; they also demanded compensation for confiscations during the conflicts of 1718 and 1726.[71] The Spanish agent for asiento affairs in London, Tomás Geraldino, broached the possibility of winding up the company and settling the demands of both parties. Under his plan, the South Sea Company would pay the King of Spain sixty-eight thousand pounds for arrears in duties and, in exchange, would receive ninety-five thousand pounds in compensation for the confiscations of 1718 and 1726. Although the proposal was approved by the shareholders, in 1737 the directors of the South Sea Company decided to request an extension of the navío de permiso concession. According to their interpretation, the agreement had been based on a period of "thirty trading years," but interruptions had reduced the number of ships sent to seven; therefore, the authorization, which according to the Spanish would expire in 1744, should be prolonged for several more years.[72] The death of Patiño in 1736 and the appointment of Sebastián de La Cuadra as Secretary of State put an end to any possibility of a friendly agreement, however. Walpole succeeded in having Geraldino's proposal endorsed by both parties through the Convention of El Pardo (14 January 1739) and then ratified by the British Parliament; however, the breakout of hostilities was precipitated in October 1739 by the opposition of the Duke of Newcastle (defending the interests of the merchant bourgeoisie), the despatch of an intimidatory squadron to the Spanish coasts and Villarias' inopportune declaration to Keene that, in future, Spain would supply its colonies without foreign help.[73]

The Anglo-Spanish Treaty of 1750, signed after a decade of war, allowed the legacy of Utrecht finally to be settled in exchange for 100,000 pounds to compensate for duties lost by the beneficiaries of the navío de permiso and the asiento.[74] One problem was thus solved—but at the price of bringing back another that had been satisfactorily resolved in the second half of the sixteenth century through the asiento system. The Crown found itself unable to come up with an efficient alternative system that would guarantee a regular supply of slave labor to the Spanish colonies, which would continue to be a market with great potential demand but scarce effective demand. By 1770, Spanish America was home to 66.3 percent of the American population but a mere 12.4 percent of the slave population; much of the African-American population was concentrated in the Caribbean, however, so Spanish settlements were in a minority. The failure of the return to the original licensing system led landowners in the Spanish Caribbean to turn increasingly to Jamaica to cover their needs.

Table 1.1. Slave Population in the Caribbean (1770)[75]

Colonies	Slaves	Percentage of Colonial Population
French	379,000	88.1
British	428,000	85.6
Dutch	75,000	83.3
Danish	18,000	72.0
Spanish	50,000	34.7

Source: Robin Blackburn, *The Overthrow of Colonial Slavery, 1776–1848* (New York, 1988), 5.

The most far-reaching measure of those adopted during the second Bourbon reform period (1788–1792) was the inclusion of the slave trade within the free trade system. In an *Instrucción reservada*, the first Secretary of State, Floridablanca, maintained that the surrender under the Treaty of San Ildefonso of the islands of Fernando Po and Toniobongia (Annobon) by the Portuguese government accorded Spain the right to participate in "the firsthand trade and purchase of negroes" and, therefore, to remove foreign intermediaries who, in addition to raising prices, used the slave trade as an excuse for contraband activities.[76] However, a way of managing the slave trade had to be found before it could be nationalized.

In the period before the Seven Years' War, the fact that the Indies had not been efficiently supplied with forced labor by private asientos helped to foster contraband trading with non-Spanish colonies. A return to the system of private concessions, although profitable from the royal treasury's perspective, only served to encourage smuggling activities on the part of the foreign colonies. After the Peace of Paris (1763), the problem of the slave trade took on a new dimension within the framework of the new priorities of enlightened politics because an appropriate solution would depend on whether the project could successfully make colonial administration in the Caribbean regions profitable. Bibiano Torres has studied in depth the various projects that were considered by the Spanish government between 1763 and 1765 to organize a logical way of supplying the Spanish colonies; finally endorsed was a proposal by Miguel de Uriarte, a merchant based in Puerto de Santa Maria.[77] The asiento contract, approved by Charles III in June 1765, gave rise to the first attempt to organize a triangular trade route from Spain. Uriarte, acting as agent for a powerful group of Cadiz-based traders that became consolidated as the Compañía Gaditana de Negros a few months after the contract was signed, undertook to transport thirty-five hundred slaves per year from the coasts of Guinea and Cape Verde to mainland and island possessions in the Caribbean in exchange for a levy on each slave called the *derecho de marca* (depending on the destination, this amounted to around 15 percent of the established sale price). The company was a complete failure, partly due to the limitations and tax burdens imposed upon it by the contract but, above all, due to the high transaction costs facing Spanish traders who, without their own sources of supply, had to acquire slaves on the Guinean coast. The first and only expedition to comply with the terms of the contract acquired a mere 250 of the 700 slaves it should have delivered. The problem was not so much the refusal of the African trading posts to negotiate with the company's buyers, but rather that the operation was frustrated because the goods brought from Cadiz—agricultural products and ironmongery—fell outside African import trading conventions, under which cotton textiles were the main component.[78] By 1770, accumulated losses—around one million pesos sencillos—forced the company to change tack; abandoning any hope of making a profit from the triangular trade, it began operating as a monopoly redistributor of slaves and flour acquired in the foreign possessions of the Caribbean.[79] During the 1770s and until the demise of the asiento, the beneficiaries earned more from collateral businesses—trade in flour, export of fruit from the colonies and contraband trading—than from the slave trade itself.[80]

The end of the concession to the Compañía Gaditana de Negros and Portugal's handover of Fernando Po and Annobon to Spain allowed for a new approach that was based on the possibility of establishing Spanish trading posts on the coast of Guinea. Floridablanca examined various proposals to nationalize the slave trade, all of which coincided in recommending the creation of a major company that would manage the trade exclusively.[81] However, participation in the U.S. War of Independence forced Spain to establish emergency policies aimed at preventing a collapse of supplies to the colonies. To this end, a Royal Order dated 25 January 1780 authorized American landowners to buy slaves directly from non-Spanish colonies.[82] This decision limited the possibilities of Spain, now at peace, regaining effective control over the slave trade. Under the protection of this authorization, "Anglo-Americans [suppliers from Baltimore and Philadelphia] poured into Havana in unprecedented numbers"[83] to provide Cuba with all the necessary inputs for its plantations; a frustrated Gálvez ordered this trade to be interrupted in August 1782, although this did not come about, in fact, until 1785.[84] In the ensuing years, protected by legal but informal networks, North American trade with Cuba continued uninterrupted despite being prohibited under Spanish law[85] and the legal slave trade—once again organized on the basis of private, region-based licenses—was incapable of competing with the contraband trade because it depended on the same foreign suppliers who were behind the clandestine importation of slaves.[86] It is ironic that Cuba, potentially the most attractive market, was being supplied by an asiento signed by the Spanish Crown with the Liverpool firm Baker and Dawson—"possibly the world's leading slave trader"[87]—which, between 1786 and 1789, delivered 5,786 Africans to Cuba.[88]

The Compañía de Filipinas led Spain's final attempt to exploit a private license obtained in mid 1787 to supply the River Plate area. The firm had decided to try its hand at the slave trade as part of a diversification strategy devised following its difficulties with the Asian trade. According to J.M. Azcona, the company's directors had previously studied the characteristics of the slave market and the difficulties they would have to overcome to enter the business. On the premise that it would be practically impossible to operate without foreign infrastructures, given the lack of information and support of trading posts on the African coast,[89] the company negotiated a concession that would allow it to organize its expeditions from England, use English materials and marine infrastructure, and make the return voyage directly to its point of departure without putting in at a Spanish port.[90] Despite the backing of Baker and Dawson,[91] the enterprise could not have had a more disastrous outcome. The two frigates purchased to transport slaves departed Bristol on 25 February 1788 bound for Bonin on the coast of Guinea, where they loaded one thousand slaves to take to Montevideo.[92] Of the 848 slaves who finally made the crossing, 16 percent died on the high seas and a further 19 percent perished on land as a result of the hardships of the voyage. The 548 survivors, therefore, represented less than 55 percent of the slaves the company had estimated it would need to sell to make a profit. The results of another four expeditions between 1788 and 1789 were no less heartening. Of 2,773 slaves taken on board in Benin, 47.4 percent died either during or as a result of the voyage. Added to these problems was the fact that the River Plate market was already fairly well supplied with illegally traded Brazilian slaves and could not absorb these imports, so most of the slaves had to be sent on to Peru and Chile at the firm's expense.[93]

Floridablanca was approached with private-sector proposals to regroup all the private concessions in a single asiento. Perhaps the most representative proposal was that of creating a Real Compañía para el Asiento de Negros, made in December 1787 by the Catalan trader Bonaventura Fuster.[94] Fuster, like Floridablanca, considered that the objective of this company should be to control all slave trading with the Spanish colonies by establishing "one or more strongholds" on the African coast. To this end, he proposed setting up a company with a fund of 1 million pesos fuertes in shares of two thousand pesos to which foreigners would not be allowed to subscribe. The proposal was rejected, mainly because Fuster had requested public backing that the treasury was not willing to give. In addition to making no reference to any payment of the derecho de marca, Fuster wanted valid private licenses still in force to be suspended and the general asiento to be granted a twenty-five-year monopoly over the slave trade. And as if this were not enough, Spain would have to provide three war frigates to accompany the expeditions and bear the costs of building one or more trading posts on the African coast. Furthermore, calculations regarding the company's profitability were highly uncertain: Fuster had estimated an annual net profit of around 304,000 pesos sencillos, based on an improbably low figure of only 4 percent of the slaves dying as a result of the crossing. On the basis of extrapolations from very recent experiences, such as those of the Compañía de Filipinas, probable losses were more likely to be around 40 percent of captured slaves; the expedition would therefore have found itself with debts of 95,600 pesos, not including "office and other expenses that the company will have in Europe."[95]

The Spanish government may well have opted to retain the traditional system of private asientos based on a close relationship with major international suppliers had the abolitionist movement in Great Britain not gone on the offensive, sparked by the *Zong* scandal, provoked when news spread of slavers who had thrown captives overboard and then claimed compensation from the insurer.[96] One of the emblems of the anti-slave-trade movement was the diagram of the slave ship *Brookes*. The *Brookes*, a slave ship registered in Liverpool, gained notoriety for a voyage in 1783: of the six hundred slaves crammed on board, seventy died during the crossing.[97] There was a public outcry against the inhumanity of the slave trade, led by the influential Quaker pressure group that in the same year had formed the first Abolition Committee. This event provided the group with powerful arguments that led to an increase in the number of supporters for the abolitionist cause, including William Wilberforce and Thomas Clarkson, who were instrumental in bringing the abolitionist debate into mainstream British politics. In 1788, Clarkson printed a diagram of stowage in the *Brookes* that was used by Captain Perry, commissioned by the government to investigate the case.[98] Clarkson's engravings and Perry's report, which described the horrors of the slave trade in detail, were widely distributed by the Abolition Committee and reached the Spanish government.[99] Repercussions soon followed. Baker and Dawson, which in 1788 had applied for renewal of the asiento to supply the Cuban market, saw its proposal refused by the nascent Cuban sugarocracy, who argued that the island's development would be jeopardized by putting the supply of slaves into British hands just as Britain was moving toward abolition.[100]

Finally, a Royal Cedula of 28 February 1789[101] broke with almost three hundred years of slave trading practices by including slaves as a new merchandise within the free-trade model. This regulation, which theoretically only affected Caribbean ports, authorized all subjects of the king of Spain to organize, on their own initiative, expeditions to "buy negroes in any place where there is a market or a supply of them" and to use any means of payment for the transactions. Although the delivery of slaves to America was not liable for tax, some restrictions did apply, such as the requirement to center the trade in a single port for each authorized area—whether Havana, Puerto Cabello, Santo Domingo, or Puerto Rico—and the ban on loading goods for the return voyage. Slave ships sailing from Spanish ports could carry "fruit and commodities" to authorized ports and use profits to acquire slaves in foreign colonies. Foreign trade was authorized on a provisional basis for a period of two years, although foreign ships were not permitted to bring other goods into Spanish ports. With news of the massive uprising of Saint-Domingue on 22–26 August 1791, the concession was extended to Santa Fe and Buenos Aires[102] and the permission granted to foreign traders was prolonged for a further six years.

Although the importance of these measures for the development of slave-based agriculture in the Spanish colonies has been sufficiently documented in the historiography, not so well documented are the repercussions on the trade between Spain and America.[103] Between 1790 and 1796, an average of seventy-seven ships delivered 5,677 Africans to Havana each year, with a third of the vessels and a quarter of the cargo belonging to Spanish traders. In this period, the slave trade became part of mainstream commercial activities associated with colonial trade; unfortunately, it is not easy to document how this interdependence actually developed. The traders' scrupulous care to cover up the nature of their operations is a major obstacle to identifying asientos related to the slave trade in merchants' accounts.[104] In addition, the fact that Spanish traders in the 1790s preferred to confine their coastal trading operations to the British West Indies, particularly Jamaica and the Hispanic Atlantic ports,[105] makes it difficult to trace their movements from Spanish sources. From the information available we can distinguish two distinct phases in what Fradera describes as the "legal period." Until 1796, the demand for slave labor was met by intercolonial trade out of British *entrepôts* in the Caribbean, especially Jamaica. The war with Great Britain and the fear of receiving slaves contaminated by the rebellions that had swept non-Spanish colonies led the Spanish authorities to adopt measures that would affect the slave trade circuit. Las Casas, governor of Cuba—the largest imperial market—prohibited the importation of slaves acquired in non-Spanish colonies and ordered the expulsion of slaves who had been brought to the island from places where uprisings had been reported. Thus only *bozal* (African-born) negroes arriving directly from the coasts of Africa would be admitted in future.[106] This decision was preceded by a series of measures that, although not prohibiting imports from non-Spanish colonies, aimed to stimulate Spanish participation in the triangular trade. Two Royal Orders dated 30 January 1793 and 20th January 1794 attempted to reduce relative costs for Spanish slave trading companies by removing the tariff barriers that raised the cost of acquiring foreign goods destined for the purchase of slaves.[107] A further two provisions in 1793 authorized the purchase and registration of foreign vessels for slave trading and exempted their owners from the *alcabala* sales tax.[108]

The impact of these measures would not be felt until a decade later. Until 1809, successive wars against Great Britain made ocean crossings practically unviable for Spanish ships, except during the short intervals of peace that followed the Treaty of Amiens (1801);[109] neutral North Americans, meanwhile, guaranteed the continuity of the slave trade and redistribution in the European market of colonial goods obtained from the sale of slaves.[110] Thereafter, the entry of French troops in Spain and the consequent change in alliances diminished the risks to Spanish slave trading, which also indirectly benefited from the prohibition of slave trading in Great Britain (1807) and the decline in Dutch activity.

For four centuries, the trafficking of slaves had been regarded as a royal prerogative that was used to reward loyalty, pay off loans, and make tacit alliances with European maritime powers. By the second decade of the nineteenth century, this "odious commerce" occupied a central role in Spanish transatlantic trade and was a regular activity and major source of income for a Spanish merchant class attempting to adapt to the reality of a shrunken empire eclipsed by Britain, which enlightened thinkers, like the Count of Campomanes, considered to set an example for all.

Notes

This essay forms part of the R&D&I project HAR 2009-14099-C2-00, funded by the Spanish Ministry of Science and Innovation.

1. *Extending the Frontiers: Essays on the New Transatlantic Slave Trade Database* (New Haven & London, 2008). See also David Eltis's essay, "The U.S. Transatlantic Slave Trade, 1644–1867: An Assessment," *Civil War History* LIV, no. 4 (2008): 347–378.
2. David Eltis, Stephen D. Behrendt, David Richardson, Herbert S. Klein, eds., *The Transatlantic Slave Trade* (Book & CD-ROM) (Cambridge, 2000).
3. A circumstance that the abolitionist James Stephen was indeed well aware of in *The Slavery of the British West India Colonies Delineated as it Exists Both in Law and Practice, and Compared with the Slavery of Other Countries, Ancient and Modern*, 2 vols. (London, 1824–1830). Both volumes were republished in 2010 by Cambridge University Press in its prestigious Slavery and Abolition Collection.
4. *Extending the Frontiers*, 63–94
5. Manuel Lobo Cabrera, "Los mercaderes y la trata de esclavos. Gran Canaria. Siglo XVI," in *Homenaje a Alonso Trujillo* (Santa Cruz de Tenerife, 1982), 49–50. For a review of the literature on slavery in the Iberian Peninsula in the decades prior to Atlantic expansion, see Alfonso Franco Silva, "La esclavitud en la Península a fines del medievo. Estado de la cuestión y orientaciones bibliográficas," *Medievalismo: Boletín de la Sociedad Española de Estudios Medievales* 5 (1995): 201–210.
6. Gustav Ungerer, *The Mediterranean Apprenticeship of British Slavery* (Madrid, 2008). On the pivotal role of English traders in traffic between Lisbon and Seville, see Consuelo Varela, *Ingleses en España y Portugal, 1480–1515. Aristócratas, mercaderes e impostores* (Lisbon, 1998).
7. Georges Scelle, *La traite négrière aux Indes de Castille. Contrats et traités d'Asiento* (Paris, 1906), 1: 208–288.
8. Elena F.S. Studer, *La trata de negros en el Río de la Plata durante el siglo XVIII* (Buenos Aires, 1958), 49.

9. Antonio de Almeida Mendes, "The Foundations of the System: A Reassessment of the Slave Trade to Spanish America in the Sixteenth and Seventeenth Centuries," in *Extending the Frontiers*, 64.
10. Daviken Studnicki-Gizbert, *A Nation Upon the Ocean Sea: Portugal's Atlantic Diaspora and the Crisis of the Spanish Empire, 1492–1640* (Oxford, 2007), 17–66.
11. Ana Hutz, "Os cristãos novos portugueses no trafico de escravos para a America Espanhola (1580-1640)," Ph.D. dissertation, UNICAMP (2008) 54–55.
12. Bartolomé Yun, *Marte contra Minerva. El precio del imperio español, c. 1450–1600* (Barcelona, 2004), 321–322.
13. "We have it that the *asiento* accorded with Hernán Ochoa has been a good negotiation." Charles V to Prince Philip, Metz, 25 December 1552, Manuel Fernández Álvarez, ed., *Corpus documental de Carlos V* (Salamanca, 1977), 3: 578. Ochoa had made a down payment of 100,000 ducados in May during the fair at Medina del Campo.
14. AGS, Cámara de Castilla, Div. 6, doc. 62. Dictamen de Fray Alonso de Castro. Felipe Cereceda, SJ. "Un asiento de esclavos negros para América el año 1553 y parecer de varios teólogos sobre su licitud," *Missionalia Hispánica*, III (1946): 580–597; Isacio Pérez Fernández, *Fray Bartolomé de Las Casas O.P.: De defensor de los indios a defensor de los negros*, Madrid, San Esteban Editorial (1995): 99–101
15. Fray Alonso de Castro (1495–1558) was undoubtedly one of the most distinguished theologians and juristas in the Salamanca School. In addition to his intellectual authority, he held great personal influence over Charles V and Philip II, to whom he had given outstanding service. He accompanied the former at his coronation as Emperor of Bologna in 1530 and shortly after this ruling, he would form part of Prince Philip's entourage on his journey to England for his marriage to Mary Tudor (1550).
16. Archivo General de Simancas (hereafter AGS), Cámara de Castilla, Div. 6, Doc. 62, opinion expressed by Fray Alonso de Castro.
17. Lorenzo del Mármol's memorial from New Granada expounding the need for five hundred slaves to work in the mines, approved by the full audiencia, led to a consultation of the Junta de Contaduría Mayor to decide on the most appropriate way of effecting supply, whether under the license system, or the asiento. The Junta advised referring the concession to Francisco Duarte for publication in Lisbon and awarding it to the highest bidder. Archivo General de Indias (hereafter AGI), Indiferente General, 741, no. 157. On Duarte, see Enriqueta Vila Vilar, *Hispanoamérica y el comercio de esclavos* (Seville, 1977), 29.
18. In 1586, the abbess of the Convent of Santa Clara of Trujillo applied to Philip II for a license to sell 100 slaves in Peru, which would enable her to remedy the financial hardships of her community. Despite a favorable ruling from the Council of Indias, which agreed to the concession because "it is a holy work" the king's response was emphatic: "tell them to look elsewhere." AGI, Indiferente General, leg. 741, no. 129.
19. Maria da Graça Mateus Ventura, *Negreiros Portugueses na rota das Indias de Castela (1541–1556)* (Lisbon, 1999), passim.
20. AGI, Indiferente General, leg. 737.
21. On litigations involving Manuel Caldeira (also spelled Caldera) in Spanish sources, see, AGI, Patronato, legs. 282 to 289, and AGI, Justicia, legs. 848, 853, 855, 857, 875, 888, and 1182.
22. AGI, Justicia, 865, no. 2
23. Eufemiano Lorenzo Sanz, *Comercio de España con América en la época de Felipe II* (Valladolid, 1979), 1: 136–139; Manuel Lobo Cabrera, "Compañías andaluzas en el comercio canario-americano," *Historia, Instituciones, Documentos*, no. 20 (1993): 197–206; Esteban Mira Caballos, "La Real Compañía Sevillana de azogues y esclavos: un proyecto non nato de 1563," at http://estebanmiracaballos.iespaña.es.

24. AGI, Justicia, 864, no. 7. Luís de Mercado requested authorization to deliver thirty slaves to Mexico under Vazquéz's license.
25. Manuel Lobo Cabrera, "Compañías andaluzas," 201.
26. *Memorias históricas sobre la legislación y gobierno del comercio de los españoles con sus colonias en las Indias* (Madrid, 1797), 137–138. Antúnez mistakenly gives the year of the concession as 1586 and the number of slaves authorized in the license as 208.
27. AGI, Indiferente General, leg. 2060, no. 31, with the text of the contract.
28. In 1576, Peralta took over the purchase and delivery of two slaves to Santo Domingo, under the license obtained years previously by the judge of the audiencia of the island, Pedro de Arceo. AGI, Indiferente General, leg. 2059 no. 103.
29. In 1590, Gaspar and his son Alonso obtained a license from the Council of the Indies to move to Riohacha to take charge of the pearl extraction business (AGI, Santa Fe, 16, R. 27, no. 9; AGI, Indiferente General, 2098, no. 97). Six years later, his nephews Agustín and Gaspar would follow the same path (AGI, Indiferente General, 2060, no. 31).
30. Mª Cristina Navarrete, "La granjería de perlas del Río de la Hacha: rebelión y resistencia esclava (1570–1615)," *Historia Caribe* 3 (2003): 35–50.
31. AGI, Indiferente General, leg. 741, no. 241
32. Vila Vilar, *Hispanoamérica y el comercio de esclavos*, 24–27.
33. In 1609, an asiento was signed with Agustín Cuello, from Salamanca, who had offered the highest bid. However, it was soon discovered that he was merely a front man for the Portuguese merchant Manuel de Cea Brito, in prison for debt. This led to a new period of reflection over whether it was appropriate to continue with the asiento system, during which the Consulado de Sevilla played its last cards. The interruption of legal trading between 1610 and 1614 left the way open to widespread contraband activity. See Vila Vilar, *Hispano-América y el comercio de esclavos*, 42–47; Hutz, "Os Cristãos Novos Portugueses no tráfico de Escravos," 57–58.
34. Vila Vilar, *Hispano-América y el comercio de esclavos*, 53–54.
35. Studnicki-Gizbert, *A Nation upon the Ocean Sea*, 151–174.
36. Vila Vilar, *Hispano-América y el comercio de esclavos*, 77–91.
37. Almeida Mendes, "The Foundations of the System," 82–83.
38. Georges Scelle, *La traite négrière aux Indes de Castille* 1: 484.
39. Linda Heywood and John K. Thornton, *Central Africans, Atlantic Creoles, and the Foundation of the Americas, 1585–1660* (Cambridge, 2007), 167.
40. Wim Klooster, *Illicit Riches: Dutch Trade in the Caribbean, 1648–1795* (Leiden, 1998), 106.
41. AGI, Santo Domingo, leg. 58, r.1, no. 10
42. AGI, Mexico, leg. 76, r. 13, no.71
43. On this issue, see Ana Crespo Solana, *Mercaderes atlánticos. Redes del comercio flamenco y holandés entre Europa y el Caribe* (Córdoba, 2009), 110–111.
44. AGI, México, leg. 370, r. 11, no. 76.
45. The viceroy to royal officials in Veracruz, Mexico 30 May 1658, AGI, México, leg. 76, r.13, no. 71b.
46. Saul S. Friedman, *Jews and the American Slave Trade* (New Brunswick, 1992), 66–69.
47. Johannes Postma, *The Dutch in the Atlantic Slave Trade, 1600–1815* 2nd ed. (Cambridge, 2008), 26–30.
48. Friedman, *Jews and the American Slave Trade*, 64–65.
49. The audiencia to the King, Santo Domingo, 6 February 1661, AGI, Santo Domingo, leg. 59, r. 1, no.3
50. P.C. Emmer, *The Dutch Slave Trade, 1500–1850* (Oxford and New York, 2006), 27.
51. On the Grillo-Lomelin asiento, see Marias Vega Franco, *El tráfico de esclavos con América: asientos de Grillo y Lomelin, 1663–1674* (Sevilla, 1984).
52. K.G. Davies, *The Royal African Company* 1957 (London, 1999), 329.
53. Postma, *The Dutch in the Atlantic Slave Trade*, 37.

54. Postma, *The Dutch in the Atlantic Slave Trade*, 41–42; Hugh Thomas, *La Trata de esclavos. Historia del tráfico de seres humanos de 1440 a 1870* trans. Víctor Alba and C. Boune (Barcelona, 1998), 213–216.
55. AGI, Contratación, 5616, no 6. Postma, *The Dutch in the Atlantic Slave Trade*, 47; Ana M. Rodríguez Bñazquez, "Penetración portuguesa en América a través del asiento firmado por la Real Compañía de Guinea en 1696," *Temas Americanistas*, no. 4 (1984): 18–21.
56. Stanley J. Stein and Barbara Stein, *Plata, comercio y guerra: España y América en la formación de la Europa moderna* trans. Natalia Mora and Luis Noriega (Barcelona, 2000), 150. José Manuel de Bernardo Ares provides an in-depth analysis of the colonial dimension of the conflict in "Tres años estelares de política colonial borbónica (1701–1703)," *Cuadernos de Historia de España*, No. 80 (2006): 171–196; and "Las monarquías francesa e inglesa entre Europa y América desde 1689 hasta 1713: Necesidad y utilidad de la historia atlántica," in León Carlos Álvarez Santaló, ed., *Estudios de Historia Moderna en homenaje al profesor Antonio García Baquero* (Sevilla, 2009), 51–62.
57. Before formalizing the asiento with the Compañía de Guinea, Philip V had to cancel the contract in force with the Portuguese company of the same name, which would not expire until March 1703. "Transacción ajustada entre España y Portugal sobre las dependencias e intereses de la Compañía de Asiento de Negros en la América Española," Lisbon, 18 June 1701, in Alejandro del Cantillo Jovellanos, *Tratados, Convenios y Declaraciones de Paz y Comercio que han hecho con las potencias extranjeras los monarcas españoles de la Casa de Borbón desde el año de 1700 hasta el día* (Madrid, 1843), 32–35. See also in the same volume, "Asiento con la Compañía francesa de Guinea," Madrid 27 August 1701, 35–43. See Carlos Malamud, "España, Francia y el 'comercio directo' con el espacio peruano (1695–1730)," in Josep Fontana, ed., *La Economía Española al final del Antiguo Régimen. III, Comercio y colonias* (Madrid, 1982), 36–37; E. Arcila Farias, *Reformas económicas del siglo XVIII en Nueva España* (México, 1977), 1: 52–53; J. A Rawley, *The Transatlantic Slave Trade: A History* (New York and London, 1981), 65–68 and 105–108.
58. Stein and Stein, *Plata, comercio y guerra*, 145.
59. Scelle, *La Trate négrière aux Indes de Castille*, 2: 335.
60. Malamud, "España, Francia y el 'comercio directo,'" 36.
61. Stein and Stein, *Plata, comercio y guerra*, 166.
62. The text of the *Asiento de Negros* with Great Britain, in *Colección de los Tratados de Paz, Alianza, Comercio . . . ajustados por la Corona de España con las potencias extranjeras* (Madrid, 1796), 1: 99–123; and Cantillo Jovellanos, *Tratados, Convenios*, 58–69. The navío de permiso concession appears as an appendix to Art. 42 of the *Asiento*, 69. The English version, in Charles Jenkinson, Lord Liverpool, *A Collection of Treaties between Great Britain and Other Powers* (London, 1785), 1: 375–99.
63. Colin Palmer, *Human Cargoes: The British Slave Trade to Spanish America 1700–1739* (Urbana, 1981), 9–16 and 59–82; and G. Walker, *Política española y comercio colonial, 1700–1787* (Barcelona, 1979), 111–123; as well as the now classic works by B. L. Brown, "Contraband Trade: A Factor in the Decline of Spain's Empire in America," *Hispanic American Historical Review* 8 (1928): 178–189; and "The South Sea Company and Contraband Trade," *American Historical Review* 31, no. 4 (1926): 662–678; J. O. McLachlan, *Trade and Peace with Old Spain, 1667–1750* (Cambridge, 1940), particularly 44–77, for a detailed study of all the negotiation and renegotiation processes for the asiento; G. H. Nelson, "Contraband Trade under the Asiento, 1730–1739," *American Historical Review* 51 (1945–-1946): 55–67; and C. Nettels, "England and the Spanish American Trade 1680–1715," *Journal of Modern History* 3 (March 1931): 1–31. Particularly thought-provoking are the conclusions drawn by D.W. Jones, *War and Economy in the Age of William III and Marlborough* (Oxford and New York, 1988), 308–317.
64. "Tratado de Declaración y Explicación sobre algunos artículos del antecedente de paz y comercio entre esta Corona y la de Inglaterra," Madrid, 14 December 1715, ratified

by England on 24 January 1716, in *Colección de los Tratados de paz, alianza y comercio*, 1: 359–362 ; Lord Liverpool, *A Collection of Treaties*, 2: 173–175.
65. "Tratado de Comercio y Amistad, firmado en Utrecht el 9-XII-1713, y ratificado en Madrid el 21-I-1714," in *Colección de los Tratados de paz, alianza, y comercio*, 1: 269–355. It is interesting to compare this text with that of the initial proposals made by Lord Lexington. See Cantillo, *Tratados, Convenios*, 115–126, to evaluate the negotiating skills of the English diplomat. See also Lord Liverpool, *A Collection of Treaties*, 2: 66–87. There was a still later Anglo-Spanish treaty signed in 1721, following the War of the Quadruple Alliance (1718–1720), which ratified all previous treaties from 1667 to 1716. See Cantillo Jovellanos, *Tratados, Convenios*, 198 onward; Lord Liverpool, *A Collection of Treaties*, 2: 264–267.
66. Studer, *La trata de negros en el Río de la Plata durante el siglo XVIII*, 180.
67. Arthur S. Aiton, "The Asiento Treaty as Reflected in the Papers of Lord Shelburne," *Hispanic American Historical Review* 8 (May 1928): 167–177; Dionisio de Alcedo y Herrera, *Descripción de los tiempos de España en el presente décimo octavo siglo (1763)* José Mª Sánchez, ed., Molledo (Madrid, 2003), 278–282.
68. Sergio Villalobos, *El comercio y la crisis colonial. Un mito de la independencia* (Santiago de Chile, 1968), 56–57.
69. Palmer, *Human Cargoes*, 137–138.
70. Ibid., 137.
71. Richard Pares, *War and Trade in the West Indies, 1739–1763* (London, 1963), 53; McLachlan, *Trade and Peace*, 117–118.
72. Studer, *La trata de negros en el Río de la Plata durante el siglo XVIII*, 186.
73. On the repercussion of the asiento problems at the beginning of the War of Jenkins' Ear, see E. G. Hilddner, "The Role of the South Sea Company in the Diplomacy Leading to the War of Jenkins' Ear," *Hispanic American Historical Review* 18 (1938): 322–341; Pares, *War and Trade*, 10–28; and McLachlan, *Trade and Peace*, 78–121.
74. McLachlan, *Trade and Peace*, 134–138.
75. Source: Robin Blackburn, *The Overthrow of Colonial Slavery, 1776–1848* (New York, 1988), 5.
76. José Moñino, Count of Floridablanca, *Instrucción reservada que la Junta de Estado deberá observar en todos los puntos y ramos encargados a su conocimiento y examen* (1787), CVIII.
77. Bibiano Torres Ramírez, *La Compañía Gaditana de Negros* (Seville, 1973), 15–38.
78. On this question, see J.E. Inikori, "Slavery and the Revolution in Cotton Textile Production in England," in J.E. Inikori and S.L. Engerman, eds., *The Atlantic Slave Trade: Effects on Economies, Societies and Peoples in Africa, the Americas, and Europe* (Durham and London, 1992), 145–181; David Eltis, "Trade between Western Africa and the Atlantic World before 1870: Estimates of Trends in Value, Composition and Direction," *Research in Economic History* 12 (1989): 197–239. J.E. Inikori, *Africans and the Industrial Revolution in England: A Study in International Trade and Economic Development* (Cambridge, 2002), 435, states that in 1739, 82.2 percent of English cotton textile exports were sent to the African continent.
79. Torres Ramírez, *Compañía Gaditana*, 71–118.
80. Between 1774 and 1779 the average number of slaves delivered per year was around 2,291, well below the 3,500 agreed in the 1765 contract. Ibid., 3.
81. On these projects planned during the first six months of 1778, see Sylvia Vilar, "Los predestinados de Guinea," *Mélanges de la Casa Velásquez* 7 (1971): 304–316.
82. AGI, Indiferente General, leg. 2436.
83. James A. Lewis, "Anglo-American Entrepreneurs in Havana," in J.A. Barbier and A.J. Kuethe, eds., *The North American Role in the Spanish Imperial Economy, 1760–1819* (Manchester, 1984), 115.
84. Ibid., 123–124.

85. Linda Salvucci, "Anglo-American Merchants and Stratagems for Success in Spanish Imperial Markets, 1783–1807," *The North American Role*, 127–133.
86. One of the few proposals from Spanish trade that came into effect was from the Cadiz firm Jaime Boloix y Ciª in 1785, for the supply of negroes to Puerto-Rico and Santo-Domingo over a five-year period (AGI, Indiferente General, leg. 2821).
87. Rawley, *The Transatlantic Slave Trade*, 216; and Manuel Moreno Fraginals, *El Ingenio. Complejo económico social cubano del azúcar* (Havana, 1978), 1: 51.
88. Rawley, *The Transatlantic Slave Trade*, 216–217. John Dawson tried to negotiate a new asiento in 1788, but opposition from merchants in Havana frustrated his effort.
89. J. M. Azcona, "El comercio de negros en tiempos de Carlos III," *Letras de Deusto* 19, no. 45 (1989): 79–91.
90. M. L. Díaz-Trechuelo, *La Real Compañía de Filipinas* (Sevilla, 1965), 222–223.
91. Inikori, *Africans and the Industrial Revolution*, 239–240.
92. The director to the Count of Floridablanca, Madrid, 21 August 1788, Archivo Histórico Nacional, Madrid, (hereafter AHN), Estado, leg. 2821.
93. Further information on these expeditions in Díaz Trechuelo, *La Real Compañía de Filipinas*, 224–225.
94. Ventura Fuster to Antonio Valdés, Madrid, 15 January 1788, AGI, Indiferente General, leg. 2821.
95. Calculations based on the "Estado y cálculo de lo que podrá producir a la Compañía el Asiento de Negros, en los términos que va propuesto," AGI, Indiferente General, leg. 2821.
96. Roger Anstey, *The Atlantic Slave Trade and British Abolition, 1760–1810* (London, 1975), 246 onward; and James Walvin, *The Zong: A Massacre, the Law, and the End of Slavery* (New Haven, 2011).
97. Rawley, *The Transatlantic Slave Trade*, 283. Compare this loss with the appalling number of deaths on the slave ships of the Compañía de Filipinas.
98. Rawley, *The Transatlantic Slave Trade*, 283–284.
99. The engraving accompanied by the "Descripción del navío *Brooks*, harto conocido en el comercio de esclavos, hecha por el capitán Perry enviado expresamente por la cámara de los comunes a Liverpool para tomar las dimensiones de los bastimentos empleados en dicho tráfico," in AGI, Indiferente General, leg. 2821.
100. Pablo Tornero, "Emigración, población y esclavitud en Cuba (1765–1817)," *Anuario de Estudios Americanos* XLIV (1986): 10–11.
101. The content of the decree was debated and approved by the Junta de Estado in the session of 19 February, in the minutes of which the text of the provision is noted, but no motives are presented. AHN, Estado, lib. 3, fols. 4 v. and 5 r. Entire copies in AGI, Indiferente General, leg. 2436, and AHN, Estado, leg. 235(1). I do not analyze here the political reasons that might have influenced the Spanish government's decision to define slaves as free-trade merchandise, although there are indications to suggest that the measure was already under consideration prior to the rebellion in Haiti as a key factor in a strategy to gain the loyalty of Creole plantation owners. Neither do I examine the impact of pressure brought by Cuban plantation owners for the liberalization of the slave trade.
102. Royal Order of 24 December 1791, AGI, Indiferente general, leg. 2821. Another Royal Order, dated two days later and sent by Floridablanca to the Viceroy of Santa Fe, gave the first instructions in response "to the news received of the commotions on the island and the French establishments, and of the Negroe insurrection in el Guarico" (AHN, Estado, leg. 3222-1). The free trade of slaves would be subject to successive extensions in the following years. A RO of 21 May 1795 (AGI, Indiferente General, leg. 2827) authorized the port of El Callao for the delivery of Africans in Peru. Finally, a RD of 22 April 1804 gave a twelve-year extension to the conditions granted to Spanish shipowners who

participated in the slave trade and added Valparaiso, Guayaquil, and Panama to the list of authorized ports (AGI, Indiferente General, leg. 2821).
103. Neither J. R. Fisher, *Commercial Relations between Spain and Spanish America in the Era of Free Trade* (Liverpool, 1985) nor A. García-Baquero, *Comercio colonial y guerras revolucionarias. La decadencia económica de Cádiz a raíz de la emancipación Americana* (Sevilla, 1972) appear to attach a great deal of importance to this measure in the evolution of the situation of the slave trade or in its organization. The exceptions are two works by Josep M. Fradera, "La participació catalana en el tràfic d'esclaus," *Recerques*, no. 16 (1984): 118–139; and *Industria i mercat, Les bases comercials de la indústria catalana moderna (1814–1845)* (Barcelona, 1987), 54–78, whose opinion I share.
104. Fradera, *Industia i mercat*, 66.
105. Some examples in AGI, Indiferente General, leg. 2826.
106. David R. Murray, *Odious Commerce: Britain, Spain and the Abolition of the Atlantic Slave Trade* (Cambridge, 1980), 18; Herbert S. Klein, "The Cuban Slave Trade in a Period of Transition, 1790–1843," *Revue Française d'Histoire d'Outre-Mer* LXII (1975): 72–75; and Tornero, "Emigración, población y esclavitud," 18.
107. Matilla Tascón, *Catálogo de la Colección de órdenes generales de rentas* (Madrid, 1950), no. 4851, 452 and no. 5014, 466.
108. Royal Orders of 20 January 1793 and 20 March 1797, AGI, Indiferente General, leg. 2826. Another, dated 14 March 1804, likewise permitted exemption from the alcabala tax for sales from slave ships that had previously made five expeditions to the African coast and delivered a minimum of 250 slaves to America.
109. On the Spanish slave ship expeditions in these years, AGI, Indiferente General, legs. 2821 to 2827.
110. Herbert Klein estimates that between 1790 and 1809, 853 North American vessels brought slaves into Havana: "The Cuban Slave Trade," 72–73.

– *Chapter 2* –

PORTUGUESE MISSIONARIES AND EARLY MODERN ANTISLAVERY AND PROSLAVERY THOUGHT

Luiz Felipe de Alencastro

Among the European Atlantic empires, Portugal established a unique and complex relationship with Africa. Well before the ships and merchants of other European maritime regions, traders from Lisbon, the Algarves, Madeira, and the Cape Verde Islands started exchanges with the sub-Saharan ports. Soon, Portuguese institutions were transplanted in the African continent. The early dioceses of Cape Verde (1533), São Tomé (1534), Congo and Angola (1596), whose seat was in São Salvador do Congo (Mbanza Congo) and was the first to be established in continental Africa, as well as the municipal councils of Luanda (1589), Massangano (1589), and Benguela (1619) strengthened the Portuguese colonial enclaves. Built in 1671, two hundred miles Southeast of Luanda, the fort of Pungo Andongo became the most central European outpost in Africa until the mid nineteenth century. At the same time, the transatlantic slave trade to the Portuguese colonies, mostly through bilateral exchanges between Brazil and Angola, increased steadily, transforming Luanda into the most important slaving port on the west coast of Africa. This context led Portuguese authorities and missionaries, mainly the Jesuits, who traded enslaved Africans and possessed slave properties in Angola and Brazil, to elaborate an articulate justification of the slave trade, connecting colonial exploitation on both sides of the South Atlantic.

As is well known, the Jesuits played a fundamental role in building the framework of Portuguese expansion. São Paulo de Piratininga, São Paulo de Luanda, São Paulo de Goa, São Paulo de Malacca, and São Paulo de Macao: all over the world, the Society of Jesus was erecting churches and colleges in honor of the saint consecrated as the apostle of the gentiles. Moreover, an interpretation of verses 18 to 23 of Saint Paul's first epistle to the Romans led some theologians to maintain that overseas gentiles would have had a previous knowledge of the Christian God even before the arrival of the missionaries.[1] However, gentiles' reactions would change from one longitude to the other. Early on, the missionaries realized—and vindicated—the specificity of missionary work overseas.

From India, the Lisboan Father Luís Fróis warned with refined objectivity, showing his perfect awareness of the cultural limits of sacred rhetoric: "As to the course of studies [at the college of São Paulo in Goa] and the order of them, I truly believe that they should not expect the renown of the ceremonies at Coimbra [University] nor the large number of classes and scholars there, for that is the proper place to acquire the sciences, and here to practice them, there to dispute and raise questions, here to give solutions to those who live in the valley of the shadow of death."[2]

Certainly, the duty to catechize imposed on missionaries a social reflection to understand overseas cultures. Still, it was not only regarding natives that the process of evangelical transculturation took place. Just as significant was the pro-slavery doctrinal adjustment that the Jesuits in Angola and Brazil carried out.

As David Brion Davis points out, the process of transforming human beings into slaves has generated, since antiquity, a dualism in religious and philosophical thought. The peak of this dualism, continues Davis, occurred in the sixteenth and seventeenth centuries, as the distance between the rising cult of freedom in Europe and the expansion of colonial slavery in America was greater.[3] In the Iberian Peninsula, this contradiction took shape within the framework of the Counter Reformation. In fact, the sixteenth-century Catholic Reformation revived the practice of the seven sacraments, against the Protestant doctrine, which recognized just two of them (Eucharist and baptism) and questioned if they were mandatory.[4] Yet, missionary practice had to overcome the impasses that arose with regard to the effects of the sacraments of marriage, baptism, and confession on the status of slaves and the rights of masters.

Soon, the Jesuits met with a serious reverse in Central Africa. At King John III's request, a Jesuit mission departed to Mbanza Congo in 1548.[5] Setting out even before the first Jesuits came to Brazil, the Congo mission brought fervent hopes to the Society of Jesus' colleges.[6] Written by Father Cornélio Gomes, a Portuguese Jesuit born in Mbanza Congo, the *Doutrina christã na língoa do Congo* (1556) appeared as the first book printed in a Bantu language.⁷ The book was published some years later than the *Arte da língoa malabar em português* (1549), by the Jesuit Henrique Henriques, and the *Cartilha em tamul e português* (1554), authored by three Hindus converted by the Jesuits, but forty years before the *Arte da grammatica da língua mais usada na costa do Brasil* (1595) by Father Anchieta S.J., about the Tupi language, and fifty years earlier than the *Arte da língoa de Japam* (1604–1608) by the Jesuit João Rodrigues.

The decline of Latin as the universal language of Europe and contact with the new cultures revealed by the Age of Discovery had transformed the world into a new Babel. As Carvalhão Buescu has noted, scholars of the Society of Jesus would methodically translate overseas languages, preliterate in most cases, into sixteenth- and seventeenth-century Portuguese. Guided by the linguistic model provided by Latin grammar, the missionaries tried to decode all languages.⁸

The fact that the Jesuits took a pioneering role in the study of native languages derived from their privileged position in Iberian overseas expansion. As will be seen, it also had to do with the importance Jesuit doctrine attached to the sacraments of Eucharist and confession. In the post-Tridentine doctrine followed by the Society of Jesus, confession presupposed a direct and private contact between confessor and penitent, so required a substantial knowledge of native tongues.⁹

In any case, the early effort to create a grammar of the Bakongo language demonstrates the strong interest in that Central Africa kingdom. Upon setting foot in the territory of Bahia, after having crossed the Atlantic, Father Manuel da Nóbrega asked anxiously in one of his first letters to the metropolitan superior: "[I]s there news from the Congo mission?"¹⁰ There was news, but not pleasant news. One of the Jesuits sent to the Bakongo kingdom had returned to the metropolis. The other two missionaries, converted to the slave trade, ended up expelled from the Company of Jesus.¹¹ Except for some visits, they resettled in the region only in 1618 and only for a short time because the Jesuits closed permanently the college of São Salvador do Congo in 1669.¹²

In 1559, the first group of Jesuit missionaries traveled to Angola.¹³ Wary after the fiasco in Congo, the superior of the mission opted for military conquest. "Without subjugation, neither this nor any other barbarian people, no matter how well inclined, will be able to remain steadfast in faith, as it can be clearly seen in Congo, where Christianity has been so ill attained."¹⁴ Angola—the Ndongo kingdom—suffered the consequences of the affronts the Jesuits received in Congo. Together with the villages, the *sobas* (local Mbundu rulers with authority over a territory and its inhabitants [a *sobado*]) were removed from the sovereignty of the King of Ndongo and handed over to the Jesuits and Portuguese captains. Governor Paulo Dias Novais made official this subjection to vassalage through the system of Portuguese *amos* (masters), a sort of Angolan *encomienda*.[15]

Unlike their European contemporaries, Portuguese sailors, merchants, and missionaries had some knowledge of communities on the African littoral in the mid sixteenth century. In addition to experience acquired in the Atlantic Islands and Upper Guinea, many priests had already had daily contact with black and Moorish captives sold by three generations of slave traders in some parts of the Iberian Peninsula.[16]

Consequently, the clergy in Brazil professed the doctrine propagated by the papal bull *Romanus pontifex* (1455).[17] The enslavement of black Africans was tolerated because it made catechesis easier. Taken from the Dark Continent, the Africans' souls would be saved in the Christian environment of the Iberian kingdoms and its Americans enclaves. Still, it was also necessary to adapt the pontifical doctrine to the American colonial scene, where slavery, unlike that which prevailed in Iberian cities like Seville and Lisbon, progressively assumed a systemic character. It is noteworthy that the involvement of the Portuguese in the slave trade during the sixteenth century was severely criticized by the Dominican friar Fernando Oliveira (1507–1581) in his pioneering treaty on sea power, *Arte da guerra do mar* (1555).[18]

On landing in Bahia, Nóbrega was shocked at what he saw and heard. "All, or almost all" settlers had a guilty conscience for owning slaves illicitly. Without delay, he asked the Portuguese court to send inquisitors of the Holy Office to free the natives who had been "illicitly enslaved" and kept in paganism by unjust masters,[19] a clear antislavery attitude without concessions that would be abandoned subsequently. In fact, a year later the Jesuit superior was dealing with a new dilemma: the masters prevented slaves from marrying, afraid of being compelled to manumit both spouses.

In fact, the sacrament of marriage was changing. Feudal customs of Roman origin, which characterized marriage as a *connubium legitimum*—union of free individuals decided between persons of the same social status—had fallen into disuse.[20] As a source of divine grace and remedy for concupiscence, marriage had to be facilitated by the church. For this reason, the mutual consent of spouses was enough to sanction their union before a parish priest.[21] This practice, favorable to morganatic, socially unequal marriages, threatened lineages and social hierarchies. Hence, French participants in the Council of Trent (1545–1563), formalizing the nobility's complaints, requested a stricter canon law on marriage. In the end, the bishops decided on the presence of witnesses and of the parish priest during the ceremony but maintained the prevalence of mutual consent. For the prelates, parental, family consent was not a necessary condition to validate the sacrament. The French monarchy rejected the Council's decrees, considering them offensive to the rights of the secular power. A royal ordinance of Henry III established a norm to guarantee patrimonial interests that would last until the French Revolution: marriage without parental consent was linked to abduction and punished with death.[22]

A totally different conflict concerning marriage arose in slaveholding colonies. What was the social autonomy granted to an enslaved family started under the sacrament of marriage? Did the captive married by the church assume the status of *pater familias*, being given freedom and control over his wife and children?

Following the pre-Tridentine Thomist doctrine, Nóbrega and the Society of Jesus in Brazil did not believe so. Wishing to reconcile the duty of catechizing and the will of slave masters, the Jesuit superior suggested a new charter to King John III: it should be clear that marriage between slaves would not exempt spouses from bondage nor force their masters to manumit them. Attentive to the overseas context, Nóbrega recommended the enforcement of this law in Brazil, São Tomé, and other slaveholding regions.[23] This would be the court's purpose. At the turn of the seventeenth century, the Jesuit Jorge Benci wrote in his breviary on Luso-Brazilian slavery that masters used to prohibit slaves from marrying and, if they were already married, the masters would care little about separating couples when selling them.[24]

Subsequently, the constitutions of the Archbishopric of Bahia ruled in 1707 to codify the canonical norms that endured until the abolition of slavery in Brazil (1888): slaves who get married "remain slaves, as they were before."[25] In the middle of the nineteenth century, the jurist Perdigão Malheiro summarized the legal doctrine prevailing in Brazil with regard to slave marriages: "The Civil Law ... as a rule has almost no effect on them." Some years later, in 1869—three hundred years after the beginning of the slave trade—Brazilian law granted legal rights to enslaved parents: in the auction of slave families, it was not allowed to separate spouses or children of less than twelve years of age from the father or the mother.[26]

Apparently contradictory, Nóbrega's judgments illustrated the tortuous process of adjusting a religious doctrine to the colonial order. On the one hand, Nóbrega firmly stated the justification for evangelization: bondage would be legitimate only if followed by catechesis. On the other hand, he established the primacy of the right of property—of the full right to enslave—over the contractual norms implicit in sixteenth-century religious practice. Here, it is worth recalling Orlando Patterson's analysis:

the slave was a slave not because he was property, but because he could not possess; not because the slave was an object of property, but because he was prevented from becoming the subject of property, since he did not hold the essential rights in the acts in which he appeared as a contracting party.[27] On restricting the social and legal effects of the religious marriage between slaves, Nóbrega stimulated an institutional movement of adjustment of Christian doctrine to slavery. From the same perspective, the royal letter of 1557 to the governor of India determined that converted Moorish slaves and gentiles could only be resold to Christian masters, to prevent them from returning to heresy and paganism. Yet baptism did not change slaves' status. They would not become "free Christians for that reason."[28]

To the contrary, baptism opened a path of no return to slavery, a problem the Jesuits had resolved in Luanda. The Jesuits believed that slaves donated to them by settlers would teach harmful habits to the priests' other slaves. Therefore, it was better to sell them right away.[29] The option of manumitting the captives donated to the Society of Jesus did not cross the clergymen's minds. Even being of little value, slaves could be exported and taxed by the Crown. A captain in Angola reported that native merchants sold so-called "pieces" (slaves) in lots, good ones mixed with bad ones. However, slave traders would reject the "bad pieces" — the sick, the old, and children — compelling merchants to resell them to free Mbundu, who used these slaves in their lands. For the captain, "bad pieces" should be exported to Rio de Janeiro and subject to the royal tribute, thus preventing these individuals from returning to paganism in the Angolan hinterlands.[30] Captive, the native was baptized and became a Christian, which rendered him unable to return to natural freedom, a den of idolatry.

Friar Vitoriano, bishop of Cape Verde in the beginning of the eighteenth century, would be sleepless merely thinking of fornication among the colonists of his island. Moved by his ardor to break up sexual liaisons, he used to get up and "leave during the night to remove, personally, the concubines out not only from priests' houses, but also from those of laymen, even in distant places and out of town." The free concubines would be exiled to other islands of the African archipelago, whereas the slaves would be banished and sold in Rio de Janeiro.[31]

Concerning the Portuguese attachment to the commodity slave, some authors stressed the discrepancy of the Iberian legislation on the status of slaves belonging to defendants before the Holy Office. In Spain, the tribunals would manumit them eventually. In Portugal, in contrast, they were confiscated and later sold by royal foremen to the benefit of inquisitors.[32] Freeing rebel slaves and the so-called refuse composed of old slaves, children, concubines, and heretics' captives was unthinkable.

The Antislavery of the Holy Sacraments

Far from the theologians of Coimbra and Salamanca, more worried with securing the material bases of overseas residences, the second generation of Jesuit missionaries managed slaves directly. In Europe and Asia, the Society of Jesus succeeded in obtaining privileges that provided missionaries with revenues, as was the case with the *contrato de Japão* (sale of Chinese silk from Macao to Japan) and land revenues in Portugal and India, such as the revenues from *namoxin* lands confiscated from Hindu temples in Goa.[33] The maintenance of missions justified the order sidestepping Tridentine guidelines and even the restrictions of the Superior General Francisco de Borja, who prohibited Jesuits from commercial activity.

In Southern Africa and, to a lesser scale, in Portuguese America, the Jesuits' resources came from the compulsory labor of natives and also, in Luanda, from the Atlantic slave trade.[34]

Property donated to the missionaries or acquired by them included a growing number of slaves. In the higher spheres of the society, the missionaries' involvement in Atlantic slave transactions was embarrassing to the point of making Francisco de Borja (1565–1572) protest against the owning of slaves by the Society of Jesus. In this context, antislavery reactions arose at the college of Bahia, especially the incidents triggered by Fathers Miguel García and Gonçalo Leite. Deciding to impose a strict obedience to the sacrament of confession, these two Jesuits understood that absolution suited only those masters able to prove they owned slaves legally.[35] It was not only the general status of slavery in Renaissance Europe that was under discussion; more precisely, they debated the problems caused by the daily witnessing of slaveholders' violence.

Outraged by the missionaries who herded black and Indian slaves, Father Miguel García warned Rome in 1583: "The mass of slaves the Society owns in this Province, particularly in this college [of Bahia] is something I cannot swallow by any means." In his opinion, all natives and Africans employed in Bahia had been illicitly enslaved. From the beginning, he refused to hear the confession of any slave master, including his own fellow Jesuits.[36] He was not the only Jesuit to take such actions. From Lisbon, the procurator of the missions, Father Jerônimo Cardoso, wrote to the superior general to criticize the fact that the Society of Jesus owned slaves in Brazil. "We ask the king to order that all [Indians] be freed, yet, we have many captives and make more use of those from the villages, than all other whites do." In Angola, all say "we trade and practice commerce *sub praetextu conversionis* [under the pretext of conversion]: and I would say that if we cannot maintain many [missionaries] without them having [slaves] then we should maintain fewer [missionaries] without [slaves], for so did the ancients."[37]

Sent from Lisbon to Bahia to settle the conflict, the *Visitador* (Itinerant Inspector) Father Cristovão de Gouveia, carrying opinions written by the Society's treatise writers, met the most prominent missionaries.[38] Again, the Jesuits decided that slavery was a "safe contract," as the Board of Conscience (*Mesa de Consciência*) had determined.[39] Thus, Father García's opinions seemed "quite contrary to common sense, dangerous and scandalous in these parts." Consequently, the superiors of the order decided to send García back to Spain.[40]

Gonçalo Leite's antislavery discourse created a more serious incident. Master of the novices, first professor of arts in the college of Bahia, superior of the residences of Porto Seguro and Ilhéus, he had a significant influence on his fellows. Other priests, close to Miguel García and Gonçalo Leite, also decided to deny the sacrament of confession to slaveholders who could not justify the enslavement of their captives. The Visitador tried to disqualify those missionaries, determining that they would hear confessions only at the college entrance hall, prohibiting them from exercising their ministry inside the church.

At that point, the sacrament of confession, as in the case of marriage, was going through transformations. Tridentine reforms established the individual confession in closed cubicles inside the church—confessionals date back from that time—abandoning the collective or domestic acts in the residences.[41] The penitents submitted to contrition, to confession proper, and to compunction for the sins committed. Influenced by Baius (1513–1589)—a theologian at the University of Louvain and precursor of Jansenism—clerical thought understood that, in the absence of the penitent's repentance, without real contrition, confessors should refuse or postpone the sacrament. *Contrito caritate perfecta,* the rule of the Council distinguished the perfect contrition, characterized by sincere and disinterested hostility to sin, from *attrition,* regret motivated only by fear of divine punishment.[42] Tolerated in the baptism of natives, mere attrition seemed to some priests insufficient to make confession effective.[43]

The Jesuits stood out for their action in favor of assiduous communion and confession.[44] Influenced by the Society of Jesus, Cardinal Infante Dom Henrique, regent of the Kingdom and inquisitor-general, issued in 1556 a royal provision in which he summoned Catholics to confess and partake of the Holy Communion regularly, "finding very odd the contrary abuse."[45] Yet, there were missionaries in Bahia who insisted on refusing the sacrament to the many faithful settlers who owned slaves. It was urgent to resolve the impasse: Gonçalo Leite ended up being banished to Lisbon by decision of the Visitador.

Father Fernão Cardim, who traveled from Lisbon with Father Cristovão de Gouveia, was laconic about this serious antislavery dissent: "the Visitador has sometimes, together with some prelates and scholars, dealt with cases of great importance about enslavement, baptism, and marriage of Indians and Guinea slaves, from their resolutions followed veritable fruit and improved Christianity after we arrived in Brazil."[46] In fact, the "resolutions" of the Visitador did not convince Father Gonçalo Leite at all. From Lisbon, he continued to protest to the head of the Society of Jesus in Rome, demanding confessions based on contrition: "I see our priests confessing homicides and robbers of someone else's freedom, property and sweat, with neither restitution of the past nor remedy for future evils of the same sort that are committed every day."[47] As he observed in Bahia, slaveholders refused to demonstrate the necessary regret and did not restitute past sins, maintaining their property in illicitly enslaved individuals. Therefore, they were prevented from confessing.

At first, the antislavery missionaries' protest produced the desired result in Rome. Against the opinion of Visitador Gouveia and of the most influential Jesuits in Brazil and Angola, the superior of the order in Rome, Claudio Acquaviva, determined that the Jesuits would neither own nor trade persons enslaved under doubtful conditions nor absolve their masters. Besides, Jesuits should not follow those who said that it was better to maintain these individuals in bondage than to let them live free as pagans. However, Acquaviva eventually went back on his word and authorized missionaries to own slaves.[48]

The refusal to confess slaveholders, an extreme measure, does not seem to have been applied collectively again, as had happened in Bahia. Miguel García, Gonçalo Leite, and their Jesuit fellows in Bahia saw in slavery an obstacle to the teaching of the gospel overseas. Amador Arrais and Pedro Brandão, Carmelite bishops, expressed their criticism based on a different ideological foundation, grounded in conservative, seigniorial, antimercantilist thought. For them, what mattered were the evils engendered by slavery in the heart of traditional Portuguese society. Moreover, on attributing a redeeming legal effect to the baptism of slaves, the two bishops also expressed the antagonistic character that existed between catechesis and slavery.

Friar Pedro Brandão had direct knowledge of the slave trade in the diocese of Cape Verde, where he performed Episcopal functions (1589–1594). Based on his familiarity with the ports of Upper Guinea, he concluded that it was "humanly impossible" to deter the unlawfulness of the enslavement and the trade in Africans. Brandão's reflections were influenced by his professor, Friar Amador Arrais, bishop of Portalegre, in Alentejo, affiliated with the antihumanist thought of the sixteenth century.

In his *Diálogos* (1589), Friar Amador Arrais condemned slavery because it endangered the seigniorial order and the traditional communities. To him, the introduction of Africans in Portugal took away jobs and occupations from poor white men: "In earlier times, before that canaille [the slaves] came to the kingdom, there were as many Portuguese people as now, nobody begged ... the poor lived with the rich, and the rich maintained them and all had the necessities for living." Moreover, evangelical reasons proper intervened: the traffic had brought illicitly enslaved people, offending Christian morals from the beginning: "[B]ringing them [the Africans] to become Christians is not an excuse, since Christianity cannot be exchanged for bondage."[49]

In the same vein, Bishop Brandão coupled his reactionary convictions with antislavery arguments. Slavery seemed reprehensible to him because it increased the disorder of seigniorial society, intensifying the evils caused in Portugal by the prevalence of the merchants' interests and new forms of enrichment generated by the discoveries. Thus, Brandão listed the troubles the African slave trade caused Portugal: economic disequilibrium, shortages of food, monopoly of the wheat business by foreigners, unemployment for poor whites, because the rich would only make use of slaves: "hence so many lost [poor] without means of living," degradation of manual crafts performed by slaves, "mixing of blood," the miscegenation that "uglified" Portugal, concubinage, public immorality, and discredit of the Kingdom before Europe, because "[W]e do not know of a nation other than the Portuguese that trades slaves as commodities."

In practice, the memorial by the bishop of Cape Verde was a petition for the court to determine the manumission of converted slaves. As said previously with regard to marriage and confession, baptism was declared mandatory in the Council of Trent.[50] Nevertheless, what were the direct and indirect consequences of divine remission infused in colonial peoples by the sacrament of baptism? Understanding that baptism had an intrinsic redeeming effect—as taught by the theologian Jesuit Fernão Rebelo at the University of Évora—Brandão formulated a forceful antislavery argument: "Among Turks and Moors freedom is given to captive Christians if they adopt their damned sect, and there is more reason to give it to the gentiles of the colony, which the popes granted to this kingdom, to make them Christians."[51]

Evoking Divine Providence, Bishop Brandão asserted that Portuguese faults in the spreading of slavery had caused the misfortunes (such as the death of the Portuguese King Sebastian in North Africa and threats of war) that had befallen the kingdom as divine punishment.[52] Later, facing the hostility of Cape Verdean colonists and the Catholic hierarchy, Friar Brandão resigned the bishopric.[53] His criticisms of the slave trade were contemporary with the first Portuguese *asiento* contract with Spain (1595), which gave to the transatlantic slave trade an unprecedented volume and extension.⁵⁴

Nonetheless, the Crown's policies, especially during the union with Spain (1580–1640), and merchants' activities were not the only source of interest and legitimacy driving the early transatlantic slave trade. Despite the objections from priests such as Brandão and García from various points in the overseas empire, many of the missionaries, particularly the Jesuits in Africa and Portuguese America, played a crucial role in this process.

The Jesuits' Pro-Slave Trade Theory

I am the mantle of the world
whose sins I covered
"Auto de la Visitación de santa Isabel" (1597) José de Anchieta

In 1592, Father Pero Rodrigues embarked from Lisbon on a long sea journey that would take him to two continents to carry out two challenging tasks. Appointed Visitador of the Jesuits' in Angola, he would prepare a report on missions among the Mbundu people to the order's superior general in Rome. Then he would cross the Atlantic again to take over his position as provincial of the Society of Jesus in Brazil (1594–1603). On leaving the Tagus, he already knew of the trouble emerging on the South Atlantic horizon: the governor of Angola, Francisco de Almeida, in whose fleet Pero Rodrigues was traveling, carried categorical royal orders: the system of amos should be extinguished. The Jesuits and captains who had robbed the Angolan sobados should hand over villages, revenues, and natives to the Crown's representative.

However, instead of sailing to Luanda together with the fleet, Father Pero's ship landed in Bahia first. Thus, the Visitador heard from the missionaries of Brazil about the dispute of the amos in Angola.⁵⁵ At that point, the Society of Jesus was striving to consolidate its missions in Portuguese America by means of relocations (*descimento*), a system that subjugated Indian communities from the hinterlands to the missionaries and colonial authorities.

Although the context of Portuguese America—exporter of inert goods—was different from that of Angola—from which living "goods" were exported—settlements in Brazil resembled the system of Angolan sobados managed by Jesuit amos. Consequently, José de Anchieta, Luís da Grã, Fernão Cardim, the provincial Marçal Beliarte, and other Jesuits in Portuguese America would support their fellows in Angola. Contrary to the royal order of 1592, they decided that the Jesuits should carry on controlling the sobados.[56]

Armed with these opinions, Father Pero resumed his journey to Luanda, where events had come to a head. Thus, the Itinerant Inspector's ship crossed on the high seas two vessels from Luanda, which would call in Pernambuco before proceeding to Lisbon. Each vessel was carrying a central character of the conflict that took place in Angola: the first carried the governor Francisco de Almeida, expelled by the Jesuits and captains involved in the amos' uprising, and the second, the superior Baltazar Barreira, banished by Philip II from the colony for having headed the said rebellion.[57]

Father Baltazar Barreira had first landed in Angola 1579, together with the Captain-General Paulo Dias Novais, as superior of the Jesuits' mission.[58] Soon, the Jesuits erected the church of São Paulo de Luanda, which lent its name to the town, and fought beside the conquerors, exhorting them in the battles.[59] In spite of having baptized the first converted Ndongo nobleman as Constantino, Barreira remained skeptical regarding the possibility of Constantinism (as Charles Boxer wrote), already attempted in parts of Asia, thriving in Angola. In fact, he did not think that Christianity could be inculcated from above, cascading through the traditional native hierarchy, after the conversion of the Mbundu aristocracy.[60] On the contrary, the failure of the policy of indirect government tried in Congo made the Jesuits fight to defeat the Ndongo kingdom through a total war of economic, territorial, and ideological conquest. On providing captains with moral and material help, attentive to Mbundu war tactics, and raising soldiers and gunpowder to form armies, Barreira must be considered a real military chief who shared with Paulo Dias Novais the leadership of the offensive launched in Central Africa from 1580 on.[61]

Summoned by King Philip II to appear before the court after the amos' rebellion, Barreira went to Madrid and proceeded to Évora, where he took over the position of novice master. He was about sixty-six years old when he resumed his African apostolate in Guinea, Cape Verde, and Sierra Leone. Affectionately called the Old Saint by father Antonio Vieira and other missionaries, he died in Cape Verde in 1612, after having served the Crown and the Society of Jesus for more than half a century.[62]

An old hand in West African affairs, a tireless traveler, influential with allied chiefs, Barreira might be, in the Jesuit saga, as distinguished as Francis Xavier and José de Anchieta for their apostolates in Asia and America. This was the feeling that the Lisbon Jesuit Baltazar Telles expressed in his *Chronica* (1645), the first history of the Portuguese Jesuits written from a nationalist, anti-Spanish perspective. Years later, passing through Cape Verde, Father Antônio Vieira paid homage to the memory of Barreira, the

Old Saint, "so much to be imitated."[63] The beatification process of Baltazar Barreira would have to come to terms with the Old Saint's voluntary, considered, and decisive activity in favor of the Atlantic slave trade.[64]

To Loyola, Laínez, Borja, Mercurian, and Acquaviva—superiors general of the Society of Jesus in the sixteenth century—the fact that the Jesuits owned slaves was repugnant. "There are days in which I am resolved that it does not suit the Society to make use of slaves. To Your Most Rev. I recommend trying to gently get rid of those you have in Portugal," insisted the Superior General Francisco Borja to the provincial of Portugal in 1569.[65] Other superiors general of the society also expressed scruples on the matter, considering that the missionaries' slaveholding practices did not augur well for the work of the society in Africa.

The insertion of the human commodity in the gears of the Commercial Revolution reintroduced the concept of absolute property coined by Roman law: the slave was an integral part of the individual, private universe of property owned, exchanged, sold, pawned, and inherited, of the *universitas rerum*.[66] That situation induced Catholic theologians and regalist philosophers to consider the absolute property of a slave by a master as an obstruction to catechesis overseas and a producer of crippling effects on the plenitude of monarchical authority.

Within these legal and philosophical uncertainties, Barreira sent a memorial from Luanda to the scholars of Salamanca, Évora, and Coimbra, who were debating the lawfulness of the slave trade. For Barreira, there were no doubts about the foundation for African enslavement. Counted as money everywhere, a slave, argued Barreira, was the currency of the colony. Prisoners of war, delinquents, and descendants of other captives composed the contingents of the African hinterland traffic. Forced, sold, and resold from market to market, all these people were mixed, making it impossible to clear up the legitimacy of their bondage. Furthermore, Barreira alleged, the Mbundu asked for missionaries to convert them and, later, abjured the Christian faith, falling into paganism again, therefore incurring apostasy. Thus, the war that was made on them should be understood as a *just war*: "[T]he conclusion will be that the more involved we become with the land and trade in blacks, the more we will come to realize that slaves can be more safely bought in Angola than from anywhere else in Guinea [i.e., black Africa]." In a related text, Barreira explained that, among the peoples of Angola, there was no "legitimate marriage in the law of nature."[67] For him, the slave trade did not destroy any authentic Angolan family.

The argument according to which the Angolan traffic—given the role of native intermediaries in the markets—seemed more licit than in any other part of Africa is summed up by the provincial of Portugal, Francisco de Gouveia, influential with the Curia, and conveyed to the leadership of the Society.⁶⁸

Thus, the need for legally recognizing the just war (bellum justum) that would legitimate the enslavement of prisoners captured in battle was overcome. Supposedly already enslaved by natives, the captives were acquired through purchase and barter in hinterland markets and not through direct capture by the Portuguese, as was usual in indigenous bondage in Brazil. At the same time, at the University of Coimbra, it was taught that the slave trade regularly submitted to the royal contracts and taxes of Portugal would enjoy full legal sanction ipso facto.⁶⁹

For reasons deriving from security in maritime traffic and the Lusitanian monopoly in Central Africa, the *asientistas* invested heavily in Angola. Thus, Barreira's ideology for justifying the Angolan traffic spread as slave ships flowed in greater numbers to Southern Africa.

An assiduous letter writer, a fine thinker, a gifted author, and knowledgeable of the sugar mills in Pernambuco, São Tomé and Cape Verde, considered as the greatest Jesuit expert and, certainly, the most experienced missionary of his time in Africa, Barreira efficiently rebutted the moral and religious restrictions raised against the Atlantic slave trade. According to the Society of Jesus' procedures, his letters, as those by Jesuits in the East and America, were often reputed to be edifying. As such, they were to be read in college and seminary refectories to motivate preachers, novices, and the faithful and make them reflect.⁷⁰ Copied and deposited in libraries, a good part of this correspondence would serve as a reference on the arts of the devil among overseas pagans. For this reason, Barreira's justification of the slave trade reached opinion makers living far beyond the nominal addressees of his letters.

On commenting upon the correspondence between Loyola and Jesuits across the four corners of the world, Pierre Chaunu points out the beginnings of the modern bureaucratic system of information that the Society of Jesus established, a system centralized on the choice of ends and wisely decentralized in the choice of means.⁷¹ In this context, the pro-Atlantic slavery realpolitik of the province of Portugal—inspired by Barreira, among others—had its share of responsibility for the decided reversal made by the Jesuit hierarchy in 1599, when an instruction of long-term consequences arrived at overseas missions from Rome: "[W]e can make use of captives."⁷²

Barreira was convinced that it was necessary to destroy the Ndongo kingdom to save it for Christ. His accounts of the battles omit the presence of thousands of allied native archers to highlight the valor of the Portuguese. Divine signs in favor of the conquerors were promptly recorded: crosses in the sky, visions of the Virgin in battles, swords of fire, and similar miracles. Equally unrestricted is his praise of pillage and the conqueror's bravery—or truculence.

In a letter addressed to Father José de Anchieta, then provincial of Brazil, he narrated the battle of Ilamba (1585), in which almost all the warriors of three Ndongo armies had been killed or captured. The Mbundu aristocracy was slaughtered. Together with hundreds of severed noses of their soldiers, the chiefs' heads were placed in bags and sent to Luanda on the backs of twenty bearers. Sixty years later, the chronicler Baltazar Telles was quite startled by these mutilations, and considered them a "cruel curiosity." [73]

Patterson observes that all stratified societies are born from violent appropriation of individuals by other individuals. In most cases, this act of "original accumulation" is restricted to the prehistory of societies and is lost track of. However, in the slaveholding system, the act of reifying the dominated is continuously renewed,[74] especially in Brazil, I would add, where the slave system—closely connected to the Atlantic slave trade circuit from 1550 to 1850—remained based on the pillaging of African villages. Hence the importance of following the successive theological and legal arguments that, over those three centuries, legitimated the initial, African stage of the slave trade, a decisive moment for the legal foundation of slavery.

Within the framework of continuous violence that involved the enslavement of Africans, epistolary documents sometimes reveal the ambiguous feelings raised by raids. In bright colors, Father Baltazar Afonso, Barreira's fellow, describes one of Paulo Dias Novais's raids:

> At that time [1580] the governor already had with him 300 Portuguese and some 200 slaves of the Portuguese, and as there was a shortage of food they started to look for it at gunpoint, conducting some 4 or 5 assaults in which they caused great destruction ... and bringing plenty of food that satiated all. Here it happened that a [Mbundu] father with his son, running away from our people, and seeing that he would not be able to save his son, turned to our people and sent as many arrows as he had, until he was killed for not having moved from a place so that his son could hide. And the father died and went to hell.[75]

Straightforward language, realistic narrative, explicit rapine, and an extreme gesture of paternal heroism: the emotion that flows almost until the end of the text in the desperate fight of the Mbundu father is nevertheless stanched by a judgment without forgiveness: "And the father died and went to hell."

Adhering to Barreiras's thesis, the annual letter of 1588 from the province of Portugal emphasized the preeminence of colonial war over catechesis in Angola: "The whole kingdom should submit in order to mold (*enformar*) these gentiles more safely and pull idolatry by the root."[76] By the same token, Visitador Pero Rodrigues's report, whose draft Barreira examined closely, ordered missionaries not to baptize any nobleman of the Ndongo kingdom until the whole land was subjected to vassalage.[77]

Nonetheless, the replacement of Angolan sobas for captains and Jesuits in the tutelage of the sobados had been interrupted by the royal ordinance of 1592, which extinguished the system of amos. King Philip II himself, and not only nonconformist priests or envious settlers, refused the property and trade in slaves by the Jesuits. The Jesuit response came in a double register. On the one hand, the missionaries challenged the royal authority and fomented the amos' mutiny. On the other hand, the Jesuits' pro-slavery arguments adjusted to the coeval mercantile thought, as shown in an emblematic text written by the Jesuits of Angola after a discussion with their coreligionists in Brazil:

> There is no scandal in [Jesuit] priests of Angola paying their debts with slaves. Because, just as in Europe currency is coined gold and silver, and in Brazil it is sugar, in Angola and neighboring kingdoms it is slaves. So, when [Jesuit] priests of Brazil send us what we have asked, like [manioc] flour and lumber for doors and windows, and when merchants who come to this land sell us biscuits, wine and other things, they do not want to receive from us payment in currency other than that which is valid in the land, which is slaves. Which they carry each year to Brazil and the Indies.

Further on, the document reiterates the mercantile character of captive and deported Africans: "[I]n the custom houses of Brazil, where we have sent our slaves until now, we do not pay taxes because of the privilege bestowed by His Majesty. As, by the same privilege, [Jesuit] priests do not pay taxes for the sugar they sell in Brazil or for other things in Portugal." Finally, the text underlines the missionaries' dependence on the specific mode of exploitation in each colony: in the Indies of Castile there were the encomiendas; in India the Society of Jesus had land rents of the Salsette Island (in Maharashtra); in Portugal the Jesuits had revenues from land and some country estates in Alentejo, "and the *sobas* are [like] the country estates of Alentejo," i.e., property meant to generate income for the Society in Angola.[78]

Already appointed provincial of Brazil, Father Pero Rodrigues appears as the main signatory of this synthesis about the meaning of colonization written for the Crown. However, it is clear that the Jesuits of Brazil, gathered in Bahia, had already endorsed the document. Barreira had not signed the memorial. Besides being disliked at the court, he was not in Luanda anymore. Still, he should be considered its intellectual author because the text summarized almost literally the arguments he had formulated ten years before.⁷⁹

A concise history of the Jesuits in Angola, written in 1594 for the Superior General Acquaviva, emphasized Barreira's ideas. Only a military offensive could guarantee catechesis. Individuals made captive in war were few; most of them would come from the "extremely old and always used" trade practiced by natives in hinterland markets. Submitting sobas directly to the Crown would cost much and produce little. The artifices and apostasies of the king of Angola—of the Ndongo—had provided the obvious cause of just war to enslave all those people. At the conclusion of the document, there is a blow against the unsuccessful governor Francisco de Almeida, the Crown's counselors, and, eventually, King Philip II himself, who had vetoed the system of amos. The (Jesuit) priests were watching over Angola very well, "until those who had the obligation to protect this work obstructed it." Guerreiro endorsed the same arguments in his *Relação Anual* (1603–1611), in which he publicized the missionary epic of the Society of Jesus.⁸⁰

Back in Africa in 1606, Barreira sent to the superiors a report on Africans deported via Cape Verde. Quite probably, this document was a reply to the antislavery work by Bishop Pedro Brandão. Barreira admitted the stark reality: "What one can say in general about Blacks bought and sold in this Guinea called Cape Verde is that no examination is made of the title of their enslavement, and nobody asks for it." After narrating the ways by which natives were enslaved, the memorial concludes: "And as to slaves taken from these parts thus far, since the fairness of the reason for enslaving them is doubtful, and that *in dubio melior est conditio possidentis* [in doubt, the right of the owner prevails], it seems that nothing has to be changed."⁸¹

The Jesuit treatise authors and thinkers admitted that the owners' right to possession could prevail over the captives' right to freedom, but only in an extreme and hypothetical situation: when the buyer was totally unaware of the controversy over the Atlantic slave trade and there was no doubt in favor of the enslaved.⁸² Based on these same principles, Father Antônio Vieira developed, in favor of the Indian enslaved by the settlers of Maranhão, an interpretation diametrically opposed to Barreira's. For Vieira, the postulate *in dubio melior est conditio possidentis* guaranteed the possession of freedom by the captive: "[I]n this case one does not question whether the Indians belong to Peter or Paul, but one doubts whether the Indians are free or captive, and in this doubt is the possession of freedom."⁸³

Barreira swept such scruples aside and preached the legitimacy of the Atlantic slave traffic, although he recognized that the matter was "beset with doubts." Such is the meaning of a letter he sent to the Roman seat of the Society of Jesus: "[C]oncerning the bondage of these Blacks, a matter so beset with doubts *pro utraque parte* [on both sides], it is not possible to do other than either letting it continue or to forbid this trade completely. I say this because it is usual to sell Blacks for the misdeeds that they themselves or their relatives and children commit, this is like law among them. Sometimes it happens that they are sold in spite of being guiltless or for a misdeed that does not deserve bondage. But it is impossible to verify."[84]

By the same ship leaving Sierra Leone to Europe, he sent an account to the order's director in Portugal (provincial), stating a similar thesis.[85] In his opinion, the Jesuits could either accept the trade and the enslaving practices in Africa or face the Crown, the European merchants, and the colonists. Under the overwhelming weight of the interests galvanized by the commercial and production complex of the Atlantic slave trade—from the lobbyists for the Madrid asientos to the merchants and masters in Luanda, Rio de Janeiro, and the Río de la Plata—only one answer was possible: the Jesuits should let the slave trade continue.

Four years later, on answering the inquiry about African slavery requested from Cartagena de Indias by the Jesuit jurist Alonso de Sandoval, the superior of the Society of Jesus in Luanda, Father Luís Brandão, reiterated with conviction Barreiras' theory on the lawfulness of the Angolan traffic:

> Your Reverence would like to know whether the Blacks sent [overseas] are licitly enslaved. To which I answer that it seems to me that Y.R. should not have scruples about it. For this is something the Board of Conscience in Lisbon has never condemned, and [the Board members] are learned men of good consciences. Furthermore, the bishops who have been in São Tomé, Cape Verde and Luanda, being learned and virtuous men, have never condemned it. And we have been here for 40 years and very learned [Jesuit] priests have been here, and in the province of Brazil, where there always were priests of our order eminent in letters, who never considered this trade illicit: and thus we, and the missionaries of Brazil, bought these slaves for our service, with no scruples at all. And I say more, that if someone could dispense with having scruples, these are the settlers of these parts, because as the merchants who take these Blacks take them in good faith, they can well buy from such merchants with no scruples at all, and they can sell [the enslaved]: for it is common opinion that the owner of the thing in good faith can sell it, and it can be bought ... And losing so many souls that leave from here, of which many are saved, just because some are illicitly enslaved, without knowing who they are, does not seems to be so much the service of God, for they are few [the illicitly enslaved], and those saved are many.[86]

Sandoval included this pro-slave trade manifesto in his celebrated book. He condemned the tortures inflicted on the deported, but he also thought that the slave traffic was a lesser evil, because it allowed taking Africans from the heart of paganism.[87]

The most definitive argument in favor of the enslavement and trade of Africans emerged from "the valley of the shadow of death," as Luis Fróis called the overseas missions: the Atlantic slave trade was a fundamental link in the insertion of Africa in the world market. Suppressing it would endanger Portuguese overseas control and break the chain of exchanges set up in the Atlantic. Moreover, the souls of blacks who could be redeemed by slavery in America would be lost to paganism if they remained in African hinterlands.

Enunciated in the papal bull *Romanus pontifex*, the fifteenth-century justification for evangelization in favor of the slave trade had a univocal character. It convinced the followers of Christian proselytism, those who worried about rescuing the souls of the gentiles.[88] In turn, the sixteenth-century pro-slavery argument based on the existence of cannibalism—denaturalized to the point of presenting anthropophagy as the so-called ordinary food of warlike ethnicities and the reason for Africa's depopulation—covered a broader scope.[89] It justified the deportation of the Africans for believers and unbelievers also interested in the salvation of bodies because it rescued prisoners from African indigenous wars. Even so, this argument—like the enunciation in the papal bull—had an ideologically circumscribed character. It presupposed the opinion that it was necessary to save natives from themselves and their supposed barbarism. Based on this postulate, João Baptista Fragoso, a theologian at the University of Évora, conceived slavery as a process that "blossomed from a sentiment as delicate as mercy, introduced in the Law of Nations (*Jus gentium*) to mitigate the fury and rigors of war."[90]

In a much more efficient and universal way, Barreira started with a secular supposition that was important in the age of merchant capitalism: the circulation of the commodity legitimated the functioning of the business. It is noteworthy that, like most of the treatise writers and thinkers of the Company of Jesus such as the theologian Fernão Rebelo, Luis de Molina, assistant at the University of Évora, stated that in case of suspicious enslavements it was necessary to decide *pro favore libertatis* (in favor of freedom).[91] Living in slave trade ports in Angola and Sierra Leone, crucial places for qualifying Africans for the colonial slavery, Barreira championed the opposing thesis: in dubious cases, the right was on the side of the owner, the slave master, the slave trader. *In dubio melior est conditio possidentis*. This thesis became dominant, underlying a general justification for slave traders and slaveholders. In fact, Barreira seemed realistic and disillusioned at the same time. He had lived long enough to evaluate how little the missions had progressed in one century of catechesis in Guinea and Central Africa. He was a realist about the course of the commercial revolution he observed around him. Barreira knew that colonial dynamics would tie the future of Africa to that of the New World.

The "Relocation" of the Indians and the Traffic of the Africans

Coupled with the slave trade, the conquest of Luanda's hinterland brought about a colonial dominion based on plunder that jeopardized missionary activities. In the last quarter of the seventeenth century, the Portuguese impasse in Southern Africa was already evident. Asked the governor of Angola in 1678 in a controversy with the Jesuits, "In Angola there is not one *soba* of whom one can say that he is truly rooted in Faith; therefore, if missions are so many, why is there so little fruit and this so ruined?" Completing his criticism, the governor considered a "manifest mistake" the Jesuits' abandonment of missions in the hinterlands to settle in Luanda to assist the colonists. In their own defense, the Jesuits attributed their retreat into the college of Luanda to the "malignity of the climate" that reigned in the Angolan lands, acknowledging the failure of their missionary policy in native villages.[92] In this context, Portuguese Jesuits designed a complementary missionary system in the South Atlantic that justified the commerce in African slaves and a pro-Indian policy in Brazil.

It is well known that in Portuguese America the Jesuits joined the authorities in carrying out the relocations (descimentos) of Indian villages. This system had a threefold objective: first, establishment of settlements for tame (*mansos*) Indians to protect the colonists from the wild (*bravos*) Indians. Second, the settlements surrounded the colonized areas, preventing enslaved blacks from escaping from plantations and sugar mills into the tropical forest.[93] Finally, the descimentos played an important role in preventing the Indians' nomadism, the "greatest difficulty" for missions in Portuguese America, as Luís da Grã wrote to Ignatius of Loyola.[94] Hence, the descimentos increased the Indians' deculturation, rendering them permeable to catechesis.

Paratiý, Rerytýba, and *Tupinambá,* three short theatre plays by Father José de Anchieta, written around 1580 in the Tupi language to be staged by the natives from Espírito Santo, depicted the Indians' removal from the original village and their transfer to the colonial settlement. In *Tupinambá,* an Indian sings:

> *My people, in old times,*
> *Followed primitive customs.*
> *The missionaries, later, looked for them,*

To reveal God
[...]
Crossing the great river
I came; I wished to see you [Saint Mary]
Come, our protector!
Provided that he can meet you
My father Tupinambá![95]

"Crossing the great river" was the reason the Jesuits helped the authorities transport Indians downstream from the hinterlands to the colonial enclaves. That was also the reason why the slave trade became acceptable in the eyes of the church. In fact, what is the deportation of the Africans if not another great crossing, a lengthy maritime, transatlantic *descimento*? Removed from the Black Continent, where the resistance of native communities, the epidemiological conditions, and the slave pillaging hindered missionary activity, the African, totally uprooted in America, became permeable to the teachings of the Church.

In this sense, it is necessary to observe the specificity of the slave trade and the characteristic status of the Jesuits in Angola and Brazil. As we observed above the missions reinforced the ideological foundation of the discoveries: evangelization justified the royal monopoly over the conquests and profits obtained from overseas commerce. This opinion is clearly stated in a book written by the Portuguese Mercedarian Serafim de Freitas, professor at the University of Valladolid, *De justo Imperio lusitanorum asiatico* (1625), a Portuguese reply to the thesis of *Mare Liberum* (1608) by Grotius. The imperative of evangelization, writes Friar Serafim de Freitas sententiously, "right and duty of the kings of Portugal," justified the royal monopoly over the Asian commerce, in particular, and the overseas commerce, in general, "since this mission can be neither performed nor advanced, amid so many most powerful nations, unconquered and far distant from each other, except under the appearance of commerce."[96]

This statement emphasizes the idea formulated almost two centuries before by the papal bull *Romanus pontifex* (1455), whose text postulated that dominium and overseas monopoly were granted to the Portuguese Crown "to compensate for the great perils, efforts and expenses, with the loss of so many nationals of the said kingdoms (Portugal and Algarve) ... for the protection and growth ... of the Catholic Faith." It was this same papal bull that advanced the first evangelical justification for the slave traffic. Two centuries later, this doctrine would be retaken and updated in the "Sermon XIV," one of the sermons of the rosary that Father Antônio Vieira preached in Bahia. Latent in the religious and social practice, the justifications for the African slave trade was framed by the paraenetic and the baroque rhetoric to legitimate seventeenth-century daily colonial life.

Vieira set a cultural limit for the remission of the Africans' souls: only Christian blacks would enjoy eternal redemption in heaven. The others, who lived in paganism in Africa, were condemned to hell. After the discovery of Upper Guinea by the Portuguese in the sixteenth century, Vieira would teach, the prophecies for the salvation of the Africans' souls, inscribed in psalms 71 and 77 of the Old Testament, started to be fulfilled: "[A]nd they are being fulfilled today, more and better than in any other part of the world, in this America," where Africans were being brought in "innumerable number." Next, addressing the blacks from Bahia, Vieira enunciated one of the boldest ideological justifications for the Atlantic traffic in Africans: "Thus the Mother of God, foreseeing your faith, your piety, your devotion, has chosen you among so many others from so many and so different nations, and has brought you to the brotherhood of the Church, so that you did not lose yourselves there [in Africa], like your parents, and you save yourselves here [in Brazil], as Her children. This is the greatest and most universal miracle of all those Our Lady of the Rosary works every day, and has worked for her devotees." Further on, he reiterates: "Oh, if the Black people taken from the dense woods of their Ethiopia, and brought to Brazil, knew how much they owe to God and to His Most Holy Mother for this which can seem like exile, captivity and disgrace, but is nothing but a miracle, and a great miracle!"[97]

In the spheres of the Atlantic market, God's invisible hand guided the African to eternal redemption in Brazil. A miracle, "and a great miracle," resulted from the massive deportation of men on slave ships across the ocean. Thanks to Our Lady of the Rosary, the Africans were being saved from Africa and brought to redeeming labor in Brazilian lands. This epiphany of the slave trade has been little noticed by Vieira's present-day commentators. But it did not escape the lay humanism of the *Maranhense* historian and author João Francisco Lisboa, who wrote in his biography of father Vieira in the 1840s: "Thus, this eternal exile from their native land and all those horrors of the crossing to which from then until now the wretched Africans have been condemned were an attenuation of the evil, and a true advantage, in the conception of the Jesuit missionary!"[98]

Frequently quoted by Vieira specialists, "Sermon xiv" is studied mostly for its second part, where the slaves' sufferings in the sugar mill are compared to the martyrdom of Christ on the cross. However, the decisive moment of Vieira's doctrine is expressed in the first part of the text, in the assertion assimilating the enslavement and deportation process in Africa to evangelization in Brazil. Bought in African markets (and drawn away from paganism), branded with the royal seal upon embarkation (and baptized on the slave ship), sold in Brazil (and placed out of harm's way in a Christian land), the African was already half way toward heaven upon landing in Portuguese America. Therefore, the problem of the legitimacy of blacks' slavery becomes a subsidiary if not invisible element in Brazilian society. Enslaved by the Africans themselves and carried to the Land of the Holy Cross through mercantile operations endorsed and taxed by the Crown, the African and his offspring became slaves in fact and in law. The work and grace of Our Lady of the Rosary solved the main issue—debated by theologians and jurists—about the conditions in which the African had been tried, captured, enslaved, and sold in African factories.

In "Sermon xxvii," preached in Salvador da Bahia, Vieira calls his contemporaries' attention to the historically unprecedented events happening in their city: "One of the extraordinary things observed in the world today, and about which, due to everyday habit, we do not wonder, is the immense transmigration of Ethiopian peoples and nations who are continuously passing from Africa to this America. ... A ship from Angola enters and unloads on a single day 500, 600 or perhaps 1,000 slaves." Next, he explains the transcendental meaning of the phenomenon: "[T]he captivity of the first transmigration is ordained by Her [Our Lady of the Rosary] mercy for freedom in the second."[99] Thus, the "first transmigration," that is, selling and deporting the African to the lands of Portuguese America, appeared as a necessary stage of the second journey, the transmigration to heaven.

In the seminary, Vieira had as his master and protector Father Fernão Cardim, one of the repressors of the antislavery dissidence that emerged at the end of the sixteenth century among the Jesuits of Bahia. Later, the slave trade's legitimacy ceased being questioned and partook of the colonial order in its own right. Vieira's "Sermon xiv," formed with Latin citations, would have been preached in a sugar mill in Bahia to the Brotherhood of the Blacks of the Rosary on the day of the feast of the patron saint in 1633. "Sermon xxvii" referred to a sermon also held in Bahia on the same feast in 1680. Revised, and maybe written especially for publication in the years 1670–1690, the sermons must be interpreted as doctrinal metatexts. Years and decades after the facts, Vieira asserted that he preached for those believers, in those places, on those dates.[100] Determinedly normative, his texts assume the doctrine's propagandistic character that the author bequeathed to Christians of the kingdom and overseas.

Illustrating the scope of the propagation of Father Vieira's pro-African slave trade arguments, the *Peregrino da América* (1728), a manual of Christian principles with five editions in the eighteenth century, as such considered a bestseller in Portuguese America, quoted almost literally the arguments of "Sermon XIV" in a parable intended for masters and slaves in Brazil.[101]

Baltazar Barreira would legitimate the slave trade with arguments drawn from commercial practice: guaranteed by the act of purchase, the master was not bound to inquire into the origin of the slave owned. Antônio Vieira thought that the slave traffic made sense because it allowed the salvation of Africans condemned to paganism in their native land. Both agreed, however, with the imperative of the enslavement and trade of Africans in the Atlantic world. Vieira emerged as a brilliant novice with the Jesuits of Bahia, at eighteen years of age, when he wrote the *Carta ânua* (1626) of the Society of Jesus, in which he made clear, among other reflections, the need for the Angolan slave trade. Seventy-two years later, on the eve of his death (1697), paralyzed, blind, almost deaf, but always possessed of the brightest strategic mind in the Lusitanian Empire, he still dictated letters reiterating the same imperative. In his last text—five days before dying at the Jesuit college of Salvador—Vieira took upon himself for the very last time the defense of the Bahia planters and slave owners. Writing to the secretary of the duke of Cadaval, he considered "a manifest injustice" the attitude of Bahia merchants, who forced a reduction in the price of sugar in conjunction with an increase in price "of things from Angola," that is, Angolan slaves.[102] Indeed, throughout his long life in Bahia, Olinda, Lisbon, Paris, The Hague, London, Rome, Maranhão, Pará, Porto, and Coimbra, Father Antônio Vieira always saw the Atlantic slave trade as the unsurpassable horizon of his time.

Once the doctrinal foundation of the African's enslavement was defined, it was necessary to make clear the evangelical duties of the slave master, who was responsible for the social reinsertion of the African in colonial Christian territory.[103] So, in the same sermons of the rosary (XIV, XX, and XXVII), Vieira strongly condemned the mistreatment and contempt that the slaves suffered. For his part, in 1707, the Jesuit Jorge Benci insisted on the "Christian Doctrine masters are obliged to teach their servants": the right to own slaves "ignorant of the Commandments of the Law of God" had as a corollary the duty to supply food for the captives' body and soul, according to the broad sense taught by Augustine: *panis, ne succumbat.*[104]

A graduate in law from Coimbra established in Bahia, Father Ribeiro Rocha dedicated part of his "theological-legal" treatise *Ethiope resgatado* (1758), which sold out in Brazil, to doctrinal edicts on the evangelizing role reserved for slave owners, especially when their slaves came directly from African hinterlands: "[E]verything theologians say about Christian doctrine, that parents should teach their children, they declare that is also true for masters regarding their slaves and, specifically speaking, those who came from infidelity [in Africa]." Refuting the belief that the slaves seemed wanting in understanding and, for this reason, unable to assimilate Christianity, Father Ribeiro Rocha returned to pre-Tridentine doctrine to affirm the magical character of prayer. He related that in the Brazilian countryside a parrot taught to pray "miraculously saved its own life by repeating the Hail Mary when a hawk carried it in its claws."[105] If even American birds "miraculously" received the protection of the divine mantle when parroting prayers, Africans, too, could develop this ability. All it would take was their masters' diligence and perseverance. Hence, the Jesuit's slave trade theory helped to give shape to Luso-Brazilian seigniorial patriarchalism.

Confronted with the obstacles that the resurgence of native cults, the climate, and the slave trade created to catechesis in Africa, the Jesuits choose Portuguese America as the main target of their activity in the Atlantic. Later, after the forced retreat from Japan and China, and the isolation of missionaries in India, Brazil became the center of the Portuguese Jesuits' enterprise. Evangelization in this one colony, Brazil, explains the apparently contradictory but in fact complementary character of Jesuit policy regarding the bondage of natives on either side of the South Atlantic. This framework defined a second complementary system, which brought together slave productions zones in Brazil with slave reproduction zones in Africa.

Notes

Translated by Monica S. Martins.
This article is a modified version of chapter 5 of my book, *O Trato dos Viventes: Formação do Brasil no Atlântico Sul, séculos XVI e XVII* (São Paulo, 2000).
1. Especially the Jesuit Francisco Suárez (d. 1617), who taught at Salamanca and Coimbra. See Jacques Lafaye, *Quetzalcóatl et Guadalupe : La formation de la conscience nationale au Méxique* (Paris, 1974), 73–74.
2. Goa, December 1, 1560, *Documentos sobre os portugueses em Moçambique e na África Central 1497–1840* (Lisbon, 1971) 7, 518–555, 532. The Jesuit Luís Fróis later went to Japan, where he wrote his monumental *História de Japam* (1584–1594), 5 vols. (Lisbon, 1976).
3. David Brion Davis, *The Problem of Slavery in Western Culture* (New York, 1966), chap. 5.
4. M. Venard, "Les bases de la Réforme catholique,» in J. M. Mayeur, C. Pietri, A. Vauchez e M. Venard, eds., *Histoire du christianisme des origines à nos jours*. 12 vols. (Paris, 1992–1994), 8, 223–279.
5. Antonio Brasio, *Monumenta Missionária Africana*. 1a série, (África Ocidental central), 15 vols. (Lisbon, 1953–1988), (hereafter *MMA1*), 2, 169–173, 179–188, 209–217.
6. "Do grande fervor que houve no colégio de Coimbra para a missão de Congo," Father Balthazar Telles, *Chronica da Companhia de Jesu nos reinos de Portugal* 2 vols. (Lisbon, 1645–1647), 1, 355.
7. There is no extant copy of that book, but its existence is recorded in documents of the time. See Father V. van Bulck, "Operum Iudicia," *Archivum Historicum Societatis Iesu*, vol. 24 (48), 1955, 455; F. Bontinck and Ndembe Nsasi, *Le catéchisme kikongo de 1624—*

Réédition critique (Brussels, 1978), 17–23. About the Franciscans in Congo, J. Cuvilier and L. Jadin, *L'Ancien Congo d'après les archives romaines 1518–1640* (Brussels, 1954), 62–64.

8. M. L. Carvalhão Buescu, "A gramaticalização das línguas exóticas no quadro cultural da Europa do século xvi," *Revista de História Economica e Social*, no. 10 (1982): 15–28.
9. I agree with Alden's opinion on this subject. See Dauril Alden, "Changing Jesuit Perceptions of the Brasis during the Sixteenth Century," *Journal of World History* 3 (Fall 1992): 212–213.
10. Bahia, August 9, 1549, Manoel da Nóbrega, *Cartas jesuíticas* 2 vols. 2nd ed. (São Paulo, 1988), 1, 87.
11. "Carta do pe. Inácio de Azevedo a Inácio de Loyola," December 7, 1553, *MMA1*, 15, 167–172, and A. A. Banha de Andrade, ed., *Dicionário de história da Igreja em Portugal* 2 vols. (Lisbon, 1979), 1, 258–260.
12. *MMA1*, 2, 229, 275, 377.
13. *MMA1*, 15, 221–225.
14. "Apontamentos das cousas de Angola," (1563) *Arquivos de Angola*, 2nd series, 16, n. 67–70, (1960) : 28–31.
15. "Carta de doação de Paulo Dias ao pe. Balthazar Barreira, Luanda, 11/7/1583," *MMA1*, 15, 279.
16. A. C. de C. M. Saunders, *A Social History of Black Slaves and Freedmen in Portugal 1441–1555* (Cambridge, 1982), 59–61. Seville, with eighty thousand inhabitants in 1550–1560, had about ten thousand Black slaves (12.5 percent), maybe the highest percentage recorded in the Iberian Peninsula, A. Stella, "L'esclavage en Andalousie à l'époque moderne," *Annales E.S.C.*, 47 (1992), 35–64.
17. Published with the wrong date (1454) elsewhere and with the correct date (1455) in Antônio Brasio, *Monumenta Missionária Africana. 2a série. (África Ocidental oeste)*, 6 vols. (Lisbon, 1958-1992) (hereafter *MMA2*), 1, 277–286. The bull revisits D. Afonso V`s arguments, taken from the first version of Zurara's *Crônica da Guiné*. As demonstrated by Witte and confirmed by Saunders, popes endorsed the justifications of the slave trade advanced by the kings of Portugal, J. de Bragança, introduction to Gomes Eanes de Zurara, *Crônica de Guiné* (Oporto, 1973), LXXIX; C.M. de Witte, "Les Bulles pontificales et l'expansion portugaise au XVe siècle," *Revue d'Histoire Ecclesiastique* 53 (1958), 5–46, 443–471, 455; the preceding parts of the study in 48 (1953), 683–718; 49 (1954), 438–461; 51 (1956), 413–453 and 809–836. Saunders, *Social History of Black Slaves*, 36–37.
18. Among his compelling arguments against enslavement and the slave trade, he states, "It is not a valid excuse to say that they [the Africans] sell themselves to each other, for the one who buys the thing wrongly sold is as guilty ... because if there were no buyers there would not have sellers, nor thieves steal to sell." Fernando Oliveira, *A Arte da Guerra no Mar* (Coimbra, 1555), "Primeira Parte," 15.
19. M. da Nóbrega, *Cartas jesuíticas*, letter of 1550, 103–113.
20. Georges Duby, *Le Chevalier, la Femme et le Prêtre* (Paris, 1981), 44–47.
21. A. Duval, *Des sacrements au Concile de Trente* (Paris, 1985), 281–326.
22. Royal ordinance of 1579 in Roland Mousnier, *Les institutions de la France sous la monarchie absolue*, 2 vols. (Paris, 1974), 1, 56–60.
23. M. da Nóbrega, *Cartas jesuíticas*, letter of 1551, 123–127.
24. Father J. Benci, *Economia cristã dos senhores no governo dos escravos* (1700) (Lisbon, 1954), 82–85. Father Antônio Vieira explains that slave marriages were prohibited by masters, because the "married ones serve less well," "Sermão xxvii," *Sermões*. 5 vols. (Porto, 1993), 4, 1214.
25. Canon 303, *Constituçoens Primeyras do Arcebispado da Bahia, feytas & ordenadas pelo ilustríssimo e reverendissimo Sr. D. Sebastião Monteyro da Vide, arcebispo do dito arcebispado* (Coimbra, 1720). A. Titton, "O Sínodo da Bahia (1707) e a escravatura." *Anais do VI Simpósio Nacional dos Professores Universitários de História* (São Paulo, 1973), 1, 285–306.

26. Act of September 15, 1869, which prohibited slave sales separating husband from wife, as well as parent from children of less than fifteen years old. Next, the free womb law (1871) extended the prohibition to separations and donations derived from inheritance, but lowered the age of the children protected by law: only those younger than twelve years old would be kept together with father *or* mother. Studies on Rio de Janeiro have demonstrated that from one third to one fifth of the lots of slaves recorded in testamentary divisions correspond to groups of first-degree relatives living together after property transmission. See M. Florentino and J.R. Góes, "Parentesco e estabilidade familiar entre os escravos do agro-fluminense, 1790–1830," *Cadernos em História Social* 1 (1995), 13–19. However, the threat of division led to continuity in traditional slave management. The heirs of a plantation might not be interested in disbanding groups familiarized with labor for the same owners and even less in separating slave families. In fact, the threat of masters' retaliation against their relatives could intimidate rebellious slaves or those prone to escaping. The percentage of kindred slaves kept after the sale of slave lots could have been much lower. Eventually, the parliamentary debate on the project of the 1869 law revealed the frauds that allowed for the sale of family members separately. *Jornal do Commércio*, Rio de Janeiro, April 4, 1864.
27. Orlando Patterson, *Slavery and Social Death* (Cambridge, MA, 1982), 29.
28. Royal ordinance of March 8, 1546, on the Christianity of India, Antonio da Silva Rego, *Documentação para a História das Missões do Padroado Português do Oriente* (hereafter *DHMPPO*) 12 vols. (Lisbon, 1991), 3, 315–317; Royal letter of 1557 to Francisco Barreto, governor of India (1555–1558), *MMA1*, 2, 404. In the same vein, "Carta dos governadores de Portugal sobre a alforria dos gentios," March 15, 1580, *MMA1*, 3, 84–85. In 1560, Philip II prohibited the Moors still living in Andalusia from owning slaves to prevent the latter from being converted to Muslim customs.
29. *MMA1*, Document of 1594, 3, 471–479.
30. Report of 1618, *MMA1*, 6, 341.
31. C.J. de Senna Barcellos, *Subsídios para a história de Cabo Verde e Guiné*. 3 vols. (Lisbon, 1899–1911), 1, part 2, 173.
32. Father D. Maurício, "A Universidade de Évora e a escravatura," *Didaskalia* 7 (1977): 153–200, 172, 185.
33. Fortunato de Almeida, *História da Igreja em Portugal (1910–1928)* (hereafter *HIP*), 4 vols., (Porto, 1967–1971), 2, 169–181, 297–310. The college of São Paulo de Goa owned the revenues from villages and also the namoxins—land of an agrarian community whose product returns to religious cult—of Goa and adjacencies. See A. de Almeida Calado, "A Companhia de Jesus na Índia em meados do século xvii," *Studia*, n. 40 (1978): 349–366. In 1567, the Jesuits Superior General Francisco de Borja protested against the Japan contract, according to which Portuguese merchants would buy a certain amount of silk in Macao and sell it in Japan, handing over the revenue to the Jesuit mission. See Father J. Wicki, "Dois compêndios das ordens dos padres gerais e congregações da provincial dos jesuítas de Goa," *Studia*, nos. 43–44 (1980): 343–532, 400; C.R. Boxer, *O Grande Navio de Amacau* (Macao, 1989), 175–179.
34. Complying with a charter of July 20, 1611, which ordered Jesuits to list their properties in Angola, the Jesuits listed several farms in Luanda, Bengo, and Massangano, but declared that they did not produce anything, *MMA1*, 6, 91–102.
35. Father García was a Spaniard. See Serafim Leite, *História da Companhia de Jesus no Brasil 1549–1760* (hereafter *HCJB*) 10 vols. (Lisbon and Rio de Janeiro, 1938–1950), 2, 567.
36. *HCJB*, 2, 227–228.
37. "Carta ao geral da Companhia," Lisbon, September 6, 1586, *MMA1*, 15, 298–299.
38. Opinions about slavery written by the theologians Luís de Molina, Fernão Perez, and Gaspar Gonçalves, scholars at Coimbra and the University of Évora, Telles, *Chronica*, 2, 454–470.

39. The *Mesa da Consciência e Ordens* was the Royal Tribunal and Council for religious affairs.
40. Letter from Father Cristóvão de Gouveia, Bahia, July 25, 1583, *MMA1*, 15, 280–281.
41. "Confessionnal," G. Jacquemet, G. Mathon, G.H. Baudry, P. Guilluy, and E. Thiery, *Catholicisme—Hier, aujourd'hui, demain*, 13 vols. (Paris, 1954–1993), 2, 1507–1510.
42. Lana L. da Gama Lima, "A confissão pelo avesso—O crime de solicitação no Brasil colonial," 3 vols. Ph.D dissertation in History, Universidade de São Paulo,1990, 1, 184–185. J. Delumeau, *L'aveu et le pardon: Les difficultés de la confession XIIIe-XVIIIe siècle* (Paris, 1995), 46–71. The theologian Michel de Bay, said Baius (1513–1589), had taught at the University of Louvain, which had close relations with Spanish and Portuguese universities.
43. *MMA1*, 3, 37–38.
44. A. Duval, *Des Sacrements*, 153–154.
45. Royal provision of 1556, Telles, *Chronica*, 2, 188–189.
46. F. Cardim, *Tratado da terra e gente do Brasil* 1585 (São Paulo, 1978), 171.
47. Letter to the Society's general, 1586, *HCJB*, 2, 228–229.
48. "Our people [of the Society of Jesus] shall not possess, nor buy or sell suspicious captives, nor absolve those who own them, nor follow the opinion of those who say that it is better to hold them in bondage than being them lost, nor buy or sell them to seculars." Decision of the general Cláudio Acquaviva, 1588, Father J. Wicki, "Dois compêndios," 376.
49. Friar Amador Arrais, doctor in Theology from the University of Coimbra, joined the Calced Carmelites as a novice in 1545. In 1581, he was appointed bishop of Porto Alegre, *Diálogos* 1589 (Porto, 1974), 112–115, 207, 285.
50. "Baptême," A. Vacant, E. Mangenot, and E. Amman, *Dictionnaire de théologie catholique*, 15 vols. (Paris, 1930–1972), 2,167–377.
51. The question of manumitting slaves converted to Judaism was also put before the Jewish hierarchy in Dutch Brazil. The 1648 rulings of the congregation *Zur Israel* of Recife, the first to be written by a Jewish community in a modern slave society, dictated measures to prevent slaves converted to Judaism from being kept in bondage: trying to hinder masters from selling slaves already converted, the congregation prohibited the circumcision of slaves before they had been properly manumitted. See Arnold Wiznitzer, *The Records of the Earliest Jewish Community in the New World* (New York, 1954).
52. A. Brásio wrote that this text by Bishop Brandão is dated from 1606–1608, *MMA2*, 3, 442–445. About the manumission given to captives converted to Islam—a more complex process than that suggested here by the Carmelite, see J.R. Willis, "The Ideology of Enslavement in Islam," and idem, "Jihad and the Ideology of Enslavement," *Slaves & Slavery in Muslim Africa* 2 vols. (London, 1985), 1, 1–15 and 16–26.
53. Curiously, Bishop Brandão, retired since 1594 in Lisbon, where he established an entail (*morgado*), was accused of having become rich at the expense of his Cape Verdean diocesans and also of having trafficked slaves. See F. de Almeida, *HIP*, 2, 685. Senna Barcellos does not mention it. He says only that Brandão was a merchant and that he and his diocesans disagreed because he wished to impose religious fasting on them and prohibit concubinage. Could the accusations of slave trading have been forged by his enemies? It does not matter. Even written by a bishop who became rich through questionable means or by a regretful slave trader, the text by Friar Brandão develops a consistent argumentation, which transforms it into an exceptional document for understanding conservative antislavery thought: *MMA2*, 4, 26–27, 28–29, 50–51, 92–95, 178–181, 299–300; Senna Barcelos, *Subsídios*, 1, part 2, 159–160, 172–175, 178.
54. In his study on Father Luís de Molina, Hespanha considers the author of the *Tractatus de iustitia et de iure* (1593) as the first theologian to analyze systematically the theme of the African slave trade. He also states that the topic is approached with great delay when compared with the controversy over Amerindian slavery. In fact, the extension of At-

lantic commerce and the discussions about the establishment of the asiento gave a new meaning to the African slave trade at the end of the seventeenth century. See Antônio M. Hespanha, "Luís de Molina e a escravização dos negros," *Análise Social* XXXV (2001): 937–960.
55. The visit to Angola was decided on January 4, 1592, in Lisbon; Pero Rodrigues arrived in Africa in March 1593, coming from Bahia. He inspected the missions of Luanda and Massangano. *MMA1*, 3, 471.
56. *MMA1*, 3, 471–479, and 15, 333–338. Serafim Leite omits the Jesuits' opposition to the royal orders on the control of the natives of Angola expressed by the congregation held in Bahia, *HCJB*, 2, 502–503.
57. *HCJB*, 2, 496–497.
58. "Carta Ânua da Residência de Angola" (1579), *MMA1*, 3, 184–186.
59. "Carta do pe. Balthazar Barreira para o pe. Sebastião de Morais," Luanda, January 31, 1582, *MMA1*, 3, 208–211.
60. Document of January 31, 1582, *MMA1*, 3, 212–213.
61. In 1584, Barreira sent Father Balthazar Afonso, another bellicose missionary, to the island of São Tomé to bring men and "some support in the form of gunpowder" to help Novais, *MMA1*, 3, 265–267.
62. "Carta do governador de Cabo Verde a el-rei d. Filipe ii, 25. 7.1613," *MMA1*, 4, 507–541.
63. Letter of December 25, 1652, *MMA1*, 4, 24–26.
64. Telles, *Chronica*, 2, 617–652; See also D. Barbosa Machado, *Biblioteca lusitana* (1741–1759). 4 vols. (Lisbon, 1930–1933), 4, 435. For a more recent and more balanced article on Barreira, see Banha de Andrade, *Dicionário*, 2, 186–187.
65. Letter from Francisco de Borja to the provincial J. Henriques, 1566, *MMA1*, 3, 476–477. Another letter in the same vein to Father Gonçalo Alvarez, in November 2, 1569, letter from Acquaviva to Father Francisco Monclaro in 1588. Father J. Wicki, "Dois compêndios," 376.
66. Patterson, *Slavery and Social Death*, 27–32.
67. "Informação acerca dos escravos de Angola," (1582–1583) *MMA1*, 3, 227–231.
68. Francisco de Gouveia, "Carta ao geral da Companhia," December 16, 1596, *MMA2*, 3, 402. For ten years, Gouveia was a professor of moral theology at the college of Évora before being rector of the same college, procurator of the Province at the Curia, and, finally, provincial in Portugal. His opinions on the matter carried great authority.
69. About the Atlantic slave trade, Friar Antônio de São Domingos would teach at the University of Coimbra at the end of the seventeenth century: "Either it is acknowledged that the king does not care about this business, or it is not. If it is, nobody can buy these Blacks, except for those who want undertake this diligence; if it is not, then, one should presume that all is being done correctly, for this duty belongs to them only and one should believe they fulfill it perfectly, otherwise a manifest injury is being done to them. Consequently, we can buy Blacks with a safe conscience as long as things are thus." Father A. de C.X. Monteiro, "Como se ensinava o Direito das Gentes na Universidade de Coimbra no século xvi," *Anais*, 2nd series, 33 (1993), 26.
70. For a nonexclusive repertoire of Barreira's letters, Fathers R. Streit and J. Dindinger, *Bibliotheca Missionum*, 30 vols. (Freiburg, 1963–1975), vols. 15 and 16. About the meaning of "edifying letters," see "Instruções de Francisco Xavier," 1549, A. da Silva Rego, *DHMPPO*, 4, 292, and 5, x–xiii.
71. Pierre Chaunu, *Eglise, culture et société* (Paris, 1981), 397–401.
72. Decision taken after the fifth general congregation held in Rome in 1594, Father J. Wicki, "Dois compêndios," 376 and 431.
73. "Carta do padre Balthazar Barreira," Massangano, August 27, 1585, *MMA1*, 3, 323–325. Telles mentions this letter and says, based on a different document, that those noses formed a load carried by twenty Blacks. *Chronica*, 2, 628.

74. Patterson, *Slavery and Social Death*, 3.
75. *MMA1*, 3, 199.
76. *MMA1*, 3, 375.
77. *MMA1*, 3, art. 26 of "Instruções," 477.
78. Memorial of June 15, 1593, *MMA1*, 15, 333–338.
79. The crucial role played by Pero Rodrigues, Baltazar Barreira, and the leaders of the Jesuits in the construction of the South Atlantic slave system has been ignored. Dauril Alden does not even mention those two Jesuits in his work *The Making of an Enterprise: The Society of Jesus in Portugal, its Empire, and Beyond, 1540–1750* (Stanford, 1996).
80. *História da residência dos padres da Companhia de Jesus em Angola e cousas tocantes ao reino e à conquista,* Luanda, May 1, 1594. Visitador Pero Rodrigues wrote the first chapter and Father Baltazar Afonso, chapters 6, 7, 8, and 9. Baltazar Afonso has been a missionary in Angola for twenty-eight years and died there in 1603. A faithful fellow of Barreira, he also championed the military conquest of the territory. *MMA1*, 4, 546–581.
81. "Dos escravos que saem de Cabo Verde," (1606), text sent to the provincial of Portugal, *MMA2*, 4, 190–199. P.E.H. Hair makes a precise analysis of this and other texts written by Barreira in Cape Verde and Guinea in "Heretics, Slaves and Witches: As Seen by Guinea Jesuits c. 1610," *Journal of Religion in Africa* 28 (May 1998): 131–144.
82. On this specific point, see Father M. Ribeiro Rocha, *Ethiope resgatado, empenhado, sustentado, corregido, instruído e libertado. Discurso theologico-juridico em que se propõem o modo de comerciar, haver, e possuir validamente, quanto a hum e outro foro, os pretos cativos africanos, e as principais obrigações que correm a quem delles se servir* (Lisbon, 1758), 37–63.
83. Father Antonio Vieira, "Informação sobre o modo com que foram tomados e sentenciados por cativos os índios do ano de 1655," *Obras escolhidas*, 12 vols. (Lisbon, 1951–1954), 5, 61.
84. Letter from Father B. Barreira, Sierra Leone, March 4, 1607, *MMA2*, 4, 220–222.
85. Letter of March 5, 1607, *MMA2*, 4, 227.
86. Document of August 21, 1611, *MMA1*, 15, 442–443.
87. A. Milhou, "L'Afrique," J.M. Mayeur, C. Pietri, A. Vauchez, M. Venard, eds., *Histoire du Christianisme*, 3, 685–690. Alonso de Sandoval, *Naturaleza, policía sagrada i profana, costumbres i ritos, disciplina i catecismo evangelico de todos los etíopes* (1627). Edition by Enriqueta Vila Vilar, *Un tratado sobre la esclavitud* (Madrid, 1987), 154.
88. Luís de Molina questioned the legitimacy of the slave trade grounded on the evangelizing argument of this papal bull, cf. A. Manuel Hespanha, "Luís de Molina," 958–-959.
89. Luís Mendes de Vasconcellos wrote about the *jagas*: "[T]here are likely more [slaves] whom they eat than they deliver alive, for this is their most ordinary food," Arquivo Historico Ultramarino, Angola, box 1/74, August 28, 1617.
90. Born in 1559, João Baptista Fragoso taught theology at the college of Santo Antão de Lisboa and at the University of Évora, established in 1559 to educate Jesuit theologians. Father D. Maurício, "A Universidade de Évora," 53 and 191–195.
91. Fernão Rebelo taught at Évora from 1586 to 1596, Father D. Maurício, "A Universidade,"183.
92. *MMA1*, 13, 465–473; Biblioteca Nacional de Lisboa (hereafter BNL), Res. 2761 (P), *Ao senhor governador e capitam geral Ayres de Saldanha de Menezes, & Souza, os religiosos da Companhia de Jesu, sobre o Collegio, Missoens, & Seminario de Angola,* reproduced in *MMA1*, 13, 455–464.
93. *HCJB*, 6, 552, and 5, 23 and 165.
94. "Carta de Luís da Grã a Santo Inácio," Piratininga, June 8, 1556, Father M. da Nóbrega, *Diálogo sobre a conversão do gentio Diálogo sobre a conversão do gentio* 1557 (Lisbon, 1954), appendix B, 115.
95. J. de Anchieta, *Poesias* (São Paulo, 1954), 578–580.

96. S. de Freitas, *De Justo Imperio Lusitanorum Asiatico*, 2 vols. (Lisbon, 1983), 1, 217, 364, and 367, and 2, 94. Friar Serafim was a religious of the Order of Mercy.
97. "Sermon xiv," *Sermões*, 4, 733–769. In Sermon xxvii, Vieira contradictorily classifies the slave trade as a "diabolical trade" and then justifies it using the same arguments from Sermon xiv: "[C]aptivity in the first transmigration [deportation to Brazil] is ordained by her [Our Lady of the Rosary] mercy for freedom in the second [transmigration to heaven]." A slave should work diligently for this master, because, after death, he would receive directly from God payment for the unpaid labor performed on the farms of Brazil, ibid., 1202–1241. For other comments on this topic, see L. Koshiba, "A Honra e a Cobiça," Ph.D. dissertation, Universidade de São Paulo, 1988, 2 vols., 2, 293–298; and A. Bosi, *Dialética da colonização* (São Paulo, 1992), 143–148.
98. J.F. Lisboa, *Vida do padre Antônio Vieira* 1865 (Rio de Janeiro, 1891), 352. Published posthumously, this book was written before the end of the slave trade to Brazil in 1850. More recently, Saraiva insisted on Vieira's support to the introduction of African slavery in Maranhão, but the key point in Vieira's theory, emphasized by João Francisco Lisboa, is his justification for the Atlantic traffic in Africans. A.J. Saraiva, "Le père Antonio Vieira S.J. et la question de l'esclavage des Noirs au XVIIème siècle," *Annales E.S.C.* XXII (1967), 1289–1309.
99. "Sermão xxvii," *Sermões*, 4, 1205.
100. The wording and chronology of the sermons are objects of discussion among Vieira scholars.
101. Nuno Marques Pereira, *Compêndio Narrativo do Peregrino da América* 1728 2 vols. (Rio de Janeiro, 1988), 1, 148–150. The author lived in Bahia, where he might have been born, and in Minas Gerais: ibid., 3–22.
102. Letter to Sebastião de Matos e Sousa, Bahia, July 10, 1697, *Cartas do pe. Antônio Vieira*. 3 vols. 2a reimp. Ed. J.L. de Azevedo (Lisboa, 1997), 3, 712–714.
103. There is no contradiction at all in Vieira's ideas about slavery. To the contrary, Vieira is favorable to the slave trade as an instrument of colonial politics, at the same time as he incites masters to treat slaves humanely and opposes vigorously the enslavement of Indians. His positions are complementary, not contradictory.
104. Benci, *Economia cristã*, 63–104.
105. Father M. Ribeiro Rocha, *Ethiope*, 227, 232–233. Inocêncio Francisco da Silva, in his *Diccionário bibliographico portuguez*, reports that the edition of Father Ribeiro Rocha's book sold out in Brazil. In other words, the book had been printed in Portugal to be sold in Brazil, which shows the ways around the lack of printing presses in Portuguese America.

– Chapter 3 –

THE ECONOMIC ROLE OF SLAVERY IN A NON-SLAVE SOCIETY
The River Plate, 1750–1860

Juan Carlos Garavaglia

Introduction

What is the role of slavery in a colonial and postcolonial American society in which it did not constitute the central nucleus of the relations of production, as it did in Cuba? We will consider as an example the rural area of the River Plate from the middle of the eighteenth century until 1860, when the institution of slavery was officially abolished. Until recently, Argentine historiography treated slaves as if they were just another luxury item that formed part of the colony's patriarchal society. Their presence was justified—when it was not completely silenced—above all by their role as domestic servants. The situation was in fact quite different. We will focus primarily on two regions that present very diverse profiles of production in this immense space that made up the River Plate. On the one hand, the region of the Pampa represented an area of prime importance that was settled by different types of units of production (large, medium, and small) dedicated to wheat and livestock. The presence of slavery was widely diffused there, and slaves had a central role in the stability of agrarian productive relations. On the other, we will consider the region of Cuyo, a very rich oasis in the piedmont of the Andes that produced wine, cereals, and fruit as its principal vocation. There, slaves were the fundamental source of labor. This fact is striking, as activities such as those related to viniculture generally do not employ this type of forced labor. Map 3.1 shows the location of these two regions.

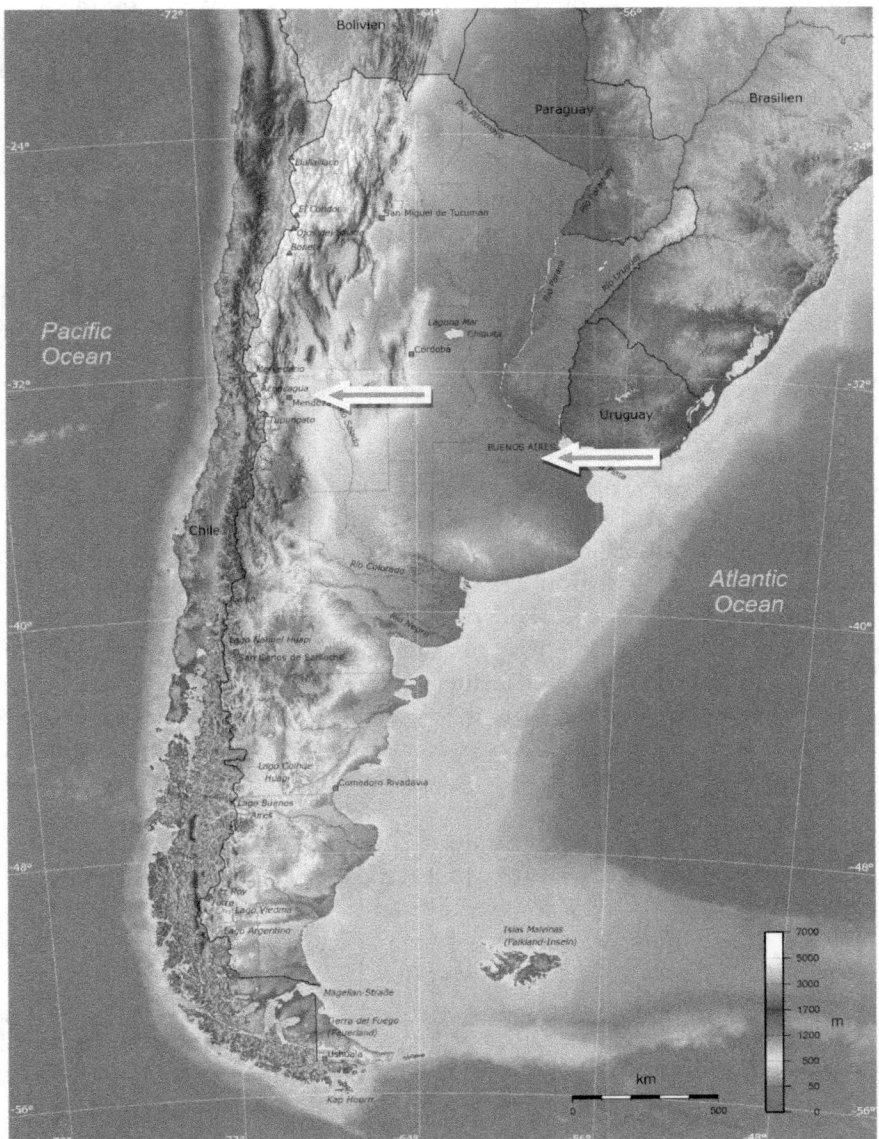

Map 3.1. Two slaveholding regions in the Río de la Plata

Slavery in the Countryside of Buenos Aires

The presence of slaves in this region and in its productive activities has been documented since the first occupation of the territory at the end of the sixteenth century. The proximity of Brazil made the traffic of slaves from Africa itself and from the Portuguese colony a very lucrative activity that even managed to excite a famous bishop of Tucumán. It is clear therefore that African slaves were indeed present in the life of the River Plate colony from its origins. Slave labor represented an indispensable tool for the farms and *estancias*[1] in a region where the sparse indigenous population could not be easily exploited as a workforce.[2] Slavery thus constituted one of the principal sources of manpower well into the eighteenth century in the very humble colony that surrounded the city of Buenos Aires, which at that time did not have more than two thousand inhabitants.

Little by little, the *mestizos* (persons of mixed race), along with migrants from Tucumán and other regions of the interior, were becoming integrated into this area also as day laborers on the farms and estancias. The descendents of these day laborers and many other migrants, as well as more than a few black freedmen, were forming a peasant population made up of small producers. In this context, it is essential to keep in mind the fundamental role that the existence of an open frontier played, as it created an offer of fertile lands that were relatively accessible to production and, though more rarely, to ownership. Possessing a certain degree of liberty, this growing peasant population thus limited in turn the supply of free labor, given that it controlled means of production such as land and a few animals. Peasants, therefore, did not have the slightest interest in selling their labor to the large farmers and *estancieros*, and they made sure that they were very well paid at the time of the wheat harvest when their presence was indispensable. This situation in turn explains the continual necessity for a stable workforce, and this group was primarily composed of African slaves.

In the middle of the eighteenth century, in a rural population of about six thousand inhabitants (the city had at that time almost twelve thousand inhabitants) there were a few more than seven hundred individuals of color, half of whom were slaves of both sexes. The population pyramid that corresponds to 1744 shows two phenomena that would be characteristic in the future: the indubitable existence of some families—including among the slaves—and a very high masculinity rate (MR) in the cohorts of workers. It indicates that even if there were domestic groups of slaves and free mulattos, the greater presence of male slaves and freedmen of working age is clear. Almost seventy years later, when the first postrevolutionary governments carried out a series of excellent censuses between

1812 and 1815, we can see that the total population of the countryside had multiplied by ten, more than forty-two thousand inhabitants (such growth can only be explained by the continuous migrations from the interior and the existence of a relatively open frontier of fertile lands).[3] And the relative proportions of the total rural population, the population of color, and the slaves continued being almost exactly the same as at the middle of the eighteenth century.

Let us now examine a series of tables and graphs that depict the slave population based on the 1813–1815 censuses, when a total of 3,364 slaves were registered as forming part of the rural population of the countryside of Buenos Aires.[4] Graph 3.1 shows us the population pyramid of slaves that inhabited the countryside in 1813–1815.

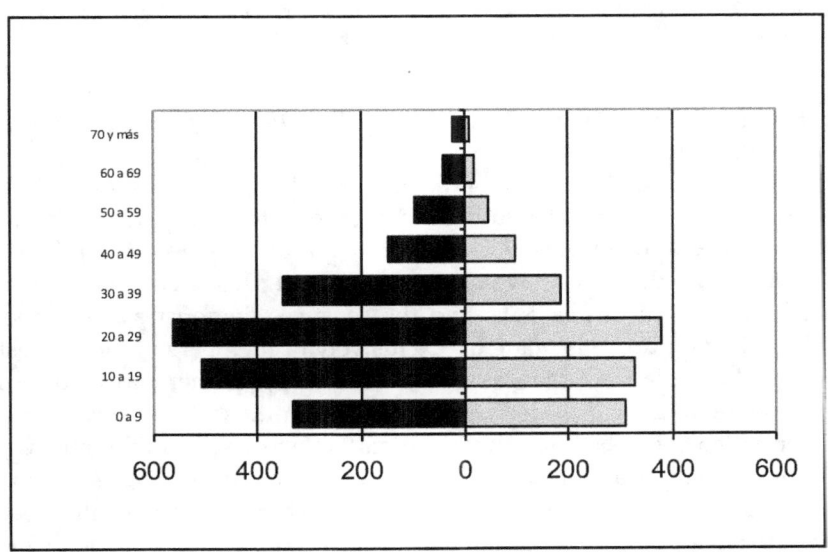

Graph 3.1. Population Pyramid of Slaves in rural Buenos Aires 1813–1815. Source: "La sociedad rural bonaerense a principios del siglo XIX."

This pyramid indicates very high masculinity rates for those of working age[5] and the presence of domestic groups with children who are slaves in the first cohort (because of the *libertad de vientres* [law of free wombs] of 1813 we already find in this census about sixty-one freed slaves who are less than two years of age, not included in this first graph). As we stated above, this pyramid almost replicates the one that represents the results from 1744,[6] thus demonstrating the continuity of the place that slaves occupied in this rural society and the regularity of their demographic profile. If we compare the preceding pyramid to the one that corresponds

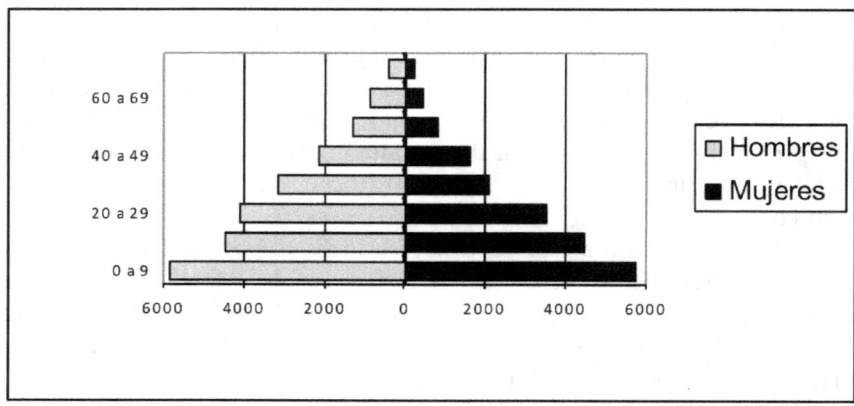

Graph 3.2. Population Pyramid in rural Buenos Aires 1813–1815. Source: "La sociedad rural bonaerense a principios del siglo XIX."

to the general population of the countryside, we will see the differences much more clearly.

We are definitely dealing here with a rural population with very pronounced masculinity rates in the labor cohorts (due in part precisely to the presence of male slaves), but it is much more balanced than the preceding pyramid. As we have already indicated, this society is predominately composed of peasants, and the censuses demonstrate that about half of the workforce is made up exclusively of members of the domestic group. What place do the slaves therefore occupy? There are two forms of dependent labor included in the censuses in those years, day laborers (often called peons) and slaves. It is remarkable to discover that there were almost as many slaves as day laborers and peons (in reality, 52.8 percent were slaves and 47.2 percent peons and day laborers). This result already gives us an idea of the central place that slaves occupied in the dependent workforce. Obviously, the total number of slaves includes children and women, but it does not mean that both categories did not form part of the workforce. In the case of the children their participation obviously depended on their age, but we should not forget that in a rural society such as this, children started to help with chores between the ages of eight and ten. As for women, we know quite well that the simple expression *domestic service* disguised quite a number of tasks (washing and ironing clothes, fetching water, cooking, etc.) that must be paid for when there were no slaves.

Let us see now how the peons/day laborers and slaves were distributed in the distinct farming and ranching zones that constitute the countryside surrounding Buenos Aires:

Table 3.1. Buenos Aires, 1813–1815, Dependent Workforce by Zones

Zones	North	Percentage	Cercana	Percentage	West	Percentage	South	Percentage	Total	Percentage
Peons	832	45.8	697	35.7	802	48.8	923	62.6	3254	47.2
Slaves	985	54.2	1255	64.3	843	51.2	541	37.4	3364	52.8
Total	1817	100	1952	100	1645	100	1474	100	6888	100
Percentage	26.4		28.3		23.9		21.4		100	

Source: "La sociedad rural bonaerense a principios del siglo XIX."

Before discussing this table, let us point out the principal characteristics of these zones. There is a clear division between two areas where the production of livestock (cows, horses, and sheep) predominated (the north, the area of early colonization near Santa Fe and the south, which was expanding vigorously but was also limited by the border with the Indian territory). The western zone was characterized by a mix of livestock ranching and production of cereals, whereas the countryside close to the city (Cercana) stands out as the wheat-producing region par excellence. Such a configuration can be seen as an expression of the theory of productive circles, which was elaborated by Johann Heinrich von Thünen in the first decades of the nineteenth century, in which livestock—which have "feet"—arrives from the more distant areas and the heavy carts loaded with wheat come from the areas that are closest to the city. Even if the peasants, workers, and shepherds could be disseminated in all of the zones, their maximum concentration, for obvious reasons, was in the areas that produced wheat or both wheat and livestock. Map 3.2 shows the locations of these different zones.

Let us consider table 3.1 now. First of all, it should be pointed out again that it only includes those who were older than ten, whether they were peons or slaves. Slaves constituted the majority in all of the zones apart from the clear exception of the south, where ranching predominated as the principal activity. They even dominated in the zone closest to the market, which the city of Buenos Aires represented. What would happen if we only discussed the male workforce?

Table 3.2. Distribution of the Masculine Nondomestic Workforce in the Countryside

Zones	North	Percentage	Cercana	Percentage	West	Percentage	South	Percentage	Total	Percentage
Peons	832	61.4	697	44.9	802	64.8	920	71	3254	60
Slaves	523	39.2	854	55.1	436	35.2	375	29	1700	31
Total	1355	100	1551	100	1238	100	1289	100	5442	100
Percentage	25.5		28.3		22.5		23.5		100	–

Source: "La sociedad rural bonaerense a principios del siglo XIX."

Regiones : censos de 1813 y 1815

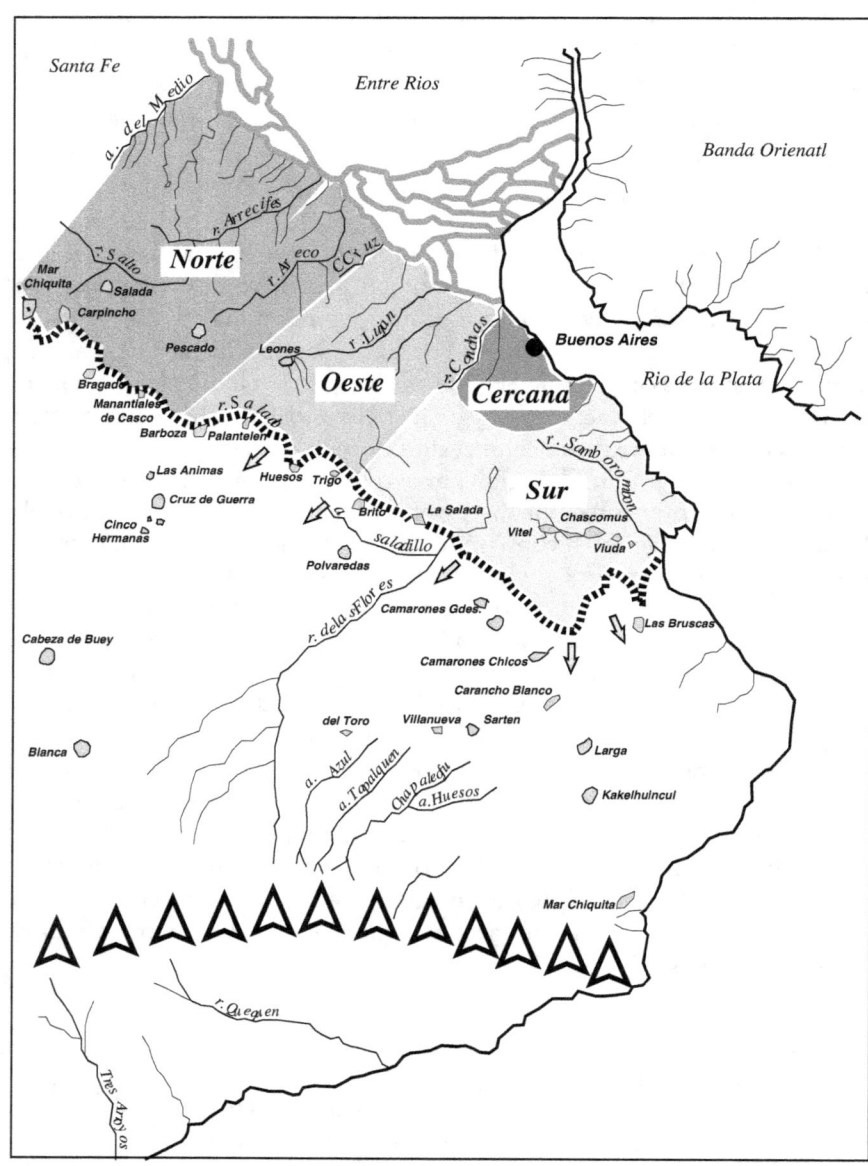

Segun el mapa de Londres de 1824

Map 3.2. Environs of Buenos Aires

Some changes can be observed, but in the case of the zone close to the city, it is obvious that there were more slaves working than freedmen, whether they were called day laborers or peons (in any case, it has to be pointed out that female slaves carried out a series of tasks that were not exclusively domestic). This chart shows us the importance of slavery in the productive agrarian relations of the countryside of Buenos Aires at the end of the colonial period. Let us continue with this line of argumentation; the third table shows us the number of male and female slaves of working age—always, as in the two preceding tables, we are speaking of those who were over the age of ten—in each zone and their respective masculinity rates (MR).

Table 3.3. Distribution of Slaves (Male and Female) by the Zones of the Countryside

Zones	North	Percentage	Cercana	Percentage	West	Percentage	South	Percentage	Total	Percentage
Men	388	22.8	589	34.6	418	24.7	305	17.9	1700	100
Women	300	29.6	214	21.1	362	35.7	138	13.6	1014	100
Total	688	25.4	803	30	780	28.7	443	16.3	2714	100
RM	1.29		2.75		1.15		2.21		1.67	

Source: "La sociedad rural bonaerense a principios del siglo XIX."

As the table clearly demonstrates, the difference in the MR among the different zones was visible and there was a greater presence of male slaves in the two quite diverse zones for different reasons: on the one hand, the Cercana zone closet to the city where the production of wheat reigned on the large farms that produced cereals and, on the other, the frontier area of the south, where the largest livestock estancias were concentrated. Producing wheat and livestock, the western zone continued to be the area where there was a greater equilibrium between the sexes for all of the people of color, slave and free. The same is true in the so-called old north where ranching predominated.

The next two graphs clearly show the differences in the population pyramids of the slaves between San Isidro, a rural area that belonged to the wheat-growing zone par excellence—that we call here Cercana—with an MR of 1.9 and Upper Areco, an area of the still open frontier in the western region where both farming and ranching were present, where we can see the relative equilibrium between the sexes as well as the presence of slaves of both sexes younger than ten; the MR in this case is 1.3. Another notable difference is that in San Isidro, more than 61 percent of the slaves were Africans, whereas in Upper Areco this proportion drops to 33 per-

82 | *Juan Carlos Garavaglia*

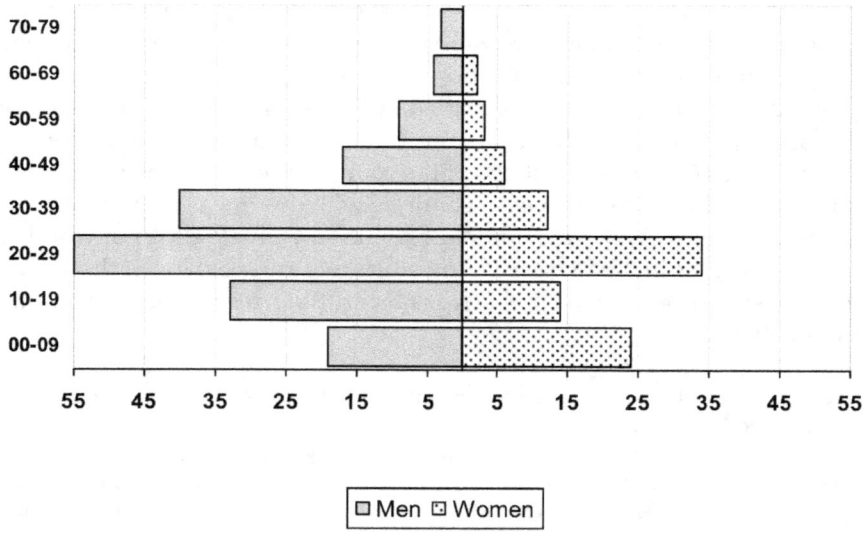

Graph 3.3. Slaves in San Isidro, 1815. Source: Archivo General de la Nación, Buenos Aires (Henceforth AGN), X-8-10-4

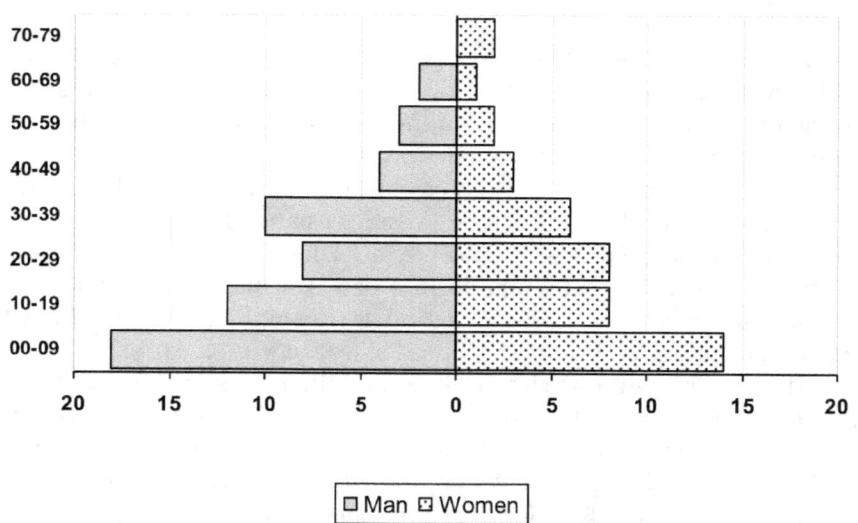

Graph 3.4. Slaves in Areco Arriba, 1815. Source: AGN, X-8-10-4

cent, thus representing a majority of Creole slaves that have already been integrated into the region for some time and demonstrate a certain degree of domestic stability.

To understand better the relation between the domestic workforce and the two forms of dependent labor, that is, slaves and peons, we can add a few more facts about San Isidro, the region that we have already seen represented in one of the preceding pyramids. It is one of the two principal nuclei of wheat production close to the city (the other is Matanza). Table 3.4 shows these data.

Table 3.4. Workforce: Domestic Workforce, Slaves and Peons, San Isidro, 1815

	Only Domestic Workforce		Peons		Slaves		Peons and Slaves	
	Members	UP	Members	UP	Members	UP	Members	UP
Totals	4.66	102	5.77	22	9.02	37	11.72	11
Percentages		59		12.8		21.5		6.4

Source: AGN, IX-19-2-5

We can see that the 171 units of production of peasants (*labradores*) that the census of 1815 enumerates can be classified in the following manner. First of all in the 102 units where the domestic group represented the only workforce (59 percent of the total), there was an average of 4.66 members per unit. These were obviously the poorest peasants. Then come the 22 units in which there was at least one peon. In this group we generally find the peasant families that are in two completely opposite moments of their life cycles: very young families that still had very small children or, at the other extreme, families whose children had already left, leaving the parents alone. In both cases, the help of a peon was indispensable. Next, we have the units of production of the middling and the so-called rich peasants—relatively speaking, of course. For this group, the presence of slaves or slaves and peons allowed them to reach 9 to 11 members respectively per unit, representing thereby 28 percent of the total number of labradores. There were also in San Isidro two millers and five *hacendados* that possessed many more slaves and peons; Table 8 (below) shows such a case, the miller and baker Guadalupe Baquero who had fourteen slaves, nine peons, and a foreman.

The examination of postmortem inventories for estancias and farms supplies even firmer evidence for assessing the importance of slavery in this society. Table 5 shows the data for a series of four hundred inventories from 1754 to 1815[7] that we studied. It reveals the percentages of the total of the capital goods in each inventory (we have subtracted the value of clothes, luxury goods, and urban real estate).

Table 3.5. Capital Goods, 1754–1815 (Percentages)

Cattle	26
Slaves	17
Constructions	16
Land	13
Horses and Sheep	11
Trees and enclosures	9
Wheat	2
Oxen	2

Source: Garavaglia, unpublished database.

It is easy to perceive that after livestock—the principal capital good of the estancias and, to a lesser degree, on the farms—slaves were the most important means of production—their value even surpassed that of the land (the offer of fertile lands was still open, which explains the low value of land). In the case of both the livestock estancias and farms, we can state that one of every two establishments possessed slaves, the average being four slaves per unit of production.

The following table shows us the importance of the slaves in the diverse types of units of production (UP in the graph) and the different levels of capitalization in relation to the presence, number, and value of the slaves.

Table 3.6. Slaves and Levels of Capitalization in the Diverse UP, 1754–1815

	Farms	Estancias	Mixed Estancias	Hacendados
Inventories	92	291	75	13
Percentage UP with Slaves	46	52	64	100
Number of Slaves per UP	3.7	4.3	5.5	9.5
Average Price for Slaves (Pesos)	215	189	208	223
Total Value of Slaves (Pesos)	796	813	1144	2118
Average Value of the UP (Pesos)	1960	3046	3540	20760

Source: *Les hommes de la pampa.*

Two clarifications: the so-called mixed estancias were those in which the presence of plows and other agricultural tools were a sure sign of dual activity—livestock and producing wheat—of the unit of production; the hacendados [8] were the owners of the establishments worth more than ten thousand pesos. The more a unit of production was capitalized, the greater the frequency of slaves (see the second row of the table); at the same time, at a higher level of capitalization, there were more slaves and of better quality—this we can measure by their prices. And the last line shows something that is obvious; the more an establishment was capitalized, the less the slaves weighed in the total of the capital goods. This table only has one explanation, and it is noteworthy: the farms were the establishments that, relatively, possessed the highest-priced slaves—only the hacendados surpassed this average—moreover, they were where the investment in slaves weighed more in relation to the total investment, reaching 41 percent. Once again, the importance of slave labor in relation to the production of wheat is made evident by these figures. And they also show that the grade of intensity of work can be measured by these indicators. Slaves were more important wherever the regular and constant need for labor was greater and where the salaries paid to the day workers and peons were the highest. Let us not forget that in the areas of the zone closest to the city where the production of wheat was centered, that is, San Isidro and Matanza, one out of every three males over the age of twelve was a slave, freedman, or free black.

Table 3.7. Capital Goods and the Slaves on the Estancia Laguna de Barragán

	1792 Pesos	Percentage	1815 Pesos	Percentage	1824 Pesos	Percentage
Buildings	199	7.7	250	3.6	300	1.1
Enclosures	201	7.8	272	4.0	350	1.3
Carts	—		135	2.0	112	0.4
Trees	4		546	8.0	339	1.3
Tools	15		20		30	
Miscellaneous	37		170		677	
Subtotal	456	17.8	1493	21.8	1667	6.3
Land	575	22.4	526	7.7	5500	21.0
Slaves	**580 (2)**	**22.6**	**1250 (5)**	**18.3**	**2230 (10)**	**8.5**
Livestock	955	37.2	3562	52.0	16811	64.1
Totals	2566	100	6831	100	26208	100

Source: AGN-Sucesiones 5561 y AGN-Sucesiones 4847

The analysis of a specific productive establishment allows us to understand better how a few aspects of this question can be visualized. Table 7 provides us with data taken from three postmortem inventories carried out at different times for the estancia Laguna de Barragán in the southern ranching region.[9] As the estancia becomes more capitalized (we can follow it through the increase of its value and of that of its livestock) the number of slaves grows—in parenthesis in the graph—their value increases also but their respective importance as part of the total diminishes.

Table 3.8. Slaves and Peons in the UP with Greatest Number of Individuals, 1813–1815

Head of the UP	Occupation	Total UP	Place	Family	Slaves	Peons	Foremen
Ortega, Julián	Livestock Breeder	30	San Vicente	11	10	8	—
Baquero, Guadalupe	Miller	32	San Isidro	7	14	9	1
Verdugo, Florencio	Farmer	32	San Vicente	1	—	30	—
Pineyro, Manuel	Farmer	36	Arrecifes	3	17	11	—
Arnoy, Jorge	Livestock Breeder	37	San Vicente	5	9	22	—
Miguez, Francisco	Hacendado	39	Magdalena	6	12	9	—
Lima, Tomás	No data	41	Arrecifes	10	19	6	1
Otalora, Felipe	Farmer and Livestock Breeder	41	Cañada de la Cruz	4	28	2	—
Chavarria, José Antonio	Livestock Breeder	41	San Vicente	1	33	1	1
Escola, Cayetano	Hacendado	44	Cañada de la Cruz	—	39	2	—
Cane, Ramón	Foreman of an ecclesiastical property	47	Arrecifes	—	33	13	1
Trillo, Eusebio	Priest	59	Arrecifes	7	27	9	1
Ramos Mejia, Francisco	Farmer	80	Matanza	4	51	15	—

Source: "La sociedad rural bonaerense a principios del siglo XIX."

How was the workforce distributed between the slaves and peons in the units of production that have the greatest number of individuals, according to the censuses of 1813–1815? Table 8 shows these data. In these units of production there are significant numbers of slaves; not coincidentally they represent the large farms—those that the census identifies as labradores—some of them located in the zone closest to the city (San Isidro and Matanza, that we have already mentioned a few pages earlier) as hacendados and breeders, that is, livestock farmers. Such numbers of slaves very clearly indicate how these large units of production resembled those that we can find in slave societies, as in the *gaucho* south of Brazil, but it is obvious that in the River Plate they were the exception, whereas in Brazil they were the norm.[10]

An Analysis of the Role of Slaves on a Large Estancia Dedicated to Livestock

We will close this part of the article by studying the estancias that belonged at one point in time to *don* Antonio Rivero de los Santos, a Portuguese merchant established in the River Plate. It unquestionably represents one of the largest farming and livestock establishments of the late colonial period, and in fact it ranks among the five largest in the sample of 281 estancias that we studied for the period 1750–1815. His lands extended over a total of 15.5 square leagues, which means around 41,850 hectares; fourteen milestones marked its extension, like the great haciendas of New Spain or the Andes. Here we clearly are faced with a true colonial *latifundio*. According to the inventory of 1805, we know that it was comprised of three different units: the *Grande* (Large) estancia, or San Antonio Fort in Samborombón, the Laguna estancia, and the winter pastures, which were located three leagues inland from the first one. All were situated very close to the frontier with the Indian lands in the south; the residence of the Grande estancia possesses a fort that surrounded it, convincing evidence of its proximity to the frontier. The inventory of 1805 (see Table 9) gives us an idea of the productive structure of these estancias. Possessing almost eighteen thousand large domesticated animals (cows, oxen, horses, and mules), these establishments demanded a great number of workers. In addition, as we already know, wheat was also grown on Rivero's estancias—there are various plows and many other agricultural tools—all of which presupposes a very considerable presence of slaves, peons, and foremen. The principal activities of the estancia were breeding and selling young bulls for the slaughterhouse of the city and the production of wheat for the same destination.

Table 3.9. Rivero's Estancias in 1805

	Value	Units	Percentage
Buildings	5,596		18.4
Enclosures	1,578	6	5.2
Trees	280		
Stores	s/d		
Miscellaneous	129		
Subtotal	7,583		25
Slaves	**4,020**	**14**	**13.2**
Land	4,500		14.8
Cattle	11,661	13,666	38.4
Oxen	156	39	
Horses	1,906	3,554	6.2
Mules	485	389	1.6
Sheep	50	800	
Subtotal	14,258		46.9
Total	**30,361**		**100**

Source: "Tres estancias del sur bonaerense."

Rivero's estancias had thirteen slaves in 1790; the majority of them had jobs related to farming and ranching—foremen, farmers, breakers, on horseback—and there is only one woman (the wife of Juan Antonio, the foreman of the Grande estancia). By 1805, several of the slaves had moved to be in service in the city at the home of his heirs, but the total number of those who lived on estancias had increased to fourteen individuals, due to the three children born to the foreman and his wife. Four of the slaves were designated as foremen.[11] The peculiarity of their situation is obvious, if we bear in mind that they supervised both slaves and free peons and that they even possessed their own brands for livestock, which in turn supposes their own animals. We have abundant, precise information[12] about the hiring of peons on the estancias for the period that begins in September 1807 and ends in the same month in 1812. About 109 peons worked during this period on the three estancias. But, obviously, the peons did not work all year long; analyzing the figures in depth, we reach the conclusion that their work on the average would equal ideally the labor of sixteen peons for all of the 365 days of the year. It means that the tasks that the estancias generated would require fourteen slaves and sixteen peons every year. But it is much more realistic to say that four free foremen, in addition to twelve slaves, worked throughout the entire year and about twenty-two peons during nine months of the year. Or, in other words, of a total of about twelve thousand annual workdays—taking into account also eight foremen—four of them slaves and four free—63 percent correspond to day laborers and free foremen and 37 percent correspond to foremen and workers who were subjected to slavery.

Once again, we see the importance of slavery as an element of regulation of the relations of production in the countryside of the River Plate. As opposed to the peons, who during the epoch of harvesting wheat demanded a higher salary (they charged 30 percent more than during the rest of the year),[13] the slaves, even if they received gifts and bonuses—yerba maté, liquor, tobacco—did not have any other choice than to be always at the orders of the foremen.

Slavery in Mendoza

The region of Cuyo, nestled to the east of the Andes, during the colonial period was home to two very important agricultural areas, Mendoza and San Juan (San Luís, more removed from the mountains, was much less important as an agricultural region). Mendoza is situated in a very dry climatic region, and therefore it is arid; nevertheless, since pre-Hispanic times human populations have known how to take advantage of the water from the rivers that run from the Andes for irrigation. Upon arriving in Mendoza from Chile, the Spaniards rapidly used these hydraulic channels and little by little constructed a verdant irrigated oasis where the vineyards, fields of cereals, and orchards, implanted at the end of the sixteenth century, made this region into the producer of wine, liquor, wheat, and dried fruits par excellence for a very extensive area (its products even reached Potosí) even though Buenos Aires represented its fundamental market. As the port city and its surrounding countryside grew, the market for these products from Cuyo likewise expanded. From the middle of the eighteenth century, the acceleration of the demographic growth of the entire coast and the Banda Oriental (present-day Uruguay) did nothing more than stimulate the economy of Cuyo, which entered into a splendid period of prosperity. Slave labor was always very important for Mendoza's wine- and fruit-based economy.

In the first place, let us see what we know about the population of Mendoza during the period that interests us. Table 10 presents the most important data.[14]

Table 3.10. Population of Mendoza, 1777–1812

	1777	(Percentages)	1802	(Percentages)	1812	(Percentages)
Whites	4491	51	5148	37	5987	45
Mestizos	789	9	4092	30		
Blacks	2129	24	2301	18	4456	33
Slaves			2140	16		
Indians	1359	16			2875	22
Totals	8765	100	13769	100	13318	100

Sources: Revello, "La población de Cuyo"; and Masini, *La esclavitud negra en Mendoza*.

In 1777, the total of the mestizos plus Indians gives us a subtotal of 24.5 percent; however, in 1802, as the table demonstrates, 29.7 percent belong to these categories (now converted into mestizos),[15] and finally in 1812 only 21.6 percent corresponds to Indians, whereas the mestizos have magically disappeared, probably hiding in part among the white population, which seems to have had a dynamism in the period 1802–1812 that it did not have between 1777 and 1802. It is obvious that here there are no demographic changes, rather alterations in the categories used to name this sector of the population that is considered neither black nor white. This situation represents hence a nominal question, as it occurs in general in the rest of Latin America, but even with these different denominations we can perceive the relatively limited increase in the mixed groups. In any case, the growth of the total population is also slow (compared, for example, with the annual rates of 3.2 percent in the countryside of Buenos Aires during the same period). It demonstrates thus a 1.8 percent annual increase between 1777 and 1802, becoming clearly negative between 1802 and 1812. If we calculate the annual growth rate for the period between 1777 and 1802, it would be 1.2 percent for the entire population.

But what do we find if we concentrate on the black population? Between 1772 and 1802, the individuals of African origin grew at an annual rate of 3 percent before undergoing the same phenomenon as the rest of the population even when there was a very slight progression between 1802 and 1812 (those considered white, meanwhile, increased at the very low rate of 0.5 percent between 1777 and 1802, for it is probable that the increase between this date and 1812, as we have just seen above, is partially hiding the passing between categories from mestizo to white). Unfortunately we do not have accurate figures for the total number of slaves in 1812—in 1802, as seen in the graph, they accounted for 16 percent of the total population—but we can suppose that this percentage had varied little by 1812. A few signs allow us to surmise that a slight increase could have occurred.

The census of 1814—of which unfortunately there only remain very incomplete data, as there is only information for several of the districts (*cuarteles*)[16]—shows a very significant presence of slaves and free people of color. In the sixth cuartel, for example, in which there are various medium-sized and large vineyards, businesses, as well as many mulatto artisans, out of a population of 551 inhabitants, almost half were of African origin (exactly 49 percent of the total), and of these 164 were slaves, which is 30 percent of the total of the inhabitants of that cuartel. To have a basis for comparison, let us recall that in the Buenos Aires countryside, in the *partido* of San Isidro, where the African presence was very strong for the local parameters, 20.4 percent of the population had this origin and one of every three males older than twelve was African. In this sixth cuartel of Mendoza, there were only two dependent workers—one peon and one day laborer—who were considered white by the census taker. And to assess the evolution of slavery in Mendoza, it is important to point out that in this same district in 1823, out of a total of 556 persons (almost the same total figure as in 1814) there were only 12 slaves and not even one free black.[17]

What is clear from this rapid description of the population of Mendoza during these years is that the presence of African Americans and of the population subjected to slavery was very great in the local economy and the daily life of the dominant sectors; moreover, the population considered white showed limited dynamism during this same period, showing a negative tendency between 1803 and 1812. It is highly probable that this demographic trend is related to the ecological factors that limited the growth of production of the vintners, with the changes of the economic cycles of that agricultural activity and with the complex relations with the markets of the coast, especially in 1778 and the first postrevolutionary decade—but here is not the place to analyze this problem.[18]

After being commissioned by the president of the Audiencia of Santiago de Chile—which exercised jurisdiction over Cuyo in those years—to carry out the inventories of the property of the expelled Jesuits of Mendoza, Juan Martínez de Rozas began the task in September 1757.[19] The very long list of their possessions demonstrates the extent to which the activity of the Company of Jesus occupied (as in all of Latin America) an absolutely central place in the local economy. The figures do indeed make one dizzy: a dozen vineyards with more than 49,000 vines, hundreds of fruit trees, various wine vaults, a flour mill, three estancias with more than 6,300 cattle, 2,000 horses and mares, 880 mules, and 1,760 sheep. These establishments required the work of 397 slaves of both sexes, of which 274 took care of the cultivation of the vineyards. To have an idea of what these numbers represented in those years, let us point out that in a sample of postmortem inventories from a research project underway, out of thirty inventories from the period 1750–1777, the average number of vines per vineyard was 4.256, the average number of slaves nine, and the quantity of livestock did not reach forty animals on the average, with rare exceptions (a few owners of vineyards also had estancias in the valley of Uco, a few leagues from the city, where there were about a dozen estancias during this period).[20] We should also add that for that very reason, such animals were much more expensive than in the countryside around Buenos Aires,[21] given the shortage of good land for raising cattle and horses, in the context of an ecosystem that is almost desert if there is no irrigation. Let us imagine the authentic revolution in the local economy brought about by the sale of these enormous Jesuit properties. As occurred elsewhere in Latin America, these sales brought about the process of shuffle and deal again that allowed those who were close to power to find themselves suddenly with juicy profits by appropriating these properties for little money, thanks to the complacency (or the complicity) of the colonial officials.[22]

To have a more realistic idea (and now distancing ourselves from the very peculiar enterprise that the Jesuits represented), let us see what a sample of the ninety-one postmortem inventories that we are now analyzing shows us about the productive structure of Mendoza.[23] They cover the period 1750–1821.

Before discussing them, it is indispensable to offer a few explanations. As for the rubric vineyards and land, it has to be noted that whenever the vineyards were evaluated, their value included the land in which the vines were planted; therefore, it is not possible to separate them. It consequently means that the rubric land that appears here refers to other lands, those that do not have vines, such as pastures, stony grounds, and in particular, lucerne fields (these were increasingly used from the end of the eighteenth century to fatten up cattle that would later be sent to Chile on the other side of the Andes).

We are dealing here with an agricultural economy that was radically different from the one that characterized the countryside of Buenos Aires during the same period. Here the vines—in addition to the lands in which they were planted—as well as the rest of the land that was not dedicated to vineyards represented the lion's share, and if we add the trees we reach almost 57 percent of the total value of the capital goods. Such a distribution is logical in an agricultural economy based on a complex system of irrigation and that therefore had very concrete limits to its expansion in the technological conditions of the period and in which there was a shortage of manpower. The value of the land was much higher than in Buenos Aires, where there was plentiful fertile land, an open frontier and relatively few people. This difference can also be demonstrated by the very humble place that livestock occupies in this table.

Table 3.11. Mendoza, Means of Production, 1750–1821 (Percentages)

Vineyards and Land	51.5
Houses and Constructions	14.4
Slaves	13
Wine Cellars/Barrels/Utensils	7.5
Livestock	5.5
Trees	4.5
Wine/Liquor	1.3
Miscellaneous	2.3

Source: Garavaglia, unpublished database.

As for the slaves, they occupy the third place, after the dwellings and adjoining buildings, but we should not forget that here we have information that goes up to 1821, a few years after the crisis of slavery, brought on by the Wars of Independence, had already started. If we consider the data until 1814, we see that slaves were equal to the economic weight of the rubric dwellings and buildings. In any case, the frequency of slaveholding was higher than in the Buenos Aires countryside, for 63 percent of the rural landowners owned slaves in Mendoza, as opposed to 52 percent in Buenos Aires. The average number per owner is a bit higher than three slaves (if we examined them in 1814, it would be about five per owner). All of the sources—including later ones[24]—testify to the importance of owning slaves for the multiple daily tasks of the vineyards. Peons were only hired in the most critical moments of the agricultural cycle, as in the countryside of Buenos Aires during the wheat harvest, during the hot spells of the summer, or in Mendoza during the grape harvest at the beginning of autumn when it was indispensable to have several additional workers in a short period of time.

The Evolution and End of Slavery in the River Plate: The Countryside of Buenos Aires

A series of decrees made during the revolutionary events of 1810—the moment when the process of independence began in the River Plate—initiated the abolition of slavery in Buenos Aires and its surrounding countryside; but this process lasted for several decades and would not reach its final stage until about 1860. First, the interdiction of the slave trade decreed on May 15, 1812 (this provision, nevertheless, would be overlooked, and, in fact, the trade would not be effectively abolished until a treaty was signed with Great Britain in 1839, which was also signed by Uruguay and Chile). Second, in February 1813, the government decreed the libertad de vientres (law of free wombs). From this moment on, we find in the parochial registries the note *Freed by the Homeland* written in the margin of the entries added for the recently born children of slave mothers. The subsequent *Reglamento del Liberto* in March of the same year (a decree that gave a concrete form to the conditions and terms of the effective liberation of these freedmen). Thus began the slow process of slavery's erosion, which would drag on for almost half a century.

On different occasions, the most important of which was the war with the Empire of Brazil between 1825 and 1828, authorities permitted the entry of slaves from captured ships destined for Brazil. Slaves seized in such a fashion would be transformed into freedmen, whose contracts possessed varying lengths of duration; these entries of slaves caused in reality the semicovert continuation of the trade until the treaty with Great Britain was signed in 1839. For example, during the war with the Brazilian Empire, more than seventeen hundred individuals reached Buenos Aires.[25]

In this manner, that is, thanks to the semicovert persistence of the trade, the tensions that the beginning of the abolition of slavery had brought to the rural economy of the River Plate were somewhat diluted. The other way to limit the effect of this process in the framework of the productive relations in the countryside was by increasing the pressure on the workers, a phenomenon that was not by chance contemporary with the preceding one and that had in the famous *papeleta de conchavo* (hiring billet) of 1815 one of its fundamental pillars. This document obligated free men of working age to present a paper signed by their bosses each and every time that they were asked, in which it was stated that the worker was working as a peon;[26] later on, the obligation to carry proof of enlistment in a regiment of the militia was added, which brings us to the other principal theme related to the end of slavery: the military question.

The military question had already started to surface a few years before the revolution of 1810, when in 1806–1807, the English intervened in the River Plate; the call to military action made to the free blacks and mulattos to defend the homeland, as well as the enlistment of many slaves turned over by their owners meant that, for the first time, the descendents of Africans participated personally in the defense of the colony. As a result of the valiant performance of the majority of them,[27] about thirty slaves were rewarded with their liberty (out of a total of 688 slaves who had participated in an official manner in combat). Even if this event had a minor importance quantitatively, it had an enormous symbolic impact on the slave population, as liberty was granted in a public ceremony that opened new horizons of freedom for those who were still enslaved.

The leaders of the revolution that began in 1810 were bearers of ideas of freedom. Moreover, the growing and immediate need for vast numbers of enlisted men to control the cities that had not joined the cause resulted in the fact that from 1813—at the same moment that the libertad de vientres order was decreed—slave owners were ordered to hand over a certain number of their slaves to support the revolutionary cause. If we note how these percentages were established, we have even more evidence of the importance of slavery in the rural area. The owners had to give up one out of every three domestic slaves, one out of every five slaves who worked in a bakery or mill, and one out of every eight of those who worked in the fields or with livestock. The cost of these slaves would be paid off within three years. At the end of 1813 and beginning of 1814, the demands of the war against the Loyalists in the north forced a new wave of purchases, and more than a thousand slaves were thus incorporated into the army as freedmen.[28] A new wave of forced liberation occurred from 1815 to 1818 in response to military necessity. We should not forget that the war had come to the River Plate beginning in 1806–1807 during the British invasion. The region would remain war torn and its inhabitants mobilized to fight for decades. Army officials knew from that date that the freedmen and free blacks were ideal for the infantry (the cavalry was reserved for the mestizo and white peasants who virtually lived mounted on a horse.)

A total of 2,074 slaves were officially incorporated into the army (we say officially, as more than a few runaway slaves also enlisted to escape from their condition). Although the former slaves were converted into freedmen once they joined the army, few could really enjoy their liberty or expect to survive their military service (though a handful of them even fought in Ayacucho in 1824—General Espejo met a former slave from

Cuyo in Lima in 1848). The masculinity rate (MR) of the negro and mulatto population of the city of Buenos Aires went from 110 to 75 between 1810 and 1822 to 58 in 1827,[29] demonstrating clearly what the true consequence of the revolutionary wars was on that segment of the population, both enslaved and free. But it should not be forgotten that these events also had an unexpected consequence: those who returned from the military campaigns—as well as those who were enlisted in the battalions of freedmen that remained in Buenos Aires—rapidly acquired a clear conscience of their new role in society.

As we have already stated, during the conflict with the Empire of Brazil from 1825 to 1828, more than seventeen hundred slaves captured at sea were converted into freedmen and sold as such in Buenos Aires and in the surrounding countryside.[30] It is possible to verify the effect of these sales on a few rural districts, where, far from diminishing, the number of people of African origin grew in the 1830s (for example, in San Antonio de Areco, we find there 18 percent of the population were blacks and mulattos when they were 16 percent of the population in 1813).

The fifteenth article of the constitution of 1853 granted complete liberty to the slaves and freedmen who still existed in the Confederation of Argentina (as we will see next, in a few provinces slavery was still completely legal, and it was indispensable to establish the conditions for the liberation of those slaves). As for Buenos Aires, given that the confederation and the state of Buenos Aires were separated after 1853, slavery ended legally in the city and its countryside in September 1860 when the representatives of Buenos Aires, after peace with the confederation, accepted the constitution of 1853[31] (even in 1856, a priest in the city, inscribed in the registry of a notary public the act of freeing his slave Rosa, freedom that would only become effective after his death).[32] It is important to note that the legal suppression of slavery in the rest of the republics of the River Plate was also late in coming, as Uruguay abolished slavery in 1842 and Paraguay in 1869.[33]

The Situation in Mendoza

We have already seen the role and importance of slave labor in the principal economic activities of Mendoza during the colonial period. When the struggle for independence made itself felt, the impact on the population of slaves would be astounding, having even greater repercussions than in Buenos Aires. For reasons of military strategy, Cuyo was the region selected by General San Martín as the point from which he would cross the Andes to attack the Loyalists in Chile and from there invade Peru by sea. The successive defeats in Upper Peru had convinced the general that the surest route to defeat Lima, the center of the Loyalist reaction in the south of the continent, was that which went through Chile. It is for this reason that San Martín arrived in Mendoza in 1815 and started preparing the army that he would lead to Lima during his long campaign against the troops that remained loyal to the crown of Spain.

Even before the arrival of the future liberator, on two occasions (in 1813 and 1815) about one hundred slaves were seized and sent to Buenos Aires to join the seventh and eighth battalions, the line troop of blacks and mulattos. San Martín's arrival stimulated this process, but now freed slaves were sent to the army that was preparing for the adventure of crossing the Andes. After considerable comings and goings, a session of the *cabildo* of Mendoza in 1816, which was joined by two deputies from San Juan, decided that they would take possession of two thirds of the slaves older than twelve from every owner (it is clearly specified that the rest were indispensable for the "cultivation of the haciendas"). About 482 slaves originally from Mendoza would thus be integrated into the army at that moment. We should also add to that number the Cívicos Pardos battalion that had about 185 men of color in its ranks and was also incorporated into the army of the Andes. This last total, however, represents the minimum because of the total of fifteen hundred freedmen who were enlisted, half arrived from Cuyo, most from Mendoza.[34]

The demographic result of war and military service is clear: in 1812, with a total of 13,318 inhabitants, the population of African origin represented 33 percent of that total; in 1823, once again in an incomplete census (but much more representative than that of 1814), 17,734 inhabitants were counted, of which only 11.7 percent were of African origin. We have already referred to the example of cuartel 6, and we repeat it here: in 1812, there were 251 blacks in this zone—46 percent of its 545 inhabitants—in 1814, of a total of 551 inhabitants, the slaves and the free mulattos represented 49 percent of the population of the cuartel (but the impact of the demands of war were already visible, as the MR of the slave population was 80 men for every 100 women); finally in 1823 we find only 12 slaves and not one free mulatto among 556 settlers. It is obvious that the decline of slavery spurred a crisis of production in the vineyards that had already started some time before, even when work contingents made up of Loyalist prisoners of war tempered the problem caused by the scarcity of laborers for agricultural tasks during the first postrevolutionary decade.

Masini's study shows that the trading of slaves continued to be a common reality in the economy of Mendoza until at least 1851, the closing date of the registry that this author presents in his study; also, of course, there continued to exist contracts for transferring years of service for freedmen.[35] On August 11, 1853, a commission "created by the Supreme Decree of July 26 to make arrangements for the slaves and freedmen, who by the Constitution sworn on the ninth of the same year, were liberated, at the same time appraising them for the indemnification that the state owes to their masters" met in the city of Mendoza. In this act thirty-nine slaves and forty-eight freedmen definitively gained their complete freedom, and the state took responsibility for the 2,482 pesos that represented their estimated value.[36]

Conclusions

First of all, we should underline the importance of the economic role that slaves had in the two productive regions that we have examined, in the countryside surrounding Buenos Aires as well as in the area of vineyards, orchards, and wheat fields of Mendoza. Slaves occupied a position of primary importance in the stability of the relations of production in the case of the countryside of Buenos Aires—given the relative freedom of the peasant family—and also a central element for the continuity of the productive activity in the vineyards and wheat fields of Mendoza. And we should also remember that the female slaves carried out essential economic functions in the bundle of tasks that tend to be classed as domestic service. This participation can be detected in the role of free mulattas during the nineteenth century in activities such as washing and ironing clothes, hawking goods, or making bread. When sheep herding was developed in the countryside of Buenos Aires, the participation of black women in their shearing became something of a platitude reported by visitors and the scarce iconography of that epoch. All of these activities were nothing more than the perpetuation of a tradition that they had inherited from slavery (their own or that of their mothers).

The consequences of the rapid erosion of master-slave relations during the struggle for independence that began in 1810 also demonstrate the weight slavery had held up until that moment. In the case of the countryside surrounding Buenos Aires, it was necessary to create a series of compulsory mechanisms to increase control over free workers, who until then had been reluctant to yield to the working conditions of a real labor market (thanks to the possibilities that the peasant economy offered them of surviving without selling their labor or making sure that it came dearly). Given the situation of Mendoza, the end of slavery in that zone was a factor in the crisis of the vineyards that ended with the conversion of local production toward pasturage and the export of livestock to Chile,[37] an activity that required much less manpower than the vineyards and orchards.

Finally, it is clear that the end of slavery was not only a result of the ideas of liberty that spread through the provinces of the River Plate during the revolution of 1810, but rather above all, of the terrible military consequences of those same events on the society of the River Plate. It was the army and the revolutionary wars that undermined slavery. After independence, the remnants of the institution of slavery continued for decades, when the ideas of liberty were no longer what they had once been. In any case, Argentine society, in spite of negating and hiding systematically until very recently the role of slavery in its past, remained influenced by the presence and culture of the descendents of Africans.[38] To take but one small example, the word *tango*, which for Argentines (and Uruguayans) represents the soul of the nation to the most sublime degree, is of African origin.

Notes

1. Estancias are units of production of cattle, horses and oxen, and wheat, which can be of any size.
2. For more about the region and slavery during this early period, see R. Gonzáles Lebrero, *La pequeña aldea. Sociedad y economía en Buenos Aires, (1580–1640)* (Buenos Aires, 2002).
3. The growth of the population of the countryside of Buenos Aires was spectacular during this period, as can be seen in the annual growth rates in the following table.

	Inhabitants	Annual Growth Rates (Percentages)
1744	6.033	
1778	12.925	2.3
1815	41.168	3.2
1838	88.232	3.4

4. We are following the most complete study of these censuses: "La sociedad rural bonarense a principios del siglo XIX. Un análisis a partir de las categorías ocupacionales," Grupo de Investigación en la Historia Rural Rioplatense, directed by Mariana Canedo and José Mateo, UNMP, published in R.O. Fradkin and J.C. Garavaglia, eds., *En busca del tiempo perdido. La economía de Buenos Aires en el país de la abundancia, 1750-1865* (Buenos Aires, 2004), 21–63.
5. Almost 61 percent of the total of the slaves were men.
6. See J.L. Moreno, "Población y sociedad en el Buenos Aires rural a fines del siglo XVIII," in J.C. Garavaglia and J.L. Moreno, eds., *Población, sociedad y familia en el espacio rioplatense. Siglos XVIII y XIX* (Buenos Aires, 1993), 22–48.
7. J.C. Garavaglia, *Les hommes de la pampa. Une histoire agraire de la campagne de Buenos Aires, 1700–1830* (Paris, 2000).
8. We use this title for the owners, and it was common that the largest be called in this manner, though the productive unit was rarely called a hacienda as it was in other parts of the Americas.
9. J.C. Garavaglia, "Tres estancias del sur bonarense en un periodo de 'transición' (1790–1834)," in M. Bjer and A. Reguera, eds., *Problemas de la historia agraria. Nuevos debates y perspectivas de investigación* (Tandil, 1995), 79–123.

10. See the excellent study of Helen Osório, *O imperio portugues no sul da america. Estancieiros, lavradores e comerciantes* (Porto Alegre, 2007). In Río Grande do Sul, of a sample of 265 postmortem inventories, slaves represented 23 percent of the total of productive goods (18 percent in Buenos Aires), but if in the countryside of Buenos Aires 52 percent of the producers had slaves, in Rio Grande do Sul, they were 94 percent—which means that there were almost no estancieiros that did not own slaves—and the average was nine individuals per exploitation, whereas it was four in Buenos Aires; see Table 8 and Table 14 about the units with the greatest number of slaves.
11. This was absolutely not an exception, as twenty-one of the sixty-six foremen who the censuses of 1813–1815 registered were black slaves; if we add the seven slaves who held the ambiguous title of estancieros, which supposes that they were in charge of an establishment, the total sum of slaves that were in charge of a unit of their masters would reach more than a third of the total of the seventy-three individuals who occupied these functions of control over the rest of the slaves and free workers.
12. AGN-Sucesiones 7776 and AGN-Sucesiones 7777.
13. We should not forget that they received their salary in cash, as the sources that we have consulted for this study indicate.
14. We have taken this information from J. Torre Revello, "La población de Cuyo a comienzos del Virreinato y a principios de la iniciación del periodo independiente, 1777 y 1812," *Boletín del Instituto de Investigaciones Históricas* XXIII, 77–78 (1938/1939):, 77–86, and from J. Masini, *La esclavitud negra en Mendoza. Época independiente* (Mendoza, 1962).
15. The term that the censuses of the epoch used in Mendoza was free mestizo to distinguish them clearly from the black slaves.
16. Archivo Histórico de Mendoza (henceforth AHM), Independiente, Legajo 14. There were seven cuarteles in the city out of eleven—and as for the countryside, there were only eleven out of thirty-three.
17. Masini, *La esclavitud negra en Mendoza*.
18. See S. Amaral, "Comercio libre y economías regionales; San Juan y Mendoza, 1780–1820," *Jahrbuch für Geschichte von Staat, Wirtschaft und Gesellschaft Lateinamerikas*, 19 (1982): 1–67; J.C. Garavaglia and M. del C. Prieto, "Diezmos, producción agraria y mercados: Mendoza y Cuyo, 1710–1830," *Boletín del Instituto de Historia Argentina y Americana "Dr. Emilio Ravignani"* 3a. serie, 30 (2008): 7–33.
19. AGN-IX-22-3-1.
20. A map from the middle of the eighteenth century lists only nine estancias, and the census of 1810 of the Valley of Uco does not count more than thirty productive units that can be considered estancias"; whether they belong to large estancieros or small and medium-sized breeders, see AHM-Colonial 10.
21. Indeed, in the Buenos Aires hintrland cows cost ten to twelve reales in 1767 and in Mendoza a bit more than twenty-one reales per head in this same year.
22. In the case of Mendoza, the ridiculous values that were given as an estimate of the probable incomes of these properties (the evaluation was done by some of the same men who would later participate in their purchase), allow us to see to what extent the dominant groups, even if they were very Catholic and attended mass daily, did not hesitate to enrich themselves at the expense of the Jesuits; but, it is well-known that *pecunia non olet*.
23. Taken from AHN-Colima and AHM-Independiente; we prefer not to cite the long list that would not make very much sense in this study, being also a sample of ninety-one inventories that is still incomplete and is presently being elaborated.
24. See, for example, J. Miers, *Travels in Chile and La Plata* (London, 1826).
25. L.M. Crespi, "Negros apresados en operaciones de corso durante la guerra con el Brasil (1825–1828)," *Temas de África y Asia* 2 (1994): 109–124.

26. "1. Any individual from the countryside that does not possesses legitimate means to insure his subsistence...shall be considered as belonging to the class of servants"; "2. Every servant of any class should have a billet from his employer, endorsed by the district judge"; "3. The billets of these peons should be renewed every three months. ..."; "4. Any individual of the peon class that does not keep this document shall be considered a vagrant"; "5. Any individual, even if he has a billet, that travels in the countryside without a permit from the district judge, or endorsed by him but being from elsewhere shall be considered a vagrant"; "6. Vagrants shall be sent to the army for five years. ..." Decree of Manuel Luis de Oliden, Governor-Intendente, Buenos Aires, 30/08/1815, AGN-X-2-10-6.
27. Given that the combat was carried out house to house in the defense of 1807, not only the enlisted slaves in the militia fought, but also those that had not been drafted because of their age and sex.
28. M. Klachko Rotman, "Le rôle de l'armée dans le processus de libération des esclaves au Rio de la Plata : le cas des 'libertos' de Buenos Aires (1806–1821), " in C. Bernand and A. Stella, eds., D'esclaves à soldats. Miliciens et soldats d'origine servile, XIII-XXI siècles (Paris, 2006), 279–300. See also M. Goldberg and S. Mallo, "La población africana en Buenos Aires y su campaña. Formas de vida y de subsistencia (1750–1850)," Temas de África y Asia 2 (1994).
29. See the classic book of George Reid Andrews, The Afro-Argentines of Buenos Aires, 1800–1900 (Madison, 1980), 74.
30. The patronage of freedman could be the object of a paid transfer during the years that this peculiar juridical condition existed; see examples of these contracts that transferred patronage for the period 1810–1860 in Buenos Aires in the book that Miguel Angel Rosal is preparing about slavery in the River Plate; I thank the author for having generously given me a copy of his manuscript.
31. The constitution of the State of Buenos Aires, approved in 1854, does not once mention the word slavery or slave but affirms the validity of the libertad de vientres and the prohibition of the slave trade (article 169), and it is noteworthy that article 146 establishes that "[a]ll the inhabitants of the State are equal before the law," without making the slightest allusion to the existence of those peculiar inhabitants that the slaves were and that, it seems even superfluous to recall, were not equal before the law. Cf. "Constitución del Estado de Buenos Aires," in Registro Oficial del Estado de Buenos Aires (Buenos Aires, 1854), 28–47.
32. Rosal, M.A. manuscript about slavery in the Rio de la Plata cited in note 30.
33. A. Borucki, K. Chagas, and N. Stalla, Esclavitud y trabajo. Un estudio sobre los afrodescendientes en la frontera uruguaya, 1835–1855 (Montevideo, 2009); and J. Pla, Hermano negro. La esclavitud en el Paraguay (Madrid, 1972).
34. See Masini, La esclavitud negra en Mendoza; and B. Bragoni, "Esclavos, libertos y soldados: la cultura plebeya en Cuyo durante la revolución," in R.O. Fradkin, ed., ¿Y el pueblo donde está? Contribuciones para una historia popular de la revolución de independencia en el Río de la Plata (Buenos Aires, 2008), 107–150.
35. Masini, La esclavitud negra en Mendoza, 37–53.
36. Ibid., 75–80.
37. We should not forget that this moment marks the beginning of the boom of Chilean mining production.
38. In addition to the pioneering work of Andrews, The Afro-Argentines, it is now possible also to consult the work of Lea Geller: Andares negros, caminos blancos: afroporteños, estado y nación: Argentina a fines del siglo XIX (Barcelona, 2010).

– Chapter 4 –

SLAVES AND THE CREATION OF LEGAL RIGHTS IN CUBA
Coartación and Papel[1]

Alejandro de la Fuente

"[T]hrough the play of custom, an abuse might always by mutation become a precedent, a precedent a right."
Marc Bloch, "The Rise of Dependent Cultivation and Seigniorial Institutions" (1966)

On August 16, 1855, doña Carlota Dascar, a resident in Santiago de Cuba, initiated a legal suit against Miguel Rodriguez, *síndico procurador* of the city, to prevent the forcible sale of her slave María. Dascar had tried to sell her slave, whom she described as a healthy criolla without vices, for seven hundred pesos, but the slave had "presented" herself before the síndico to "request her *coartación* because she had cincuenta pesos." As the municipal official charged with the representation of slave interests, the síndico then initiated the customary process of assessing the value of the slave to fix the price at which María would become *coartada*, that is, the price that she would have to pay to purchase her freedom. He invited Dascar to appoint an appraiser, whose assessment would be compared with that produced by the síndico's own assessor.[2]

As was frequently the case, the valuations were widely apart and had to be settled in court. The representative of the owner appraised María at 600 pesos; the síndico valued her at 450. The local judge then proceeded to appoint a legal assessor, who ratified 450 pesos as the right value of the slave, making this the price at which María would be coartada. Having accepted this defeat, Dascar went to the síndico's house and asked him "to return her slave," for María had not voiced "any complaints" against her. Instead of receiving her slave back, however, Dascar was presented with a new challenge, as the síndico "demanded" that she issue a sale license—"su papel de venta"—for María to seek a new owner, while daring her to take the case to court again.

Now incensed, Dascar claimed that coartación "did not limit in any sense the dominium that masters have over their slaves and if the slave who is not coartado cannot be sold against the will of his master without just cause, the same must be the case with the coartado slaves, who are subject to the same servitude as the others; this is categorical and is not open to doubt or interpretation." Yet the dominium of the master in this area was anything but categorical, as Dascar would learn to her dismay. In court, the síndico invoked article 35 of the Cuban slave ordinance, the Reglamento de Esclavos of 1842, which in his view "clearly gives the coartado slave the power to sell himself whenever he wants against the will of his master ... from which it follows that being the black María Irene coartada, she is in the situation of soliciting a new master any time she wishes."

The judge who heard the case sided with the síndico and ordered Dascar "to give the corresponding paper to her slave so that she could seek a master at her leisure" ("papel a la dicha esclava para que buscase amo a su gusto"). Although the owner persisted in her refusal to sell the slave, the judge ordered the sale to proceed. María had found someone ready to pay her price, including the taxes on the sale, which were the responsibility of any coartado who wanted to be sold against the wishes of his or her master. Frustrated, Dascar appealed to the captain general, noting that she "had complained and protested in vain against this process, mainly against the sale of the black María. I have refused to sign or authorize anything, but in vain; everything has moved forward with a rigorous inflexibility." She also used family connections to bring the case before Santiago's town council, where the husband of her stepdaughter, Regidor don Ruperto Ulecia Ledesma, presented for discussion a lengthy memorandum depicting the actions of the síndicos and the slaves' attempts to change owners as a "veritable forceful expropriation." According to the town councilor, two issues merited the attention of the municipal body. The first concerned the process of legally appraising the prices of the slaves for the purposes of coartación, a process that limited unlawfully the owner's freedom to ask whichever price he deemed proper for his property. The second referred to "the outrage of the coartado slave changing owners as many times as he wishes without having just cause," which was tantamount to an expropriation. In both instances, he noted, the "sacred ... property rights" of the masters were being "curtailed."[3]

Dascar's judicial and extrajudicial efforts were not exceptional. Her complaints were part of a large chorus of grumbling slave owners who by the 1850s were trying to resist, through litigation and through appeals to authorities, what they perceived as a growing challenge to their dominium over their slaves. They resented both their inability to prevent the municipal officials' interference in the management of their slaves and the slaves' successful invocation of legal rights that could be exercised against their wishes. Not without reason, the owners asserted that these prerogatives represented a dangerous concession to the slaves. The enforcement of what lawyers, justices, and authorities described as *derechos* ("rights") had "relaxed slavery completely" and "impaired the subordination" on which slavery was based.

The most important of these rights were coartación (gradual self-purchase) and pedir papel (request for paper) to seek a new owner, two institutions with deep roots in the island. Through coartación masters and slaves agreed on a manumission price that could not be subsequently altered.[4] The slave could then make partial payments toward his or her freedom. As the case of María illustrates, by the mid-nineteenth century these two legal practices had become linked, for some lawyers, justices, and slaves believed that coartados had the right to change masters at will. However, neither coartación nor the possibility of changing masters figured in the legal codes of Castile as slave rights. Rather, it seems that these prerogatives emerged out of constant litigation by the slaves themselves and as a pragmatic response to the slaves' initiatives, which in this way were channeled into the legal sphere. In this sense Cuba was hardly unique. As the processes of emancipation clearly show, slaves' initiatives and actions shaped legislation and produced legal consequences across Latin America.[5]

Until the promulgation of the Reglamento de Esclavos in 1842 the practices of coartación and papel were based on little other than custom.[6] They could be claimed as customary rights at best and were quite vulnerable to the whim of individual masters. But in 1842 these customary rights were written into law, codified, and henceforth treated by most justices and many jurists as true legal rights to be observed even against the will of the owners. Furthermore, some jurists and justices claimed that these rights had wide-ranging legal effects that gave slaves considerable control over their lives and labor. But how did these legal rights come to exist and how did they relate to the traditional codes of Castile or to colonial laws?

And why were these customary rights codified, and codified precisely as slave rights, in Cuban nineteenth-century slave society, despite the opposition of the slave owners?

This paper attempts to answers these questions. It does so by focusing, first, on the evolution of the law to establish the possible bases for the practices of coartación and papel. I find that until the Reglamento de Esclavos of 1842, these laws provided only a very tenuous foundation to what María and other slaves attempted to claim as personal rights. The slave owners' systematic rejection of these claims resulted in litigation, forcing justices to define which practices conformed to the law and what entitlements, if any, the slaves had under Spanish law and legal customs. These conflicts are best studied through the legal processes themselves, which show that justices did not share a uniform view about these issues. The conflicts surrounding these legal practices peaked in the 1840s and 1850s, after the Reglamento of 1842 codified them unequivocally as slave rights, in terms that many masters deemed openly confiscatory. The very codification of these potentially favorable legal practices in a slave society such as Cuba is something of a puzzle. Instead of treating coartación and the practice of pedir papel as static, abstract rights, this paper studies these practices as contested legal institutions in which different interests—those of slave owners, colonial authorities, legal experts, and slaves—clashed.[7]

It is difficult to offer chronological precisions about the evolution of these institutions. The first debates about their legal contours took place in the 1780s, when the Spanish crown reviewed the slaves' legal status as part of its codifying efforts. By then, however, the practices of coartación and papel had evolved into customary rights—again, highly contested and with little foundation in written law.

The transformation of these practices into customary rights took place during Cuba's long early colonial period, between the sixteenth century and the late eighteenth century. Conditions in early colonial Cuba were relatively favorable for the creation of these customary rights. Prior to the development of plantation slavery in the western section of the island after the late 1700s, Cuba was a society with slaves, not a slave society, to use a problematic but nonetheless graphic distinction.[8] Slavery was mainly urban in character, and a large proportion of slaves were used in the service economy of Havana and other cities. Limited Spanish migration to the island required slaves to perform economic activities that might otherwise have been closed to them and that implied some degree of autonomy and their active participation in the mercantile life of the cities. In the sixteenth and seventeenth centuries, slaves and free blacks monopolized important sectors of Havana's booming service economy. They were also conspicuous in the trades, not just as day laborers, but as master artisans with their own shops. An indeterminate but significant number of slaves hired themselves out, lived in their own houses, and operated inns, taverns, and other commercial establishments.[9]

Through their participation in market transactions and other social relations, slaves gained critical knowledge about the market economy and the dominant culture. Included in this cultural background was the knowledge that under Spanish law masters had obligations and slaves had the right to appeal to authorities—to an authority higher than their masters—to denounce mistreatment or abuse. This may have been the slaves' "only right," as a Cuban justice stated, but it was a critical one.[10] The practice of papel seems to have evolved as a consequence of this right of petition, as slaves repeatedly requested authorities to be sold to a different master due to abuse.

Slaves contributed to the definition of coartación as well. One can easily understand that slaves would want their manumission price to be fixed once they had reached an agreement with their masters. It is also understandable that they would seek to inscribe such agreements in the public sphere by noting them in the sale contracts. As early as the 1590s some contracts noted that slaves were entitled to buy their freedom once they had paid a given amount. Slaves who had begun to make payments toward their freedom, in turn, began to claim that they had purchased a portion of their time and labor and were entitled to some autonomy. By the late seventeenth century some contracts acknowledged this reality and made reference to the fact that coartados had in fact purchased a portion of themselves. We also know that a century later some coartado slaves were claiming that any limitation on their ability to complete payments constituted abuse, which allegedly entitled them to request papel and change owners. Each claim created a precedent that made subsequent claims more likely, creating in the process what Sherwin Bryant calls "a corpus of case law."[11] Thus by the eighteenth century these two practices were frequently linked.

These practices did not vanish with the transformations experienced by Cuban society during the early nineteenth century, when the island became a leading producer of sugar. They were part of a "heritage" that, as Rebecca Scott states, "would influence society in the nineteenth century." To be sure, recently imported Africans in the deep plantation zones would have limited access to authorities and the law, but as I have claimed elsewhere, the new economic and social order had to be imposed on and reconciled with previous customs and social mores.[12]

Paradoxically, slaves' opportunities to press claims probably increased after the 1760s with the creation of the office of síndico procurador. A municipal institution transplanted to the colonies in 1766, the síndico was to provide legal representation for the slaves and mediate in their conflicts with masters. The Real Cédula of 1789 "on the education, treatment, and occupation of the slaves" referred to the síndicos as "protector[s] of the slaves" and established that no slave could be criminally prosecuted without the intervention of the síndico, who was also responsible for charging slave owners and overseers in cases of excessive punishment. Since the síndicos were elected by the town council, their position considered an honorable public duty, one must assume that many were themselves slave owners and not particularly concerned with the well-being of the slaves.[13] At the same time, the very existence of the institution created clearly delimited institutional channels for enterprising slaves to claim rights and the possibility of expanded state intromission into the master-slave relationship. As will be shown below, with time the síndicos seem to have developed procedures and values that many owners deemed intolerable. In the midst of Cuba's slave society, the síndicos' actions contributed to reproduce customary legal practices such as coartación and papel while surrounding them with a mantle of legality.[14]

In trying to understand how slaves positioned themselves as legal subjects and tried to take advantage of the limited legal recourse available in colonial societies, this article joins a fast-growing body of scholarship concerning slavery and the law in Latin America. In contrast to a previous generation of scholars who, in reaction to celebratory accounts of Iberian legal culture, were skeptical if not cynical about the importance of the law to the study of slavery, the most recent scholarship concentrates on the slaves themselves and on their attempts to find cracks within the Spanish normative system.[15] These scholars emphasize that under Spanish absolutism slaves were constituted as subjects who were "socially not so dead," that civil and religious authorities encroached on the masters' control over slaves, and that slaves learned how to navigate the contradictory Spanish legal maze and to use it to their advantage.[16]

Many of the slaves seeking to take advantage of these normative cracks were women, who were disproportionately represented in the urban labor force.[17] This facilitated the development of valuable networks within and without their social group, increased their chances to purchase freedom, and, above all, gave them easier access to authorities and legal intermediaries such as the síndico procuradores.[18]

Furthermore, legal decisions and opportunities were informed by gender ideologies and family considerations. The Spanish legal culture concerning slave families contained significant ambiguities that slaves sought to use to their advantage. Some slaves and free blacks invoked the sanctity of marriage to press claims on behalf of their enslaved spouses.

Others invoked paternal or maternal bonds to demand the manumission of a child. After all, as Bianca Premo states, "Spanish law preserved a measure of patriarchal authority within the slave family itself," so slaves could petition the courts to uphold their authority over their own children.[19] Under some circumstances, masters actually agreed. In those cases, they argued, the enslaved mothers—not them—should be financially responsible for raising the child. State authorities had their own views on this as well, however, for these children were also subjects of the king and were entitled to his benevolence and protection. As a result, these cases witnessed the clash of different notions of patriarchy, property rights, and family rights, a conflict that slaves and their legal representatives sought to use for their own purposes. As historian Herman Bennett puts it, "[T]he enslaved gained an acute awareness of competing obligations and rights, a form of ambiguity they willingly exploited by deploying regulatory devices in a manner that the Spanish monarchs never intended."[20]

This is precisely what happened with the poorly studied practices of pedir papel and coartación. Historians of slavery in Cuba have known of coartación for a long time, but debates have centered on its frequency and on the institution's role in facilitating the integration of Africans into colonial society.[21] Determining the proportion of coartado slaves is nearly impossible, for it is likely that only a fraction of the slaves under coartación ever completed their payments and obtained their freedom. According to the census of 1871 only 2,137 slaves were coartados in a slave population of over 280,000. In their study of the Cuban slave market, however, Laird Bergad and his collaborators found that in a random sample of notarized sales between 1790 and 1880, coartados represented 13 percent of the total. "Significant numbers of slaves became coartados, and this was no doubt critical for the hopes and aspirations of slave communities." Some contemporaries shared the view that many slaves were becoming coartados, although their perceptions were tinged by the fear of losing control over slaves in general. "It happens with frequency," asserted a lawyer in 1830. "Slaves are becoming coartados in large numbers," a town councilor from Santiago concurred in 1855.[22]

Whatever the proportion of slaves who became coartados, it is difficult to sustain the claim that this represented, in quantitative terms, a major avenue toward freedom in nineteenth-century Cuba. According to various sources, the number of slaves manumitted in the island each year during the 1850s and early 1860s was around two thousand, which would suggest annual manumission rates below 1 percent.[23] These figures of course included all sorts of manumission, not just gradual self-purchases, so the annual number of slaves obtaining freedom through coartación was probably small.

But the significance of coartación went beyond ratios and the number of slaves who obtained freedom through it. As with marronage or revolts—which always involved a small proportion of total slaves—the impact of coartación cannot be reduced to a question of percentages.[24] Slave owners resented coartación and its concomitant practice of papel so much not because large numbers of slaves used it to obtain freedom, but because they could do it without the acquiescence of the masters. With coartación manumission ceased to be an expression of the generosity of the owner, no longer a pious act to serve God, as the letters of freedom frequently stated. With coartación manumission was imposed on masters by entrepreneurial slaves, not given to slaves by God-fearing and humane masters. To make matters worse, coartación produced—or in the eyes of some slaves and justices was understood to produce—a number of poorly defined and much contested rights that gave slaves significant control over their labor and personal lives, including the alleged right to change masters at will, the source of much litigation in nineteenth-century Cuba. For the slave owners, at least, the significance of coartación resided in its serious attack on the property rights of masters.

Slave Owners' Obligations

The masters' outrage was not without foundation, for as they repeatedly claimed, the rights that slaves and some justices attempted to impose were not explicitly regulated in Spanish law. Although the possibility of manumission was long recognized in the Castilian codes and in tradition, it was always dependent on the goodwill and benevolence of the master. It was a master's prerogative, not a slave right. The traditional codes of Castile granted slaves a few rights that were not conditional on their masters' wishes—such as the right to marry and to petition authorities in cases of abuse—but these were the exception rather than the rule.

What the codes did regulate in a fairly systematic manner were the obligations of the masters. In addition to religious instruction, the master's most important duty concerned the physical well-being of the slave. According to Law 6, title 21, of the Fourth Partida, a master had "complete authority" over his slave "to dispose of him as he pleases." But there were limits to the master's power: he was not supposed to wound, kill, or mutilate his slaves, at least not without proper judicial order, and he could not starve them to death. In cases of severe abuse, which the law defined as starvation and intolerable physical punishments, slaves could complain to a judge. The judge in turn was to inquire about the complaint and, if it was corroborated, order the forcible sale of the slave to another master.[25]

These three principles—that masters should not abuse their slaves, that slaves could complain to a judge, and that justices should hear these claims and proceed accordingly—were ratified by numerous subsequent regulations. The obligation to feed, house, and care for infirm slaves was confirmed in the ordinances issued by the Audiencia of Santo Domingo in 1528 and 1535, by the town council of the same city in 1768, and in the Código Negro of 1784. The ordinances issued by the audiencia also charged municipal officials with visiting the farms and gathering information about excessive punishments, "ill treatments," and failure to provide enough food to the slaves, in which case they should notify local authorities and justices to proceed "according to justice." The 1784 Code referred to the usefulness of these visits and spoke of them as something that was "frequently" done.[26] Whether justices actually ordered the sale of abused slaves is not known. The old principle contained in the Siete Partidas was also reproduced in regulations issued by the crown for the colonial territories, the so-called Leyes de Indias.[27]

When the first comprehensive ordinances for Cuban villages were issued in 1574, they basically replicated the language that the Audiencia of Santo Domingo had used in its own regulations. This is not surprising, for the Cuban rules were drafted by a visiting judge from that court, the Oidor Alonso de Cáceres y Ovando. His "ordenanzas" made reference to two forms of "ill treatment." The first concerned the lack of proper nourishment and clothing for the slaves; the second to cruel punishments, particularly to excessive flogging and to "burning with different types of resins." To prevent these abuses Cáceres ordered municipal officials to visit the farms in their jurisdiction twice every year. As in La Española, the purpose of these visits was to gather information concerning "the treatment" of the slaves and whether the ordinances concerning food and clothing were being observed. In cases of cruelty and "excessive punishments," the justices should forcibly sell the slave and proceed legally against the owner.[28]

It is difficult to establish whether these visits were performed in Cuba as regularly as mandated and whether the municipal officials inquired about the treatment of slaves, as they were supposed to do. But two things should be noted. The ordenanzas continued to be invoked as the law of the land well into the late eighteenth century. Second, by then the visits continued to be seen as one of the responsibilities of town councilors. A colonial official noted in 1762, for instance, that these visits allowed authorities to "watch over the good treatment of slaves, whether they are assisted in terms of food and clothing, matters that require the presence and authority of the judge himself." Ten years later the custom was still observed. In January of 1772 the governor commissioned one of the councilors to visit the farms to "inspect the slaves ... and see if they were well dressed and treated as stated in ordinance sixty" of the 1574 Cáceres ordinances. A case of egregious abuse was detected in one of these inspections in 1754, when the visiting justice initiated a case ex-officio against landowner Fernando Ramos for mistreating one of his slaves, a child five or six years old who he had "punished with fire and other cruelties."[29]

Regardless of the frequency and concrete impact of these visits, it appears that the justices continued to uphold the centuries-old notion that masters were to treat their slaves properly. Local regulations reproduced the traditional parameters for acceptable treatment, which required adequate nourishment and clothing and forbid unusually cruel punishments. The 1789 Real Cédula on the treatment of slaves ratified the same principles. As usual, the physical well-being of the slaves was identified, among other things, with a given quantity and quality of food and clothing, as well as with their physical integrity. Following the letter of the Partidas, the excessive punishment of a slave would result not only in the forcible sale of the slave, but also the criminal prosecution of the master "as if the injured party was free."[30]

Thus by the late eighteenth century, a well-established legal doctrine regarding what constituted acceptable treatment for slaves existed in colonial law. Equally well established was the principle that the justices not only had the power to interfere in cases of excessive punishment or mistreatment, but that they indeed had an obligation to interfere and, if circumstances warranted, to impose on abusive masters the forcible sale of the slave. A subtle but telling distinction had taken place since the Partidas, however. While maintaining the preoccupation with the physical well-being of the slave, the colonial ordinances and the Real Cédula of 1789 had shifted the initiative in mistreatment cases from the slaves themselves to justices and local officials. What the Partidas had envisioned as a limited slave prerogative later regulations treated as a duty of municipal officials.

Slaves' Customary Rights

In Cuba and elsewhere in the Iberian colonial world, however, slaves did not wait for local officials to detect and prosecute instances of abuse and mistreatment. They seized the initiative and approached justices to complain about abusive masters and to seek redress from authorities. In some cases this redress consisted simply in the mediation of an outsider to improve conditions in the workplace or replace an abusive overseer, but in other cases slaves' demands went further. What all these cases had in common, however, was the slaves' attempt to transform what the law had envisioned as obligations of the masters into personal rights.

Particularly for rural slaves, presenting a complaint before local authorities was not an easy task. They had to abandon the farm where they worked, walk for hours or days, find a justice in a nearby town, and elicit his sympathy. Extant cases in Cuban nineteenth-century judicial records suggest, however, that at least occasionally rural slaves turned to authorities to complain of mistreatment and that these complaints were worded in terms that echoed the dominant legal culture. The case of eight slaves who walked out of the San Miguel sugar mill and presented themselves before the local justice in the town of Corral Falso, Matanzas, in 1846 exemplifies this. The slaves had come "to complain against the administration" of the mill, arguing that they did not receive enough food, that they were forced to perform "excessive work," and that they did not get proper clothing or medical attention. Something similar happened in the sugar mill Buenavista, in the municipality of Trinidad in central Cuba. In 1879 nineteen slaves escaped from the mill and told authorities that the overseer abused them and gave them "bad food." In yet another case, Pablo, a slave in the Caridad sugar mill, municipality of Colón, presented himself before a local official in 1865 to complain against his overseer, who he claimed had punished him excessively by giving him over one hundred lashes and abused the slaves in a variety of ways. Asked to elaborate on the conditions at the mill, Pablo declared that the overseer and the driver had mutilated two slaves in the past "without anybody notifying the authorities" and that slaves only got plantains and rotten jerked meat twice a day.[31]

In his deposition Pablo charged that the overseer also punished those slaves who sought the sponsorship and protection of local authorities (the verb he used was *apadrinarse*). He mentioned the case of Secundino Criollo, who had asked a local authority to intercede on his behalf to avoid a punishment. Even though the authority had called the overseer and reprimanded him, Pablo continued, Secundino had been shackled and punished "a lot" as a result.

Pablo's testimony suggests that even though sympathetic authorities could not guarantee the protection of the slaves, the latter were very much aware of the existence of these authorities and of the possibility of seeking their sponsorship and mediation. It is possible that slaves reserved this recourse for extreme situations, perhaps for those conflicts that could result in life-threatening punishments or severe physical abuses. In any case, local justices seem to have treated these as routine cases. They opened dossiers, took the slaves' depositions in the presence of witnesses, and called on medical experts to examine those slaves who claimed to have been abused. These were time-honored procedures: it is what local justices in Spain and the colonies had done for centuries. Nowhere in the proceedings do we get the sense that these cases were exceptional or that the local justices were outraged by the insolence of the slaves. As the instructing judge in one of these cases reported, appealing to authorities in cases of abuse was the slaves' "only right"—their *único derecho*.[32]

Slaves not only tried to transform the masters' responsibilities into bases for legal claims, but took matters a step further. By the late-eighteenth-century slaves who complained about abuses of various kinds frequently requested authorities' assistance to change owners. This practice was sometimes referred to as buscar papel or pedir papel, the paper in question being a written document issued by the master or a judge authorizing the slave to find a party interested in purchasing him or her for a price previously agreed with the owner. As mentioned above, the Siete Partidas and subsequent regulations allowed judges to forcibly sell slaves who had been subjected to severe abuses, but nowhere did they suggest that slaves themselves were entitled to pursue a change of owners even in cases of flagrant abuse. The initiative belonged to the judges. In the practice of seeking papel, however, it was the slaves who took action, as if the masters' negligence of their legal duties entitled slaves to select a new owner.

The available evidence suggests that this practice was much more common in the cities than in rural areas, where opportunities for mobility and for the creation of the social networks needed to elicit the interest of a new (and potentially more favorable) buyer were more restricted. But rural workers also attempted to change owners when abused or neglected by their masters. One such case concerns the slave Manuel de la Trinidad, who in 1795 escaped the sugar mill where he worked. He wanted his master to "give him paper to find another whom he would serve, for they do not attend to him as is required and they give him too much work."[33] Trinidad's reference to the attention that owners were required to give to their slaves follows closely the letter of the law. In addition to excessive work, he denounced the lack of "necessary food" plus "the cruelest treatment that can be imagined." In 1850 the slave Andrés Criollo, who worked on a tobacco farm in western Cuba, presented himself before the síndico procurador of Havana "to complain against the treatment he receives from his master" and to "solicit paper" to seek a new owner. Ignacio, a slave employed on a cattle ranch in the jurisdiction of Havana, also presented himself before the síndico to seek paper, in his case for excessive punishment. Cristobal del Castillo, a slave in another cattle farm, offered a much laxer definition of abuse in 1836. He complained of mistreatment because his owner did not allow him to "earn a few reales with which to buy his freedom nor would he give him paper to search for a new master."[34]

It was in the cities where slaves attempted more frequently to turn what the law had conceived as a limited judicial power in cases of extreme abuse into a potential right to be claimed before authorities. Foreigners who visited the island in the early nineteenth century reported to be surprised when slaves approached them with the question, "Would you like to buy me?"[35] A síndico in Havana reported in 1861 that out of 307 complaints presented by slaves before him during the previous year, 66 had resulted in slaves "receiving paper" and another 28 in owners pledging to sell the slave to another person. In all these cases, the transfer of ownership was a direct consequence of the slaves' initiatives.[36] An extreme case is that of Ciprián Castillo, who bluntly stated in 1852 that he was requesting papel because he was not pleased with his new master: "no siendo de su gusto el nuevo amo." Equally extreme was the case of Luisa Vázquez del Castillo, who in 1858 solicited paper and a judicial assessment of her price because it "was not convenient for her to remain in the house" of her current owner. In some of these cases there was not even an attempt to demonstrate mistreatment or the notion of abuse had been stretched by the slaves well beyond the tight limits regulated in the codes.[37]

To many masters these demands for papel must have seemed a display of the worst kind of insubordination and insolence, an assault on their property rights. Juan Francisco Manzano, the author of a famous slave autobiography published in 1840, recalled the negative reaction of his master when he raised the possibility of obtaining paper "in order to advertise for a new master." His mistress was reportedly "quite astonished" by his "boldness" and denied the request. For some masters, however, giving papel may have represented the possibility of selling a slave under favorable conditions. It is possible that this custom developed in part as an extension of the widely practiced hiring out system, by which a slave sought work, and therefore a temporary master, with the authorization of his or her owner. The testimony of novelist Cirilo Villaverde suggests that the two practices could be easily mixed. "The first thing that doña Rosa did in the city was to give license or paper to María de Regla to seek employment (*acomodo*) or master (*amo*). The paper ... stated, more or less, what follows: I give paper to my slave María de Regla so that in the next ten days she can look for employment or master in the city. She is criolla, rational, intelligent and agile, healthy, strong, has never suffered any contagious disease, does not have known defects (*tachas*), knows how to sew, understands about washing, ironing, and taking care of children and infirm. She is being given paper because she has requested it. She has not known any master other than the one under whom she was born and who is now selling her." Thus María de Regla could either try to find a convenient job, a new master, or both.[38]

Finally, there were also masters who, faced with the possibility of legal proceedings and outside interference, resigned themselves to selling an otherwise unmanageable slave. Joaquina Pimienta admitted as much when she finally agreed to her slave Micaela O'Farrill's demand for papel: "I would rather miss her services than suffer her impertinence." As a síndico reasoned in a one of these cases, allowing a slave to change masters was frequently in the best interest of the owners, whose "tranquility" and "security" might otherwise be at risk.[39]

As a customary right claimed by slaves who declared to be the victims of various forms of abuse, the practice of papel had some foundation in law, however flimsy. The slaves attempted to invoke rights born out of the masters' unfulfilled duties, which were clearly established in legal doctrine. The legal bases of coartación were even flimsier. No written law referred to this institution, although a law in the Siete Partidas mentioned the sale of slaves "under the condition that they be emancipated within a certain time" and established that such conditions could not be altered—one of the main elements of the institution as it evolved later. The contours of coartación seem to have become defined over time as masters and slaves negotiated the implications of the slave's gradual purchase of his freedom. Indeed, the institution was known in Havana and in southern Spain since the late sixteenth century.[40] Changes in terminology reveal some of the changes undergone by coartación. A 1581 Málaga population count and seventeenth-century royal decrees refer to slaves who were cortados. The 1729 edition of the Dictionary dictionary of the Spanish Royal Academy defined *cortarse* as the action by which a slave "adjusted" with his master the terms of his freedom. Cortarse referred to the action by which slaves cut or divided their price into pieces. By the late eighteenth century, however, the practice was known as coartación, which literally means hindrance or restriction. Whereas cortar evokes the action of the slave, *coartar* refers to limitations on the master's power. Over time, the slaves' actions had become a constraint on the master's dominium.[41]

Because of its lack of precise definition, coartación should be seen as a legal institution in the making with poorly defined and contested legal effects. The one element of the institution that seems to have been accepted by all involved was the invariability of the price. In 1640, for instance, an owner acknowledged in his will that his slave Miguel Angola had "arranged his freedom" with him in 1636 for 400 ducados, of which he had already paid 228. He ordered the slave to be given his freedom letter as soon as he paid the difference. Another slave, Juana, a twenty-year-old resident of Guanabacoa, agreed with her master in 1690 on a freedom price of three hundred pesos, of which she paid half. The owner issued a notarized receipt, declaring that he would grant her freedom whenever she paid the other half. It was understood that a slave who had paid a fraction of his redemption price could not be mortgaged or sold for a higher value. That is why when the slave Juan, a seventeen-year-old criollo, was sold four times in 1690, it was always on condition that he was to be freed as soon as he was able to pay the two hundred pesos remaining for his total value. The typical sale contract established that the buyer of the coartado bought the slave "under the said condition" and that he could "possess and mortgage" the slave but not in an amount higher than the remaining price. Royal regulations ratified the invariability of the price and reinforced the principle that coartado slaves could only be sold under this condition.[42]

Much less clear was the status of a slave while coartado and the legal implications of this status. One subject of litigation concerned the coartados' possible control over the portion of time and labor for which they had already paid. Some slave owners believed that because the coartado had purchased a portion of himself or herself, they owned only part of the slave. The sale of Juana, a coartado mulatto slave who had paid half of her price in 1690, exemplifies this custom: "[C]oncerning this sale it is only on half of the said mulatto woman. The buyer must use her in the same form and if he uses her whole service or rent, collecting it entirely, he must grant her half of the time that belongs to her and discount it from her price." In a 1590 sale of another coartado woman, the buyer agreed to discount four ducados monthly from her manumission price to enjoy her services full time.[43]

The special status that many individuals identified with coartación is perhaps best illustrated by the fact that since the late eighteenth century non-coartado slaves were referred to as *enteros* (complete, entire). This designation suggested that coartados were only partially enslaved or, as a local official reported in 1826, that coartados "not being free can barely be called slaves." As a síndico argued in 1861, having paid a portion of his price, the slave "became associated to the dominium of himself."[44]

Some owners, however, rejected the notion that coartados were entitled to a portion of their labor. In 1826 master don Francisco Prado went to court over the earnings generated by his slave José Genaro. The síndico representing the slave demanded a portion of the profit he had produced for the last two and a half years—the time during which he had been coartado—to be credited toward his coartación. The owner refused. Some lawyers supported their position and decried the custom of linking the slaves' obligations with the price differential for their freedom. As one of them stated in 1830, "[S]ome síndicos have attempted to alleviate slavery, so as to pretend to concede a half of their time to slaves who are bound in service of their masters (when they have paid half of their value to their owners); but this opinion is not in conformity with the law.... The coartación ... was not established to reduce slavery into halves, but only to prevent any alteration in the price of the slaves."[45]

In practice, however, at least some of the coartados managed, if not to reduce slavery by half, to credit a portion of their time and labor toward the manumission price. Although this issue continued to be litigated well into the nineteenth century, the custom that slaves should retain a fraction of their earnings proportional to the payments they had already made persisted. By the nineteenth century in Cuba, as in Puerto Rico, the coartado slaves who were hired out paid a reduced rent to their masters. This rent was fixed at one real daily per 100 pesos of the remaining price for their manumission.[46]

Another contentious point concerned the situation of pregnant coartada women and whether this condition was transferred to their unborn children. Some jurists in Havana understood that the value of the child should be reduced in a proportion similar to the payments already made by the mother. Governor José de Ezpeleta issued a decree in 1786 supporting this view and based it on the legal principle that children always followed the condition of the mother. But the Consejo de Indias, sensitive to allegations concerning the need for workers for colonial agriculture, reversed this ruling as "contrary to law, for coartación in mothers is something only for them, so personal that it cannot be transmitted to their children," a principle that was ratified by a royal cédula of 1789. Although a few slaves attempted to claim freedom based on the condition of their mothers as coartadas, these cases did not prosper.[47] Later litigation and conflicts concentrated rather on a different question: the mothers' ability to coartar their recently born children.

Two additional elements of coartación, also poorly defined, were litigated in the courts of Havana in the early nineteenth century. The first concerned the masters' obligation to accept their slaves' payment toward coartación. Although some owners clearly resented any attempt to treat manumission as a slave right, instead of a prerogative of the master, the síndicos were invariably successful on this point. They invoked the traditional principle of *favor libertatis,* contained in the Siete Partidas, and forced reluctant masters to issue freedom letters and coartación papers to those slaves who could pay for them.[48] As a síndico put it in a demand against a master who claimed outstanding debts to refuse a payment from a coartado slave, "[N]either this motive nor any other of greater importance can have the effect of delaying or creating obstacles" for freedom. On this point legislation had been consistent: freedom was to be favored. The Consejo de Indias ratified the principle in a 1778 pronouncement concerning coartación: masters were "obligated, according to custom, to give [slaves] their freedom whenever they showed the corresponding price."[49]

By far the most contentious issue was the coartado's alleged right to seek papel and change masters at will. It is difficult to ascertain how these two legal practices became intertwined, but it is likely that as part of their drive for increased self-control, the coartados felt entitled to claim abuse or mistreatment whenever the owners attempted to reassert control over them. The claim of abuse would then be used to request papel. Already in 1766 Governor Antonio María Bucareli made reference to the disputes generated by the "voluntary and involuntary sales" of the coartados. Although the Council of Indies stated unequivocally that coartación did not entitle slaves to change masters without the latter's consent, the slaves and the síndicos who represented them continued to invoke this customary right. In some cases they did so by claiming abuse, which was construed broadly as any limitation on the coartado's ability to work toward his freedom. In other cases they simply alleged that the right to change masters was inherent to the status of coartación.[50]

Of the first kind was the case of Micaela O'Farril, an urban slave who in 1835 presented herself in the palace of the Captain captain General general to request assistance to obtain her paper to change owners. She claimed to have suffered unbearable but unspecified ill treatments at the hands of her owner and that "the laws allow the slave to change owners, particularly when … she is coartada." Claiming distaste for judicial proceedings, the master agreed. The case of the coartado Pedro López the same year exemplifies the second kind, in which demands to change owners were not based on claims of mistreatment. Here the síndico argued that the slave should receive his paper because this was "in his unfortunate situation, the only relief that the law gives him." Other síndicos put it in more forceful terms, as in this 1837 case: "[H]is master must give her paper to search for a new master because this is a prerogative of the coartado slaves." No abuse whatsoever was alleged.[51]

Masters resented this assault on their dominium and litigated against their slaves and the síndicos who, representing them, invoked rights without foundation in the codes. They found a sympathetic ear in those lawyers, justices, and even síndicos who shared their view that coartados were not entitled to change owners against the master's consent without just cause. As lawyer and magistrate José Serapio Mojarrieta stated, "The question may also be asked if slaves (coartados) have the right to go out of the power of their masters whenever they desire, and the answer is not difficult, if we consider that the slaves (enteros) entirely so are obliged to allege some great reason to compel their masters to sell them. And what difference can there be between one and the other, when we see that the yoke of slavery on all is the same? If the slaves (coartados) do not enjoy the rights of freemen, on what principle can they claim the right of changing masters at their pleasure?" A síndico concurred with this assessment in 1836, arguing that coartación's only legal effect was to limit the sale price.

In his view the institution did not "give a slave the right to change owners, just for his pleasure" nor did it force masters to give slaves a portion of their earnings.⁵²

According to Mojarrieta, who in the 1820s worked as a lawyer at the Audiencia of Puerto Príncipe, this appellate court always rejected the coartados' demands to change masters. Indeed there is evidence that in the early decades of the nineteenth century masters managed to litigate successfully against this practice. In 1820, for instance, don Leandro Garcia agreed to the petition of his slave Bernardo Lucumí to become coartado, but rejected his request of paper to change owners. Because the síndico failed to reach an agreement, the case went to a judge, who found the slave's petition without merit: "[N]ot being sufficient the causes alleged by Bernardo Lucumí to compel his master Leandro García y Sanabria to this alienation ... it does not proceed, informing don Leandro that he has to accept the amounts that his slave may give him for his freedom." Equally successful in rejecting his slave's petition for papel was the Marquis of Campo Florido in 1833. He alleged that "he could not be forced by the síndico" to the sale and that his petition did not conform to reason, the law, or the "delicate political order" in a country in which slaves outnumbered masters by the hundreds. The judge concurred, stating further that the síndico did not have jurisdiction in this case to begin with.⁵³

As long as these practices remained anchored just in custom or in fragmentary royal regulations, masters could successfully curb their slaves' insolence through litigation, as the Marquis of Campo Florido and other owners did in the early decades of the nineteenth century. The Reglamento de Esclavos of 1842 modified the legal landscape, however, creating new bases for the slaves and the síndicos to claim rights. The masters responded with vigorous litigation and demanded the suspension and repeal of a law that they perceived as an assault on property rights.

Codification: The Reglamento de Esclavos of 1842

Approved by Governor Gerónimo Valdés in 1842, this slave ordinance was Spain's response to "a series of concurrent pressures" from within and without.⁵⁴ Internally, the colonial state sought to control more effectively a fast-growing slave population that, particularly in the sugar districts, was exploited brutally. Several revolts, frequent rumors of conspiracy, and the specter of another Haiti underlined the precarious balance of colonial society.⁵⁵ To make matters worse, the international context was not favorable. Great Britain was determined to halt the slave trade and abolished slavery in its own colonies in the 1830s. The arrival in Havana of British Consul David Turnbull in 1841 was greeted with alarm by planters and authorities, and the central government instructed the Captain captain General general to counteract his efforts in favor of emancipation. As historian Jean-Pierre Tardieu states, to prevent "the worst," the colonial administration "had no choice but to propose a reform of the slave system that was favorable to both the slave and the master."[56] A few months later Valdés promulgated the Reglamento de Esclavos.

The reglamento was approved over the objections of the planters, who realized that the new regulations would control not just the slaves but the slave owners as well—"an attempt to rein them in," as Robert Paquette puts it. The owners resented almost any form of state interference in their properties, including any attempt to regulate slavery legally, claiming that slaves would always understand such regulations as a "bill of rights and a tacit accusation against masters."[57] On this point there was consensus among slave owners: discipline was a private matter to be decided exclusively by the master as the supreme authority. As a slave owner explained in 1842, "It is well known that public authorities cannot interfere between masters and slaves without grave risks." The mere act of regulating slavery was tantamount to the creation of "rights that slaves could claim" and therefore a direct attack on their authority. "Any direct intervention by the government, which in any way allows a slave to suspect that he has rights against the master" would automatically result in an increase of those demands, a slave owner warned. As soon as slaves knew that there existed an authority that protected them and watched over the masters, "all the links of subordination" would be lost and the very survival of the institution of slavery would be endangered.[58]

The very approval of the reglamento illustrated the diminished political power of Cuban planters and the expansion and consolidation of the absolutist power of the Captain General in the island, particularly after the 1830s.[59] Valdés himself referred in the introduction of his *Bando* to the governor as "the center of power and action" and as the interpreter of "the *true interests* of this rich and important part of the monarchy."[60]

Many slave owners and planters in the island did not see those interests as their own. Once it was approved, they fought against the reglamento and sought to have it repealed or suspended. In 1844, a commission of planters issued a report to the colonial governor in which they blamed the reglamento for several slave insurrections and for the conspiracy of La Escalera, which resulted in the repression of hundreds of free blacks and mulattos.[61] The members of this commission claimed that, following the royal cédula of 1789, the reglamento had transformed "the protective mission" and "the rights" of masters into obligations that could be claimed by the slaves. Indeed the reglamento had followed the traditional principles of Castilian law, asserting that masters should feed, clothe, and provide medical care for their slaves. As the Siete Partidas and colonial regulations had repeatedly stated, in cases of excessive punishment or cruelty the justices were authorized to order the forcible sale of the slave. All this, the commission elaborated, eroded the authority of the owners to the point that slaves did not see masters as "the absolute and legitimate power" any longer. Their recommendation, however, was not to repeal the reglamento. This would alarm the slaves and create international problems, a clear reference to British pressures. Better to put it on hold so that it would quietly fall into disuse.[62]

This did not happen, however. The reglamento continued to be invoked as the law of the land by slaves, by the síndicos, by the justices, by authorities, and by masters well into the 1860s.[63] The articles that masters attacked the most were those dealing with coartación. Article 34 defined coartación as a true slave right, for it was stated that owners "may not refuse" the coartación of any slave who offered at least fifty pesos toward his or her price. A practice that was initially known as "cortarse" — the action through which slaves cut or divided their price into pieces — had become coartar, which literally means hindrance or restriction, a limitation on the master's dominium. The coartación price, the following article asserted, could not be altered, although "if the slave wished to be sold against the will of his master and without just cause," the master could add the sales tax to the price. Following the principle established by the Consejo de Indias and the king in 1789, coartación was to be understood as a personal benefit that was not to be inherited by the children of coartado mothers.[64]

The slave owners' opposition to the reglamento resulted in litigation and in efforts to have it modified or repealed. One of the principles over which some slave owners continued to litigate concerned their obligation to accept their slaves' payments for coartación and freedom under all circumstances. Plantation owners, for instance, complained that by becoming coartados slaves acquired the right to seek new masters, leaving the units and disrupting production. Others used coartación to evade the mills altogether. Máximo Arozarena, owner of the sugar mill Mercedes, faced this situation. When in 1859 he tried to transfer nineteen slaves from a cattle farm to the mill, they abandoned the unit, presented themselves to the síndico Antonio Bachiller y Morales in Havana, and requested their coartación. The owner worried that, once coartados, they could invoke the right to seek a new master, a possibility that he characterized as "the most terrible and destructive weapon against territorial property."[65]

Slave owners also resisted slaves' attempts to coartar young children. They reasoned that children were assessed at very low prices that then could not be changed. As a result, once grown up these slaves could easily complete payments for their freedom. In the meantime, however, the owner was responsible for the sustenance and all the expenses associated with raising the slave. In 1861 Angela Vázquez Prieto, a resident of Bayamo, complained to the governor that the síndico was forcing her "to the coartación of a two-months old" unnamed girl. Vázquez protested against the "mistaken" application of articles 34 and 35 of the reglamento and explained how detrimental they were when applied to children. Furthermore, she claimed to be willing to grant manumission to the child for "her [market] value, because in this case she will leave my power in the day," but not to coartación, a status that made her financially responsible for raising the girl.[66]

Vázquez Prieto's concerns reflected not just the fact that slave prices increased with age, but also the suspicion that average slave prices would continue to rise. Coartación could work to the advantage of masters, as the price did not change despite the slave's depreciation due to age, but only if the slave waited long enough to complete his payments after his prime age (when depreciation began) and in an environment of price stability. Slave prices remained stable between 1800 and 1850, but they increased significantly afterward. Between 1850 and 1858 the average price of prime-age slave doubled.[67] In the early 1840s, when the reglamento was approved, the average price of prime-age slaves was about 350 pesos. Thus the minimal amount a slave needed to offer to become coartado (fifty pesos) represented about one seventh of his or her price. In the late 1850s, however, when prices grew to over eight hundred pesos, the amount needed to become coartado had declined to just six 6 or seven 7 percent of the price. Alarmed, in the 1850s several owners and local officials proposed to the central government to raise the coartación amount to at least ten 10 percent of the market price or to a minimum of 200 pesos. Following the same logic, masters also argued that the customary amount that slaves had paid for the freedom of an unborn child, set at 25 twenty-five pesos, should be raised. As a slave owner explained in 1857, "[W]hen the price of a slave used to be only 400 pesos what was carried in the belly was assessed in 25, but having tripled the value of the mother to 1,200 it is obvious that the daughter's triples as well."[68]

By far the most common point of litigation continued to be the coartados' alleged right to change owners at will, a prerogative they used to gain some control over their labor, avoid unfavorable occupations, and escape abusive masters. In 1862 Paulino Criollo presented himself before a síndico in Havana to complain that his master had taken him to a sugar mill to use "his services as if he was a complete slave" even though he had been coartado in 250 pesos. In a similar case, the mother of a coartada slave who had been taken to the interior demanded in 1869 that she be returned to Havana, where she could effectively earn her freedom. The slave Filomeno Lula, a cigar maker, requested papel in 1852 because, being coartado, his master was sending him to *el campo*—the countryside. To secure that his children and their mother, slave Clara Diago, were brought back to Havana from el campo, free black Felipe Herrera deposited 150 pesos with the síndico to proceed to their coartación and to demand that they be sold thereafter in the city.[69]

Slave owners resented these prerogatives and mobilized their considerable influence to try to modify articles 34 and 35 of the reglamento. In the 1850s several individual owners, frustrated by unfavorable judicial outcomes, appealed to the Captain General to promote the modification of the law. Some of them took their cases to the highest courts of the land, only to be rebuked.[70] The town councils of Puerto Príncipe and Santiago supported their views, which were shared by some councilors and other authorities in Havana as well. The prosecutor of the Real Audiencia (the court of appeals) of Havana asserted in 1853, for instance, that these articles had been detrimental to the interests of "all social classes" and recommended their repeal. Slaves should still access coartación, but only if they paid one fourth of their market value. Moreover, masters could only be forced to sell the slaves if they hurt, mistreated, or inflicted on them punishments "contrary to humanity." A legal advisor to the governor of the eastern department referred to coartación in 1855 as an evil suffered "by all owners of slaves" that the courts were unable to remedy due to the existing law. A councilor from Havana concurred: "[O]ur charitable laws, which have modified slavery allowing emancipation and coartación, are being used to demoralize the country and to sow confusion, intrigue, conflicts and revenge in the households." This official suggested that to "conserve with all strength the links of respect and subordination to the masters, principle and foundation of the social order," the síndicos should inquire whether the funds collected by the slaves had been honestly earned, that the minimum amount for coartación should be raised, and that the coartados should not enjoy any particular rights due to their status.[71]

The controversy over coartación spilled over to the press in the mid 1850s, when several jurists debated the nature of the institution and its legal effects. From the pages of the influential *Diario de la Marina,* Juan Olavarría from Santiago de Cuba and Antonio Bachiller y Morales from Havana criticized the way in which the síndicos and justices understood the institution. The crux of their argument remained the same used by lawyers like Mojarrieta since the early nineteenth century: slavery was a total status. People were either free or slave, there was no so-called half-way slavery, and consequently the coartación's only legal effect was to fix the manumission price of a slave. The coartado, Olavarría stated, was as enslaved as the entero. Recognizing that the reglamento clearly rejected these principles, Bachiller claimed that this ordinance was not technically a law and that it did not supersede previous regulations on the matter.[72]

A group of legal experts disputed these arguments and, taking sides "with the Courts of the Island and with the Síndicos," asserted that the reglamento was in fact "the only current law on the matter."[73] To the notion that slavery was a totalizing status, they responded that coartación represented one exception to this general principle.[74] Through coartación the slave acquired partial dominium over his body, labor, and time, constituting a form of concurrent ownership. "The coartado slave is not as slave as the entero," explained lawyer José I. Rodríguez.[75] This condition had several legal effects, the most important of which was the possibility to change masters at will, a possibility that the various authors repeatedly described as a derecho.[76] Rodríguez referred to it as "a right of the coartado slave, established by the law and sanctioned by an old custom." Nicolás Azcárate concurred: "Custom, more than the law, because the Reglamento has only confirmed customs, is the origin of the right that the coartado slave undoubtedly has among us to change masters." In turn, Ramón de Armas, who had been síndico when Governor Valdés published the reglamento in 1842, spoke of the "faculty" that coartado slaves had to change owners. Armas further mentioned that Valdés was familiar with the tract of Mojarrieta, disagreed with it, and that he understood coartación and the possibility of changing masters as entitlements that were not contingent on the consent of the masters.[77]

Another jurist, José M. Céspedes, criticized the reasoning of these lawyers by recycling some of the arguments that Mojarrieta, Barchiller, and Olavarría had made before.[78] The efforts of those opposing the reglamento were not without effect. The court of appeals of Havana—the Real Audiencia—issued a statement in 1853 endorsing the need to modify articles 34 and 35 of the reglamento. In 1855 a commission appointed by the governor to revise the *Bando*, which included the reglamento, accepted the notion that both articles should be repealed. Coartación, the commission argued, had not been created by royal regulations "to reduce slavery to half" nor did those regulations "concede slaves prerogatives as free … the right to change owners without just cause relaxes the subordination to which [slaves] should be subject." Thus the commission proposed the following changes to the law. Article 34 would read: "[N]o master may refuse to coartar his slaves whenever they pay him one fourth of their value, acquired by legal means." As for the controversial article 35, the reversal was complete: "[T]he masters of the coartado slaves cannot be forced to sell them unless there is just cause, as is regulated for those who are not coartados."[79]

The need to modify the reglamento was felt, of course, because these articles were being invoked by the slaves and by the síndicos who represented them. The latter insisted that it was their duty to enforce the law, even if that meant, as one of them put it, becoming "an accomplice" of the slave. A typical argument was offered, successfully, by a síndico on behalf of the slave José Casanova in 1846: "[A]ccording to article 35 ... the coartados can change masters at will." When the síndicos of Havana were asked to issue a pronouncement about whether slaves could demand coartación "in any case," their answer, which they qualified as "very easy," was unequivocal: "[T]he síndicos of this city have always made to be declared coartado any slave who gives his master the amount of fifty pesos according to the reglamento." When, years later, they were asked again to issue a statement concerning the application of this right to small children, their reply was again definite: the articles did not make an exception of small children, who could not be excluded from this benefit. Invoking the principle of favor libertatis, they also noted that it was a principle of law that all doubts should be resolved in favor of freedom.[80]

When attacked for contributing to the erosion of property rights and the social order in the island, the síndicos countered that they were simply performing their duties and enforcing the laws. As one of these officials put it in 1858, "[B]ecause I see in the delicate question of coartación a principle of freedom for the slave and I find article 34 to be explicit I feel the imperious need to press a demand ... for the coartación of Evaristo." Or as another síndico stated in 1850, "[T]he duty of my ministry, which I cannot ignore, compels me to initiate a claim on behalf of the said slaves." When the síndico of Santiago de Cuba Miguel Rodriguez, who represented the slave María in her quest to change owners against Carlota Dascar, was accused of protecting the slaves who asked for papel, he claimed to be "astonished." He had simply "enforced what is regulated in the reglamento and Royal Cédulas of slaves."[81]

The síndicos' argument that laws had to be upheld reinforced the perception that it was necessary to repeal or modify articles 34 and 35 of the reglamento, as the Real Audiencia and the Comisión Revisora—the commission for the revision of the *Bando*—recommended in 1853. The governor acknowledged receipt of the recommendations by the commission, but "reserve[d] approval" for a future moment, when revisions of the entire *Bando* were finished.

Yet this approval was never issued. In 1862, when the recently created Consejo de Administración issued a final report about coartación, it deemed it inadvisable to modify the reglamento.[82] Addressed to the governor, the report offered a careful assessment of the conflicts of interests that surrounded coartación. On one side there were "private interests" that, invoking property rights, discipline, and order, aspired to "curtail concessions given to the slaves." On the other side there was "a well-understood public interest" supported by the laws, which the members of the council depicted as monuments to humanity and Spanish civilization. Beyond these abstractions, however, the councilmen acknowledged the weight of practical reasons. They noted that the island was living through "difficult circumstances" and "an evidently transitional period" in which it was not prudent to attack "rights or concessions sanctioned by law," particularly when they affected a numerous sector of society. Although they acknowledged that some owners may be irritated by the possibilities linked to coartación, particularly when it involved children, they deemed those interests "too secondary to influence a matter of such social importance." The council thus recommended that neither the articles concerning coartación, nor the custom of allowing the manumission of unborn children "in the terms established by custom"—that is, for a price of twenty-five pesos—should be altered. They further stated that even if the child of one of their slaves was born free, it was the master's responsibility to keep them until they turned seven, at which point they could be transferred to a master artisan to learn a trade or to a public institution.[83]

The council's statement did not represent an end point, but a new stage in the longstanding conflict surrounding the implementation of coartación in nineteenth-century Cuba and the legal effects of the institution. An ordinance issued in 1863 to regulate the activities of the síndicos codified the pronouncements of the Consejo and wrote into law some of the most restrictive interpretations concerning the effects of coartación on masters. For instance, unborn children could be liberated for the customary amount of twenty-five pesos. The owner remained responsible for the upbringing of the child and could not prevent enslaved mothers from breast-feeding them. Those who employed coartado slaves had to pay them a salary proportional to the portion for which the slaves had already paid. This arrangement had been long observed in the island, but it had not been written into law before. Furthermore, appraisers were instructed that in cases of coartación or self-purchase the price of slaves should be based only on their age and physical condition, regardless of qualifications and abilities. Masters could be compensated for the expenses associated with training their slaves, but skilled slaves should not be penalized by assessing them with a higher manumission price. Finally, article 13 stipulated that if a slave—any slave, not just a coartado—was being sold without fault on his part, then he had "the right to be authorized to look for a new master for three days," after which the owner could sell the slave to whomever he pleased.[84] It is unknown to what extent these regulations were enforced. What seems clear, however, is that this ordinance restricted further the dominium of slave owners and represented another expression of a thread of legal thinking that subordinated the rights of the property owners to the stability and "true interests" of the colony.

The slave owners, of course, did not resign themselves to what they perceived as repeated assaults on their sacred rights and continued to challenge the slaves' right to change masters. At least in the case of rural slaves, they seem to have had some success. As late as 1867 a justice from the sugar zone of Colón, in Matanzas, inquired whether rural slaves who were coartados "could ask for papel to seek a new master and to abandon the farm as a result," warning that this created a disastrous example for the farmhands. The very existence of this consultation suggests that justices continued to be ambivalent about this right, its codification in law notwithstanding. Although the Consejo de Administración ratified, again, that articles 34 and 35 continued to be valid and that they applied to all slaves, including those in the countryside, the planters' pressures eventually bore fruit. A circular issued by the governor in 1871 declared that rural slaves "did not have the right to change owners," even if they were coartados.[85] By then, however, the slave owners faced a threat that was far more serious than coartación. The anticolonial revolt that erupted in eastern Cuba in 1868 threatened in fact the slave system as a whole.

Colonial authorities rationalized the practices of coartación, buscar papel, and others, as concessions grounded on the humanitarian spirit of the Spanish laws, a characterization that was at best partially correct. Although some of these practices, such as seeking paper and a new owner, were tenuously linked to Spanish legal codes and mores, they had developed in ways that were frequently quite different from those intended by the law. These customary rights, in turn, were widespread enough that by the mid nineteenth century, when colonial authorities felt the need to regulate slavery—that is, its survival—they codified some of those customs into law. Once included in the reglamento there was no turning back. As the Consejo de Administración acknowledged later, it was not prudent to revoke rights already legitimized by custom and law. A concession this was, but a concession to fear.

For the slaves, however, the codification of these rights represented a stronger ground on which to base claims. This is what slave owners resented the most. Slaves could now claim rights that could be exercised even against the will of the master, and rights that produced other rights in turn. Slavery was supposed to be a neatly defined social and legal status; coartación complicated this considerably. That is probably what síndico Antonio Bachiller y Morales had in mind when he asserted that slavery "was not compatible with the rights of the coartado slaves."[86] Masters realized that any right that slaves could claim came at the expense of their dominium and therefore at the expense of their own rights.

Notes

1. This article originally appeared in *Hispanic American Historical Review* 87 (November 2007): 659–692.
2. Doña Carlota Dascar al Gobernador, 3 May 1856, in Expediente sobre la coartación, 1853–1862. Archivo Nacional de Cuba (hereafter ANC), Intendencia, leg. 960/3.
3. Representación del Regidor de Santiago Ruperto Ulecia Ledesma, 23 August 1855, in ibid.
4. The invariability of the price was absolute. This could be beneficial to the master if the slave aged or became ill or incapacitated, conditions that lowered his market price. But it could be detrimental to the owner as well due to changing market conditions or the slave's acquisition of new skills.
5. For a few significant examples, see Carlos Aguirre, *Agentes de su propia libertad: los esclavos de Lima y la desintegración de la esclavitud 1821–1854* (Lima,1993); Christine Hünefeldt, *Paying the Price of Freedom: Family and Labor Among Lima's Slaves 1800–1854* (Berkeley, 1994); Camilla Townsend, "'Half My Body Free, the Other Half Enslaved': The Politics of the Slaves of Guayaquil at the End of the Colonial Era," *Colonial Latin American Review* 7, no. 1 (1998): 105–28. For Cuba, see the pioneering work of Rebecca J. Scott, *Slave Emancipation in Cuba: The Transition to Free Labor, 1860–1899* (Princeton,1985).
6. Other aspects of slaves' lives were regulated in the Siete Partidas and in subsequent civil and religious regulations, some of which I mention below. The Partidas were not just a collection of abstract legal principles, but a code that was invoked by legal actors and the courts well into the nineteenth century. See Norman A. Meiklejohn, "The Implementation of Slave Legislation in Eighteenth-Century New Granada," *Slavery and Race Relations in Latin America*, ed. Robert Brent Toplin (Westport, 1974), 176–203; Olga López Vera, "La esclavitud en la jurisprudencia civil del Tribunal Supremo" (Ph.D. dissertation, University of Navarra, 2001); and Alejandro de la Fuente, "Slave Law and Claims-Making in Cuba: The Tannenbaum Debate Revisited," *Law and History Review* 22 (Summer 2004): 339–369.
7. For studies of slavery and the law in Cuba see Gloria García, *La esclavitud desde la esclavitud* (Havana, 2003); Jean-Pierre Tardieu, *"Morir o dominar": en torno al Reglamento de Esclavos de Cuba (1841-1866)* (Madrid, 2003); María del Carmen Barcia, *La otra familia: parientes, redes y descendencia de los esclavos en Cuba* (Havana, 2003); Manuel Barcia Paz, *Con el látigo de la ira: legislación, represión y control en las plantaciones cubanas, 1790-1870* (Havana, 2000); Scott, *Slave Emancipation;* Verena Martínez-Alier, *Marriage, Class, and Colour in Nineteenth-Century Cuba: A Study of Racial Attitudes and Sexual Values in a Slave Society* (New York, 1974); Franklin W. Knight, *Slave Society in Cuba during the Nineteenth Century* (Madison, 1970), 121–36; Herbert Klein, *Slavery in the Americas: a Comparative Study of Virginia and Cuba* (Chicago, 1989); Fernando Ortiz, *Los negros esclavos* (Havana, 1975); de la Fuente, "Slave Law and Claims-Making."
8. On the distinction between societies with slaves and slave societies, see Ira Berlin, *Many Thousands Gone: The First Two Centuries of Slavery in North America* (Cambridge, MA, 1998), 8. For some critiques, see Herman L. Bennett, *Africans in Colonial Mexico: Absolutism, Christianity, and Afro-Creole Consciousness, 1570–1640* (Bloomington, 2003), 14–15;

Sherwin K. Bryant, "Enslaved Rebels, Fugitives, and Litigants: The Resistance Continuum in Colonial Quito," *Colonial Latin American Review* 13, no. 1 (2004): 36–37 (note 11).
9. The significance of these activities has been assessed through the regulations issued by the town council of Havana on slavery-related matters between 1550 and 1700. See de la Fuente, "Slave Law and Claims Making," 353–363.
10. This case is discussed at length in Alejandro de la Fuente, "Su único derecho: los esclavos y la ley." *Debate y Perspectivas* 4 (December 2004): 7–22.
11. Bryant, "Enslaved Rebels," 21.
12. Scott, *Slave Emancipation*, 13, note 20; de la Fuente, "Slave Law and Claims Making."
13. José Serapio Mojarrieta, *Esposición sobre el origen, utilidad prerogativas, derechos y deberes de los síndicos procuradores generales de los pueblos* (Puerto Príncipe, [1830]). For the síndicos' functions in the Real Cédula of 1789, see articles 9, 11, and 13; for the Reglamento of 1842, articles 37, 42, 43, and 46. Both in Ortiz, *Los negros esclavos*, 412–414, 447–448. See also Klein, *Slavery in the Americas*, 78–84; L.1, T. 18, L. 7 of the *Novísima Recopilación*.
14. For a critique of the síndicos and an appeal for them to cooperate with the submission of the slaves, see Mojarrieta, *Esposición*, 16–17.
15. Older studies concentrated for the most part on Spanish legislation and on the prescriptive aspects of the law. Important contributions include Frank Tannenbaum, *Slave and Citizen: The Negro in the Americas* (Boston, 1992) (original edition New York, 1946); Ortiz, *Los negros esclavos* (original edition 1916); Luis M. Díaz Soler, *Historia de la esclavitud negra en Puerto Rico (1493–1890)* (Madrid, 1953); Carlos Larrazábal Blanco, *Los negros y la esclavitud en Santo Domingo* (Santo Domingo, 1967); Javier Malagón Barceló, *Código Negro Carolino (1784)* (Santo Domingo, 1974). Scholars of derecho indiano have continued this tradition. For a recent overview of colonial law see M. C. Mirow, *Latin American Law: A History of Private Law and Institutions in Spanish America* (Austin, 2004). Two useful compilations have been recently issued in CD by Fundación Histórica Tavera of Madrid: Ismael Sánchez Bella, *Textos clásicos de literatura jurídica Indiana* (1999) and José Andrés Gallego, ed., *Nuevas aportaciones a la historia jurídica de Iberoamérica* (2000).
16. Bryant, "Enslaved Rebels," 7–46; Renée Soulodre-La France, "Socially not so Dead! Slave Identities in Bourbon Nueva Granada," *Colonial Latin American Review* 10, no. 1 (2001): 87–103; Brian P. Owensby, "How Juan and Leonor Won Their Freedom: Litigation and Liberty in Seventeenth-Century Mexico," *Hispanic American Historical Review* 85, no. 1 (2005): 39–79; Bennett, *Africans in Colonial Mexico*; Kris Lane, "Captivity and Redemption: Aspects of Slave Life in Early Colonial Quito and Popayán," *The Americas* 57, no. 2 (2000): 225–246; Aguirre, *Agentes de su propia libertad*; Hünefeldt, *Paying the Price of Freedom*; María E. Díaz, *The Virgin, the King, and the Royal Slaves of El Cobre: Negotiating Freedom in Colonial Cuba, 1670–1780* (Stanford, 2000). See also the contributions to the special issue of the journal *Debate y Perspectivas* 4 (2004) titled "Su único derecho: los esclavos y la ley." For Brazil see Sidney Chalhoub, *Visões da Liberdade: as últimas décadas da escravidão na Corte* (São Paulo, 1990); Hebe Mattos, *Das Cores do Silêncio: os significados da liberdade no Sudeste escravista—Brasil século XIX* (Rio de Janeiro, 1998); Keila Grinberg, "La manumisión, el género y la ley en el Brasil del siglo XIX: el proceso legal de Liberata por su libertad," *Debate y Perspectivas* 4 (2004), 89–103.
17. Women represented 60 percent of the slave population of Havana in 1792 and 50 percent in 1817 and 1861. Their proportion in the island as a whole was 44, 38, and 41 percent, respectively. In 1855 women represented 53 percent of urban slaves in the island, compared with 36 percent among rural slaves. Calculations made from census data in Comité Estatal de Estadísticas, *Los censos de población y vivienda en Cuba* (Havana, 1988), 1, 2, 71, 73, and 112; Kenneth F. Kiple, *Blacks in Colonial Cuba, 1774–1899* (Gainesville, 1976), 61. See also Knight, *Slave Society*, 79.
18. Laird W. Bergad, Fe Iglesias García, and María del Carmen Barcia, *The Cuban Slave Market, 1790–1880* (New York, 1995), 124, 128–131. As numerous studies confirm, women

represented between 55 and 68 percent of slaves manumitted across Latin America. Given that about two thirds of imported Africans were males, women's manumission rates were in fact much higher than those of males. For a recent contribution that summarizes previous findings, see Frank "Trey" Proctor III, "Gender and the Manumission of Slaves in New Spain," *Hispanic American Historical Review* 86 (May 2005): 309–336. For a useful overview, see Herbert S. Klein, *African Slavery in Latin America and the Caribbean* (New York, 1986), 227. For early colonial Havana, see my "A alforría de escravos em Havana, 1601–1610: primeiras conclusões," *Estudos Econômicos* 20 (Jan.–April 1990): 139–159.

19. Bianca Premo, *Children of the Father King: Youth, Authority, and Legal Minority in Colonial Lima* (Chapel Hill, 2005), 211. In addition to the cases in this article, see Townsend, "Half My Body Free," 105–128; Camillia Cowling, "Negotiating Freedom: Women of Colour and the Transition to Free Labour in Cuba, 1870–1886," *Slavery and Abolition* 26 (December 2005): 377–391; Bryant, "Enslaved Rebels," 20–31. On manumissions as a gendered process see also Proctor, "Gender and the Manumission," and Kathleen J. Higgins, *"Licentious Liberty" in a Brazilian Gold-Mining Region: Slavery, Gender, and Social Control in Eighteenth-Century Sabará, Minas Gerais* (University Park, 1999).

20. Bennett, *Africans in Colonial Mexico*, 4.

21. The best empirical research on coartación during the nineteenth century is Bergad et al., *The Cuban Slave Market*, 122–142. For other contributions see Klein, *Slavery in the Americas*, 196–200 and the critical reading of Scott, *Slave Emancipation*, 13–14; Ortiz, *Los negros esclavos*, 285–290; de la Fuente, "Slave Law and Claims-Making," 358–359; Leví Marrero, *Cuba: economía y sociedad*. 15 vols. (Madrid, 1975–1992), 13, 163–168. A study that emphasizes the economic advantages of coartación for the masters is Rafael Duharte. *El negro en la sociedad colonial* (Santiago de Cuba, 1988), 53–61.

22. The 1871 figure is quoted by Scott, *Slave Emancipation*, 14, note 26; Bergad et al., *The Cuban Slave Market*, 123. The other testimonies are from Mojarrieta, *Esposición*, 19, 23; Representación del Regidor de Santiago Ruperto Ulecia Ledesma.

23. According to an 1861 report, the number of slaves manumitted in the island between 1851 and 1858 was 16,243. The census of 1862 registered 9,462 manumissions between 1858 and 1861 and estimated a slave population of ca. 370,000. See Expediente promovido por Juan Manuel Rodríguez y Francisco Ravirosa para introducir ocho mil negros libres en la Isla, 1861. ANC, Miscelánea de Expedientes (hereafter ME), leg. 4412; *Noticias estadísticas de la isla de Cuba en 1862* (Havana, 1864).

24. A point suggested to me by Stanley Engerman, for which I am grateful. A similar statement concerning runaway slaves is made by Eugene D. Genovese, *Roll, Jordan, Roll: The World the Slaves Made* (New York, 1974), 598.

25. I have used here the English translation of the pPartidas edited by Robert I. Burns, *Las Siete Partidas* 5 vols. (Philadelphia, 2001), 4: 979. For a useful analysis of this regulation, see López Vera, "La esclavitud," 99–101 and Ortiz, *Los negros esclavos*, 312–13. Here the law of Castile followed Roman precedents, where city prefects heard slaves' allegations of starvation. See Keith Bradley, *Slavery and Society at Rome* (New York, 1994), 100.

26. These regulations are reproduced in Malagón Barceló, *Código Negro*, 134, 141, 225–229.

27. See for instance a Real Cédula of 1710 in Malagón Barceló, *Código Negro*, 255; Real Cédula 15 April 1540, later L. 8, Tit. 5, Lib. 7 of the *Recopilación de Leyes de los Reinos de las Indias*.

28. The ordenanzas are reproduced in Marrero, *Cuba: economía y sociedad*, 2, 429–444. Compare articles 22 and 23 of the Ordinances of Santo Domingo of 1528, and article 34 of the Ordinances of 1535 with articles 60 and 61 of the Cáceres ordinances of 1574. The language used by Cáceres in his text is almost identical to a report he had issued four years earlier about sugar slaves in Santo Domingo. See Cáceres to Juan de Ovando. Santo Domingo, 1570, in *Colección de documentos inéditos, relativos al descubrimiento, conquista*

y organización de las antiguas posesiones españolas de América y Oceanía. 42 vols. (Madrid, 1864–1884), 11:55.
29. Cargos, descargos y sentencias de esta ciudad de la Habana, 1762. Archivo Histórico Nacional, Madrid (hereafter AHN), Consejos, leg. 21467, pieza 6, fol. 28v. The reference to the 1754 case is taken from "Pieza de diligencias preparatorias para la residencia de esta ciudad de la Habana," 1762, ibid.; Cargos y Exculpación del Sr. Marques de la Torre, 1777. AHN, Consejos, leg. 20892.
30. This Royal Cédula is reproduced by Ortiz, *Los negros esclavos*, 408–415, and Barcia, *Con el látigo*, 85–94.
31. Expediente sobre haberse presentado al capitán de Macurijes ocho negros del ingenio San Miguel. 1846. ANC, Gobierno Superior Civil (hereafter GSC), leg. 944, no. 33,303; Barcia, *Con el látigo*, 57; Criminales por sevicia al negro Pablo del ingenio Caridad, 1865. ANC, ME, leg. 2851, no. J.
32. Expediente... de Macurijes, 1846; de la Fuente, "Su único derecho."
33. "Para que le diese papel para solicitar otro a quien servir atento que no le asistían como era necesario y le daban mucho trabajo." Don Francisco de Ponce de León y Maroto con don Manuel Dueñas sobre pertenencia de dos esclavos. AHN, Consejos, leg. 20839.
34. Expediente sobre el negro Andres criollo, que se queja de maltrato, 1850. ANC, GSC, leg. 33373; Autos promovidos por el Síndico a nombre del negro Ignacio, 1848. ANC, Escribanías, leg. 581, no. 14; Expediente en que el moreno Cristóbal del Castillo solicita carta de libertad, 1836. ANC, GSC, leg. 937/33080.
35. See Alexander von Humboldt, *Ensayo político sobre la isla de Cuba* (Paris, 1827), 279; Robert F. Jameson, *Letters from the Havana during the Year 1820* (London, 1821), 41.
36. We do not know how many of the 307 demands concerned change of ownership. The possible maximum would be 263, for we know that the remaining 44 cases dealt with other matters (usually freedom). This would indicate that at least one third of the slaves requesting to change masters before this official succeeded in doing so. This data is taken from Expediente promovido por el Sr. don José Morales Lemus, síndico segundo, 1862. ANC, GSC, leg. 954, no. 33747.
37. Expediente en el que el negro Ciprian Castillo pretende variar de amo, 1852. ANC, GSC, leg. 947/33429; Expediente en que la negra luisa Vázquez pretende variar de dueño, 1858. ANC, GSC, leg. 949/33545.
38. Edward Mullen, ed., *The Life and Poems of a Cuban Slave: Juan Francisco Manzano, 1797–1854* (Hamdem, 1981), 98; Cirilo Villaverde, *Cecilia Valdés*, quoted by Ortiz, *Los negros esclavos*, 350.
39. Correspondencia sobre esclavitud, 1834–1842. ANC, GSC, leg. 937/33052; Expediente en el que el síndico procurador solicita que doña Felicia Jáuregui le de papel para buscar amo al moreno Pedro López, 1835. ANC, GSC, leg. 937/33057.
40. See L. 45, tit. 5, P. 5, in Burns, *Siete Partidas*, 5, 1045. The existence of cortados in Spain is reported by Bernard Vincent for Málaga in 1581, in his *Minorías y marginados en la España del siglo XVI* (Granada, 1987), 253, although most scholars of slavery in Iberia do not make reference to the institution. For the evolution of this legal practice, see Manuel Lucena Salmoral, "El derecho de coartación del esclavo en la América Española," *Revista de Indias* 59, no. 216 (May–August 1999): 357–374; Watson, *Slave Law in the Americas*, 51; de la Fuente, "Slave Law and Claims-Making," 339–369; Marrero, *Cuba: economía y sociedad*, 13, 163–168. I thank Vincent for sharing his work on Málaga slaves with me.
41. I thank Joseph Miller for suggesting this line of reasoning. See Vincent, *Minorías*, 253. The first time I have seen the institution mentioned in a royal decree is in a Real Cédula of 18 April 1673 mentioned by Ortiz de Matienzo to the King, Havana, 23 November, 1673. ANC, AH, leg. 89/548; Real Academia Española, *Diccionario de la Lengua Castellana* (Madrid, 1729), 626.

42. ANC, Protocolos Notariales de la Habana (hereafter PNH), Escribanía Fornaris, 1640, fol. 721; 1690, fol. 45, 140, 144, 262, 363; 1693, fol. 114. See Real Cédula of 21 June 1768 and its analysis in Lucena Samoral, "El derecho de coartación," 366–366; and Real Cédula of 8 April 1778 reproduced by Mojarrieta, *Esposición*, 21.
43. ANC, PNH, Escribanía Fornaris, 1690, fol. 44; Escribanía Regueira, 1590, fol. 26v.
44. The term enteros is used by the Consejo de Indias in a 1778 consultation and was frequently used during the nineteenth century. See Marrero, *Cuba: economía y sociedad*, 13, 164; Lucena Samoral, "El derecho de coartación," 358; García, *La esclavitud*, 42–43; Mojarrieta, *Esposición*, 19. The 1826 report is quoted by Marrero, *Cuba: economía y sociedad*, 13, 166. The statement of síndico José Morales Lemus in ANC, Intendencia, leg. 760/3.
45. El síndico contra Francisco Prado sobre la coartación del pardo José Genaro, 1826. ANC, Escribanías (Galleta), leg. 814/7; Mojarrieta, *Esposición*, 19. I used here the translation of Richard Madden as it appears in Mullen, ed., *The Life and Poems of a Cuban Slave*, 201.
46. For examples, see Expediente en que la negra Tomasa Amaya se queja de su amo, 1854. ANC, GSC, leg. 948/33533; Expediente promovido por el Síndico de Sagua la Grande en consulta de introducir mejoras en la compra de esclavos coartados, 1877. ANC, ME, leg. 3946/Ar. See also José I. Rodríguez, "La coartación y sus efectos," *Revista de Jurisprudencia*, 1 (1856), 355. In Puerto Rico this custom was formalized in a circular issued by the Governor in 1849. See Lucena Samoral, "El derecho de coartación," 372.
47. Mojarrieta, *Esposición*, 23; Lucena Samoral, "El derecho de coartación," 367–370; Marrero, *Cuba: economía y sociedad*, 13, 165; El moreno Pedro Pascasio sobre su libertad, 1835. ANC, GSC, leg. 937/33074.
48. The Partidas's first "rule of law" was "that all judges should aid liberty, for the reason that it is a friend of nature." The code also acknowledged the possibility that slaves may purchase their freedom. See Rule 1, tit. 34, P. 7 and L. 8, tit. 2, P. 3, Burns, *Siete Partidas*, 5, 1478 and 3, 548. See also Ortiz, *Los negros esclavos*, 315–316; López Vera, "La esclavitud en la jurisprudencia," 107–108, 116–120.
49. El síndico procurador general del común a nombre del moreno Santiago, 1826. ANC, Escribanías (Salinas), leg. 676/7858. For additional examples see Diligencias promovidas por el síndico procurador general a nombre de la negra María del Carmen, 1831. ANC, Escribanías (Bienes de Difuntos), leg. 196/3437; El moreno Cristóbal del Castillo sobre su libertad, 1836. ANC, GSC, leg. 937/33080; El síndico procurador general sobre la libertad del negro Carlos Ferregat, 1839. ANC, Escribanías (Junco), leg. 78/1248. For the pronouncement of the Consejo, see Marrero, *Cuba: economía y sociedad*, 13, 164.
50. Bucareli's report is mentioned by Marrero, *Cuba: economía y sociedad*, 13, 164; on the Consejo's recommendation, see Lucena Samoral, "El derecho de coartación," 365–366.
51. Micaela O'Farril al Capitan General, 1835 in Correspondencia sobre esclavitud, 1834–1842. ANC, GSC, leg. 937/33052; El síndico procurador solicita que Da. Felicia Jauregui le de papel al moreno Pedro López, 1835. ANC, GSC, leg. 937/33057; Incidente a la testamentaría de Pedro Santo, 1837. ANC, Escribanías (Junco), leg. 309/4743.
52. Mojarrieta, *Esposición*, 20–21, using here Maddan's translation in Mullen, ed., *The Life and Poems of a Cuban Slave*, 202; Expediente en que el moreno Cristóbal del Castillo solicita carta de libertad.
53. Bernardo Lucumí sobre su coartación y venta, 1820. ANC, Escribanías (Daumy), leg. 778/3; El síndico sobre que el Marqués de Campo Florido le otorgue escritura de venta a su esclavo Francisco, 1833. ANC, Escribanías (Salinas), leg. 672/7776. It is interesting to note that in this last case the judge nonetheless mediated to persuade the Marquis to sell the slave, an arrangement to which he agreed.
54. Knight, *Slave Society*, 126. See also Tardieu, "Morir o dominar"; Robert Paquette's, *Sugar is Made with Blood: The Conspiracy of La Escalera and the Conflict Between Empires over Slavery in Cuba* (Middletown, 1988), 77–80; Ortiz, *Los negros esclavos*, 339–340; Moreno Fraginals, *El ingenio*, 2, 83–90.

55. Gloria García, *Conspiraciones y revueltas: la actividad política de los negros en Cuba (1790–1845)* (Santiago de Cuba, 2003); Gwendolyn Midlo Hall, *Social Control in Slave Plantation Societies: A Comparison of St. Domingue and Cuba* (Baton Rouge, 1971), 55–57; Gabino La Rosa Corzo, *Runaway Slave Settlements in Cuba: Resistance and Repression* (Chapel Hill, 2003). On the lasting impact of Haiti on Cuban slave society see María Dolores González-Ripoll, Consuelo Naranjo, Ada Ferrer, Gloria García, and Josef Opatrný, *El rumor de Haití en Cuba: temor, raza y rebeldía, 1789–1844* (Madrid, 2004).
56. El Ministerio de Marina al Capitán General, Madrid 28 July 1841. Archivo del Museo de la Ciudad de la Habana (hereafter AMCH), Colección Esclavitud, leg. 64, no. 7; Paquette, *Sugar is Made with Blood*, 131–157; Tardieu, "*Morir o dominar*," 123.
57. Paquette, *Sugar is Made with Blood*, 77; Parecer de la Real Junta de Fomento sobre el Reglamento de Esclavos, 1845. ANC, GSC, leg. 943/33271. Reproduced by Tardieu, "*Morir o dominar*," 264–271, quote on 265.
58. "Encuesta sobre ... los siervos," 1842. ANC, GSC, leg. 940/33158. This whole dossier, which includes reports by twelve plantation owners, is reproduced by Tardieu, "*Morir o dominar*," 206–263.
59. On the varying political fortunes of the planters and their relationships with the state, see Josep M. Fradera, *Gobernar colonias* (Barcelona, 1999), 95–120; Christopher Schmidt-Nowara, *Empire and Antislavery: Spain, Cuba, and Puerto Rico, 1833–1874* (Pittsburgh, 1999), 16–17; Manuel Moreno Fraginals, *Cuba/España, España/Cuba: historia común* (Barcelona, 1995), 165–169, 190–198; Paquette, *Sugar is Made with Blood*, 47–49.
60. Gerónimo de Valdés, *Bando de gobernación y policía de la Isla de Cuba* (Havana, 1842), 4. My emphasis. I have used the translation of Knight, *Slave Society*, 127, for the second quote.
61. The best study of the conspiracy is Paquette's, *Sugar is Made with Blood*. See also Daisy Cué Fernandez, "Plácido y la conspiración de la escalera," *Santiago* 42 (1981), 145–206; José L. Franco, *Plácido: una polémica que tiene cien años* (Havana, 1964).
62. Parecer de la Real Junta de Fomento sobre el Reglamento de Esclavos, 1845.
63. Ortiz asserts mistakenly that the reglamento was repealed and replaced by a new set of rules issued by Governor Leopoldo O'Donnell in 1844. See Ortiz, *Los negros esclavos*, 347–348. On the 1844 rules see also Tardieu, "*Morir o dominar*," 183–196, 272–278; Barcia Paz, *Con el látigo*.
64. Valdés, *Bando de gobernación*. The reglamento is reproduced by Ortiz, *Los negros esclavos*, 442–452; by Barcia Paz, *Con el látigo*, 95–104; and by Marrero, *Cuba: economía y sociedad*, 13, 193–195. For a discussion of the reglamento see Tardieu, "*Morir o dominar*," 178–200. Lucena Samoral and Knight note that the reglamento owed much to an 1826 slave ordinance from Puerto Rico. See Knight, *Slave Society*, 136–132; Manuel Lucena Salmoral, *Los códigos negros de la América española* (Madrid, 1996), 140–159.
65. Máximo Arozarena al Capitán General, 8 March 1859. ANC, Intendencia, leg. 960/3.
66. Instancia de Angela Vázquez Prieto, Holguín, 2 October 1861. ANC, Intendencia, leg. 960/3.
67. Bergad et al., *The Cuban Slave Market*, 47–56. See also Manuel Moreno Fraginals, Herbert S. Klein, and Stanley L. Engerman, "The Level and Structure of Slave Prices on Cuban Plantations in the Mid-Nineteenth Century: Some Comparative Perspectives," *American Historical Review* 88, no. 5 (1983): 1201–1218.
68. El síndico procurador sobre la libertad de la criatura que lleva en su seno la morena Isabel, 1857. ANC, Escribanías (Luis Blanco), leg. 334/7. On proposals to alter the coartación minimum, see El Consejero ponente a la sección de gobierno, 30 August 1862 in Expediente de informe para revisar las leyes vigentes sobre coartación de esclavos, 1862. ANC, Consejo de Administración, leg. 3/108; Parecer de la Comisión Revisora del Bando de Gobernación, 22 October 1853 and the Memorial de Jose Matos, 5 April 1859, both in ANC, Intendencia, leg. 960/3.

69. García, *La esclavitud,* 147; Expediente promovido por la morena Isidra Lazo, 1869. ANC, ME, leg. 4004/I; Expediente en el que el negro Filomeno Lula pide licencia para buscar nuevo amo, 1852. ANC, GSC, leg. 947/33417; Expediente promovido por el moreno libre Felipe Herrera, 1864. ANC, ME, leg. 4105/Ñ.
70. All the cases mentioned in the previous note were favorable to the slaves. A notable case, involving a prominent member of the local elite, was that of the Marquis of la Real Proclamación against his slave Filomeno. The Marquis appealed the case unsuccessfully, and Filomeno obtained his paper to change masters. See Marrero, *Cuba: economía y sociedad,* 13, 167. See also the cases included in Expediente sobre la coartación, 1853–1862. ANC, Intendencia, leg. 960/3.
71. These testimonies are included in Expediente sobre la coartación, 1853–1862.
72. *Diario de la Marina,* November 2 and 6, 1856; Barchiller y Morales, "De la coartación y sus efectos," *Revista de Jurisprudencia* 1 (1856), 426–430.
73. N. Azcárate, untitled entry, *Revista de Jurisprudencia,* 1 (1856), 363.
74. Azcárate, "Réplica al Señor don Antonio Bachiller y Morales," *Revista de Jurisprudencia,* 1 (1856), 477–481.
75. Rodríguez, "La coartación y sus efectos," 353–362, quote on 355.
76. Additional effects included, according to Rodríguez ("La coartación," 355), the existence of a fixed price, the inability of the owner to collect all the earnings of the coartado slaves, and the limitation on the master's dominium, for the slave owned a portion of himself.
77. Rodríguez, "La coartación," 356; Azcárate, untitled entry, 363; Ramón de Armas, "Sres. Directores de la Revista de Juriprudencia," *Revista de Jurisprudencia,* 1 (1856): 431–434. See also, in the same issue of the journal, the contribution of José Cintra, "Coartación," 474–476.
78. Quoted in Bachiller y Morales, *Los negros* (Barcelona, [1887]), 151–161.
79. Expediente sobre la coartación, 1853–1862.
80. Expediente sobre la queja del negro José Casanova, 1846. ANC, GSC, leg. 944/33306; Expediente sobre la coartación, 1853–1862. See also García, *La esclavitud,* 147.
81. El síndico procurador sobre la coartación del esclavo Evaristo, 1858. ANC, Escribanías (Luis Blanco), leg. 334/3; Incidente al intestado del presbítero don José Luis Abad, 1850. ANC, Escribanías (Gobierno), leg. 362/17; Doña Carlota Dascar al Gobernador.
82. The Consejo de Administración consejo included the most important civil, military, and religious authorities in the colony. On its composition see Julio A. Carreras, *Historia del estado y el derecho en Cuba* (Havana, 1981), 81–84.
83. El Consejo de Administración al Gobernador Superior Civil, 27 October 1862, in Expediente sobre la coartación, 1853–1862.
84. "Decreto del Gobernador Superior Civil que comprende el Reglamento para las Sindicaturas de la Habana a la presentación de esclavos en queja contra sus amos," January 28, 1863, reproduced in Bienvenido Cano and Federico de Zalba, *El libro de los síndicos de ayuntamiento y de las juntas protectoras de libertos* (Havana, 1875), 42–46.
85. Consulta sobre la coartación del negro José Salas, 1867. ANC, Consejo de Administración, leg. 13/1493; "Circular del Gobierno Superior Civil declarando que los esclavos de campo no adquieren por la coartación el derecho de cambiar de dueño," 1 May 1871, in Cano and Zalba, *El libro de los síndicos,* 59.
86. This statement appears in a marginal note that Bachiller wrote on Maximo Arozarena's letter of 8 March 1859 to the Captain General, in Expediente sobre la coartación, 1853–1862. The text was reproduced with some variation in Barchiller, *Los negros,* 156–157.

– Chapter 5 –

CUBAN SLAVERY AND ATLANTIC ANTISLAVERY[1]

Ada Ferrer

The nineteenth century, as is well known, was the century of antislavery. For centuries, the institution of slavery had been the companion of empire and colonialism in the New World and had served as a motor of capitalist development in Europe. But starting at the turn of the nineteenth century, the structures that had undergirded the global economy were profoundly transformed, and in the process slavery came under assault. In the short and medium term, the attack on slavery had two distinct but interrelated sources: British abolitionism and the Haitian Revolution. These were the twin pillars of Atlantic antislavery in the nineteenth century.

Both movements had roots in Enlightenment thought, in which slavery figured as a powerful political metaphor for the most extreme denial of human rights and for the persistence of old-regime absolutism. But in contexts where slavery as metaphor encountered slavery in fact, powerful political and social movements emerged. In the British world, a growing movement of abolitionists mobilized in effective and unprecedented ways to challenge a central institution of British power. By the 1790s, widely publicized parliamentary debates took up the question routinely and began to make clear that the end of the system would come in relatively little time. By 1807, the British had abolished the slave trade and over the next decade secured the legal (if not always practical) end of the trade of rival states. By 1834, it abolished slavery itself in all its New-World colonies.[2]

In the French world, the revolution that began in 1789 issued an equal challenge, as revolutionaries obliterated the monarchy, struck at the church and nobility, and created the institutional space for the discussion and potential exercise of the rights of man and citizen. Nowhere was this particular challenge appropriated and transformed more radically than in the French colony of Saint-Domingue. At the time of the French Revolution, it was the New World's most profitable colony and the globe's largest producer of sugar, the most important staple commodity of its time. In this colonial society, with about half a million slaves, slaves and free people of color eagerly seized the revolution's promise and, combining it with other emancipatory practices both creole and African, produced the era's most radical instantiation of the emerging notion of human rights. It was here that the modern world's first wide-scale slave emancipation took place in 1793, not so much decreed from above as forced from below. It was here that a former slave named Toussaint Louverture took the reins of government and attempted against great odds to implement not only slave emancipation but an ambitious project of colonial autonomy that, in the end, proved too ambitious for the metropole. When France tried to reassert absolute control and reimpose slavery, former slaves and other non-white colonists exposed what they cast as the false universalism of the metropole and in 1804, after a bloody war of independence, founded the world's first black republic. Its foundational and justifying principle was antislavery.[3]

Together these two developments—the Haitian Revolution and the growing hegemony of British abolitionism—constituted a powerful challenge to the institution of slavery. With one, the most powerful country in the globe committed itself to the gradual erosion and eventual elimination of the institution. With the other, the world's newest and least powerful republic stood as an example of the power of slaves' themselves to achieve liberation. The Haitian example also further fueled abolitionist debates, as advocates of the end of slavery argued that it was wiser to end the institution gradually than to risk the emergence of other Haitis. With the destruction of the world's most significant slave economy in 1791, with the declaration of Haitian independence in 1804, with the 1807 and 1808 abolition of the British and North American slave trades, respectively, and the naval campaigns for the suppression of the trade that followed, with the illegalization of the Spanish trade in 1817 and the French and Dutch in 1818, and finally with the end of slavery in the British West Indies in 1834, it would seem that the nineteenth century came in spelling the death knell of slavery. Clearly, the nineteenth century was the antislavery century.

Yet it was precisely in this context, with slavery under political, intellectual, and economic assault, that slavery in Cuba underwent its most dramatic expansion. Starting modestly with the British occupation of Havana in 1763, but then inexorably with the collapse of Saint-Domingue sugar in 1791, the Havana planter elite and the Spanish colonial state allied to usher in a massive expansion of sugar production based on the forced labor of African men and women. By any measure—the importation of Africans, the number of sugar mills, the amount of sugar produced, and so on—the intensification was manifest and transformative. As the British assault on slavery became the age's hegemony, more and more men and women labored under slavery on larger and more mechanized plantations producing more and more sugar. Havana became a principle receiving point for Africans arriving in the New World; and its hinterland became home to the world's largest and most modern plantations. By the 1820s, Cuba had become the world's principal producer of sugar.[4]

This dramatic transformation in Cuba, occurring in a context that seemed to point to its antithesis, cannot, however, be seen as a paradox or contradiction. Slavery's expansion here must be viewed as part and parcel with its decline elsewhere. As Dale Tomich has persuasively argued, the destruction of slavery in the British Empire and its virtual elimination in the French did not represent the end point in a single coherent narrative of the rise and decline of slavery. In fact, the end of the slave trade and then slavery in the British and parts of the French world actually encouraged and fueled the expansion and intensification of slavery in emerging zones of commodity production, most notably in the U.S. South (cotton), southern Brazil (coffee), and Cuba (sugar). This new wave of slave systems that emerged in the context of an increasingly hegemonic antislavery Tomich aptly calls the "second slavery."[5] The significance of this conception is not only its insistence on considering the simultaneity or coexistence of both the destruction and expansion of slavery in the nineteenth century, but also its attention to the ways in which both processes were linked. The decline of sugar and slavery in Saint-Domingue and the British West Indies actually fed the demand for slave-based commodity production elsewhere. That decline and, more generally, the erosion of colonial trade monopolies (even in Cuba, one of the last colonies of the region, free trade became the default policy in 1817) meant that those societies doing the most to suppress the slave trade were also the biggest consumers of cheap commodities, "without regard to the form of labor that produced them."[6] The assault on slavery and its simultaneous expansion in places like Cuba were thus not contradictory processes, but rather different manifestations of an emerging global division of labor.

This essay examines the expansion of Cuban slavery in the context of the rise of nineteenth-century antislavery, taking as its point of departure the simultaneity of Cuban slavery's ascent and the rise of the twin pillars of antislavery: the Haitian Revolution and British abolitionism. That simultaneity is key for several reasons. The most obvious is causal and structural: it was the disappearance of Saint-Domingue sugar followed by British slave trade and slavery abolition that directly fed the demand for slave-based sugar production in Cuba. Another was infrastructural: as Saint-Domingue sugar and British slave ships disappeared significant parts of the infrastructure of those two industries were transferred to Cuba. Thus in a physical and material sense, the artifacts of antislavery in the British and French contexts literally helped sustain slavery's expansion elsewhere. Finally, the fact that Cuban slavery became entrenched precisely at the moment that those two major antislavery forces took root shaped the very character and experience of enslavement in Cuba.

Cuban Slavery and the Haitian Revolution

The Haitian Revolution (1791–1804) did not create or directly cause the sugar boom that transformed Cuban society. Seeds for that change had already been planted decades earlier. For example, the British occupation of Havana in 1762 opened up the slave trade and eliminated the longstanding trade restrictions of the Spanish. In the ten months of British occupation, approximately ten thousand Africans arrived in Havana harbor for sale, about as many in ten months as would have normally arrived in ten years. With more enslaved laborers to produce the sugar and with obstacles to trade removed, the amount of sugar exported also witnessed gains that would later come to seem modest but at the time were unprecedented.[7]

Although the boom was short-lived, the sudden gains reaped by planters made this group the most vociferous proponents of reform. Of these none was more prominent or effective than Francisco Arango y Parreño. From a prominent Havana family, Arango traveled to Madrid in 1787 and soon became the official agent of Havana's town council. In that capacity, he immediately began lobbying the metropolitan government for a free trade in slaves and in agricultural machinery. With sectors of the government open to the development of colonial agriculture, Arango's labors were successful. In 1789, the slave trade monopoly was provisionally ended, and the trade was opened to Spaniards and foreigners for a trial period of two years. In a very real sense, the path of sugar and slavery had already been chosen for Cuba by both the colonial and metropolitan governments.[8]

In 1791, the provisional opening of the trade came up for review. In May, Arango wrote an appeal for its expansion and its renewal for a period of six to eight years. The appeal had already been judged favorably at various levels of government, and it was slated for final discussion in the Council of State when unexpected news of the outbreak of revolution in Saint-Domingue arrived. With dramatic and lurid accounts circulating in Madrid as elsewhere, Arango and the planter class for whom he spoke worried that ministers in Madrid would close the trade and thus thwart Cuba's new economic boom. The news arrived in Madrid from Havana on November 19, and Arango went to work immediately. In about a day, he drafted a treatise on the causes of the revolution and its implications for Havana and Madrid. Forgoing the customary channels of the Consejo de Indias, Arango placed a copy of his essay in the hands of every individual member of the Council of State.[9] Thus, the very first discussion of the Haitian Revolution at the highest levels of the Spanish government was mediated by the intervention of the Cuban planter class. Arango actions suggested that before the metropolitan government decided on a response to the revolution, it must first consider the interpretation of Havana planter class. He succeeded: at that first meeting on the revolution on November 21, 1791, the ministers read the reports of the revolution from Havana's governor together with Arango's brief and utilitarian treatise on the Haitian Revolution.[10]

Arango's essay flatly denied that Saint-Domingue's troubles were cause for fear in Havana. Spanish subjects were content with their king and their system of government; Cuban planters were not engaged in political folly before the eyes and ears of their slaves; and the enslaved in Cuba were better treated by wiser planters and a magnanimous king. Because there was no danger of repetition or contagion, the revolution in Saint-Domingue was simply an opportunity to be seized. It was this pragmatic argument, more than any historical or sociological comparison between the French and Spanish colonies, that most interested Arango. His immediate purpose was to prevent the ministers from either postponing or rejecting the renewal and expansion of the open slave trade. Three days later he had his response in the new Real Cédula extending the open slave trade for six more years and granting many concessions that Arango had long requested.

Beyond the immediate question of the 1791 extension, Arango also sought to persuade the king to realize more permanent reforms that would allow Cuban planters to take long-term advantage of Saint-Domingue's collapse. At the time, observers could not yet imagine that Saint-Domingue would never recover, much less that it would soon become an independent and antislavery black republic. Thus Arango's purpose was to take intense advantage of what he saw as a significant but temporary opening, so that when France recovered, Cuba could retain its newfound advantage. To this end, Arango's essay expressed his willingness to write a more detained and careful exposition of the means by which the state could give Cuban agriculture a definitive advantage over the French, for the good and in the interest not only of the planters but of the Spanish state. Arango's offer was discussed and approved at that same meeting of November 21, 1791. Thus the first Spanish state discussion of the Haitian Revolution explicitly linked that revolution with the expansion of slavery and plantation culture in the now ascendant Cuban colony. Several months later Arango submitted his famous paper on Cuban agriculture, *Discurso sobre la agricultura de la Habana y los medios de fomentarla*. The long essay is generally and rightly seen as a foundational document of Cuban history.[11] Its critical genealogy—that is, its direct origin in the very first metropolitan-colonial conversation about the Haitian Revolution—is less often noted. Thus the dominant intellectual approach to Cuban society and economy at this critical juncture and for more than half a century to come required a particular reading of the Haitian Revolution and its relation to Cuba. In this view Saint-Domingue was a model to emulate, Haiti did not pose a danger, and Cuba could indeed follow in the footsteps of the former without becoming the latter.

Arango's vision would be eagerly embraced in Havana and Madrid. The collapse of Saint-Domingue became synonymous with the entrenchment of the plantation economy in Cuba. A key in the transformation was, as Arango and his companions knew, a regular and relatively inexpensive supply of labor. Approximately 325,000 Africans were legally brought to Cuba as slaves between 1790 and 1820 (more than four times the number brought in the previous thirty years. The bulk of these men and women were fated for work in sugar. In the late eighteenth and early nineteenth centuries the nucleus of the boom was Havana. Overtaken by what one witnessed called a furor to establish *ingenios*, or sugar mills, the number of mills in its outskirts jumped from 237 in 1792 to 406 in 1806. Their average productive capacity more than doubled from 58 metric tons per mill in 1792 to 136 in 1804. The largest mills, owned precisely by men such as Arango, had production capacities of two and almost three times that average. The island's export figures are equally dramatic. From about fifteen thousand metric tons exported in 1790 to almost forty thousand by 1804, the island's share of the world's sugar market grew and grew; and by 1830, producing almost 105,000 metric tons, it was undisputedly the world's largest producer of sugar.[12] The antislavery import of the Haitian Revolution notwithstanding, in Cuba the revolution contributed directly and decisively to the entrenchment of slavery. With one system destroyed, the architects of another rushed in and eagerly filled the void left in an expanding and profitable market.

Although the ruin of Saint-Domingue sugar industry was almost total, material artifacts of that system survived: planters, technicians, machinery, technologies of production and slave control, and even men, women, and children who for one reason or another would be denied the possibility of liberation and remain enslaved, if not generally, in Saint-Domingue. The infrastructure of sugar and slavery that survived the conflict was fanned out from that territory. Cuba—close by and embarking on a boom that required this material—was well placed to benefit. Thus as Saint-Domingue's system of sugar and slavery collapsed, significant parts of its infrastructure were transferred to a rival system just emerging.

From the outset of the revolution and at subsequent critical junctures, Cuban authorities, especially in Havana and Santiago, received requests from Saint-Domingue planters and technicians, who had heard rumors of the land and hospitality offered by the Spanish government in Cuba. In them, the refugees stressed their familiarity with sugar and coffee cultivation, their experience in curing the diseases of slaves, or their affinity for managing black workers. The response was fairly receptive. The Cuban governors listened with interest and made it relatively easy—and certainly easier than it should have been by law—for French planters from Saint-Domingue to migrate to Cuba. The motivation was less humanitarian than it was to expand the production of sugar and coffee with people who knew that production and those industries intimately. The Cuban governor said so explicitly, encouraging the minister of war and the king to favor the migration of the French, arguing that the island was in a position to accept some of these families, "whose best recommendation is that they are voluntarily abandoning their country and the disunity of those inhabitants, in addition to the fact that they bring with them, their industriousness and their knowledge of cultivation."[13]

With the blessing of the colonial state, these French citizens established themselves in Cuba and, as has been amply shown, provided a great impetus to Cuban agriculture. The technicians brought with them extensive knowledge of sugar manufacture and their willingness to collaborate with Cuban planters. It is not surprising then that the Real Consulado routinely appealed to the governor to grant or extend permission for these French citizens to live and work in Cuba.[14] For example, Nicolás Calvo, perhaps the second-most-important sugar planter after Arango, supported the residency of Julian Lardiere before the Consulado. Lardiere served as engineer on the ingenios La Ninfa and Nueva Holanda, two of the most technologically advanced mills on the island. A now famous anecdote captures the euphoria that marked the collaboration between Cuban planters and Saint-Domingue technicians. Calvo and Lardiere were riding in a carriage through the valley of Güines, central node of the boom and home to the most formidable plantations on the island and soon the globe, when Lardiere was overcome with the certainty of their success. He practically leapt from the carriage, announcing, "[T]his is the land, this is the site where nature has provided everything for the cultivation of cane and the manufacture of sugar." By the late 1790s he was collaborating with planters and the colonial state on the construction of a canal in Güines meant to simplify the transport of sugar, coffee, and tobacco in the days before the railroad. By 1815 Lardiere was established enough in this world to own his own plantation.[15]

Esteban LaFayé was another French sugar genius who allied with men like Arango. The three most important men on the island collaborated closely with him: Arango, Calvo, and the governor himself, Luis de Las Casas, who on his arrival in 1790 had been given a plantation (with slaves) as a gesture of welcome from Havana planters and who in the years that followed was able to purchase a second one. Both had false owners to evade the law. His interest in promoting the boom was thus as much personal as it was political. LaFayé worked on the invention and construction of a new kind of *trapiche* on one of Las Casas's estates. Contemporary sources describe LaFayé's workshops as one of the regular meeting places of the Havana elite. At demonstrations of LaFayé's prototypes, Las Casas himself was said to hold the stopwatch and even help adjust levers. LaFayé worked as well on projects to construct roads (the better to transport sugar) as well as on innovative and more efficient means for calculating the yield of sugar cane.[16]

As Moreno Fraginals calculates, of the ten most productive sugar mills on the island at the turn of the century, eight had been designed by French technicians such as LaFayé and Lardiere.[17] The importance of the French input notwithstanding, it bears emphasizing that the role of the French technicians was to facilitate and accelerate the realization of a vision of Cuban society that was already well developed among the creole planter class. But the French also played a key role in the cultivation of coffee, and there, their role was more generative. In eastern Cuba, individual refugees as well as societies (or protocooperatives) of French subjects purchased unused virgin land and began the cultivation of coffee. In western Cuba, even in the sugar mecca of Güines, refugees also contributed to the expansion of coffee culture, though it remained always secondary to sugar. French refugees published and translated treatises on scientific methods for cultivating the new crop.[18]

So, it was that the collapse of Saint-Domingue provided both a new and expansive space in the world market and at the same time transferred to an emerging zone of production the technicians and technologies that would allow the Cuban planter elite to take full advantage of the new opening. At times this goal of extending the momentary advantage seemed to take priority over more clearly imperial ones. One would think, for example, that the openness to receiving these French migrants would have been curtailed by the declaration of war between France and Spain in 1793. Yet though Madrid ordered the expulsion of these temporary French residents, the Real Consulado continued to consider their petitions to remain and work in Cuba. Las Casas thus wrote to Madrid announcing that despite the expulsion order, he had granted permission to Estaban Lafayé to remain on the island, given that he had been contracted to complete a project that would be of enormous utility to local planters. He did not add that he was one of the investors in the project and that the final product was to be used on his own sugar plantation.[19] Havana planters sometimes found their technicians not just from the community of refugees but even among French prisoners of war. When French prisoners from Saint-Domingue were taken by Spanish forces in Santo Domingo, they were transported to Havana to be held in the numerous forts of the colonial city. Many were French citizens taken in border towns recently reverted to Spanish control: Fort Dauphin, for instance. But to the Cuban men who were members of institutions such as the Havana town council or the Real Consulado, these men were more than French prisoners; they were also potential assets in the quest to expand Cuban agriculture. One such prisoner was Jean Lage, who at the urging of Nicolás Calvo was liberated to work on a major road construction project in Güines.[20] If the geopolitics of war and empire required their confinement or expulsion, the exigencies of the emerging economic boom required their integration.

The war helped transfer Saint-Domingue's sugar infrastructure to Cuba in another way as well. During the war, the Spanish and creole men from Cuba, as officers and members of the Havana and Santiago regiments, traveled to the island of Hispaniola to fight the war on the frontier between French Saint-Domingue and Spanish Santo Domingo. Though they were military men by career, the most prominent ones had links to the Havana sugar elite. The world from which they came shaped their encounter with a crumbling slave economy and an ascendant slave revolution.

One such man was the Marqués de Casa Calvo. He was from a prominent Havana sugar family; he owned a plantation in the Havana countryside and was the brother of Nicolás Calvo. As brigadier of the Havana Infantry Regiment, he was named governor of Bayajá, the Spanish name for Fort Dauphin just seized from the French. Suddenly physically present for the collapse of Saint-Domingue sugar, Calvo seemed to take Arango's insistence that the revolution was an opportunity to be seized as a literal call to action. He quickly entered into business deals with the slave insurgents, buying from them the latest sugar equipment looted from plantations they had just destroyed even, said one particularly hostile source, as the bodies of their white French victims still steamed. The business had become so regular that the hallways and patios of his residence were lined with drums, cylinders, and other sugar-making equipment. He then shipped them to Havana, perhaps for use in his own mill, or his brother's, or to be sold to fellow Havana planters.[21]

Calvo also seized the opportunity to acquire men and women he could send to Cuba as slaves. Other high-ranking Cuban officers positioned on the French border of Saint-Domingue, among them Juan Lleonart and José María de la Torre, appear to have done the same. Some of the black men and women they purchased were sold by French prisoners being sent to Havana who sought to recoup funds by selling them to eager Cuban officers. Others were women and children stolen from insurgent armies by rival groups and sold illegally in the same manner. Sending these slaves to Cuba violated any number of restrictions against the entry of French slaves in Spanish territory. Yet high-ranking Cuban officers regularly flouted such laws, eager as they were to increase their stake in the nascent boom back home. It is difficult to know the scale of the practice. Some shipments of slaves purchased in this manner were turned away in Havana, but still such slaves seemed to have entered. Colonial records are full of references to French slaves in this period, so much so that the colonial state had to keep reissuing the restrictions against their entry, an implicit but powerful admission that the policy was in effect failing. In Saint-Domingue Toussaint himself, as well as his officers, regularly referred to the practice of Spanish officers and soldiers purchasing people as slaves from the insurgent armies and then shipping them off to Cuba or other Spanish territory.

The practice appears not to have been confined to these Cuban officers. In fact at several critical junctures of the Haitian Revolution, men, women, and children were taken out of Saint-Domingue and sold in Cuba as slaves. At the start of the revolution, slave traders appear to have taken advantage of the uncertainty to purchase slaves cheaply and resell them in Cuba. The official Havana gazette, as well as the records of the captain of the port, recorded the entry of slave ships from Saint-Domingue in Havana during the early phases of the revolution. In addition, French planters who fled to Cuba often managed to bring with them or send for some slaves. Although the entry of the latter was prohibited by law, the state often turned a blind eye to the infractions. Finally, in the final phases of the revolution, with the conflict transformed into a war of independence, French officers illegally took black men and women from Saint-Domingue to sell them in Havana. Thus some of what one might call the human infrastructure of sugar and slavery in Saint-Domingue was also captured and transferred to the emerging sugar zones in Cuba.

As this brief analysis should make clear, to study the transformation of Cuban slavery in the late eighteenth and early nineteenth centuries is of necessity to come to face to face with the Atlantic's impact. In terms of structural questions about the market, Saint-Domingue's loss was critical. But the transfer of tropical commodity production from declining zones to emerging ones also involved the literal transfer of some of the infrastructure of that production, as slaves, technicians, machinery, and techniques from a collapsing Saint-Domingue were shipped to or recreated in a Cuba whose power holders were eager to remake in Saint-Domingue's image, even as they sought to avoid becoming another Haiti.

But on another level as well, the simultaneity of slavery's collapse and slavery's entrenchment in Saint-Domingue and Cuba, respectively, reminds us that these processes were more cross-cutting and mutually constitutive than they were discrete. The collapse of slavery in Saint-Domingue and the intensification of it in Cuba unfolded each within view of the other, in a context in which encounters between the protagonists, ideas, images, and rumors filtered back and forth. The presence of French slaves, technicians, and planters, each with a particular experience and vision of slavery and revolution, now lived out and remade the institution of slavery in Cuba. French planters brought the French *foete*. French slaves bragged to their new companions of their participation in the revolution that had set them free in Saint-Domingue.[22] These kinds of encounters and flows would shape the very experience of slavery in Cuba.

At many critical junctures of the revolution the enslaved in Cuba seemed to know of those events and think about their own enslavement and liberation with them in mind. In multiple examples of slave conspiracies and rebellions, the enslaved made regular reference to the Haitian Revolution. In 1795 slaves in Puerto Príncipe confronted masters and governors announcing that the French had made them all free. And there in 1798 rebel slaves combined stories of the heroism of Charlemagne, the faith of Jesus Christ and Carabalí Viví, and the daring of French slaves in Saint-Domingue to plot their own liberation in Cuba. In Bayamo in 1805 rebel leaders recruited fellow slaves by offering them positions of command similar to those held in Saint-Domingue by Toussaint or Jean-François. They dared each other to prove their worth and show their courage by doing as Toussaint had done — taken the land away from the whites. In 1806 in Güines three enslaved men — one a Saint-Domingue native, another a literate Cuban creole, the third Congolese born — led an effort, they said, to win their freedom like their *compañeros* in Haiti. And in 1812 in perhaps the most significant conspiracy of the period, free men of color traveled to the plantations of the Havana countryside, wearing alleged Haitian uniforms, taking on the name of Haitian heroes, telling stories and sharing images of Haitian leaders both past and present, and organizing a network of rebellion designed to rival any the island had yet seen.[23]

Even absent a conspiracy or rebellion, in casual encounters on country roads and city squares, brief mentions of the Haitian Revolution were used to convey meaning among the enslaved and between masters and slaves. When in Havana in 1795 an elderly enslaved man entered a school and with his machete murdered or injured thirteen children, the city went into a panic, and masters began turning to authorities with stories about once loyal slaves who were now invoking the school attack and the example of the rebels in Haiti, both as things that might be imminently repeated in Havana. On street corners, black strangers murmured threats: here whites can behead blacks too; don't think we won't do what they did in Guarico (Cap Français). Authorities lamented that slaves and free people of color knew the events of the Haitian Revolution as if by heart; the names of its leaders resounded in Havana like the names of invincible heroes. And all seemed to know that the French (and, increasingly, the British) had aligned themselves with the freedom of slaves.[24] The revolution that had destroyed sugar and slavery in Saint-Domingue was thus regularly named in Cuba. Haiti had become part of the cognitive landscape in Cuba precisely in the period in which both sugar and slavery were taking off. Wide-scale black rebellion thus became thinkable precisely as more and more black men and women were arriving in chains to work in a labor regime rapidly intensifying in response to booming market conditions.

For masters to think about the Haitian Revolution was thus far from an abstract exercise. Certainly for Arango in 1791 that revolution was synonymous with economic opportunity; the stakes were palpable, not hypothetical. But from the start, he and his fellow planters understood that that opportunity was not necessarily permanent or risk-free. They opted to live dangerously and dove headfirst into the boom. But they kept part of their vision trained on the risks. Thus they met regularly to discuss the progress of Saint-Domingue's revolution. They commissioned reports on how best to reconcile the new growth with the continued tranquility of the ever-higher number of slaves upon which they now depended. They advocated things like the creation of rural schools, to soften the habits of overseers (so as to not instigate rebellions about slaves), or projects for rural police, or for a more efficient system for the capture of runaways. Increasingly, especially after 1795, they did this in a climate that encompassed not only the hefty example of Saint-Domingue but also homegrown instances of rebellion and conspiracy on Cuban soil. It was out of these efforts to reconcile prosperity with survival that the most interesting intellectual projects of the planter elite emerged.

For slaves, as well, Haiti was not just an abstract hope or model. For them the invocation of Haiti came to be as much about the gripping example set by men like Toussaint, Jean-François, Dessalines, Christophe, and their followers, as it was a means by which to think about their own experience of enslavement in Cuba. In the conversations of slaves that are condensed and recalled in slave testimony, we see repeated references to the Haitian Revolution: to the daring and bravery (and manliness) of its protagonists who had defeated the whites and become "absolute lords" of the land. Most often, however, such conversations were prompted by immediate local concerns—by a lack of proper food, the imposition of a violent or stingy overseer, the loss of free time for worship or independent agriculture, or the increasing brutality of corporal punishment.[25] It was in discussions about these kinds of conditions, amidst expressions of complete exhaustion and frustration, that Haiti was invoked. Those invocations then were as much about quotidian and local experiences as about Atlantic revolution. If Haiti could be used by statesmen and planters to advance particular arguments—the need for a growth in the African trade, the imperative of white immigration programs, the necessity for coastal security, and so on—it could also certainly be used by slaves: to assert their worthiness vis-à-vis other slaves, to manipulate the fears of white overlords, to express immediate and urgent grievances, or, maybe, to help imagine a place without whites or a place without slavery.

It is, of course, likely that slaves had long imagined such a place. But the power and proximity of Haiti meant, among other things, that masters and statesmen now imagined that slaves were imagining that place all the time. That Haiti had happened shaped the way slaves discussed punishment, the way they voiced their contempt, the way they understood their own sense of power and powerlessness. It shaped the way slaves and masters viewed one another and the world in which they lived. A global force, Haiti was used as a way to give voice and social meaning to local conditions.[26]

The collapse of slavery in Saint-Domingue and its entrenchment in Cuba occurred on distinct geographical terrains, but they were not isolated, discrete processes. They were rather cross-cutting, mutually constituting, and both undeniably enmeshed in the transformation of a capitalist world economy. One space's collapse created the definitive space in the market to feed the frenzied boom of the other. That collapse moreover had physical and tangible effects, as the very human and material artifacts of one system were transferred (to the extent possible) to the emerging zone of production nearby. At the level of the quotidian experience of slavery, the simultaneity of the two processes has further meaning, as the example of black revolution and the content of a radical antislavery circulated in a context in which black enslavement intensified and expanded. No consideration of the transformation of Cuban slavery at the turn of the nineteenth century then is complete without an examination of the ways in which that transformation occurred under the shadow of an ever-present Haitian Revolution.

British Slave Trade Abolition

Slavery's expansion in Cuba unfolded also in the growing ambit of British abolitionism. At the very juncture in which Cuban slavery had become firmly implanted and was sustaining the island's first economic boom, planters and the state collided with the power of the British to extend the reach of their new convictions. Following decades of effective abolitionist campaigns and with the declining influence of British West Indian interests, Parliament abolished the slave trade in 1807. (The Americans followed suit in 1808). The British then turned their attention to enforcing the ban on their own traders, to persuading other nations to abolish theirs, and to suppressing the trade by force on the coast and high seas of the South Atlantic. If the Haitian Revolution represented radical and insurgent antislavery, British slave trade abolition was antislavery of a different sort: imposed by the most powerful naval and economic power in the world after a long period of dominating the slave trade.

Like the Haitian Revolution, it was a profoundly transformative event with which emerging slave societies like Cuba had to contend of necessity. The 1807 abolition came in the context of the rapid expansion of slavery and only eighteen years after the appearance of an open slave trade to Havana in 1789. It was in that year that after much lobbying by the planter class, the Spanish monarchy abolished the slave trade monopoly and granted permission to both Spaniards and foreigners to transport and sell slaves in designated Cuban ports free of duty. As we saw, in 1791, the king expanded and renewed the provision for another six years, thanks in part to Arango's deft handling of the news of the slave uprising in Saint Domingue. In the fifteen-year period of the French and Haitian revolutions from 1789 to 1804, a total of eleven royal decrees reformed and further expanded the slave trade to Cuba.[27]

The clamor for more and more Africans and the policies that brought them to Cuban shores were, of course, part and parcel of the expansion of Cuban agriculture in the late eighteenth and early nineteenth centuries. As the sugar industry of Saint Domingue was devastated by revolution and, more gradually, as production declined in the older British colonies, Cuban agriculture boomed and the number of Africans imported skyrocketed. The expansion of the slave trade to Cuba was both cause and effect of the boom in which it unfolded. Between 1790 and 1806, the year before the abolition of the British trade, just under 100,000 Africans arrived as slaves in Cuba, about as many as had arrived in the two and a half centuries of the trade before that.[28] These Africans arrived principally in Havana, the center of the boom in sugar and the seat of a colonial government intimately and personally involved in the business of sugar. Local papers carried regular announcements about the arrival of slave ships and about the sale of their cargo at determined places and times. Though the trade was legal at this point, the ships often arrived under cover of night—the only ships in Havana given the privilege of doing so. The captured Africans were then disembarked and taken to warehouses newly built for just this purpose. It was said that the island's captain-general in the 1790s often went himself or had his agents go to the warehouses to take first pick from the new arrivals.[29]

It was as this trade solidified and expanded that British and American slave trade abolition came and suddenly eliminated Cuba's main suppliers of Africans. One would expect that the sudden disappearance of the British and then the Americans would produce an immediate and precipitous decline in the number of captives arriving from Africa and the Caribbean. Initially it did; in the two years following abolition the number of ships arriving in Havana from Africa became sights almost as infrequent as they had been in the days of the monopoly trade. But this initial decline notwithstanding, British (and later American) slave trade abolition did not in fact produce the abolition of the slave trade to Cuba. Rather than signal the trade's demise, the 1807 abolition appears only as a minor blip in an otherwise steady and often escalating supply of enslaved Africans through much of the nineteenth century. Of all the captured Africans that ever arrived in Cuba over the whole period of the slave trade starting in the sixteenth century, 86 percent arrived after the British abolition of the trade in 1807.[30] Clearly, the slave trade to Cuba, and to Havana as the major Cuban port of entry, not only did not abate with abolition and suppression, it grew and acquired its most profitable and dynamic form specifically in the context and the aftermath of British slave trade abolition. And it was with a flourishing—if increasingly threatened—slave trade as a foundation that Cuba became by the 1820s the world's largest producer of sugar.

Though the abolition of the trade did not have its intended effect in Cuba, the event did mark the way in which that trade was carried out. The trade rather than principally British or American became principally Spanish and Creole. Creole planters had long advocated the establishment of a Spanish and Cuban slave trade; now, they reasoned, doing so was a matter of urgent necessity.

Although official registers seem to demonstrate the withdrawal of British participation in the Cuban slave trade, in fact that participation continued, if in diminished and covert form. First, British subjects invested heavily in the emerging Spanish-Cuban trade, selling their expertise and their equipment to the eager latecomers. As had already been the case since the start of the legal trade in 1789, the new Spanish and Cuban slavers hired British crews, sending along Spaniards and Cubans as apprentices, a process that accelerated after 1807. In fact, slave ships with Spanish flags were often owned in part by British and American companies and manned by British or American crews. As David Eltis and others have shown, a significant proportion of British and American traders hid behind fraudulent Spanish flags and papers, only to be discovered when they were captured by the British navy.[31] The prevalence of this practice made all slave ships flying the Spanish flag suspect and therefore susceptible to capture by the British. Havana merchants and planters protested this policy vigorously, not only because British practice threatened their labor supply, but also because, despite covert British and American involvement, there was by about 1815 a predominant Cuban and Spanish protagonism in the slave trade. Thus whereas roughly half the slavers coming into Havana in the 1807–1815 period were Spanish/Cuban, after that date, they were almost entirely so.

British slave trade abolition had helped make the planters' vision of a Cuban slave trade to provision Cuban agriculture a reality.[32] However, as in the case of the Haitian Revolution, that shift was enabled at least in part by the transfer of the trade's infrastructure to new regions and new actors. In the same manner that sugar-making technology and infrastructure was transferred from older to newer zones, the technology, experience, and infrastructure of the slave trade were similarly transferred from old to new players to the financial benefit of both.[33]

Increasingly the British brought pressure to bear on Spain to abolish the trade, and in 1817, the two countries negotiated a treaty to end the slave trade to Spanish territories by 1820. Faced with an imminent abolition, the slave trade to Cuba accelerated even further, producing the highest import figures yet seen in Cuba, of between fifteen thousand and almost twenty-six thousand a year in that brief interlude. The frenzy to capture and import Africans before the treaty took effect ushered in what Moreno has called the "most tragic era" of the Cuban slave trade. Reports from the doctors assigned to vaccinate and examine incoming Africans give a sense of the conditions on board Cuban slavers of this period. Moreno cites the case of the *Amistad* (a different *Amistad* from the one treated by Michael Zeuske and Orlando García Martínez in this volume), which held 733 Africans and arrived in Havana fifty-two days later with only 188.[34]

But in fact the fear that the Spanish would work in tandem with the British to suppress the trade proved ill-conceived. And, as in the first decade of the century, the trade continued to flourish. But now it did so illegally, with the violation of the law a foundational feature of its day-to-day operation. As before, slavers continued to arrive at night, but now they employed new layers of deceit. Sometimes they stopped first in Puerto Rico, where there was less vigilance and where they obtained a kind of passport, making it seem on their arrival in Havana that the slaves on board had been purchased in another Spanish territory rather than on the now prohibited African coast. Another common ruse was to arrive and disembark slaves outside Havana on some stretch of deserted coast and then march the Africans into Havana in broad daylight as if they were the slave force of a sugar mill that was being liquidated.[35] Such subterfuges would not have worked if authorities had pressed even minimally, but the fact is that they rarely did. Take for example, the case of the slave ship *Minerva*, examined by Cuban scholar Fernando Ortiz. This ship left Havana for Africa in April 1826 and was denounced to Havana authorities by British commissioners. In August, the ship was captured by the British and escorted to Havana, where a British officer demanded to board and inspect it. But the Spanish captain of the ship required that he get authorization from the captain of the port. When the British official requested that authorization, however, he was sent to the *jefe del apostadero*, who then said he had to consult with the governor about the case. The governor was conveniently absent, so a file was started and several Spanish officials were consulted. When the governor finally appeared he refused to rule without first consulting the captain of the port and the jefe del apostadero. By the time authorization was given for the British captain to board and inspect the ship the following morning, there were no Africans on board.[36] The protection of the illegal slave trade became a key function of the colonial state, shaping the local practices of rule.

The prevalence of the illegal trade even left physical traces in the Cuban landscape. Take for example the case of the only surviving *barracón* in Cuba today, located in the small town of Juraguá, just south of Cienfuegos. Barracónes were the large, usually rectangular structures that served as the slave quarters in the period of sugar's expansion in the nineteenth century. This particular barracón, which belonged to the plantation called Caridad de Juraguá, is essentially intact—and in fact, inhabited—today. It is, however, less a testament to the history of nineteenth-century Cuban slavery than to the history of the illegal slave trade. Its proportions were much too large for the size of the estate on which it sat. Local historians and archeologists believe that this barracón was an illegal holding area for Africans brought illegally to Cuba. There they were housed until they recuperated from their transatlantic journeys, and then they were sold to Cuban plantations. It was the money from this illegal venture that built some of the principal landmarks and institutions of nineteenth-century city of Cienfuegos.[37]

From the perspective of the colonial state, the attitude of noncompliance was a natural extension of its decades-old practice of fomenting the new plantation economy. With a relatively new boom and a relatively new slave trade, continued growth was seen as reliant on an ample and steady supply of fresh laborers arriving from Africa. When British policy began to threaten the core of that vision, planters, traders, and colonial bureaucrats opted to circumvent the law. Thus no consideration of economic policy in this period of continued expansion can ignore the pressure of the British and the concerted work of the Cubans and the Spanish in resisting it.

Because of that Cuban boom and despite the growing British pressure, the Cuban slave trade continued to flourish and expand after both British slave trade abolition and the legal (if not actual) Spanish abolition of the trade in 1820. It received another major impetus in the late 1830s, with the construction of the first railroad in Cuba, built, as is well known, expressly to meet the needs of the sugar industry and enable rapid transport of sugar cane to mills and of processed sugar to ports. With the capacity to open more and more land to new sugar production, the slave trade to Cuba underwent another violent period of growth. It was not until the late 1860s that the journeys of enslaved Africans to Cuban coasts ended, more than half a century after British slave trade abolition.

To view slave trade abolition from Havana reminds us of the insufficiency of examining such events from a purely national or imperial focus. The 1807 law may have ended the importation of Africans to British territory, but it did not spell the death knell of the trade more generally. In fact, it can be argued that it served as impetus for the invigoration of the slave trade, now directed to new centers of tropical production. Like the Haitian Revolution, the event represented a major assault on slavery, but part of its effect was the emergence of new actors and new zones of slavery and the slave trade. And, as in the case of the Haitian Revolution, that transfer was to some extent facilitated by the transfer of infrastructure from declining to expanding zones.

If British slave trade abolition did not have an immediate and deterring effect on the rapid expansion of Cuban slavery, it did affect the way the slave trade was carried out. It changed how, when, and where ships landed, and where and how slaves were received. And it made everyone—from planter to trader to bureaucrat—complicit in the violation of international law. The same might be said of British abolitionism more generally. Slave trade abolition and suppression unfolded within the much broader and increasingly powerful movement of British abolitionists. Although that movement did not result in the end of slavery in places like Cuba, its existence did shape the character and experience of enslavement there. Starting in the 1790s, Cuban authorities began identifying abolitionism—in a manner somewhat similar to the Haitian Revolution itself—as a force with the potential to stir unrest among the enslaved. Facing a growing number of conspiracies and rebellions among Cuban slaves, they posited that the cause of this mounting problem lay less with anything inherent in Cuban slavery than with the growing presence of foreign slaves who seduced Cuban ones with subversive ideas. In 1795 the governor reissued the ban on the entry of French slaves but expanded it to include slaves of the British Caribbean as well. After significant consultation with Havana planters, he further ordered the expulsion of French slaves brought after 1790 and British ones brought after 1794, the date, he surmised, when resistance and abolitionism became more endemic in the British islands. He believed that in colonies like Jamaica, planters were confronting the new crisis by conspiring to sell off the most troublesome slaves to places like Cuba.[38] In fact in the same manner that records of local slave conspiracies and rebellions note the presence and participation of French slaves, so, too, do they refer to British slaves. In the 1805 Bayamo rebellion, for instance, many of the conspirators were slaves from the British colonies. When they were deposed, some did not have enough Spanish to answer the questions, and the search for people with the linguistic abilities to translate found only other British slaves.[39]

The world of Cuban slavery was broad and fluid enough to encompass multiple encounters not only with the radical antislavery of the Haitian Revolution but with the growing hegemony of British abolitionism. Among the enslaved, rumors circulated not just about freedom and revolution in and emanating from Haiti, but also about forces of emancipation in the British world. Rumors about emancipation decreed by the British king or parliament shared space in the political imagination of the enslaved with emancipation issued by the French government, or won by force of arms by slaves, or enacted by new black heads of state in Haiti. For example, in the Aponte conspiracy of 1811–1812, by far the most significant of the early nineteenth century, slaves and free people of color often alluded to rumors of both British and Haitian emancipation decrees that were to be implemented in Cuba.[40]

This particular combination was likelier to surface precisely after British slave trade abolition. With the British navy becoming more and more aggressive in seeking out and punishing infracting slave ships, news of the encounters between the slave trade and official British antislavery circulated widely in port cities like Havana. Even in a context where enforcement was lax, the visible world now included British commissioners who escorted ships into the harbor, inspected them, and cast themselves as authorities equal to the planters and the colonial state. The British did this before the eyes and ears of the slaves and free people of color who frequented the docks and in a context in which Haiti had already achieved its independence. In fact, sometimes the projects of British slave trade abolition and Haitian antislavery became linked not only in practice but in the minds of those who saw themselves as potential objects of those policies.

Early in 1811, news began arriving in Havana about new and daring acts by Henri Christophe, the head of state in northern Haiti, who was intercepting slave ships bound for Cuba, liberating the Africans on board, bringing them to Haitian soil as free men and women, and sending the crews and empty ships on their way. In 1810–1812 such was the fate of at least three ships: the *Nueva Gerona;* an unnamed Portuguese ship en route with 440 Africans from Rio to Havana; and the *Santa Ana,* whose shipment of 205 slaves was liberated and taken by Christophe's forces to the port of Gonaïves. In addition, Havana's Real Consulado decried the capture of "various slave ships" prior to the interception of these three. With several similar cases in a relatively short space of time, members of the Real Consulado also commented that news of the captures was circulating widely in Havana.[41] If the news circulated, we can be sure that one of its key points of transmission would have been the docks, where the arrival of empty slave ships, whose original human cargo had been taken to Haiti, would have found a most attentive audience. One should not perhaps automatically cast these Haitian interceptions of slave ships as an alternative or counterhegemonic antislavery. The reality is probably much murkier. The Spanish sometimes protested to Haiti directly, but more often to the British, whose protection, they believed, enabled the captures. At least one of the Haitian ships engaged in capturing the slave ships was named *Wilberforce,* rather than, say, *Toussaint.* Interestingly, references to the Haitian seizures appear in the testimony of conspirators in the Aponte rebellion, in which many of the participants frequented those same docks. Francisco Xavier Pacheco, allegedly one the principal conspirators, confessed shortly before his execution that when Aponte showed him a portrait of King Christophe, he had explained "that England was intercepting the ships that came loaded with blacks because it no longer wanted slavery, sending them to [Haiti] to be governed by the black king."[42] Slave trade abolition and the campaigns of suppression it established were thus on the minds not just of planters, traders, or officials, but also clearly in the consciousness of slaves, who likely welcomed them as another force, after the Haitian Revolution, that might signal the possibility of liberation in their own lifetimes.

Conclusion

British slave trade abolition, like the Haitian Revolution, was less a signal of slavery's decline than part of the mutually constituting processes of the decline *and* expansion of slavery. While slavery and the trade were abolished everywhere in the hemisphere, the nineteenth century was nonetheless the apogee of its development, as slavery expanded on a massive scale in emerging zones to meet the growing world demand for coffee, sugar, and cotton. This second slavery, as Tomich has aptly labeled it, however, is not just a counterpoint in an otherwise coherent and unified narrative of antislavery. Rather, the two processes were directly linked.[43]

The Cuban boom is particularly instructive in this regard. The island became the world's largest producer of sugar and one of the nineteenth century's principle consumers of African slaves specifically in the context of the rise and growing hegemony of antislavery. Rather than coincidence or contradiction, that economic boom can be linked directly to the progress of antislavery elsewhere. The dramatic destruction of slavery in Saint-Domingue created the market space and strengthened the incentive to expand the institution in Cuba. The British and American abolition of the slave trade rather than end the importation of Africans to Cuba merely changed the players, as Spanish traders first filled in and then exceeded the gap left by their former suppliers. Inextricably linked to that abolition, the general decline of British West Indian sugar, in a context in which old colonial trade monopolies were disappearing, also greatly expanded the global market for Cuban sugar. Thus the very same forces of Atlantic antislavery fed the entrenchment of slavery in Cuba, as in other formerly more marginal zones of the Atlantic economy. But the simultaneity of the rise of both antislavery and the second slavery was also local, material, and quotidian. The protagonists, the technology, and the knowledge central to a waning system became physically present for the expansion of an emerging one. And the enslaved often found themselves positioned at a kind of meeting ground, living the intensification of their enslavement even as they witnessed and participated in the growing power of antislavery, occupying as it were plural time and space in the history of global slavery and capitalism.

Notes

1. This article originally appeared in *Review: Journal of the Fernand Braudel Center* XXXI, no. 3 (2008): 267–295.

2. Eric Williams, *Capitalism and Slavery* (New York, 1966); David Brion Davis, *The Problem of Slavery in the Age of Revolution, 1770–1823* (Ithaca, 1975); Seymour Drescher, *Econocide: British Slavery in the Era of Abolition* (Pittsburgh, 1977); and David Eltis, *Economic Growth and the Ending of the Transatlantic Slave Trade* (Oxford, 1987).
3. C. L. R. James, *The Black Jacobins: Toussaint L'Ouverture and the San Domingo Revolution* 2nd ed. (New York, 1963); Carolyn Fick, *The Making of Haiti: The Saint-Domingue Revolution from below* (Knoxville, 1990); David Geggus, *Haitian Revolutionary Studies* (Bloomington, 2002); Sibylle Fischer, *Modernity Disavowed: Haiti and the Cultures of Slavery in the Age of Revolution* (Durham, 2004); and Laurent Dubois, *Avengers of the New World: The Story of the Haitian Revolution* (Cambridge, Mass., 2004).
4. Manuel Moreno Fraginals, *El ingenio: Complejo económico social cubano del azúcar* 3 vols. (Havana, 1978).
5. Dale Tomich, *Through the Prism of Slavery: Labor, Capital, and World Economy* (Lanham, MD, 2004), 56–71.
6. Ibid., 62, 82.
7. Franklin Knight, *Slave Society in Cuba in the Nineteenth Century* (Madison, 1970), 6–7; Moreno Fraginals, *El ingenio*, 1, 35–36, 3:43; David Murray, *Odious Commerce: Britain, Spain and the Abolition of the Cuban Slave Trade* (Cambridge, 1980); Louis A. Pérez, Jr., *Cuba: Between Reform and Revolution* (New York, 1988), 57–58.
8. Moreno, *El ingenio*; Francisco J. Ponte Domínguez, *Arango Parreño, el estadista colonial* (Havana, 1937); and Dale Tomich, "The Wealth of Empire: Francisco Arango y Parreño, Political Economy, and Slavery in Cuba," *Comparative Studies in Society and History* XLV (January 2003): 4–28.
9. Francisco Arango y Parreño, "Representación hecha a su majestad con motivo de la sublevación de esclavos en los dominios franceses de la isla de Santo Domingo," *Francisco Arango y Parreño, Obras* (Havana, 2005), 1, 140–143; and Ponte Domínguez, *Arango Parreño*, 24–27.
10. Archivo Histórico Nacional, Madrid (hereafter AHN), Estado, Libro 4, Actas del Supremo Consejo de Estado, November 21, 1791, f. 131v; Archivo Histórico de la Oficina del Historiador de la Ciudad de la Habana (hereafter AHOHCH), Actas Capitulares del Ayuntamiento de la Habana, Tomo 51, February 17, 1792, ff. 50v–52.
11. Arango y Parreño, "Discurso sobre la agricultura en la Habana y medios de fomentarla," *Obras*, 1, 144–226; Ponte Domínguez, *Arango Parreño*, 30–45; Moreno Fraginals, *El ingenio*; Tomich, "The Wealth of Empire."
12. Moreno Fraginals, *El ingenio*, 1, 68; 3, 43–44; Tomich, *Through the Prism*, 75–94.
13. Las Casas to Conde Campo de Alange, November 16, 1791, in Archivo General de Simancas, Fondo Guerra Moderna (hereafter AGS, GM), leg. 6846, exp. 73.
14. Pedro Larrieu and Santiago de la Roche to Junta Económica del Real Consulado, August 25, 1795, in Archivo Nacional de Cuba, Fondo Real Consulado y Junta de Fomento (hereafter ANC, RCJF), leg. 201, exp. 8914; "Expediente promovido por D. José de Echegoyen para que este cuerpo recomiendo al Govierno permita al cultivador francés D. N. Raúl pasar a su Yngenio," December 2, 1795, in ANC, RCJF, leg. 201, exp. 8916; "Expediente sobre licencia que solicita el francés D. Esteban Lafaye para ocuparse en las artes de su inteligencia en este país," January 18, 1797 (this is for renewal of original license granted July 2, 1793), in ANC, RCJF, leg. 201, exp. 8917; and "Expediente sobre licencia que solicita D. Luis Lecesne para radicarse en este país," October 2, 1798, in ANC, RCJF, leg. 201, exp. 8918; and Actas de Sesiones de la Junta de Gobierno del Real Consulado," August 26 and September 2, 1795, in ANC, RCJF, Libro 161, ff. 37v–38v, 41–41v.
15. Moreno Fraginals, *El ingenio*, 1, 60, 75. The story of the carriage drive appears in ANC, RCJF, leg. 94, exp. 3954; Calvo's support of Lardiere before the Real Consulado is in Nicolás Calvo pide que se recomiende al Gobierno a los extrangeros D. Julián Lardiere y D. Juan de Lage," November 11, 1795, in ANC, RCJF, leg. 201, exp. 8915.

16. "Expediente sobre licencia que solicita el francés D. Esteban Lafaye para ocuparse en las artes de su inteligencia en este país," January 18, 1797 (this is for renewal of original license granted July 2, 1793), in ANC, RCJF, leg. 201, exp. 8917; and Actas de Sesiones de la Junta de Gobierno del Real Consulado, August 26, 1795, in ANC, RCJF, libro 161, ff. 37v-38v. See also Moreno Fraginals, *El ingenio*, 1, 58, 73n, 75n, 85–86, 204; and María Dolores González-Ripoll Navarro, *Cuba, la isla de los ensayos* (Madrid, 1999), 202–204.
17. Moreno Fraginals, *El ingenio*, 1, 73n.
18. Francisco Pérez de la Riva, *El café: Historia de su cultivo y explotación en Cuba* (Havana, 1944), 23–28, 149–150.
19. Las Casas to Conde de Campo de Alange, August 12, 1793, in AGS, GM, leg. 6850, exp. 96.
20. "Nicolás Calvo pide que se recomiende al Gobierno a los extrangeros D. Julián Lardiere y D. Juan de Lage," November 11, 1795, in ANC, RCJF, leg. 201, exp. 8915; and Moreno Fraginals, *El ingenio*, 1:73n.
21. Ada Ferrer, *Cuban Slavery in the Shadow of the Haitian Revolution* (Cambridge University Press, forthcoming), chap. 3.
22. Francisco J. Ponte Domínguez, *La huella francesa en la historia política de Cuba* (Havana, 1948), 49; Ada Ferrer, "La societé esclavagiste cubaine el la revolution haïtienne," *Annales* LVII (2003), 333–356.
23. Matt Childs, *The 1812 Aponte Rebellion in Cuba and the Struggle against Atlantic Slavery* (Chapel Hill, 2006); and Ada Ferrer, "Slavery and Freedom in Cuban Slave Testimony," *The World of the Haitian Revolution*, eds., Norman Fiering and David Geggus (Bloomington, 2009), 223–247.
24. The description of the incident and the aftermath described below is taken mostly from Las Casas to Conde del Campo de Alange, November 12 and November 25, 1794, both in AGS, GM, leg. 6853, and from Ylincheta to Las Casas, 1795, in AGS, GM, leg. 6854. Other examples are from Las Casas to Príncipe de la Paz, December 16, 1795, in Archivo General de Indias (hereafter AGI), Estado, leg. 5B, exp. 176; *Gaceta de Madrid,* May 18, 1804, 439; Actas del Consejo Supremo de Estado, August 1, 1794, AHN, Estado, Libro 8, ff. 81–82.
25. Ferrer, "La societé esclavagiste."
26. Ibid.
27. Murray, *Odious Commerce,* 13.
28. Murray, *Odious Commerce,* 18; and Herbert S. Klein, *The Middle Passage: Comparative Studies in the Atlantic Slave Trade* (Princeton, 1978).
29. Moreno Fraginals, *El ingenio*, 1, 58; and Fernando Ortiz, *Los negros esclavos* (Havana, 1987), 163.
30. *Voyages: The Trans-Atlantic Slave Trade Database.* Total slaves disembarked in Cuba over full time period 563,551; number disembarked in Cuba 1801–1867 is 516,184. Total slaves disembarked for the period 1807–1867 is 483,870. I arrived at this figure using single-year totals for the period 1807–1810; five-year totals for 1811–1825 and twenty-five-year totals for 1826–1850 and 1851–1875.
31. Murray, *Odious Commerce*; Eltis, *Economic Growth*; José Luciano Franco, *Comercio clandestino de esclavos* (Havana, 1996).
32. Moreno Fraginals, *El ingenio*, 1, 263.
33. Ibid., 262–263.
34. Ibid., 264.
35. Ortiz, *Los negros esclavos,* 164.
36. Ibid.
37. My thanks to Cienfuegos historian and archivist Orlando García Martínez for taking me to see the site, talking to its current residents, and for sharing with me his and

his colleague's conclusions on its history. See also http://www.azurina.cult.cu/out_sites/PATRIM/patinmueble/resclavo/caridad.htm.
38. "Expediente relativo a las precauciones y seguridad en orden a los negros en general y en particular a los introducidos de las colonias extrangeras," in ANC, RCJF, leg. 209, exp. 8993; "Acuerdo de Junta de Gobierno del Real Consulado, Sesión de 2 de diciembre 1795," in AGI, Cuba, leg. 1459; and AHOHCH, Actas Capitulares del Ayuntamiento de la Habana, November 20 and 21, 1795, Tomo 54, ff. 198–199, 201v–202v.
39. "Testimonio de la criminalidad seguida de oficio contra el negro Miguel, Juan Bautista y José Antonio sobre la conjuración que intentaban contra el Pueblo y sus moradores [Bayamo]," August 25, 1805, in AGI, Cuba, leg. 1649.
40. Childs, *The 1812 Aponte Rebellion;* and José Luciano Franco, *La conspiración de Aponte* (Havana, 1963).
41. On these three examples, see Junta Consular to Capitán General, February 23, 1811, and June 26, 1811, in Biblioteca Nacional José Martí (hereafter BNJM), Morales, Tomo 79, nos. 23 and 26, respectively; and Claudio Martínez Pinillos to Real Consulado, 24 March 1812, in ANC, Asuntos Políticos (hereafter AP), leg. 106, exp. 21. Haitian interception of slave ships is discussed briefly in José Luciano Franco, *Comercio clandestino de esclavos,* 106–107. The fate of the *Santa Ana,* which was taken to the port of Gonaïves, may be linked to the history of the famous village and ritual center of Souvenance, a few miles from that city. In oral and popular history the origins of the place are associated with a slave ship whose human cargo was liberated and taken to that area in roughly this period. Personal communication, Patrick Tardieu, November 2006; Michel Hector and Jean Casimir, February 2007.

To my knowledge, no one has worked on the Haitian capture of slave ships, and it is thus impossible at this point to know how widespread or rare the practice was, whether it affected other slave-holding powers, the extent to which such acts were carried out by north or south, or the fate of those Africans aboard the ships captured. Years later, Christophe, in correspondence with British abolitionist Thomas Clarkson, appears to deny involvement in such practices, writing on March 20, 1819, "Though it is only with the greatest grief that I can bear to see Spanish vessels engaged in the slave trade within sights of our coasts, it is not my intention to fit out ships of war against them." This was in reply to Clarkson's recommendation that he consider doing just that. See E. L. Griggs and C. H. Prator, eds., *Henry Christophe and Thomas Clarkson: A Correspondence* (New York, 1968), 128, 115–117. For this same period, José Luciano Franco (*Comercio clandestino,* 107) briefly discusses an 1819 case in which Boyer's naval forces (on the warship *Wilberforce*) intercept a Cuban-bound slave ship and free and take its hundreds of captives to Port-au-Prince.
42. The quote is from the testimony of Francisco Xavier Pacheco, in "Autos sobre el incendio de Peñas Altas," in ANC, AP, leg. 13, exp 1, f. 291.
43. Tomich, *Through the Prism,* 56–71.

– *Chapter 6* –

WILBERFORCE SPANISHED

Joseph Blanco White and Spanish Antislavery, 1808–1814

Christopher Schmidt-Nowara

In 1810, the abolitionist and parliamentarian William Wilberforce wrote to the British Foreign Minister, Lord Wellesley, to ask for his help in promoting antislavery in Spain. British abolitionists and governments would focus on Spain for the next several decades. In 1789 the Spanish crown for the first time deregulated the slave traffic to its American colonies. The result was a huge surge in African captives to Cuba, the largest slave society in Spanish-American history. From the later eighteenth until the mid nineteenth century, slave traders would disembark almost eight hundred thousand African captives in the island. Despite years of foreign invasion, imperial collapse, civil war, and treaties with Britain, Spanish governments managed to keep the slave trade flowing to Cuba, finally taking effective steps to suppress it only in 1867. Yet when Wilberforce wrote to Wellesley, he and many other British abolitionists and officials were hopeful that they could persuade Spain to close the traffic because of the tremendous leverage they might exercise over the Spanish government during the joint resistance to the French occupation of the Iberian Peninsula that had commenced in 1808. The Peninsular War (what Spaniards would later dub the War of Independence) was an opportunity to thwart Napoleonic France and also bring great pressure to bear on the two most recalcitrant European slave trading powers: Portugal and Spain. To that end, Wilberforce planned the translation of an antislavery tract that could be circulated in Spain with Wellesley's assistance: "I will endeavour to have a little leisure to draw up something for the purpose, which perhaps you will have the Goodness to use your influence to get Spanished."

To Spanish, or translate, his work, Wilberforce had in mind an exile recently arrived in London who worked closely with the Foreign Office on matters pertaining to Spain and the revolutions in Spanish America. Joseph Blanco White (1775–1841) was a former Catholic priest known in Spain as José María Blanco y Crespo, who Anglicized his name upon his arrival in England in 1810 in flight from the French occupation of his hometown, Seville. In 1812 he would convert to Anglicanism because he was also escaping from the Catholic Church, as his priesthood had led to a profound religious crisis brought on by preaching a creed that he found artificial and impious. He would remain in the British Isles for the rest of his life, never returning to his native land. To support himself in the early years of his exile he published the lively political journal *El Español* with Foreign Office assistance. He also benefited from the patronage of the Whig grandee Lord Holland and his secretary John Allen, both of whom exercised considerable influence over Blanco's ideas about Spanish and Spanish-American politics. Like his British patrons, Blanco believed that during the war against the French, Spain must concede home rule and free trade to its American colonies. Though the bonds of Spanish control would be loosened, common loyalty to the deposed monarch Ferdinand VII and the struggle against France would continue to hold Spain and Spanish America together. Such views earned Blanco considerable enmity from the Spanish government in Cadiz, committed to the monopolistic privileges of the Cadiz merchants and to reasserting Spanish authority over the colonies through a centralizing constitution drafted during Ferdinand's captivity.[1]

There was much to recommend Blanco to Wilberforce. Blanco commanded Spanish and English and moved with some facility between the languages and the history and politics of the two empires. His paternal grandfather, William White, was an Irishman who migrated to Seville in the early eighteenth century in flight from the Penal Laws that punished Catholics under British rule. William White—Joseph's father Guillermo changed his name to Blanco in the following generation—set up a trading house with Irish relatives. Many years later, Joseph briefly worked there as a youth before dedicating himself to an ecclesiastical career. The English language and familiarity with the British world were thus an important aspect of his early life. Blanco also had an acute knowledge of Spanish politics and politicians, many of whom he knew from clerical and literary circles in Seville or from the years he spent in Madrid's court before the French invasion in 1808. During the first two years of the Spanish resistance, he served as editor of the *Seminario Patriótico* in Madrid and Seville, the official publication of the provisional governments. Wilberforce also mentioned to Wellesley that Blanco's previous religious vocation would serve him well in tailoring evangelical British antislavery ideas and rhetoric to a Catholic Spanish public. Surely there was some precursor to be found in the Spanish church: "It has occurred to me as worthy of Consideration whether as Bartholomew (the Early Conveyor if not the first Spanish originator of the Sla. [sic] Trade) de la [sic] Casas, pleaded however the Cause of the Blacks, there might not be found in his Writings or those of some other of the Spanish divines, passages likely to have weight with the Ecclesiastics of the Country. Yr. Lordship knows, whether Mr. White is likely to be at all versed in Spanish Literature, especially in Ecclesiastical."[2]

Blanco White did indeed undertake the translation of Wilberforce's work, his 1807 *Letter on the Abolition of the Slave Trade*.[3] He printed excerpts in *El Español* and then in 1814 published a lengthy pamphlet called the *Bosquexo del comercio en esclavos y reflexiónes sobre este tráfico considerado moral, política y cristianamente,* which the Foreign Office and the abolitionist African Institution proposed to circulate among Spanish political leaders. But "spanishing" a British abolitionist was the same as writing the work anew. The African Institution, which provided financial assistance for Blanco's undertaking, acknowledged as much in its 1814 report:

> Believing his countrymen to be wholly unacquainted with the real nature of this nefarious traffic, he offered to endeavour to enlighten them by translating into the Spanish language such parts of Mr. Wilberforce's Letter upon the Slave Trade as might seem applicable to the circumstances of Spain and her colonies. This handsome offer the Director most willingly accepted, but Mr. White soon found the circumstances of Great Britain and Spain so different that in order to render the work serviceable to the great cause of the Abolition in the latter country, it became necessary to alter it very considerably—indeed, almost to compose a new work.[4]

What adds interest to this translation/rewriting of Wilberforce into Spanish is that Blanco had come to share aspects of the evangelical religion that animated the leading British abolitionists.[5] In letters to his brother Fernando and to Wilberforce himself, Blanco expressed a strong desire to carry out a mission to the Americas and work among the enslaved and the recently liberated. At the top of his list was Trinidad, a Spanish colony taken over by Britain in 1797. There he could bring Christianity to pagans while also leading misguided Catholics to the true religion: "I imagine that an opening presents itself for the spreading of the seeds of a Religious

Reformation in South America, which may on the one hand enlighten the ignorant and the superstitious in that Country, and on the other reclaim many of those whom the absurdity of Catholicism has driven into absolute infidelity."[6] To his brother Fernando he related an appealing offer from the representative of the Emperor of Haiti with whom he dined in London:

> Yesterday, Sunday, I dined with Mr. Moore. I met Mrs. Smith and Mr. Sanders, the king of Hayti's envoy. He was trying hard to persuade me to accept a professorship in the University, which his Most Black Majesty is establishing. The state of that Colony is very prosperous. The King is certainly a man of strong natural sense and abilities, and spares neither money nor pains to civilize the country. Were it not for you and your name-sake perhaps I might be tempted by the prospect of doing good in a tropic climate which would certainly increase my powers in that way.[7]

What these letters show is that at least for a time, Blanco fully shared the evangelical enthusiasm of Wilberforce and other leading British abolitionists. Like them, he hoped to spread the gospel among the enslaved population of the West Indies. Yet he was fully aware that such an outlook would have little appeal in Catholic Spain. How did Blanco transform Wilberforce in such a way that antislavery might appeal to other Spaniards, and what does his translation of British ideas tell us about the sources of Spanish antislavery in the revolutionary era? Wilberforce's *Letter* to his Yorkshire constituents recounted the cruelty of the slave trade and also warned Britons that such indifference to human suffering was a sure sign of imperial decadence. Abolition would benefit the African victims of the traffic, while also regenerating Britain by restoring it on the path of moral progress.[8] Blanco, too, dwelled at length upon the violence done to Africa and Africans by slave trafficking, but he did so within a more specifically Spanish political and historical framework. I will describe two facets of the *Bosquexo* and explore what they reveal about the origins of antislavery in Spain: first, the equation of African slaves with Spaniards imprisoned, exiled, and dominated by the French and second, the polemic Blanco unleashed against Cuban defenders of the slave trade that echoed with other Spanish criticisms of the traffic.

War and Slavery

Where the *Bosquexo* more closely resembles Wilberforce's original *Letter* is in the thorough descriptions of the machinations of the slave trade *in* and *from* Africa. Wilberforce relied heavily on the testimony of the Scottish explorer Mungo Park, who traveled in West Africa at the end of the eighteenth century and provided detailed accounts of enslavement and embarkation upon the slave ships. Blanco reproduced and translated these sections of Wilberforce closely, yet inflected their meaning for Spanish readers. His strategy was to equate the plight of African captives with the experience of Spaniards under French rule. This shift in emphasis was apparent already when he printed excerpts from Wilberforce's *Letter* in *El Español* in 1811, inspired partly by the short-lived debate in the Spanish Cortes about abolishing the slave trade. In introducing an excerpt in which Wilberforce recounted Park's observations, Blanco used the language of slavery to suggest that Spaniards under the French occupation must necessarily sympathize with the Africans victimized by the slave traders: "Spain, though oppressed beneath a heavy slavery, and fighting to escape from it, yet hears the cries of humanity on behalf of the blacks."[9]

When he published the *Bosquexo* three years later, he noted in the opening pages that "[a] great part of the slaves purchased by Europeans are prisoners of war."[10] Warfare and prisoners of war figured constantly in his depiction of the slave trade not only because they did in Wilberforce's but also because he hoped that the Spanish war against the French might turn Spaniards against the slave trade, a connection that he made explicit in his final plea to Spanish readers:

> Do not forget that you too have seen foreigners set foot in your homeland. Leave in peace that of others. Leave those unhappy Africans the scarce portion of goods that Heaven has bestowed on their land. Leave them in peace so that they can advance little by little along the road of civilization. Just because they are poor and ignorant, can you treat them worse than you would the beasts in the wilderness? They are poor and ignorant. But the same blood runs in their veins that runs in yours. The tears that their eyes shed are just like yours. Like you, they are parents, children, and siblings. Martyrs of Spanish patriotism! ... From this day forward stop the *Spaniards* from going to the coast of Africa where they surpass in cruelty and injustice those invaders that destroyed your soul. You, who know what it is to have [your families] ripped from your homes by foreign soldiers, leave to the father his children, and to the husband his wife.[11]

Though drawing a broad parallel between the condition of Spaniards and Africans, Joseph was also speaking from quite intimate knowledge: his own family's experience of warfare, exile, and captivity. When France invaded the Iberian Peninsula in 1808, it shattered the family's life. The most stunning development for the Blancos was the capture of Joseph's younger brother Fernando in Madrid in 1808. Fernando joined a unit of Seville volunteers and marched to Madrid, which the French had evacuated after unexpected setbacks during the early months of the invasion. However, in the autumn of that year, the French, led personally by Napoleon Bonaparte, routed Spanish forces in the capital's environs and retook the city. Fernando was one of the many Spanish soldiers and officers taken prisoner.[12]

He would spend the next five years of his life as a prisoner of war in eastern France, among the some sixty thousand Spanish prisoners held there during the war.[13] Not until the arrival of Russian and Austrian forces in the neighborhood in early 1814 would he find an opportunity to escape. Then, under Austrian protection, he and several other Spanish officers crossed eastern France, Switzerland, Germany, and the Netherlands before finally reaching England, where Fernando was reunited with his brother Joseph.

During his long captivity, Fernando wrote regularly to his parents and to his brother. Though the correspondence is copious and regular, it is marked by constant uncertainty: Did my letters arrive? I received letters from you, but are there others? What about the money I requested? What news? These letters, and later his journal of his escape that he composed in London in 1815 and 1816 (held in the Blanco White Family Collection at Princeton), convey the account of his capture, the forced march from Madrid to Burgundy, his hunger, disorientation, and sense of abandonment, all elements that would reverberate through Joseph's depiction and attack on the slave traffic.[14]

In one of his letters home Fernando tells his family that in the first months of his captivity that he was "dying of hunger" until they were able to supply him with funds. He also described the hard march to eastern France after being captured in Madrid:[15]

> They would give us bread and meat when there was some, and we would cook it with water and sometimes with salt. Every day we walked seven leagues on foot ... and on the days when the march was long they would not allow us any rest on the road so that it was necessary to eat a piece of black bread, like *pan de munición*, while walking. The cold was insufferable, as strong as here, and the ice so hard that we stumbled with every step. To sleep on the ground was now customary.

Only the family's support saved him from the most abject suffering: "My brother wrested me from misery though not from slavery, by sending me aid from his own pocket ... Every hour of the day that I look from my window and see myself surrounded by snow and ice and then turn my eyes to my stove, finding myself free from the cold, I feel myself moved upon thinking that this and so much more I owe to you who have given me the means and to my brother who has sent them to me."[16]

Fernando's captivity was clearly not the same as capture in Africa, the Middle Passage, or enslavement in Cuba: far from it. He was not sold as property. His captivity, though protracted, was temporary and not hereditary. He seems not to have been physically mistreated—at least according to his letters and to his diary of his escape. He did express fear that he might suffer the same fate as that of Spanish officers who tried to escape: imprisonment in the Fortress of Joux in the Jura Mountains (the place where Napoleon imprisoned Toussaint Louverture and where he perished in 1803).[17] Because he had given his *parole d'honneur* that he would not seek to escape, he was at liberty to billet with local families and was free to move within a certain radius from the town. He could receive letters from his family and, most importantly, financial support so that he could purchase food, clothing, and pay his rent; though as the uncertain and at times desperate tone of the letters indicate, such contact was tenuous under the circumstances of war.

Rather than draw a literal comparison between Fernando's captivity and African slavery, I would suggest that Joseph and Fernando's experiences of exile and captivity made Joseph more receptive to abolitionism and provided him with a means by which to translate imaginatively Wilberforce's evangelical outlook into an idiom more immediately comprehensible to Spanish readers struggling against the French. Wilberforce's emphasis on warfare, the long overland marches witnessed by Mungo Park, the separation of captives from their families and homes, the deprivation and uncertainty that they endured was slightly transmuted by Blanco to establish connections between the plight of Spaniards and Africans. That is to say, the language and images that he used to denounce the slave trade merged easily with his attacks on the French occupation of Spain: both were forms of invasion, warfare, usurpation, and enslavement. The difference from the British experience was significant. Though captivity was an important theme in British imperial writings, during the French Revolution and the wars against Napoleon, Britons were far less likely to be prisoners of war than were Spaniards and the enemy never occupied their country.[18] The many Spaniards with personal knowledge of invasion, war, exile, and captivity could perhaps share his outrage that because of other Spaniards, Africans were "torn from their homeland, deprived of their parents, children, and siblings, and transported to a remote region, without hope of returning to the country where they were born ... !"[19]

Blanco versus Arango

Blanco inflected the *Letter* by drawing upon personal experience in an effort to illicit Spanish sympathies for African captives. He more thoroughly rewrote it by focusing on the specific historical dimension of the Cuban slave trade, at the core of which was the fierce polemic with the most vocal defender of Cuban interests, Francisco de Arango y Parreño (1765–1837).[20] Arango was a Cuban planter who also held key administrative posts on the island and in the metropole in the late eighteenth and early nineteenth centuries. He was the highest-profile Cuban advocate of a deregulated slave trade to the island. Spanish officials had contemplated such a reform of the colonial economy since the Seven Years' War as a way of bolstering revenues that would pay for more robust imperial defenses against the rapacious British foe. After several years of gradual measures, the Crown finally threw open the trade in 1789 and recommitted to the policy soon thereafter.[21] Arango lobbied Madrid and wrote eloquently on how a robust plantation economy would benefit not only his class but also the imperial regime by promoting trade and enhancing revenues. Cuban planters thus held considerable influence in Spain during this period but during the resistance to the French occupation of the peninsula they encountered an unexpected rival: Spanish and Spanish-American advocates of abolishing the slave trade and of gradual measures against slavery itself, openly debated in the Cortes of Cadiz in 1811. These debates drew a swift response from Arango, who penned a ringing defense of the slave traffic on behalf of the Havana planter class. His *Representación* was effective, as it quelled further debate in Cadiz. Indeed, the Constitution of Cadiz ratified the following year was completely mute on the question of abolition.[22]

As editor of *El Español* in his London exile, Joseph Blanco White frequently received communications and documents from Spain and from the Spanish colonies. Among these was a manuscript copy of Arango's 1811 *Representación*. His rebuttal to it was at the core of the *Bosquexo*.

In responding to the challenge from Cadiz, Arango emphasized the centrality of Cuba's booming plantation economy to the imperial regime's well-being. Tampering with it would be disastrous not only for the planters but also for Spanish coffers at an especially delicate moment. With rebellion raging in Venezuela and Mexico and metropolitan control weakened throughout the Americas, Spain was now more dependent upon Cuban productivity and the largesse of the planters. This was leverage that Arango knew how to use well. He also argued at length that Cuban planters should not be punished for taking advantage of policies put in place by the Spanish crown. Slaves were property, and property was sacred, its "inviolability one of the great objects of any political association."[23]

Arango went beyond the question of political and economic interest and spelled out why the slave traffic was a means of rescuing and civilizing Africans, the section of his argument that would draw Blanco's sharpest retort. The Cuban author expressed outrage that when the Spanish delegate Agustín de Argüelles attacked the slave trade in the Cortes of

Cadiz, he coupled it with debates over banning the use of torture: "What connection can there be between such different matters?"[24] Arango argued that Cuban slavery could not be equated with torture because Spanish laws and local customs dictated the humane treatment of the enslaved. Moreover, captivity and transportation across the Atlantic to Cuba was beneficial to the enslaved Africans because of the worse fate that awaited them in their homeland: "In all of the centuries past and probably in all of the centuries to come, the benefits that the blacks receive by being left on their native soil are imaginary." Abolishing the slave trade would leave them to their "unhappy destiny," demonstrated by the failed British colony in Sierra Leone.[25] In contrast, by being brought to Cuba, Africans were converted to Christianity and over time acquired the trappings of civilization and the protection of Spanish laws that might one day lead to their emancipation and integration.[26] Spanish detractors might claim that slavery was contrary to natural law, but in truth, slavery had existed throughout human history, including among "the peoples who have given us the most enlightenment."[27]

Blanco responded to this defense of Cuban interests and of the immutability of slavery by affirming that liberty, not slavery, was the natural condition of all people: "[I]n the so called state of nature every individual is *free;* that is to say, the absolute owner of his person, and therefore of the fruit of his personal labor."[28] Arango believed that left to their own devices, Africans would live in a state of barbarism that only enslavement and transportation to European colonies could overcome. Blanco, in contrast, believed that all peoples were essentially the same and possessed the same innate capacities: "[N]o matter how great the difference in the nose or the skin color of Blacks and Europeans, the affections and sensations characteristic of nature are absolutely equal in both."[29] In addition to these affirmations of natural liberty and equality, Blanco sought to counter Arango by showing that European slavers, not Africans, had plunged Africa into a state of war and barbarism. The manipulations of unscrupulous merchants, ships captains, and adventurers provoked constant warfare among Africans as a means to provide captives for the transatlantic trade. What Arango would present as the state of nature in Africa was in reality a situation created by European manipulations: "[T]he Europeans brutalize the blacks through the traffic ... and then they defend the traffic by alleging that the blacks are *semi-brutos*. The impartial reader ... will soon be convinced that the blacks are possessed no less than other men of *rationality* and *humanity*."[30] This state of warfare and brutalization impeded the very justification for the slave traffic that Arango adduced: conversion to Christianity. Indeed, Blanco, echoing Bartolomé de las Casas's attack on the conquistadors and their violence against the American Indians, wrote that Africans were driven away from Christianity by the Christians who enslaved them.³¹

More was at work in the *Bosquexo* than the point-by-point rebuttal of Arango's assault on Africa and Africans. The deep history of slavery in the Iberian world shaped Blanco's, and other Spaniards', criticisms of the changes to the Cuban slave trade implemented by Bourbon officials at the end of the eighteenth century. In the Iberian overseas empires, there always existed major institutional checks on the power of slaveholders: right of self-purchase by the enslaved, a rich religious and associational life, military service, and the church's insistence that the enslaved receive the sacraments. Geopolitical factors were also influential. The Treaty of Alcáçovas (1479) between Portugal and Castile had sanctioned Portuguese preeminence in the eastern Atlantic islands and the West Coast of Africa, an agreement that would shape the development of the Iberian empires in the Americas.³² Portugal and Brazil carried out the most unbridled slave traffic over the centuries, but Spain was always more cautious and controlling. Relying more on the exploitation of the indigenous population in its core Andean and Mesoamerican colonies, the Spanish Crown placed quotas on the numbers of enslaved Africans that could be legally imported into its American domains. It also farmed out slaving to foreign merchants: Genoese, Portuguese, Dutch, British, and French. In the sixteenth century jurists and theologians such as the Dominican friar Tomás de Mercado defended this situation because they had profound doubts about Portuguese machinations in Africa and the treatment meted out to the captives in the Middle Passage.³³ The apparently contradictory formula of slavery without slave trading thus had deep institutional and intellectual foundations in Spain's Atlantic empire. The link to Africa, slaving, and enslaved labor was thus relatively weak compared not only with Portugal's but also with Britain and France's. All of this changed dramatically because of the reforms carried out in Cuba beginning in 1763 and culminating with the complete liberalization of the slave traffic in 1789. The slave trade escalated, and Spanish slavers and the Spanish flag were at the heart of the new business.³⁴

Blanco's *Bosquexo* was very much a response to the changes taking place in Cuba and did indeed bear a family resemblance to ecclesiastical writings about the problem of slavery during the early period of Spanish overseas colonization, though nowhere does he cite the work of Bartolomé de las Casas, as Wilberforce speculated that he might.³⁵ The resemblance shows up more in the sense of historical rupture from the era of Habsburg rule that frames the criticisms made by Blanco and other Spanish writers in the early nineteenth century. When Blanco wrote that "this is a Memorial directed to every Spaniard in the name of the victims torn every day from the coast of Africa by the greed of some of their country men,"[36] the implication was that Spaniards were engaging in the slave traffic in an unprecedented manner, violating the patterns established in the fifteenth and sixteenth centuries. "One must keep in mind that no other European nation has had fewer slaves, considering the extension of its colonies, nor has any other based less of its prosperity on the labor of those unhappy beings than the Spanish nation." Cuba, particularly Havana, was thus an anomaly within the broad history and structure of Spanish rule in the Americas: "[I]n the political balance of Spain there is no interest that weighs against the reasons of humanity and against the morality opposed to the commerce in blacks other than the benefit and interests of the city of Havana."[37] Blanco was voicing objections shared by other Spaniards. If we look at other Spanish protests against the Cuban slave trade from this period, we find similar criticisms, casting the deregulated traffic as a historical deviation that should be reversed.

Isidoro de Antillón was a geographer active in Madrid's learned societies before the French invasion; he and Blanco were coeditors of the *Semanario Patriótico* before Blanco's exile. Among his writings was a brilliant anti-slave-trade tract that sought to demonstrate that the deregulated slave traffic was not only anomalous but also unnecessary when understood within the broader history and structure of the Spanish colonial empire. Where Blanco appealed to Spanish sympathies, Antillón focused on the politics, economics, and demography of colonial labor. Antillón insisted in his work, originally written and publicly delivered in 1803 but printed for the first time in 1811, that Spain must ban the traffic and instead rely on the indigenous population of the colonies, which had grown considerably in the eighteenth century, as the backbone of the labor force, in a sense reverting to the forms of labor and exploitation characteristic of the Spanish Empire before the deregulation of the slave trade: "Thus," he argues, "the Indians will be what they should be: the great treasure, the true gold mine of the Americas."[38] Such a policy would of course have had little appeal in Havana because the indigenous population had virtually perished in the first century of colonization. But to such objections Antillón had a ready answer, one inspired not only by the Abbé Raynal but more recently, and dramatically, by Toussaint Louverture during the Haitian Revolution: "There can be no doubt. The blacks will one day find a valiant leader who will avenge them and assure their independence through force. And we must fear that finding the Crassus to this new Spartacus will not be easy."[39] Antillón believed that Spain enjoyed considerable advantages over its French and British rivals. They relied too heavily on dangerous and unreliable enslaved African labor. The Saint-Domingue rebellion and the frequency of uprisings and marronage in the British and French islands showed that the only way to stabilize tropical production in the rival empires would be by moving the plantations from the Antilles to Africa itself, where free laborers could be recruited. In contrast, Spain's American empire still had a large indigenous workforce. If Spain would effectively and faithfully apply its own venerable colonial legislation, the Laws of the Indies, then Indian workers would not only be more productive but also receive more just treatment from their employers and royal officials. The Bourbon reformers were mistaken in emulating Britain and France's Atlantic empires by turning toward the slave traffic; instead, Spain should take advantage of its superior human and institutional resources, implanted not by the Bourbons but by the Habsburgs, in its effort to catch up to its rivals.[40]

Such reservations about the wisdom of unleashing the slave traffic appeared in official discussions as well. After the defeat of France and the restoration of Ferdinand VII in 1814, Britain negotiated hard with Spain to sign a treaty outlawing the traffic.[41] Ferdinand finally relented in 1817 in return for substantial British payments, though his government would never take any action to uphold its end of the treaty. Indeed, the volume of the slave traffic to Cuba would remain large in the 1820s and then reach its highest point in the 1830s. Nonetheless, Spanish deliberations did reveal that some officials shared Blanco and Antillón's perspective. In 1816, the Council of the Indies issued a strong majority opinion stating that Spain should agree to ban the slave trade immediately. Interestingly, the author of the minority opinion that urged holding out against British demands was Arango, who reiterated many of the arguments in his 1811 *Representación*. In justifying its recommendation, the majority provided a brief history of Spanish and European slave trading, like Blanco and Antillón calling attention to the peculiarity of the traffic to Cuba. At the beginning of colonization, "the Spanish Court viewed with horror a commerce so contrary in its nature, to every feeling of humanity;—so much so, indeed, that, notwithstanding the repeated Applications from our American Colonies, the encouragement of such a Trade was constantly refused." The Emperor Charles V relented in 1516, but he and his successors put heavy restrictions on the extent of the trade, so much so that although other European powers followed the Portuguese in slave trafficking "for upwards of 3 centuries, in spite of the law of nature, and of every sentiment of humanity," Spain kept its distance: "[W]e have limited ourselves to receiving Slaves from their hands, for a price regulated by the circumstances of the moment."[42] Immediately abolishing the slave trade would bring to a close a relatively brief experiment that was more characteristic of Spain's imperial rivals.

Spanish Antislavery between Past and Present

The impact of Blanco White's *Bosquexo* in Spain was probably slight. In spite of the 1817 treaty with Britain, Spain maintained a strong commitment to the Cuban slave trade. The British minister in Madrid complained to the Foreign Office that even as he negotiated with the Spanish minister of state to suppress the trade, the government published in its official gazette articles meant to discredit any such agreement.[43] He also fretted about the influence of the Havana planters and the counteroffers their agents were making to the government. Organized opposition to the slave trade and to slavery would not crystallize until the 1860s, so one could hardly conclude that Blanco catalyzed his countrymen to take action. What his work shows is conviction but not mobilization.[44] It is not clear when or how many Spaniards read it. The African Institution printed copies for distribution among Spanish political and religious leaders (a Portuguese edition was also printed in the 1820s for circulation in Portugal and Brazil) but its reports indicated that the mood in Spain was not initially receptive to British abolitionist agitation, though in 1817 it sent a large number of copies to Spain because "a farther supply of copies has been called for, and has been readily furnished to those persons whose weight and influence in the Spanish Councils may, and, as the Directors hope, will speedily lead to the total Abolition of the Spanish Slave Trade."[45] The year 1817 did indeed see the completion of a treaty but in fact it did nothing to impede the flow of slaves into Cuba, a reality quickly registered by British abolitionists.[46]

What, then, is the significance of the *Bosquexo*? Rather than influential, Blanco's *Bosquexo* was reflective of broader Spanish opposition to the Cuban slave trade. Analyzing it allows us to uncover the roots of metropolitan criticisms, keeping in mind that defenders of the traffic in Madrid and Havana were able to overcome such opposition, not only in the metropole but also in the colony, until well into the nineteenth century.

Scholars of abolitionism have shown that antislavery language and symbolism could merge with other forms of protest and critique and take on new meanings in distinct social and political situations.[47] Blanco White's translation of Wilberforce throws into relief the forces that shaped early Spanish expressions of antislavery and how different they were in motivation from the British ideas he was supposedly rendering for Spanish readers: Blanco and others wrote in a time when Spaniards were entering wholeheartedly into the Atlantic slave trade, breaking with centuries of quotas and regulations, while they were also confronting a powerful enemy on their home soil. Blanco responded to the overtures of Wilberforce and other British abolitionists by translating the 1807 *Letter* into a Spanish idiom of warfare, captivity, and exile; such a rendering was intensely personal but also potentially forceful for other Spaniards who confronted the French.

Beyond the immediate family drama of the Blanco Whites, the *Bosquexo* was congruent with other contemporary Spanish attacks on the Cuban slave trade and like them was enmeshed in longstanding debates. When Blanco White "spanished" Wilberforce, he kept much of his depiction of the cruelties of the trade, the mechanisms by which it functioned, and its brutal impact on the peoples, lands, and economies of Africa. However, he profoundly altered the British abolitionist's evangelical outlook. For Spanish readers he drew upon Spain's historic distance from the African slave trade to present the late Bourbon reforms as an historical anomaly. Though Wilberforce was a goad, Blanco could tap into Spanish doubts about the slave trade that had roots in the fifteenth- and sixteenth-century era of conquest and colonization in the eastern Atlantic and the Americas.

The leading scholar of Blanco White's political thought has argued that Blanco transposed Bartolomé de las Casas's defense of America and the Indians onto Africa and the Africans.[48] While compelling, what this view neglects is that debate over the treatment of Indians and the development of the slave trade from Africa were not separate issues in the Spanish colonial empire but always profoundly linked by the constant demand for servile labor in the colonies. Indeed, the critics of Las Casas denigrated him because early in his career he advocated African slavery as a substitute for *encomienda* and Indian slavery, a recommendation that he later bitterly regretted when he learned more about Portuguese slaving in Africa.[49] The Spanish had a long history of engagement with African slavery in Spain and in the colonies—though not in Africa like the other European empires—and significant legal and moral commentary on the slave traffic dating from the sixteenth century. Though accepting slavery, these commentators, including Las Casas, were generally hostile toward the slave trade because of the way in which the Portuguese were thought to violate the principles of just war and because of the possibility that some of the captives were Christians. The Habsburg rulers negotiated this dilemma— acceptance of slavery and rejection of the slave trade—by regulating the traffic and farming it out to foreign slavers active on the West Coast of Africa, a position that the Castilian monarchy had already ceded to the Portuguese in the later fifteenth century. This situation allowed Spaniards to have their cake and eat it too: they benefited from the slave trade without actually engaging in it. They could thus pretend to occupy a moral high ground in relation to the Portuguese and other Atlantic empires. Among the social and economic consequences of this position was that until the later eighteenth century, the Spanish Indies, as Blanco and Antillón noted, were far less reliant on enslaved African labor than were rival colonies.

The explosion of the Cuban slave trade at the end of the eighteenth century upset this legal, moral, and social equilibrium. A few years later, the crisis of the Spanish monarchy opened by the French invasion in 1808 provided critics like Blanco with the opportunity to publicize their opposition to the Cuban traffic, in their view a historical aberration of monstrous proportions. They demanded that Spain bring this experiment in colonial emulation to an end. Blanco's experience of exile and captivity and his engagement with Wilberforce and other British abolitionists were the immediate, and emotional, motives for authoring, spanishing, the *Bosquexo*, but to understand fully this cogent attack on Spanish and Cuban slave trading it is necessary to situate it in the debates over the mission and wealth of empire originating in the fifteenth century.

Notes

1. The most cogent biographies of Blanco White are Martin Murphy, *Blanco White: Self-Banished Spaniard* (London, 1989); and Francisco Durán López, *José María Blanco White, o, la conciencia errante* (Sevilla, 2005). Both explore the religious dimension of his life and thought with care. On Blanco's editorship of *El Español* and his views on Spain and Spanish America, the indispensable works are by the late André Pons, *Blanco White y España* (Oviedo, 2002); and *Blanco White y América* (Oviedo, 2006). On the impact of British thought on Blanco, see also Manuel Moreno Alonso, *La forja del liberalismo en España: los amigos españoles de Lord Holland, 1793–1840* (Madrid, 1997). On his antislavery and his preparation of the work, see André Pons, "Blanco White, abolicionista," *Cuadernos Hispanoamericanos* no. 559 (January 1997): 63–73; "Blanco White, abolicionista (2)," *Cuadernos Hispanoamericanos* no. 560 (February 1997): 29–38; and "Blanco White, abolicionista (3)," *Cuadernos Hispanoamericanos* nos. 565–566 (July–August 1997): 143–158; and Manuel Moreno Alonso, "Introducción," *Bosquejo del comercio de esclavos y reflexiónes sobre este tráfico considerado moral, política y cristianamente* ed. Manuel Moreno Alonso (Sevilla, 1999), 11–66. More recent perspectives on his antislavery writings include Emily Berquist, "Early Antislavery Sentiment in the Spanish Atlantic World, 1765–1817," *Slavery and Abolition* 31, no. 2, (2010): 181–205; and Joselyn M. Almeida, *Reimagining the Transatlantic, 1780–1890* (Burlington, VT, 2011), chap. 3.
2. Wilberforce to Lord Wellesley, August 1, 1810, National Archives, FO 72/104, folio 1.
3. *A Letter on the Abolition of the Slave Trade; addressed to the Freeholders and other inhabitants of Yorkshire* (London, 1807).
4. *Report of the Committee of the African Institution* 8 (1814), 21.
5. On the British evangelicals who first agitated against the slave trade in the aftermath of the American Revolution, see Christopher Leslie Brown, *Moral Capital: Foundations of British Abolitionism* (Chapel Hill, 2006). Their leader was James Ramsay, an Anglican minister driven from St. Kitts by the planters because of his efforts to evangelize among the slaves.
6. Letter from Joseph Blanco White to William Wilberforce, dated June 21, 1815, MS Wilberforce, Bodleian Library, University of Oxford, d. 14, folios 348–349. See also letter from Blanco White to Wilberforce dated December 27, 1817, d. 17/2, folio 271. On Blanco's plan to work in Trinidad, a request rejected by the Colonial Secretary, see Murphy,

Blanco White, 104–106. More broadly on his religious travails during his early exile, see 104–113; and Durán López, *José María Blanco White*, 143–148.
7. Letter from Joseph Blanco White to Fernando Blanco White, dated Holland House, March 27, 1816, Blanco White Family Collection, Princeton University Library C0075, Series 3, Subseries 3A, Box 7, Folder 2. Wilberforce and Thomas Clarkson were enthusiastic supporters of the independent Haiti. See Karen Racine, "Imported Englishness: Henry Christophe's Educational Programme in Haiti, 1806–1820," Eugenia Roldán Vera and Marcelo Caruso, eds., *Imported Modernity in Post-Colonial State Formation: The Appropriation of Political, Educational, and Cultural Models in Nineteenth-Century Latin America* (Frankfurt am Main, 2007), 205–230.
8. On these preoccupations in British antislavery see David Brion Davis, *The Problem of Slavery in the Age of Revolution, 1770–1823* (Ithaca, 1975); and Brown, *Moral Capital*.
9. "Extracto de una Carta de W. Wilberforce Esq. sobre el comercio de esclavos," *El Español* III no. XVIII (September 30, 1811), 467. See Moreno Alonso, "Introducción," on Blanco's inclusion of Wilberforce in *El Español*.
10. Blanco White, *Bosquejo*, 75.
11. Ibid., 195–196. Emphasis in the original.
12. On the military situation in Spain, see Charles Esdaile, *The Peninsular War: A New History* (Basingstroke, 2003).
13. See Jean-René Aymes, *Los españoles en Francia (1808–1814): la deportación bajo el Primer Imperio* trans. Araceli Ramos Martin (Madrid, 1987).
14. On the conditions of deportation and captivity in France, see ibid., passim.
15. Letter to Guillermo Blanco, dated Dijon, February 28, 1810, Blanco White Family Collection, Princeton University Library, C0075, Series 3, Subseries 3G, Box 7, Folder 4.
16. Letter dated Chalon SS Enero de 1813 (no date). Blanco White Family Collection, Series 3, Subseries 3G, C0075, Box 9, Folder 6.
17. Fernando related to his family how his friend Juan María Maestre was imprisoned at the fortress after an escape attempt: "El pobre Juan María emprendió un viage muy arriesgado que le ha costado su total libertad. Irá a un castillo, y lo peor es que no tiene un quarto. Al momento le he mandado lo que he podido." See letter dated Chalon SS November 10, 1812, Blanco White Family Collection, Princeton University Library, C0075, Series 3, Subseries 3G, Box 9, Folder 6.
18. Linda Colley, *Captives* (New York, 2002); and Michael Lewis, *Napoleon and His British Captives* (London, 1962). Taking a cue from Colley, how other Spanish accounts of captivity might have influenced Blanco is an avenue worth exploring. For a learned Spaniard the works of Álvar Núñez Cabeza de Vaca and by Miguel de Cervantes, on captivity in the Indies and in North Africa respectively, would be likely reference points.
19. Blanco White, *Bosquejo*, 91.
20. On Arango's role in constructing the plantation complex and his views on Cuba's place in the imperial and world economies, see Manuel Moreno Fraginals, *The Sugarmill: The Socioeconomic Complex of Sugar in Cuba, 1760–1860* trans. Cedric Belfrage (New York, 1976), 47–62; and Dale Tomich, "The Wealth of Empire: Francisco Arango y Parreño, Political Economy, and the Second Slavery in Cuba," in Christopher Schmidt-Nowara and John M. Nieto-Phillips, eds., *Interpreting Spanish Colonialism: Empires, Nations, and Legends* (Albuquerque, 2005), 55–85.
21. See Josep M. Delgado's contribution to this volume. On Spanish decision making and Cuban influence, see also Allan J. Kuethe, "The Early Reforms of Charles III in the Viceroyalty of New Granada, 1759–1776," in *Reform and Insurrection in Bourbon New Granada and Peru* eds. John R. Fisher, Allan J. Kuethe, and Anthony MacFarlane (Baton Rouge, 1990), 19–40.
22. See Josep M. Fradera, "Raza y ciudadanía. El factor racial en la delimitación de los derechos de los americanos," in *Gobernar colonias* (Barcelona, 1999), 51–69.

23. "Representación de la Ciudad de la Habana a las Cortes, el 20 de julio de 1811, con motivo de las proposiciónes hechas por D. José Miguel Guridi Alcocer y D. Agustín de Argüelles, sobre el tráfico y esclavitud de los negros; extendida por el Alferez Mayor de la Ciudad, D. Francisco de Arango, por encargo del Ayuntamiento, Consulado y Sociedad Patriótica de la Habana," in *Obras de Francisco de Arango y Parreño* (Havana, 1952), 2, 151.
24. Ibid., 153–154.
25. Ibid., 167.
26. Ibid., 168.
27. Ibid., 172.
28. Blanco White, *Bosquejo*, 139. Emphasis in the original.
29. Ibid., 96.
30. Ibid., 93. Emphasis in the original.
31. Pons, "Blanco White, abolicionista (3)," 144–145.
32. See the contribution by Delgado in this volume. See also Nicolás Wey Gómez, *The Tropics of Empire: Why Columbus Sailed South to the Indies* (Cambridge, MA, 2008).
33. Antonio Domínguez Ortiz, "La esclavitud en Castilla en la Edad Moderna," *Estudios de historia social de España* II (1952), 406–418; David Brion Davis, *The Problem of Slavery in Western Culture* (New York, 1966), chap. 6; and Rolena Adorno, *The Polemics of Possession in Spanish American Narrative* (New Haven, 2007), chap. 3. On the contrast between Spanish critics of the trade and Portuguese defenders, see A. J. R. Russell-Wood, "Iberian Expansion and the Issue of Black Slavery: Changing Portuguese Attitudes, 1440–1770," *American Historical Review* 83 (February 1978): 16–42.
34. On the scale of Spanish involvement, see Josep M. Fradera, *Indústria i mercat: les bases comercials de la indústria catalana moderna (1814–1845)* (Barcelona, 1987), 54–78; and David Eltis and David Richardson, "A New Assessment of the Transatlantic Slave Trade," in David Eltis and David Richardson, eds., *Extending the Frontiers: Essays on the New Transatlantic Slave Trade Database* (New Haven, 2008), 34–42.
35. But Blanco's friend, the Mexican patriot Fray Servando Teresa de Mier, compared Blanco to Las Casas in their exchange of pamphlets over Spanish American independence, which Mier advocated and Blanco thought premature, in 1812. See Pons, *Blanco White y América*, 150–151. Pons argues elsewhere that Blanco's antislavery ideas were essentially lascasian. See Pons, "Blanco White, abolicionista (3)," passim. I will return to this argument in the conclusion.
36. Blanco White, *Bosquejo*, 70.
37. Ibid., 152.
38. Isidoro de Antillón, *Disertación sobre el origen de la esclavitud de los negros, motivos que la han perpetuado, ventajas que se le atribuyen y medios que podrían adoptarse para hacer prosperar nuestras colonias sin la esclavitud de los negros* (Mallorca, 1811), 67.
39. Ibid., 75.
40. Ibid., 53–67. On Spanish debates over policy toward the indigenous population in the late eighteenth and early nineteenth centuries, see David Weber, *Bárbaros: Spaniards and Their Savages in the Age of Enlightenment* (New Haven, 2005). For a recent discussion of emulation and the Bourbon reforms, see Gabriel Paquette, *Enlightenment, Governance, and Reform in Spain and its Empire, 1759–1808* (Basingstroke, 2008).
41. David R. Murray, *Odious Commerce: Britain, Spain and the abolition of the Cuban slave trade* (Cambridge, 1980), chaps. 1–3.
42. "Proceeding of the Council of the Indies of Spain, relative to the expediency of the Abolition by His Catholic Majesty, of the Slave Trade carried on by Spanish Subjects. Madrid, February, 1816," *British and Foreign State Papers* IV (1816–1817), 520–521.
43. Vaughan to Castlereagh, Madrid, September 5, 1816, National Archives, FO 72/187, folios 149–152.

44. Seymour Drescher points to the centrality of effective political mobilization rather than ideological transformation in judging the impact of antislavery. See *Capitalism and Antislavery: British Mobilization in Comparative Perspective* (New York, 1987).
45. *Report of the Directors of the African Institution Read at the Annual General Meeting* 11 (1817), 5. See also Pons, "Blanco White, abolicionista (3)," 153–156.
46. Thomas Clarkson, *The Cries of Africa to the Inhabitants of Europe, or, A Survey of the Bloody Commerce Called the Slave-Trade* (London, 1822).
47. Seymour Drescher, "Cart Whip and Billy Roller: Antislavery and Reform Symbolism in Industrializing Britain," *Journal of Social History* 15 (Autumn 1981): 3–24.
48. Pons, "Blanco White, abolicionista (3)," 145–146.
49. Adorno, *Polemics of Possession*; Silvio Zavala, "¿Las Casas esclavista?" *Cuadernos Americanos* 3 (March–April 1944), 149–154; Marcel Bataillon, "The *Clérigo* Casas, Colonist and Colonial Reformer," in Juan Freide and Benjamin Keen, eds., *Bartolomé de las Casas in History: Toward and Understanding of the Man and His Work* (DeKalb, Ill., 1971), 415–418; and Lawrence A. Clayton, *Bartolomé de las Casas and the Conquest of the Americas* (Chichester, UK, 2011), chap. 6. On the attacks on Las Casas concerning his role in the slave trade's origins, see Christopher Schmidt-Nowara, *The Conquest of History: Spanish Colonialism and National Histories in the Nineteenth Century* (Pittsburgh, 2006), chap. 4.

– Chapter 7 –

SPANISH MERCHANTS AND THE SLAVE TRADE
From Legality to Illegality, 1814-1870[1]

Martín Rodrigo y Alharilla

Throughout the nineteenth century, Cuba was only second to Brazil as a major American destination for African slaves. Moreover, legal prohibition of the slave trade (agreed by Spain and Great Britain in 1817 and a reality from May 1820) failed to short-circuit the transatlantic trade in slaves destined for Cuba.[2] According to Cuban census data, there were fewer than fifty thousand slaves in Cuba in 1774; this number doubled by 1792, again by 1817 and yet again by 1841, resulting in a population of some four hundred thousand slaves in Cuba in the middle of the century.[3]

A number of studies have tried to establish accurate numbers for African slaves arriving in Cuba, the largest of the Antilles islands. For the legal slave trading period, data published in 1826 by Alexander von Humboldt and modified some years later by José Antonio Saco have been used as a departure point for calculations made by authors such as H.S. Aimes, Juan Pérez de la Riva, and Philip Curtin.[4]

Humboldt's figure was based only on slaves disembarked in Havana, but this was not the only port used by slave traders. In 1978, Herbert S. Klein produced a new figure for the number of slaves landed in Cuba between 1790 and 1820 that was based on documents held in the Archivo General de Indias.[5] In 1984, Josep Maria Fradera used the same documentation to propose an alternative figure of 203,432 slaves disembarked in Cuba between 1790 and 1820;[6] this number was higher than Klein's but very much lower than the 272,541 slaves calculated by Juan Pérez de la Riva.

Locating sources documenting the slave trade becomes problematic from the point when trading was prohibited. Researchers largely rely on two sources to quantify the number of slaves landed in Cuba in the period after 1820: Cuban population censuses, on the one hand, and on the other hand, British records based on regular reports submitted by British consuls in Cuba and reports by British commissioners dispatched to Havana to ensure Spain's compliance with the antislave-trading treaty. In 1907, H.S. Aimes reported that 199,954 slaves were landed in Cuba between 1821 and 1864;[7] however, seventy-two years later (1969), Philip Curtin more than doubled this figure, reporting that 470,100 slaves had arrived in Cuba between 1821 and 1870.[8]

The latest and most accurate data on the number of slaves traded across the Atlantic come from research by David Eltis, whose first figures were published in 1999.[9] His original data are now contained in an exhaustive online database (www.slavevoyages.org), which has been updated with further information over the last decade. According to this database, 547,288 African slaves disembarked in Cuba between June 1820 and 1866, to which can be added the 14,178 slaves who arrived in Puerto Rico between 1823 and 1842, giving a total of 561,466 individuals. These figures represent a significant increase over the figures calculated by previous authors. The data also underline the fact that Cuba was the only Atlantic slave trade destination remaining after 1852, yet the Spanish-Cuban slave trade has been and continues to be largely absent from research into the nineteenth-century slave traffic.[10]

Despite prohibition, clandestine trade in slaves to Cuba continued as an important economic—and profitable—activity from the 1820s to the 1850s and even into the 1860s. However, what were the profits obtained by those who benefited from illegal slave trading? Using data and calculations proposed by David Eltis, Luis Alonso quantified direct profits arising from the sale of slaves in Cuba between 1821 and 1867.[11] Nevertheless, Alonso's quantification of earnings is underestimated, as it is based on a smaller number of slaves than given in the above-mentioned database. Using manuscripts from the Kew Public Record Office and Parliamentary Papers, Alonso took 287,773 to be the number of slaves landed in Cuba between 1821 and 1852; in comparison, the most recent figure proposed by Eltis is 392,787 slaves, representing an increase of 36.5 percent over Alonso's figure. Using Eltis' figures and applying Alonso's methodology, I arrive at a figure of some 61 million 1821 constant dollars in direct profits obtained from illegal slave trading to Cuba between 1820 and 1867.

Table 7.1. Estimate of Direct Profits Obtained from African Slave Sales in Cuba, 1820–1867

Year	No.(1)	Profit(2)	Total(3)	Year	No.(1)	Profit(2)	Total(3)
1820	6,472	55.3	357,901	1844	9,897	68.1	673,986
1821	8,471	55.3	468,446	1845	2,865	68.1	195,106
1822	10,729	55.3	593,314	1846	432	68.1	29,419
1823	4,021	55.3	222,361	1847	1,510	68.1	102,831
1824	11,747	55.3	649,609	1848	2,010	68.1	136,881
1825	24,192	55.3	1,337,818	1849	7,621	68.1	518,990
1826	15,203	55.3	840,726	1850	3,098	68.1	210,974
1827	11,115	55.3	614,659	1851	7,820	68.1	535,542
1828	12,424	55.3	687,047	1852	8,098	68.1	551,474
1829	19,841	55.3	1,097,207	1853	15,455	68.1	1,052,485
1830	18,638	55.3	1,030,681	1854	12,706	68.1	865,279
1831	13,096	55.3	724,209	1855	5,343	68.1	363,858
1832	14,320	55.3	791,896	1856	7,008	305.8	2,143,046
1833	13,314	55.3	736,264	1857	10,448	305.8	3,194,998
1834	16,375	55.3	905,537	1858	15,396	305.8	4,708,097
1835	24,959	55.3	1,380,233	1859	26,290	305.8	8,039,482
1836	23,414	68.1	1,594,493	1860	18,260	305.8	5,583,908
1837	20,545	68.1	1,399,114	1861	14,621	305.8	4,471,102
1838	22,582	68.1	1,538,038	1862	10,382	305.8	3,174,815
1839	19,834	68.1	1,350,695	1863	5,649	305.8	1,727,464
1840	17,739	68.1	1,208,030	1864	3,895	305.8	1,191,091
1841	14,124	68.1	961,844	1865	1,855	305.8	567,259
1842	4,739	68.1	322,726	1866	722	305.8	220,787
1843	8,012	68.1	545,617	**TOTAL**	547,288		61,617,339

1) Total number of slaves landed in Cuba.
2) Net profit per disembarked slave (in 1821 constant USD).
3) Total slave trade profits (1 x 2).

Source: Author, based on data as follows: slave numbers from the www.slavevoyages.org database; annual net profit data from David Eltis, *Economic Growth and the Ending of the Transatlantic Slave Trade* (New York, 1987), 280–281.[12]

Despite prohibition, therefore, in the middle years of the nineteenth century the African slave trade to Cuba continued to be a highly lucrative source of earnings for traders. Noteworthy also is the fact that illegal slave trading with Cuba was most profitable between 1856 and 1864, that is, when—with the exception of Cuba—African slaves were no longer landed in the American continent. In the nine-year period 1856–1864, direct profits from the sale of African slaves in Cuba amounted to around

34 million (1821 constant) dollars. And a substantial proportion of these profits flowed to Spain.

Slave Trading and Capital Accumulation in Catalonia

A significant proportion of slave trade profits—in both the legal phase up to 1820 and in the illegal phase thereafter—flowed into Spain. As the Spanish historian and republican leader, Fernando Garrido, wrote in 1867: "There was a time when negroes cost less in Africa ... in which, of twelve voyages, if one gave good results, the loss of the eleven was covered and one even made a considerable fortune.... Only thus can we explain the immense fortunes with which nobodies—who went there, as the saying goes, with only the shirt on their backs, to enrich themselves through the perpetration of an inhuman crime—returned to Spain, transformed into bigwigs."[13]

One of the regions of Spain most closely associated with nineteenth-century slave trading was Catalonia. Below I examine the impact of slave-trading profits in Spain by analyzing Catalan links with slave trading. To do so, however, requires much more than a mere case study. Catalonia became established as the only industrialized region in Spain in the middle decades of the nineteenth century. Its capital, Barcelona, was not only the main industrial city of Spain but also the most important such city in southern Europe. Catalonia in general, and Barcelona in particular, had a complex class structure and both were characterized by a great diversity of economic activities. Catalonia was not just Spain's factory and economic engine; it also had a strong trading tradition, especially across the Atlantic.

An eminent industrialist in the dynamic city of Barcelona in the second half of the nineteenth century was the former slave trafficker Antonio López y López (1817–1883). Having accumulated capital in Cuba, he came to Barcelona in 1855, where he was involved in various business activities. With his brother Claudio and two other former partners whose wealth had likewise been acquired in Cuba, López created a steamship enterprise that soon became the leading Spanish company in the sector. He also participated in the founding of two banks (of which he eventually became president), namely, Crédito Mercantil and Banco Hispano Colonial, which furnished him with sufficient funds to create a large holding company; this company was known by contemporaries in the rest of Spain as the *grupo catalán*,[14] indicating the extent to which López' name and companies were identified with Catalonia.

Thanks to his presidency of the Banco Hispano Colonial, founded in 1876 and directly linked to the Cuban slave trade, Antonio López was able to create a holding company with interests in finance (Crédito Mercantil and Banco de Castilla), shipping (Compañía Trasatlántica), shipbuilding (Arsenal Civil de Barcelona and Factoría Naval de Matagorda), railways (Caminos de Hierro del Norte de España, Crédito General de Ferrocarriles, and Ferrocarriles de Asturias a Galicia y León), insurance (La Previsión and Banco Vitalicio de España), mining (Sociedad Hullera Española), and tobacco growing and trade (Compañía General de Tabacos de Filipinas). The Compañía General de Tabacos de Filipinas was, incidentally, Spain's first transnational company as well as the most important company in the Philippine archipelago.[15]

The capital used by Antonio López to develop his vast industrial empire from Barcelona had been amassed in Cuba, to a large extent in slave trafficking. An interesting firsthand testimony has been left to us by his brother-in-law, Francisco Bru Lassús. In response to the publication, shortly after Antonio López' death in 1883, of a commemorative book titled *Homenaje que la ciudad de Barcelona tributó a la memoria del Excmo. Sr. D. Antonio López y López, Marqués de Comillas,* Francisco Bru counteracted by publishing his own book. Ominously titled *La Verdadera Vida de Antonio López*,[16] it denounced what was common knowledge in Barcelona at the time: the obscure origins of the fortune of the deceased Marquis de Comillas. "Would you like to know what the illustrious D. Antonio López traded in? [Bru asked]. He traded in human flesh; yes, readers, he was a slave trader. López had agreements with the captains of slavers and, when their ships docked, he would purchase the entire cargo, or most of it.... In Santiago de Cuba he would purchase negroes cheaply and send them to Havana and other parts of the island for sale—at a greater or lesser profit, but always at a profit." In another part of the book, Bru adamantly claimed that "Santiago de Cuba has never witnessed a crueller, more hardened, savage and brutish slave trader than López," concluding that "the square could well be called the 'Plaza de los Negreros', as it represents no less than a monumental rehabilitation and radiant apotheosis of all those who trade in human flesh."[17]

Cuban notarial and judicial documentation confirm Francisco Bru's condemnation. On 27 April 1850, for example, María Josefa Villada unsuccessfully petitioned the court of Santiago de Cuba to prevent the company Antonio López y Hermano from embarking the slave Balbina, whom Villada claimed to own, on the steamship *Guadalquivir* to Cienfuegos, the vessel's next port of call. The brothers Antonio and Claudio López, partners in the above-mentioned firm, had been trading regularly in slaves for the previous three years. In August 1847, for example, Antonio López had revoked a power of attorney awarded some months previously to the lawyer Joaquín Galain regarding "a suit against Doña Petrona López referring to the auction of some slaves." And in January 1848, Antonio López, as a partner in the firm Valdés y López (predecessor of Antonio López y Hermano) of Santiago de Cuba, had granted a power of attorney to Ramón Valdés from Asturias and to Captain Francisco Villar "so that the former could sell, in the town of Matanzas where he is resident, 12 negroes belonging to the said company [Valdés y López] at prices and conditions which would previously be notified to him, in the event that the latter failed to dispose of said slaves in any other part of the island where he is obliged to dock as captain of the steamship *Guadalquivir*."[18]

The number of slaves sold by Valdés y López and subsequently by Antonio López y Hermano continued to grow, escalating particularly after 1851: the files of just a single notary (Rafael Ramírez, referred to above) contain documentation recording the participation of the partners in Antonio López y Hermano in all 348 auctions of both adult and child slaves recorded for 1851.[19] In June 1851, for example, Antonio López requested the Escribanía Real de Manuel Caminero to draw up a power of attorney authorizing Antonio Giró, public and government notary, to sell, in López' name, "a negro called Clara, from Africa, 30 to 35 years old, with her sons Miguel, 3 to 4 [years old] and Patricio, 1 to 2 [years old]." And in September 1852 María Josefa Luzando granted a power of attorney to the partners in Antonio López y Hermano "to sell a negro of her property called Nicolasa, a *criolla* aged 13 years." Such transactions were often conducted, as can be read in bills of sale, "*con la condición de alma en boca, huesos en costal y a uso de feria,*" a phrase meaning that the seller was not responsible for diseases, blemishes, or other defects in slaves newly arrived from Africa.[20]

The increase in the number of slaves sold coincided with Antonio López y Hermano commissioning a steamship called the *General Armero* from Philadelphia (it was, apparently, the first steamship fitted with a screw propeller in the Spanish merchant navy).[21] It is quite possible that the two developments were related and that the *General Armero* was used to transport slaves to Cuba illegally. Be that as it may, the López brothers were documented in powers of attorney as having authorization to sell large numbers of slaves. On 15 May 1850, for example, Juan de Mena Garibaldo authorized the brothers to sell forty-seven slaves as a single lot; shortly thereafter, in March 1851, Luisa Cassard de Giraudy granted a power of attorney to Claudio López to sell forty-two slaves; and in May of the same year, Ramon Couroneau authorized the López brothers to sell twenty-one slaves. On 22 January 1851, Antonio López himself, acting under a power of attorney granted to him by a previous partner, Domingo Valdés, authorized Antonio Zuznárregui, based in Matanzas, to sell eighty-three slaves on his behalf. The power of attorney was the instrument used to legalize cargoes of slaves landed in the eastern part of Cuba and dispatched, as denounced by Francisco Bru, to other parts of the island.[22]

Among the beneficiaries of this "odious commerce" were Spanish employees and functionaries posted to the Cuban administration, who obtained generous extra pay in the form of bribes. John T. Crawford, a British judge in the Mixed Tribunal of Justice of Havana set up specifically to prosecute trade in African slaves, wrote as follows in 1861: "Your Majesty's government has been apprised that typically encountered among Spanish employees are some who would stoop so low as to sell their honor for a price. Many who have been thus corrupted have been dismissed from their posts, yet we have witnessed no example of such employees … being punished or otherwise demeaned. And thus it is that, having held their post for sufficiently long to enrich themselves through bribes, once dismissed from their post they retain the moneys so acquired and are permitted to retire having made their fortune."[23] Going beyond the testimony of Crawford, corruption on a general scale was a defining feature of the Spanish colonial administration in nineteenth century Cuba and was, essentially, an indirect way of benefiting from the illegal slave trade.[24] It was the traders themselves, however, who obviously extracted the greatest profits from the illegal slave trade.

What percentage of slaves landed in Cuba were transported in vessels flying the Spanish flag? Josep Maria Fradera has documented the fact that in the thirty years immediately prior to the prohibition of the slave trade, ships owned by Spaniards were gradually displacing slavers from other countries. Thus, whereas Spanish ships represented a mere 12.8 percent of the total number of slave ships operating in the Spanish colonies in the period 1790–1809, in the period 1810–1820 the total of 393 Spanish slave ships accounted for 92.2 percent of all vessels plying the trade.[25] In other words, Spanish ships had come to practically monopolize the Atlantic slave trade to Cuba by May 1820, when the Anglo-Spanish Anti-Slave Trade Treaty entered into force.

It is undeniable that slave trading attracted the interest and participation of a large number of Spanish traders, most particularly in the illegal phase after 1820. Also beyond question is the fact, exemplified by Antonio López, that Spanish slave traders based in Spain, Cuba and even Africa obtained profits that were subsequently invested in Spain. Havana was not the only port to serve as an important operational center for slave trading; prominent slavers also plied their trade through the ports of Cadiz, La Coruña, Santander, and Barcelona, to name just the most important Spanish ports. To document these practices, I will focus on the trajectories of a number of native-born or adoptive Catalan merchants who participated in the slave trade.[26]

With the definitive liberalization of the slave trade by the Spanish Crown in 1789, slave traders of different origins began to operate in Havana and in Cadiz, the Spanish city with the closest trading ties to the Spanish colonies in the Americas. Some of the best-known traders in nineteenth-century Havana had, in fact, been born in Cadiz, for example, Joaquín Gómez and Manuel Pastor. Catalans who wanted to carve out a niche for themselves in slave trading had to work either with Cadiz-based traders or with the Basque traders who had commenced trading in the closing decades of the eighteenth century. In order to fit out slave-trading expeditions to Cuba, for example, Jaime Tintó from Barcelona entered into partnership with José de la Vega, José de Hano Sierra, and Francisco A. de la Concha, all three resident in Cadiz, and with Spanish traders resident in Havana, namely, Joaquín Gómez from Cadiz and José Irineo de Yrigoyen from the Basque region. These were not the only partners to finance initiatives by Tintó. Catalans to do so were Pelegrín Marqués, resident in Cuba and manager of Marqués Ferrer y Cía of Havana, and partners of the firm Vilardaga, Julià y Reynals, originally from Barcelona. Basques such as José María Urzaingui and Andalusians, like Antonio J. Guerrero, also furnished capital for a number of slave-trading expeditions undertaken by Tintó. Captains of slave ships, mostly from Catalonia or the Balearic Islands (among them, Jaime Ricomá and Francisco Granell) also participated in risky undertakings organized from Barcelona.[27] It is no coincidence, for example, that the celebrated Ramón Ferrer, captain of the slaving brig *Amistad* (the subject of Michael Zeuske and Orlando García Martínez' article in the collection) was born on the island of Ibiza in the Balearic archipelago, which has linguistic and historical ties with Catalonia.[28] Between 1827 and 1832, Jaime Tintó fitted out a total of thirteen slave-trading expeditions using ships registered in Barcelona or Mahón (Minorca).

It is not known, however, what profits were made by agents and investors, irrespective of whether they lived in Cadiz, Barcelona, or Cuba. Because the activity was illegal, participants were careful not to leave too much of a paper trail. Letters exchanged between Barcelona, Cadiz, and Havana attest to this; in one letter dated March 1831, Jaime Tintó wrote that "in this business, it's all word of honor and good faith."[29] It was probably for this reason that this triangular partnership came undone in the 1830s in a sea of conflicts between the different partners. Catalans who, like Jaime Tintó, participated in slave trading through the Havana firm Marqués Ferrer y Cía, typically returned to Catalonia. Gregorio Ferrer Soler, after twenty-four years in Havana, returned to Barcelona in 1833 to live off his earnings; he died in 1853 in Vilanova i la Geltrú, leaving a fortune of over 320,000 pesetas.[30] His partner, Pelegrín Marqués, also Catalan, died nine years later in January 1862, leaving a fortune amassed in Cuba that was valued at almost 750,000 pesetas.[31]

Catalans other than Jaime Tintó and his partners participated in the slave trade during the same period, for example, Manuel Ramón de Llano Chávarri and Juan Roig Jacques. Juan Roig Jacques fitted out the brig-schooner *Semirámide*, which commenced slave trading in March 1829. The instructions issued to its captain, Juan Ferrer Roig, also a Catalan, exemplify the clandestinity in which slave traders operated after 1820. Capitan Ferrer was to ensure that the slaves were landed "where ordered to do so by the Pilot, who shall await him at Cabo Francés on the Island of Pines. Said pilot will be at the designated point and, once he sights the vessel and is assured by its signals and the password, will come alongside in a jollyboat flying a white pennant from its bow [and] will have in his possession a signed letter for the Captain from the agent in Havana [the firm Roig Sobrino y Cía] with the initials F.S.S. and a known seal, which letter will contain all the requisite orders and, in particular, those regarding the point where the vessel shall land its cargo ... you will also be told, after having landed the cargo, whether you should proceed to Havana or Matanzas, according to whatever pretext is to be used for mooring." Added was the following: "[A]t the landing point, every effort will be made to have one or two boats waiting to assist the jollyboat in landing the cargo as fast as possible."[32]

Captain Ferrer was, as it happens, the uncle of the reputable industrialist and politician, José Ferrer Vidal, who had a very active public life; he was the first president (1880–1882) of the powerful Catalan business federation, Fomento del Trabajo Nacional, and was also a deputy in the Cortes Generales in a number of legislatures (1857, 1863, 1865, and 1871) and subsequently a senator (in 1876–1877, 1881–1882, 1884–1885, and 1886).[33] Some years before the *Semirámide* expedition captained by Ferrer set sail in 1821, the family firm Mariano Flaquer e Hijo had organized at least one expedition to the coasts of Africa from Barcelona. It succeeded in consigning a total of 315 slaves to the Havana-based firm Domingo Martorell y Cía in an operation that yielded more than a 100 percent return on the invested capital.[34] The fact that slave trading was clandestine from May 1820 makes it difficult for researchers to document reliably the participation of specific individuals as slavers. Frequently we only have indications or indirect testimonies. We can deduce, for example, that the *indiano* Esteban Gatell, a Torredembarra-born Catalan who made his fortune in Havana, and the six Riera Robert brothers, who amassed their fortune in Santiago de Cuba, also participated in the slave trade. Rafael, José, Juan, Salvador, Sebastián, and Miguel Riera Robert, who were born between 1780 and 1798 in Sitges, a small coastal town near Barcelona, crossed the Atlantic between 1810 and 1820 to try their fortune in Santiago de Cuba. There they set up corner shops and other retail establishments. Their success in the Americas was such that they could all eventually return to their hometown.

In the 1840s and 1850s, the Riera Robert brothers, now established in Sitges, ran a cotton import business. Nonetheless, a brief sentence featuring in a deed of agreement dating from 1853 suggests that, some years previously (either from Cuba or from Catalonia), the brothers had tried their hand as slave traffickers. We know, for example, that they had capital of over seventy-five thousand pesetas in February 1840, of which at least fifteen thousand pesetas corresponded to credit, still to be repaid, extended to finance slave-trading expeditions. Recorded by a notary in Sitges years later was the fact that "the five brothers, D. Rafael, D. Juan, D. Salvador, S. Sebastián and D. Miguel [Riera Robert] recovered a mere 201.75 [duros] of the 600 [duros] invested in *expeditions to the African coast,* and hence their capital is reduced in an amount corresponding to the resulting loss" (my italics). The accounting practices of the brothers, moreover, indicate opaque and probably inadmissible trading practices. As noted by the same notary, from "the loose sheets and his [Rafael Riera Robert's] informal bookkeeping, it can be deduced ... that D. Rafael held the capital and was responsible for the accounts corresponding to the business activities common to all the brothers, done jointly and without any clearly marked separation in the name of another brother, D. Miguel, and under the exclusive rights of some of the same brothers." Maybe this was why, on the death of Rafael Riera in 1852, his brothers and partners were obliged to appoint a compositor to resolve this complicated tangle—similar to the conflict that had affected Jaime Tintó and his partners.[35]

There is also little doubt concerning Esteban Gatell Padrinas' implication in slave-trading expeditions. The son and grandson of merchants, Gatell left Torredembarra, a small coastal town south of Barcelona, to make his fortune in Havana. After fate smiled on him in Cuba, in 1837 at the age of forty he returned to Catalonia. Settling in Barcelona, he continued to be active in business. In 1855, for example, he became a member of the governing board of the Banco de Barcelona, the leading private commercial bank in Spain. In the same year, he jointly financed a slaving expedition to the coasts of Guinea with three other industrialists (José Vidal Ribas, Carlos Torrents Miralda, and Domingo Mustich). The venture was unsuccessful—on this occasion at least—as the English captured the barque *Fernando Po* and brought her to Sierra Leone, where a court declared its dedication to the slave trade as proven; Esteban Gatell never recovered the 12,500 pesetas he had invested in this expedition.[36] One of his nephews, Jaime Badia Padrines, also spent some of his youth in Cuba; he was documented by the plantation owner, Domingo del Monte, as being involved in the illegal importation of slaves to Matanzas.[37] In time, Jaime Badia would also return to Catalonia, where he made a name for himself in politics (he was a member of the Spanish Congress of Deputies for several legislatures) and, above all, as a merchant. In 1844, in fact, Badia became one of the administrators of the recently created Banco de Barcelona, Spain's first commercial bank, and was also one of the first investors in the gas company, Sociedad Catalana para el Alumbrado por Gas.[38]

Esteban Gatell's partners in the failed *Fernando Po* expedition were all respectable Catalan merchants in Barcelona. José Vidal Ribas, for example, belonged to an extended family with interests in different economic sectors in Catalonia. He was one of the founders, in 1856, of the Sociedad Catalana General de Crédito and also actively participated in Fomento del Ensanche de Barcelona, a company involved in the planning and construction of the Eixample area of Barcelona. He combined these activities with the remote management of a slave factory located near Ouidah on the African coast. Esteban Gatell's partner, Carlos Torrents Miralda, who belonged to a manufacturing dynasty based in Manresa (an industrial city in the Catalan hinterland), was founder of the firm Pau Miralda y Cía. By 1839 he was one of the three highest payers of tax on trading and manufacturing interests in Barcelona. These are just some examples of wealthy merchants from respectable Catalan families who participated in the slave trade.

Significant also was the number of Catalan slave traders resident in and operating from Havana, among them Pancho Martí Torrents, Jaime Villardebó Ferrer, Manuel Roig Milà, Isidro Anglada, Pablo Forcadell, Josep Maria Borrell, Miguel Pous, and José Baró Blanchart.[39] The most prominent, however, was Salvador Samá Martí, an outstanding member of a Catalan business dynasty with interests in Cuba and in Spain. A renowned slave trader, his life and business activities have attracted the attention of several historians, resulting in the publication of three books about him.[40] José Xifré Casas (1777–1856), the possessor of one of Spain's greatest fortunes in the first half of the nineteenth century, merits particular mention, as he too had traded in slaves during his time in Cuba.[41] Indeed, his wealth was such that a popular saying of the day referred to a wealthy person as being "richer than Xifré." Son of a trader who had gone bankrupt in Cuba, José Xifré emulated his father by departing for Cuba as a young man in 1798. He established himself in Havana and, five years later, was active as a trader on his own behalf. He remained in Cuba until 1823 and then moved to New York, where he invested part of the capital amassed in Havana in property, trade, and finance. He eventually returned to Europe, where he transferred a large proportion of his capital acquired in the Cuban slave-based economy—associated, at least in part, with slave trading.[42]

A trio of wealthy sisters—Mercedes, Carmen, and Maria Dolores Llopart Xiqués—could attribute the origins of their great fortune to the activities of their Havana-based slave-trading father, Roque J. Llopart. In Cuba, Llopart built up enough capital to allow him to invest in other activities, such as providing loans to Cuban plantation owners and exporting sugar to the United States. As related by Henry Coit to the New York importer, Moses Taylor, following Coit's visit to Llopart in 1843, "[H]e [Llopart] has retired completely from the African trade and now employs his capital to fund business ventures. He says that this year he will receive a large amount of sugar, including ... a plantation for which he provided capital. He will loan him [the plantation owner] 17,000 pesos, but the harvest will yield some 1,800 hogsheads. He lives in a beautiful house of his own property, and also has others in this city [Havana]. [José María] Morales [Sotolongo] reports that even though the plantation owners owe him a great deal of money he possesses abundant capital and is in a good position."[43]

Roque Jacinto Llopart died in Havana shortly thereafter in July 1846. His widow, Manuela Xiqués Romagosa, and her three daughters eventually left the island for Barcelona. Maintaining her interests in Cuba, Manuela Xiqués began to invest her revenues from Havana in sites and properties in Barcelona in anticipation of the marriages of her daughters and the division of their inheritance. In just sixteen years, between 1855 and 1871, Llopart's widow invested over 1.2 million pesetas—a veritable fortune—in property in Barcelona. Particularly noteworthy among the properties she purchased or commissioned were three houses constructed on the Paseo de Gracia as residences for her three daughters and the palace constructed on the fashionable main boulevard of Barcelona, the Ramblas.[44] In 1859 one of these daughters, Carmen Llopart Xiqués, married Leopoldo Gil Serra; brother to the owners of the Paris-based Casa de Banca, Gil was also the son of the powerful Catalan industrialist, Pedro Gil Babot (1783–1853), several of whose ships had plied the slave trade.

Pedro Gil's brig *Estrella-Diana*, for example, was captured by English cruisers hunting down slave traders off the African coast and was never recovered by the family. However, his brig *Tellus*, in a partnership with the Barcelona banker Antonio Milá de la Roca, the merchant Cristóbal Roig Vidal and the ship's captain Juan Botet, among others, met with better success. A contract signed in Barcelona on 28 March 1820 records that the *Tellus* was fitted out in the spring of 1820 to "undertake a voyage to Mozambique to purchase negro slaves and transport them to the Port of

Havana on the Island of Cuba." The partners invested more than sixty-five thousand pesos (over 337,000 pesetas of the day) in financing this expedition.[45] Years later, Pedro Gil Babot was elected a deputy to the Cortes cortes Generales generales for the province of Tarragona in several legislatures and even became vice president of the Congress of Deputies for one legislature. Gil combined his activities in slave trading and politics with an active business life in several different sectors. He is particularly noteworthy for having promoted and financed the first Catalan company to supply gas for lighting streets and homes (Sociedad Catalana para el Alumbrado por Gas) and was associated with the private Casa de Banca in Paris, founded with his capital in 1846.[46]

One of Gil's partners in the *Tellus* expedition was Cristóbal Roig Vidal, who had put up over fifty thousand pesetas for the venture; he, too, had made his fortune in Havana before returning to Catalonia in 1804. He was active in legal slave trading from Barcelona between 1815 and 1821. His main initiative, nevertheless, was launched after slave trading was abolished. In 1822, through the Ricomá brothers, captains of his slaving ships, Cristóbal Roig Vidal founded a factory in Madagascar. Between then and 1826, he commissioned five slave-trading expeditions to the Malagasy coast. Thereafter, however, until 1836 he preferred to contribute to the financing of slave-trading expeditions fitted out by partners and collaborators in Havana. Naturally, these activities were very carefully camouflaged in his accounts.[47]

Barcelona, for different reasons, came to be the destination of a number of slave traders who, although not native-born Catalans, opted to settle in the Catalan capital after having made their fortune in the Americas. Some examples are Antonio López, referred to above, and Joaquín Gómez, a native of Cadiz who died in Barcelona in August 1853 after a long residence in Havana. Another example is Pedro Blanco Fernández de Trava from Malaga, who lived between Africa and Cuba before settling in Barcelona in 1842; his intense life was related in a novel, significantly titled *El Negrero,* which went through several print runs.[48]

Spanish Traders Beyond the Catalan Case

Just as Antonio López sold *bozales* (i.e., slaves newly arrived from Africa) in Santiago de Cuba, other traders were doing the same in other ports of the island. Antonio López, in fact, often dispatched slaves to towns such as Matanzas, Cienfuegos, and even Havana. His right-hand man in Matanzas was Ramón Valdés, who returned to Spain in the mid 1850s. He first settled in his native Asturias in northern Spain, where he built up an important lending business, using, undoubtedly, capital that he had amassed in Cuba, some acquired from his activities as a slave trader. José Ramón García López documented the fact that between 1856 and 1860, Valdés issued loans in Asturias amounting to over 260,000 pesetas, making him one of the "most prominent lenders" in Asturias at the time.[49] Another example was Antonio López' attorney in Cienfuegos; he merits special mention as he returned to his native town, Santander, in 1853 to found a shipping company whose ships, 150 years later, still plough the high seas. The company is Pérez y Cía and its founder was Ángel Bernardo Pérez.

Indeed, the offices of Pérez y Cía SA are still located today on the beautiful Paseo de Pereda in Santander. An interested researcher can even consult a brief account of the history of the company—*Historial de la sociedad Pérez y Cía. SC*—dating from 1944; it was written by the son of the founder, Ángel Federico Pérez Eizaguirre, in his old age and was based essentially on his own memories. Significantly, the information provided in the history dates back only to 1853; the opening lines refer to the fact that the company, "of the name Pérez y García," was "founded by D. Ángel B. Pérez and D. José García Álvaro to import wood and cod from Norway." One wonders why there are no references to the years previous to 1853. Who was Ángel B. Pérez before he founded Pérez y García? And where did he obtain the capital that would enable him to set up as an import merchant in Santander? Cuban documentation, once again, provides the answers.

The books of the Santiago de Cuba notary Soler y Regüeiferos refer to a general power of attorney of 1848, signed by Claudio López y López, the brother of Antonio López, authorizing "D. Ángel Bernardo Pérez, a trader resident in Cienfuegos, to sell there or elsewhere on the Island [of Cuba] any slaves dispatched to him for such purpose, at prices and according to terms that will be notified to him privately."[50] The same notarial documents record numerous transactions regarding sales "a uso de feria," by means of which Ángel B. Pérez disposed of a large number of slaves on behalf of the López brothers and others.[51] We also learn, incidentally, that Ángel B. Pérez sat on a committee created in Cienfuegos in October 1850 to deal with an outbreak of cholera.[52]

It was during his time in Cuba, therefore, that Ángel B. Pérez established the contacts, amassed the capital, and acquired the prestige that would enable him to return to his native Santander and embark on a long and active public life until his death in May 1897. In the second half of the nineteenth century he held a number of different posts and responsibilities. He was an alderman in the Santander town council, deputy for the province and, from 1875, a member of the board of directors of the Santander branch of the Banco de España. When the Compañía Arrendataria de Tabacos was founded to manage the state tobacco monopoly, Ángel B. Pérez' company, appointed as its agent in Santander, safeguarded and sold official forms and stamps to the entire province of Santander. He was also appointed president of the recently created Santander Chamber of Commerce. His eldest son, Ángel Federico Pérez Eizaguirre, as well as participating in the family business, was the founder and first secretary of the Compañía Santanderina de Navegación and was also a member of the first board of directors of the Caja Cantabria provincial savings bank, created in 1898 and still in existence today.

Another Cantabrian who plied the slave trade, just as the López brothers and Ángel B. Pérez had, was Juan Manuel de Manzanedo (1803–1882). Born in Santoña, a village on the shores of the Cantabrian Sea, Manzanedo emigrated to Cuba in 1823, spending twenty years there until he returned to settle in Madrid in 1845. While in Cuba, Manzanedo was involved in four related activities: the exportation of sugarcane and sugarcane by-products, mortgage-guaranteed lending, the hiring of tools and implements to plantation owners, and the financing of slave-trading expeditions. According to his biographers, it was his involvement in slave trading that "ultimately explained Manzanedo's meteoric economic success."[53]

Back in his home country, Manzanedo began to invest a large proportion of the fortune he had amassed in Cuba—part of it earned from slave trading. For example, he purchased property in Madrid, including a number of properties located in the Puerta del Sol area in the heart of the city. He also had interests in railways; in 1864 he was awarded the license to build the León-Gijón railway and subsequently played a key role in the Alar del Rey-Santander railway company, of which he eventually became president. One of the founders of the Banco de Fomento y Ultramar in Madrid in 1846, Manzanedo was a supplier of American tobacco to Hacienda and also found time to invest in the Paris stock exchange and manage his own trading company in Madrid. Manzanedo also held a number of posts in Madrid. He was consul of the Trade Tribunal and a member of the Board of Primary Instruction, and he was elected a deputy and subsequently became a senator in the cortes generales.[54] It is hardly surprising that by 1870, Juan Manuel de Manzanedo's fortune was "the largest in the Madrid of the day and possibly in Spain, larger than that of the Duke of Alba and only equaled by that of the House of Medinaceli."[55] Indeed, on his death in 1882, his capital amounted to over 20 million pesetas, which, by the standards of the time, was a remarkable fortune.

Reputable Basque merchants, similar to Cantabrians like Pérez and Manzanedo, also had links to the slave trade. Some, like José Antonio de Ybarra, operated directly from the Basque Country.[56] Ybarra was the driving force behind what became one of Spain's most important business dynasties. His sons founded a number of companies in the iron mining, steel, food-processing, and financial sectors, amongst others. Some of these businesses continue today—for example, the powerful Banco Bilbao Vizcaya Argentaria (BBVA), successor to the Banco de Vizcaya founded by the Ybarra family. José Antonio de Ybarra participated in his first slave-trading expedition in the summer of 1833; he was even responsible for appointing the ship's captain, one Ángel Elorriaga from Santurce, whose sailing vessel, the *Cazador*, was custom-built in a Bayonne shipyard. Also involved in the expedition were José Félix de Latasa from San Sebastián, Martín Belarra (nephew of de Latasa) and Carlos Urruela from Cadiz. The shipping agent in Havana was Pedro Martínez, a merchant and owner of over thirty sailing ships, who also kept a house in the port of Cadiz.

As Bilbao suffered the consequences of the First Carlist War in early 1835, the *Cazador* put in on the African coast to load slaves for Cuba from a factory in Ouidah. Weeks later, nearly seven hundred slaves were landed in Bahía Honda near Pinar del Río in Cuba. The financiers of the expedition, including Ybarra, obtained profits amounting to twice their investment. José Antonio Ybarra was thus encouraged to participate in a second expedition; in July 1835 he informed Enrique Mier that "in the African expedition, capital was more than doubled. … The vessel has been fitted out for a second voyage and on this occasion we are considering the coast [of western Africa]. If it is as propitious as the first, Elorriaga [captain of the *Cazador*] says that he will retire with 20,000 duros. I hope it will be so, we too would do well by it, and even were it necessary to appoint a new captain, we will continue until it [the ship] falls into the hands of the infidels" (referring to the English).[57] However, luck failed Ybarra and his partners on this second expedition, as the so-called infidels did indeed capture the vessel and confiscate both it and its cargo.

A number of Galicians also plied the slave trade as traders and investors, operating in many cases, like Ybarra, directly from Spanish ports. One such individual operating from La Coruña was Juan Menéndez Fuertes, a Galician of Asturian origins, who traded in African slaves for Cuba. His earnings from slave trading and other business activities enabled him to invest in land and properties; when the Spanish government confiscated the properties of the Catholic Church, for example, Juan Menéndez became the largest purchaser of church properties in the province of La Coruña in the 1830s and 1840s. Juan Menéndez was also a director in the maritime insurance company, La Integridad, and from 1847, he held a seat in the Spanish senate. In 1850, he was described in French consular documents as "the owner of several ships and [owner of] the first banking house in Coruña," with a fortune estimated at "several million pesos" and with business interests in France, England, and the Americas. On his death in 1852, his fortune was valued at over 3 million pesetas, much if it derived from his transatlantic business activities.[58]

In sum, the prosopographical description provided here reveals the significance of slave trading in Spanish business circles in the nineteenth century. A substantial number of Spanish industrialists, based either in Spain or Cuba, participated in the transatlantic trafficking of African slaves into Cuba. In many cases, slave trading enabled Spaniards to amass sufficient capital to be able to undertake and develop business activities in their home country; in other cases, Cuban slave traders chose to leave their island and retire to Spain, where they too put their capital to profitable use in investments. Both contributed with their capital to the economic modernization of Spain and particularly Catalonia, whose capital city became the destination for slavers in particular and Cuban capital in general.[59]

From Economic Prominence to Social Prestige

In the middle decades of the nineteenth century, the slave trade augmented not only the fortunes of participants and beneficiaries, but also their social standing. As denounced in 1861 by John T. Crawford, a British judge in the Mixed Tribunal of Justice of Havana, "the most notorious of those who acquired their wealth from trafficking in African slaves are showered with honors and medals in Spain. Some have been made nobles on the recommendation of certain captain generals."[60] A number of slavers were, indeed, ennobled by successive Spanish monarchs. For example, in the final days of her reign, Isabel II granted seven notorious slave traders, Salvador Samá Martí, Miguel Aldama Alfonso, José Luis Alfonso García, Juan Manuel Manzanedo, Manuel Pastor Fuentes, Rafael Toca Aguilar, and José Baró Blanchart, the titles of Marquis of Marianao (1860), Marquis of Santa Rosa (1864), Marquis of Montelo (1864), Marquis of Manzanedo (1864), Count of Bagaes (1853), Count of San Ignacio (1865), and Viscount of Canet de Mar (1861), respectively. In his short two-year reign, Amadeo I granted José Antonio Suárez Argudín and Antonio Samá Urgellés the titles of Marquis of Casa Argudín and Marquis of Samá, respectively. And even after the abolition of the slave trade, in the early years of the Spanish Restoration (1875-1923), the young King Alfonso XII emulated his mother by granting Castilian titles to slave traders; thus, Julián Zulueta became Marquis of Álava in 1875 and Antonio López became Marquis of Comillas in 1878—and a Grandee of Spain three years later; José Baró, a viscount since 1861, was awarded the title of Marquis of Santa Rita in 1875 and, in the same year, Juan Manuel Manzanedo, a marquis since 1864, was made

Duke of Santoña.⁶¹ Involvement in the slave trade was clearly no impediment to ennoblement and former slavers were welcomed into the Spanish elite with open arms. King Alfonso XII himself spent two successive summers in the village of Comillas as the guest of a former slave trader. Fernando Muñoz, Duke of Riánsares, the second husband of Alfonso XII's grandmother María Cristina, when she was acting as queen regent, had participated in the slave trade through proxies such as Juan Antonio Parejo.⁶²

The relatively large number of former slavers among the Spanish elite reflected a broader phenomenon, namely, opposition to any kind of abolition—not so much of the slave trade (which, in any case, had been formally and legally abolished in 1820) as of the institution of slavery itself. Anti-abolitionists found support in powerful economic protectionist factions in Spain. Christopher Schmidt-Nowara has argued, in fact, that Spain's tardy and incomplete transition to industrial capitalism can be explained by seemingly anachronistic attitudes to protectionism and colonial slavery and, moreover, that there was a doctrinal and strategic overlap in the Spanish state between, on the one hand, protectionists and anti-abolitionists, and on the other hand, free traders and abolitionists.⁶³ The late abolition of slavery in the Spanish colonies of the Antilles (Puerto Rico in 1873 and Cuba in 1886) was no accident⁶⁴ and can be explained, to some degree at least, by the power and influence of the Spanish anti-abolition movement. We know much more about the affairs of the abolitionists than we do about the efforts of the pro-slavery faction; for this very reason, therefore, it is important to examine the development and dynamics of the Spanish anti-abolitionist movement.⁶⁵

The organizational capacity of the anti-abolitionist forces, particularly in Catalonia, can be appreciated in the period 1868–1875, which was marked by the Ten Years' War in Cuba, mirrored by a political crisis (*el sexenio democrático*) in Spain. Within weeks of learning of the outbreak of war in Cuba, the Provincial Council of Barcelona raised an army of young Catalans to fight against the Cuban separatists. Over three thousand men enlisted (the only requirement being to have no dependents), and in return they received a payment that was financed out of the pockets of the Catalan bourgeoisie. In this large-scale operation, the enlisted men were formed into Battalions of Catalan Volunteers that were dispatched to Cuba to defend the sugar plantations from attacks.⁶⁶ The initiative was supported by a number of prominent Catalan merchants who had become wealthy years before in Cuba (some of them as slavers), among them, José Canela Raventós, José Antonio Salom, José Amell Bou, and Antonio López y López. These indianos also participated in the creation, two years later, of a Círculo Hispano Ultramarino in Barcelona.⁶⁷

A first failed attempt to create an organization "to defend the integrity of the national territory with respect to Cuba" in Barcelona in August 1871 was the initiative of José Canela Raventós, who, years earlier, had founded the Empresa de Navegación y Fomento por la Costa del Sur, based in Havana. However, just a few months later in Madrid, a national movement initiated by a former slaver, the first Marquis of Manzanedo, led to the formation of the Círculos Hispano Ultramarinos. The idea was to create an organization that would put pressure on the authorities to maintain the colonial status quo and, hence, the institution of slavery. Individuals who had become wealthy in Cuba played a central role in this new organization—so central, in fact, that in Madrid, only Spaniards who were former residents in Cuba were admitted to the governing organs.

Likewise, the Círculo Hispano Ultramarino de Barcelona was composed of individuals who had laid the foundations of their fortune in Cuba, including its president, the industrialist and senator Joan Güell y Ferrer, and its vice president, the former slaver Antonio López. Other members included individuals who were (or had been) sugar plantation owners in Cuba or Puerto Rico, such as José Amell, Francisco Gumá, Tomás Ribalta, José Telarroja (a partner of Julián Zulueta), and Sebastián Plaja. In 1871, Joan Güell, the president of the Círculo Hispano Ultramarino de Barcelona, had written *Rebelión Cubana,* a pamphlet that exemplifies the thinking of these indianos regarding Cuban politics. Güell perceived members of the Cuban reform movement to be equivalent to the armed insurgents and, comparable, in turn, in form and in aims, to the protagonists of the Paris Commune—a historical episode that was experienced as very close to home. For Güell, war resulted from proposals for reforming Cuban-Spanish relations drawn up by the Board of Information supported by two former captains general of the island, Francisco Serrano and Domingo Dulce. There was, in fact, a broad consensus between the position of Güell (that is, of the Círculo Hispano Ultramarino of Barcelona) in Catalonia and that of the intransigent supporters of the *partido español* in Cuba: they both rejected any proposal for reform and fervently defended maintenance of the colonial status quo, including the institution of slavery, at all costs. Hence, whereas Cuban captains general (and Spanish Ministers ministers of the Overseas Territories [Ministros de Ultramar] such as Segismundo Moret y Prendergast) temporized, the Cuban volunteer militias (the armed wing defending the island's integration with Spain) acted as a powerful bulwark of Cuba's Spanishness, that is, of opposition to reforms.[68]

On his sudden death in 1872, Joan Güell was succeeded by the industrialist José Antonio Salom—enriched years before in Havana—as president of the Círculo Hispano Ultramarino de Barcelona. Salom launched an initiative to create the Liga Nacional, a political platform that aimed to destabilize the First Republic. A broad anti-government front, the Liga Nacional recruited the full spectrum of defenders of the status quo who rejected the First Republic's approval of the abolition of slavery in Puerto Rico in 1873. The first president of the Liga Nacional was José Antonio Salom himself—who, as mentioned above, was also president of the Círculo Hispano Ultramarino de Barcelona. Indeed, all the members of the governing board of the anti-abolitionist Círculo Hispano Ultramarino de Barcelona, without exception, immediately joined the management committee of the recently created Liga Nacional—a movement that soon saw its goals achieved.

Coups d'état, first by Manuel Pavía and then by Arsenio Martínez Campos, not only ended the short-lived First Republic but also restored a Bourbon—the young Alfonso XII—as head of the Spanish state. The support of most of the members of the Círculo Hispano Ultramarino de Barcelona for Alfonso XII's cause was patent;[69] their commitment to the restoration of the established order, furthermore, was richly rewarded by the new powers. One outcome was the strengthening of military operations in Cuba against the insurgency through a credit operation in which a number of industrialists lent the Spanish state 25 million pesos fuertes. This credit transaction resulted in the founding of a new bank in Barcelona, significantly called the Banco Hispano Colonial, which soon came to be the second-most-important bank in Spain, responsible, as it was, for handling Cuban customs revenues between 1876 and 1898. Its first president was no other than the former slaver, Antonio López, whose life story was related above.

The story of Antonio López, first Marquis of Comillas and Grandee of Spain, was remarkable but by no means exceptional. Many Spanish merchants had, like him, laid the foundations for their fortunes in the illegal slave trade to Cuba. And, like him, many of these merchants used their capital subsequently to build up profitable business empires in Spain. Indeed, even though slave trading was abolished in 1820, the transatlantic trade continued to be a source of profits for all those implicated, whether crews, functionaries, factors or agents—but, above all, for slaveship owners. According to my calculations, illegal slave trading into Cuba generated profits amounting to some 61 million U.S. dollars; particularly profitable was the period 1853–1864, that is, when, following the end of slave trading to Brazil, Cuba was the only possible destination for transatlantic traffic in slaves.[70]

The interests—not only economic—that grew up around the Spanish-Cuban nexus, linked as much to slave trading into Cuba as to the institution of slavery on the island, were central in shaping Spanish colonial policy in the nineteenth century, as exemplified by the fact that powerful anti-reformist and anti-abolitionist forces ensured the tardy abolition of slavery in Puerto Rico (1873) and Cuba (1886).

Notes

1. This research falls within the HAR2009-14099 and HAR2009-07013 joint research projects.
2. An indispensable publication for understanding slave trade abolition in Cuba is David R. Murray's *Odious Commerce: Britain, Spain and the Abolition of the Cuban Slave Trade* (Cambridge, 1980).
3. Alejandro de la Fuente, "Esclavitud, 1510–1886," in Consuelo Naranjo, ed., *Historia de Cuba* (Madrid and Aranjuez, 2009), 129–152.
4. Hubert S. Aimes, *A History of Slavery in Cuba: 1511 to 1868* (New York, 1907); Philip D. Curtin, *The Atlantic Slave Trade: A Census* (Madison, The University of Wisconsin Press, 1969); Juan Pérez de la Riva, *Para la historia de las gentes sin historia* (Barcelona, 1975).
5. Herbert Klein: *The Middle Passage. Comparative Studies in the Atlantic Slave Trade*, Princeton University Press, 1978.
6. Josep M. Fradera, "La participació catalana en el tràfic d'esclaus," *Recerques* 16 (1984): 119–139.
7. Aimes, *History of Slavery in Cuba*.
8. Curtin, *Atlantic Slave Trade*, 234.
9. David Eltis et al., *The Trans-Atlantic Slave Trade: A Database on CD-ROM* (Cambridge, 1999).
10. Significantly, not one of the twenty-five studies contained in Jeremy Black's *The Atlantic Slave Trade, Vol. IV Nineteenth Century* (Burlington, VT, 2006) refers to the Spanish-Cuban trade.
11. Luis Alonso, "Comercio exterior y formación de capital financiero: el tráfico de negros hispano-cubano, 1821–1868," *Anuario de Estudios Americanos* LI, no. 2 (1994): 75–92. Although Alonso provides his "own estimate of the number of slaves landed in Cuba" between 1821 and 1852, in calculating "the estimated direct profits from the sale of slaves in Cuba" between 1821 and 1867, he uses figures other than his own estimates but fails to indicate the source.
12. In 1820, 11,096 African slaves were landed in Cuba; however, I could only count 6,472 for the period June–December, when trading had become illegal. Since Eltis (*Economic Growth*, 280–281) does not provide profit data for 1866, I used his calculation formula for the ten-year period immediately before 1866, that is, 1856–1865.
13. José Luciano Franco, *Comercio clandestino de esclavos* (Havana, 1980), 310.
14. Martín Rodrigo, *Los marqueses de Comillas, 1817–1925. Antonio y Claudio López* (Madrid, 2001).
15. Miquel Izard, "Dependencia y colonialismo: la Compañía General de Tabacos de Filipinas," *Moneda y Crédito* 130 (1974), 47–89; Emili Giralt, *La Compañía General de Tabacos de Filipinas (1881–1981)* (Barcelona, 1981); Josep Maria Delgado, "Bajo dos banderas (1881–1910). Sobre cómo sobrevivió la Compañía General de Filipinas al Desastre del 98," in Consuelo Naranjo, Miguel Angel Puig-Samper, and Luis Miguel García Mora, eds, *La Nación Soñada: Cuba, Puerto Rico y Filipinas ante el 98* (Aranjuez, 1996), 293–304; Martín Rodrigo, "Del desestanco del tabaco a la puesta en marcha de la Compañía General de Tabacos de Filipinas (1879–1880)," *Boletín Americanista* 59, (2009): 199–221.

16. *Homenaje que la ciudad de Barcelona tributó a la memoria del Excmo. Sr. D. Antonio López y López, Marqués de Comillas* (Barcelona, 1883); Francisco Bru, *La verdadera vida de Antonio López y López. Por su cuñado* (Barcelona, 1885).
17. Bru, *La verdadera vida*, 62–65.
18. Archivo Histórico Provincial de Santiago de Cuba, Escribanía de Soler y Regüeiferos, Protocol 601, 19.08.1847, Fol. 212; Protocol 602, 29.01.1848, Fol. 29; and foll.
19. Rodrigo, *Los marqueses de Comillas*, 18–25.
20. Archivo Histórico Provincial de Santiago de Cuba, Escribanía Real de Manuel Caminero, Protocol 102, 3.06.1851, Fol. 198; Escribanía de Soler y Regüeiferos, Protocol 606, 13.09.1852, Fol. 124.
21. Francisco Condeminas, *La marina española (compendio histórico)* (Barcelona, 1923), 321.
22. Archivo Histórico Provincial de Santiago de Cuba, Escribanía de Rafael Ramírez, Protocol 532, 15.05.1850; Protocol 531, 18.03.1851, Fol. 66 and 14.05.1851, Fol. 119; Escribanía de Juan Giró, Protocol 281, 22.01.1851, Fol. 25.
23. Franco, *Comercio clandestino*, 384.
24. Alfonso W. Quiroz, "Implicit Costs of Empire: Bureaucratic Corruption in Nineteenth-Century Cuba," *Journal of Latin American Studies* 35 (August 2003): 473–511.
25. Author, based on data from Fradera, "Participació catalana," 132–133.
26. For the links between the Catalan business sector and the transatlantic slave trade, see Jordi Maluquer de Motes, "La burgesia catalana i l'esclavitud colonial: modes de producció i pràctica política," *Recerques* 3 (1974): 83–136; and Fradera, "Participació catalana."
27. Enrique Sosa, *Catalanes y gaditanos en la trata negrera cubana* (Havana, 1998). A first cousin of Juan Reynals, Francisco Granell would shortly thereafter retire as a captain of slavers to captain the *Balear*, the first steamship registered in Catalonia.
28. Michael Zeuske and Orlando García Martínez, "La *Amistad:* Ramón Ferrer in Cuba and the Transatlantic Dimensions of Slaving and Contraband Trade."
29. Ibid.; Sosa, *Catalanes y gaditanos*, 30.
30. Raimon Soler, *Emigrar per negociar. L'emigració a Amèrica des de la comarca del Garraf: el cas de Gregori Ferrer i Soler, 1791–1853* (Vilanova i la Geltrú, 2003).
31. Archivo Histórico Comarcal de Vilanova i la Geltrú, Notarial Protocols for J. Torrents e Higuero, 1862 manuals, 25.02.1862, Fols. 85–87; 31.03.1862, Fols. 130–140 and 11.07.1862, Fols. 321.366. Thanks to Raimon Soler for this information.
32. Maluquer de Motes, "Burgesia catalana," 126.
33. For further details of this important Catalan industrialist, see "Josep Ferrer i Vidal (1817–1893)," in F. Cabana, ed., *Cien empresarios catalanes* (Madrid, 2006), 103–113.
34. Maluquer de Motes, "Burgesia catalana," 109–110.
35. Archivo Histórico de Sitges, Notarial Protocols, Manuel Torrents de Papiol, 1853 manual, Fols. 349–365, 18.11.1853.
36. Francesc Cabana, *La burgesia catalana: una aproximación històrica* (Barcelona, 1996), 50–53.
37. Domingo del Monte, *Centón epistolario de Domingo del Monte*, 7 vols. (Havana, 1923–1957), 4, 120, 131, 150, and 156. Thanks to Michael Zeuske for this reference.
38. Yolanda Blasco *Epistolari de Jaume Badia. El pensament bancari en el segle XIX* (Torredembarra, 2009).
39. Manuel Moreno Fraginals, *El ingenio. Complejo económico social cubano del azúcar* (Havana, 1978), 1, 268–269; J.L. Franco, *Comercio clandestino*.
40. Albert Virella, *L'aventura ultramarina de la gent de Vilanova i la nissaga dels Samà* (Vilanova i la Geltrú, 1990); Martín Rodrigo, "Con un pie en Catalunya y otro en Cuba: la familia Samá de Vilanova," *Estudis Històrics i Documents dels Arxius de Protocols* XVI (1998), 359–397; Dolores M. Pérez Tarrau, *La saga cubana de los Samà (1794–1933)* (Barcelona, 2007).

41. Ángel Bahamonde and José Cayuela, *Hacer las Américas. Las élites coloniales españolas en el siglo XIX* (Madrid, 1992).
42. For a biography of this wealthy industrialist, see José Mª Ramon de San Pedro, *Don José Xifré Casas: pequeña historia decimonónica de un archimillonario* (Barcelona, 1956).
43. Reported in Roland T. Ely, *Cuando reinaba Su Majestad el Azúcar* (Havana, 2001), 330–331.
44. For further details of the investments of this wealthy widow, see my chapter titled "Trasvase de capitales antillanos: azúcar y transformación urbana en Barcelona en el siglo XIX," in Antonio Santamaría and Consuelo Naranjo, eds., *Más allá del azúcar. Política, diversificación y prácticas económicas en Cuba, 1878–1930* (Aranjuez, 2009), 127–158.
45. Josep Rovira i Fors, "El bergantí negrer *Tellus*," *L'Avenç* 75, (1984): 52–55.
46. Martín Rodrigo, *La familia Gil. Empresarios catalanes en la Europa del siglo XIX* (Barcelona, 2010).
47. For more in-depth information on Cristóbal Roig Vidal and his trading activities, see Josep M. Fradera: *Crisi colonial i mercat interior: les bases comercials de la indústria catalana moderna*, Ph.D. dissertation, Universitat Autònoma de Barcelona, 1983, 3 vols.
48. For a curious biography of Pedro Blanco, known as *el mongo de Gallinas* as a consequence of his reputation as a slaver in the Gallinas river area of Africa, see Lino Novás Calvo, *El negrero. Vida novelada de Pedro Blanco Fernández de Trava* (Barcelona, 1999).
49. José Ramón García López, *Las remesas de los emigrantes españoles en América, siglos XIX y XX* (Gijón, 1992), 76–84.
50. Archivo Histórico Provincial de Santiago de Cuba, Escribanía de Soler y Regüeiferos, Protocol 602, 30.11.1848, Fol. 310.
51. Archivo Provincial de Cienfuegos, Notarial Protocols, Escribanía de José Joaquín Verdaguer, 11.02.1850, Fols. 48–49; 14.10.1851, Fol. 535.
52. Enrique Edo, *Memoria histórica de Cienfuegos y su jurisdicción* (Havana, 1942), 131.
53. José Cayuela and Ángel Bahamonde, "Trasvase de capitales antillanos y estrategias inversoras: la fortuna del Marqués de Manzanedo (1823–1882)," *Revista Internacional de Sociología* 1 (1987): 125–148. Another biography was wriiten by Manuel Adolfo Muela, *Juan Manuel Manzanedo y González, primer marqués de Manzanedo, primer duque de Santoña* (Santander, 2005).
54. After his death, the fortune of the first Marquis of Manzanedo and Duke of Santoña was the subject of a much-talked-about suit brought by his natural but legitimized daughter against his widow, as described in the short treatise *Expoliación escandalosa. Historia del laudo dictado en la testamentaria del Excmo. Sr. Duque de Santoña por los Sres. Gamazo y Azcárate y voto particular del Sr. Montero Ríos. Nulidades que contiene y desastrosos errores* (Madrid, 1894).
55. Ibid.
56. Pablo Díaz Morlán, *Los Ybarra, una dinastía de empresarios (1801–2001)* (Madrid, 2002).
57. Javier de Ybarra e Ybarra, *Nosotros los Ybarra: vida, economía y sociedad (1744–1902)* (Barcelona, 2002), 149.
58. Alonso, "Comercio exterior," 87.
59. Martín Rodrigo, *Indians a Catalunya. Capitals cubans en l'economia catalana* (Barcelona, 2007); Àngels Solà, "Os 'americanos' cataláns e o seu impacto económico en Cataluña ó longo do século XIX," *Estudios Migratorios* 11 and 12 (2001): 141–168.
60. Franco, *Comercio clandestino*, 384.
61. Much of this information is from José Cayuela and Ángel Bahamonde, "La creación de nobleza en Cuba durante el siglo XIX," *Historia Social* 11 (1991): 57–82. Nonetheless, the authors do not refer to the creation of the Count of Bagaes (1853), the Marquis of Marianao (1860), or the Duke of Santoña (1875).
62. Bahamonde and Cayuela, *Hacer las Américas*.

63. Christopher Schmidt-Nowara, "National Economy and Atlantic Slavery: Protectionism and Resistance to Abolitionism in Spain and the Antilles, 1854–1874," *Hispanic American Historical Review* 78 (November 1998): 603–629.
64. For an analysis of the abolition process in Cuba, see Rebecca J. Scott, *Slave Emancipation in Cuba: The Transition to Free Labor, 1860–1899* (Princeton, 1985). For a collection and description of the legal texts referring to this process, see Concepción Navarro, *La abolición de la esclavitud negra en la legislación española, 1870–1886* (Madrid, 1987).
65. Christopher Schmidt-Nowara, *Empire and Antislavery: Spain, Cuba and Puerto Rico, 1833–1874* (Pittsburgh, 1999).
66. José J. Moreno Masó, *La petjada dels catalans a Cuba* (Barcelona, 1993); Martín Rodrigo, "Cataluña y el colonialismo español (1868–1899)," in Salvador Calatayud, Jesús Millán, and Mari Cruz Romeo, eds., *Estado y periferias en la España del siglo XIX. Nuevos enfoques* (Valencia, 2009), 315–356.
67. For a detailed analysis of the creation of this association, see Maluquer de Motes, "Burgesia catalana."
68. Juan Güell y Ferrer, *Rebelión cubana* (Barcelona, 1871).
69. For further details on the Cuban background to the Restoration, see Manuel Espadas Burgos, *Alfonso XII y los orígenes de la Restauración* (Madrid, 1975).
70. For details of the abolition of slavery in Brazil, see Seymour Drescher, "Brazilian Abolition in Comparative Perspective," *Hispanic American Historical Review* 68 (August 1988): 429–460.

– *Chapter 8* –

LA *AMISTAD*
Ramón Ferrer in Cuba and the Transatlantic Dimensions of Slaving and Contraband Trade[1]

Michael Zeuske and Orlando García Martínez

Introduction: Bringing Back the Caribbean, Cuba, and the Hidden Atlantic into American History

"The terrible history of our African trade."[2]

On the night of June 30, 1839, fifty-seven captives aboard a Cuban coastal schooner, the *Amistad,* rose up. Under the leadership of a man from Mendeland (today southern Sierra Leone and northern Liberia) named Cinqué, the captives killed the captain, a Catalan named Ramón Ferrer, and the enslaved cook, Celestino. After taking control, they tried to sail back to Africa, but an American ship intercepted the *Amistad* near Long Island. Three dramatic court cases later, the last one before the Supreme Court of the United States (United States vs. The *Amistad*), the surviving thirty-five men and four children sailed, with the help of very active Christian abolitionists and missionaries, back to Freetown, Sierra Leone, arriving in early 1842.[3]

The *Amistad* case has typically been discussed in U.S. historiography and other university systems as teaching material (best represented by Steven Spielberg's film *Amistad*),[4] showing a signal victory of abolitionism in a slaveholding society.[5] Because of the dramatic courtroom history and the attention paid mainly to the victims of human trafficking *in* the United States (but not *outside*) and to the construction of an abolitionist discourse, the *Amistad*'s history has come to form an elementary part of American national history.

When in 2005 we found the crucial Spanish and Cuban documents in the Archivo Nacional de Cuba,[6] new lines of analysis and also a new presentation of the themes became possible, including the Cuban, Caribbean, transcultural, and transnational dimensions of the *Amistad* case as part of huge system of human trafficking, a system that we call the *hidden Atlantic* of the nineteenth century. Of the some 12.5 million African victims of the transatlantic slave trade between 1440 and 1878,[7] the nineteenth-century traffic, mostly to Cuba and Brazil, accounted for more than one quarter of all of the captives in the modern age (i.e., over 3 million), according to the estimates from the Transatlantic Slave Trade Database (www.slavevoyages.org).[8] Almost one million were smuggled to Cuba and more than two million to Brazil.

Our subsequent Atlantic research (in Havana, London, Lisbon, Madrid, Seville, Arenys del Mar near Barcelona, Camagüey and La Guanaja in Cuba, Praia in the Cape Verde Islands, and São Tomé) took us first into the analysis of the principal actors, the captain, his businesses and ships, and the crew as well. So the captain, practically ignored by historians until now, became for us a symptomatic social type of the important group of bearers and founders of a culture of the hidden Atlantic, persons who were in face-to-face contact with captives and illegally enslaved people, and a process that we call *atlantization* of the Americas. Indeed, Ferrer and others like him, even more so than their victims, embodied this process because the slave traders and smugglers of human bodies, along with their crews and personnel, were practically living on the hidden Atlantic between Africa, the Caribbean, and the Americas.[9]

Traces of *Amistad* and Ferrer

We do not know as much as we would like about Ramón Ferrer himself. He was the captain of the schooner *Amistad* when the rebellion of the captives occurred in 1839. A search of the "Licences for embarkation for Cuba"[10] held in the archives in Seville has not turned up a record of his departure from Spain nor a date of his arrival in Cuba. But from his marriage record, a copy of which is in Havana, we know his parents' names and that he was born in the Balearic Islands, specifically Ibiza, though we had no birthdate until 2011.[11]

Alongside the analysis of the contraband slave trade, scholars have documented a large-scale migration of Catalans of humble origins to Cuba between 1790 and 1830.[12] Among them were a significant number from Ibiza. To try to imagine the moment of emigration of the man who would become Captain Ferrer, we might use the record of another Ramón Ferrer, this one named Ramón Ferrer y Xifra, a *cubero* [cooper], from the village of Blanes, near Gerona. This Ramón was from mainland Catalonia rather than the islands, but the profile was familiar: Unable to read or write, he sought permission to travel to Havana, where his brother operated a *pulpería,* that is to say, a small grocery stand.[13] The authorities from his village—including the mayor and council of the town of Blanes, of the district of Gerona, along with the parish priest—confirmed that this Ferrer was "a person of good reputation and habits." He was not a member of the volunteer militia, did not participate in the Prado uprising, did not attend any meetings of the secret juntas, denounced by the law, "nor has he given any cause whatsoever for complaint to the judicial authorities."[14] Similarly Julián de Zulueta, who was Basque rather than Catalan, arrived, like Ferrer, "pobre y animado" [poor but lively] in Cuba and accumulated wealth through marriage and the contraband trade.[15]

The Ramón Ferrer we are looking for, the one of the *Amistad,* had by October 1830 arrived in Havana, where he married one Juana González García. The marriage took place in the town of Regla, located outside the walls of the city. The bride and groom both appear in the record as the legitimate children of married parents. The bride is said to be from Regla itself, daughter of "Don José and Doña María de Regla García." There is no indication of a color category for the bride, though the use of the honorific titles don and doña suggests that they were categorized as white. The same bundle in the archives contains the baptismal records of two daughters subsequently born to Ramón Ferrer and Juana González García.[16]

Like many migrants of the epoch, our Ramón Ferrer had a brother with whom he went into business. Damián and Ramón Ferrer traded between Havana and the ports of Guanaja and Nuevitas, providing goods to Puerto Príncipe.[17] They presented themselves as modest captains and owners of a coastal schooner. In the sources about Ramón Ferrer, he appears sometimes with a kind of nickname, or *nom de guerre*—that of Roselló (sometimes as, but not always as Ramón Roselló), also a Catalan. His coastal schooner was called the *Amistad,* meaning friendship.

This was the period of the first Cuban railroads and steam-powered vessels, but the infrastructure of the coastal trade was still quite traditional. The most common vessels for this trade were schooners and launches and only a few steam-powered boats. From Havana the brothers made the journey to different ports and landing-points along the north coast.

Around 1834 Ramón Ferrer was captain of a boat making the regular passage between Havana and La Guanaja, one of the seaports providing access to the whole region of Puerto Príncipe, now known as Camagüey, a rich cattle-raising zone in the center-east of the island, where investors were just beginning to establish sugar plantations. In late September 1834, the year in which his first daughter was born, Ferrer visited the city of Puerto Príncipe. Before the notary Manuel Martínez Valdés he registered the purchase of two slaves. On September 26 he bought from a merchant named Carlos Vilaseca "a young mulatto ... named Celestino, born in Puerto Rico and about 25 years of age ... for the sum of 250 pesos ... in current silver money."[18] A few days later, on September 29, he acquired from the heirs of one Massouer "a mulatta named María del Carmen ... born in Puerto Cabello [Venezuela] age 14 ... for 300 pesos."[19] Celestino would become the shipboard cook for Captain Ferrer and is the first of the *Amistad* captives whose path to that boat we can thus trace.

In 1836 we pick up Ferrer's track in Cuba, through the bills of lading for goods carried on two journeys between Havana and Guanaja, one in February and one in December. The goods listed include "bales of white paper ... jugs of sugar cane brandy ... sacks of peppers ... salt cod ... salt pork ... lentils."[20] On the arrival in Guanaja in December 1836 a record appears in the port's entry log: "Around noon on this day there anchored in this port coming from Havana, the coastal schooner *Amistad*, captain D. Ramon Ferrer, after seven days' sailing." It held "six passengers with four servants" and cargo enumerated in twenty-four accompanying lists.[21] In this last year of its operation under the command of Ferrer, the schooner *Amistad* anchored nine times in the port of Havana and once in Matanzas, carrying passengers and products between Guanaja, Camagüey, Matanzas, and Havana, according to official Spanish records.[22] In these official papers, the Ferrer brothers are presented as modest captains and owners of a small coastal schooner.

We can get a better idea of what the schooner was actually carrying by taking a close look at a set of documents prepared by chief customs authorities in Guanaja. Their report of 8 December 1836 enumerated the cargo: Fabric, boxes of cigarettes, hats, sacks of coffee, barrels of butter, bottles of olive oil, beans, chickpeas, beer, paper, china, crystal, and Bordeaux wine all appeared on the lists of officially declared cargo intended for merchants in Puerto Príncipe, Nuevitas, and La Guanaja.[23] The documents issued by the customs office in Havana on June 26, 1839, and found on board after the uprising, make reference to fabric and food, though they also refer to iron bars, copper, *coronas, guirros,* "iron drums" for a sugarmill, and other material for the sugar industry. Ferrer himself had permission to transport "15 quintals of jerked beef, 15 *cabezas de suela,* 6 barrels of olives, 2 quintals of ham … 50 bottles of olive oil, and 20 boxes of noodles."[24] Another document reveals the names of some of his passengers and of the firms that dealt with him: Saturnino Carrías, Sebastián de la Vega, P. Marrugat, "Roig Hernández y Cia," Salvador Pera, based in Puerto Príncipe; Cristóbal Artur, from Nuevitas; "José Cuesta y Compañía," Evaristo Díaz, and Alejandro Vázquez, from the Surgidero de la Guanaja.[25] Two of these men, Carrías and Cuesta, were also known as slave traders. But the Ferrers, at first glance and at least in the cited written official records, had nothing to do with the slave trade. After Ferrer's death one of his partners, for whom Ferrer had transported a lump of bee's wax to La Guanaja—perhaps in his last voyage—started a legal proceeding for payments due.[26]

Where are, then, the African captives and the Atlantic dimension of the Ferrer story? And where was Ramón Ferrer when he was not appearing in the official sources as a petty coastal captain? We found a trace in the news daily *Diario de la Habana* in 1836: "I inform you that yesterday my father-in-law went to Boca de Camarioca where he found thirteen persons, among them my nephew R.; they had shipwrecked coming back from Puerto Príncipe to Havana in the schooner *N u e v a A n t o n i a*, her captain D[o]n RAMON FERRER, (a[lias]) R o s e l ló, whose misfortune happened at twelve o'clock on the night of Friday, May 27 [the day on which they embarked from the port of La Guanaja]."[27]

So in this written evidence another vessel with *Antonia* as a part of the ship's name is linked to Ferrer under his nickname Roselló. But the most important information of this short article in the press is that Ferrer was using the name Roselló frequently as an alias and that he had still another ship, named *Nueva Antonia*.

Ferrer's most important business was the illegal transportation of captive Africans. Celestino, the slave bought in Puerto Príncipe, was apparently aboard during this shady part of the business. In the official papers of the *Amistad* case, Celestino appears as "Selestino Ferrers, a mulatto, owned by Captain Ramon Ferrers, and employed as a cook."[28] Ferrer used Celestino both as a cook on his schooners and as a crew member. He appears on the permission to sail granted in May 1837 by the commandant in Havana, his presence not changing the regular crew requirements for such a voyage.[29] The documents from the *Comandancia de Matriculas* specify that "the mulatto Celestino Ferrer" and the two sailors Manuel Antonio Padilla and Jacinto Verdague arrived in the port of Havana eight times between July 1838 and June 1839.[30]

Celestino does not appear in the case of another ship, in which Ferrer had at least a 20 percent interest: the steamer *Principeño*.[31] In the investigation that followed an illegal landing (*alijo*) of about three hundred African captives near the coast of Havana in May 1838, Ramón Ferrer was imprudent enough to appear as a witness and to lie to the investigator, saying that he was not the captain of the *Principeño* at the moment of this illegal landing (April 1838) and that the steamer *Principeño* had not unloaded smuggled slaves, but simply loaded charcoal.[32] The investigator concluded "as a result, no charges against the owner of the *Principeño*."[33]

So for 1838 we know that Ferrer owned the *Amistad*, built in Cuba,[34] and held a 20 percent interest in the steamer *Principeño*, of which he was also captain. Perhaps Ferrer made two slaving voyages with the *Principeño* to Africa. If the term *schooner* evokes an earlier age of sail, the term *steamer* brings us into the world of modern transport. As it turns out, the wealth Captain Ferrer accumulated in the slave trade nourished his other businesses. The slave trade also offered more money in profits, but also more money in losses, as was normal in a risky business.

We also know that a witness from Guanaja in 1840 would say (to the state's attorney who was investigating the *Amistad* case from the Spanish side), "because he [Ramón Ferrer] loaded and unloaded his great ships"[35] in the port of Guanaja. That means that Ferrer owned more than one ship. And his widow stated in 1840 that Ferrer had even a third ship, which had sailed "about three years ago" (around 1837) to the coasts of Africa—the *Bella Antonia*. This ship, also with *Antonia*, the first name of Ferrer's elder daughter, in its name, is enigmatic. At least it also may be that there were two ships with *Antonia* in their names: the *Nueva Antonia*, shipwrecked in 1836, and the *Bella Antonia*, captured by English warships in 1837 or 1838. This reference and the information about the *Yumurí/Principeño* voyages suggests very strongly that Ferrer was directly involved with the contraband Atlantic trade in captives, for the widow mentions that the boat had been captured by the British off the coast of Africa.[36]

The continual shifting of the names of vessels under the control of contraband traders makes our task of tracking the *Antonia* across the Atlantic particularly difficult. British records of the capture of such ships would seem to provide the most promising evidence, but the British had no good way of knowing how many name changes lay in the history of the ships that they identified. Perhaps Ferrer and his collaborators changed the name of one of these ships into *Elisa* (or perhaps to *Irene*), which then sailed "under the Portuguese flag" and the other into *Aguila Vengadora* (*Avenging Eagle*) or *Esplorador* and sent both vessels, together with others, to a combined slaving-pirate expedition to Mozambique and Madagascar.[37] About the activities of these ships William Hervey from the British Legation in Spain provided "an account of the entry at the Havana of three slave vessels, the Portuguese Schooner *Eliza*, the Spanish Brig *Esplorador*, and the Spanish Brig *Irene*, after having, it appears, discharged their cargoes elsewhere."

The *"Irene"* is reported to be a sort of partner with the *"Esplorador"*, having been fitted out by the same owners, ironmongers of Havana, named Fernandez for Mozambique, where they were blockaded by a British Vessel of War about three Months.- She sailed from the Havana for that coast on the 7th of July 1837.... The circumstances attending the case of the "Esplorador" are of a revolting nature, and I am instructed to make it the subject of special representation to the Spanish Government.- That Vessel appears to have sailed from the Havana on the 13th of June 1837, under the name of the "Aguilar" or "Aguila Vengadora", supplied with the firearms and ammunition to the great amount. She sailed, it is said, to Madagascar and Mozambique, and not finding any Negroes on the Coast to be bought, forcibly and piratically took from other Vessels there, on the same errand, the Negroes they had collected, and gave the robbed Vessels a quantity of Gunpowder with the recommendation to them to adopt the same course. Having thus got together about 560. Negroes, the report further states that, before they got out of the Range of Monsoons, they encountered very violent whether, which lasted two days, and compelled them to shut down the hatches without being able to give the Negroes, during that time, air or food.- The consequence was, that when the storm abated, and they went to examine their condition, they found about 300 Negroes had perished of suffocation and hunger, and, with the ordinary mortality afterwards attending such voyages, the "Esplorador" arrived at the Habana with only about 200 surviving.[38]

In any event, it seems that Ferrer in 1838 had to replace the loss of a ship or two ships with *Antonia* in their names. Nevertheless he still had enough money to buy 20 percent of a very modern ship—the steamer *Principeño*.

The stretch navigated by the schooner *Amistad* and the (new?) steamer *Principeño* between Havana and Guanaja or Nuevitas in the years until Ferrer's death in 1839 was a portion of Cuba's north coast between Bahia Honda and the keys known as the Jardines del Rey, or King's Garden. For both its location and its seascape it was a coastline well suited for contraband. Indeed, between 1820 and 1860 this stretch of coast and islands was a prime location for the clandestine introduction of captive Africans (called *bozales*) from expeditions organized out of Havana and Matanzas.

Historians have tended to agree that after 1820 Catalans—along with some merchants from Cadiz, France, and the United States—controlled the Cuban slave trade. A small list from the years 1844 to 1857 of purchases and sales of Africans held as slaves reflects the predominance of Catalan names: Don Salvador Camps, from Sitges in Catalonia, Don Juan Barceló, Don Pablo Simon, from Catalonia, Don Juan Milá, from Catalonia, Don Majin Masó y Girar, from Catalonia, Don Pedro Vivó, from Catalonia, Don Ramon Mascaró y Don Manuel Pascual, from Catalonia, Don Juan Sarda, from Catalonia.[39] The saltwater slaves, to use the term from Stephanie Smallwood's book,[40] were often brought from Africa by Portuguese slavers, or the "Portuguese" served as captains, officials, and crews on "Spanish" slave vessels or ships owned by Catalans. In Cuba even today the term *Catalan* has overtones in popular memory, evoking the image of a man who is hard, greedy, and a skinflint. In the case of Ramón Ferrer, however, what we can document is not a stereotyped personality, but a clear predilection for both the illegal and the legal dimensions of Cuba's growing market sectors.

The Deaths of Ramón Ferrer and Celestino Ferrer

In mid June 1839 African captives from Lomboko had arrived on the Cuban coast aboard the notionally Portuguese slave ship *Teçora*. Fortunately for the smugglers, the ship's arrival seems to have escaped the attention of the British members of the Mixed Commission for the Suppression of the slave trade.[41]

Our best description of the events that followed comes, indirectly, from the captives themselves: "[T]he Africans all testify that they left Africa about six months since; were landed under cover of the night at a small village or hamlet near Havana, and after ten or twelve days were taken through Havana by night, by the man who had bought them, named Pipi [Pepe], who has since been satisfactorily proved to be Ruiz."[42] In their testimony we also learn the African names of the girls among the captives: "*Teme,* alias *Juanna, Kague,* alias *Josepha, Margui,* alias *Francisca.*"[43] In addition to highlighting the role of translators, this testimony suggests Cinqué's solidarity with his shipmates—indeed, the term *shipmate* had an equivalent among captives in Cuba of *carabela,* as it did in Brazil with *malungo* and in Dutch Creole with *sibbi.*[44] One of the translators was John Ferry, from New York, whom Lewis Tappan had engaged to speak with the captives.

On June 27, 1839, in Havana, one Martínez (perhaps Pedro Martínez, the famous slave trader?), on behalf of Captain General Ezpeleta, had obtained a *licencia,* which the subsequent court papers refer to as a passport, authorizing the passage by sea to Puerto Príncipe of forty-nine *negros ladinos* owned by Don José Ruiz. A similar document was drawn up listing the ladino names (and omitting the African names) of the three African girls owned by Pedro Montes.[45]

At the beginnings of the history of what would later be known as "The *Amistad* Case," the slaving captain Ramón ("Mongo") Ferrer, along with José Ruiz and Pedro Montes, had evidently obtained the papers through bribery and corruption (the technical term at the time was *cohecho*). In these

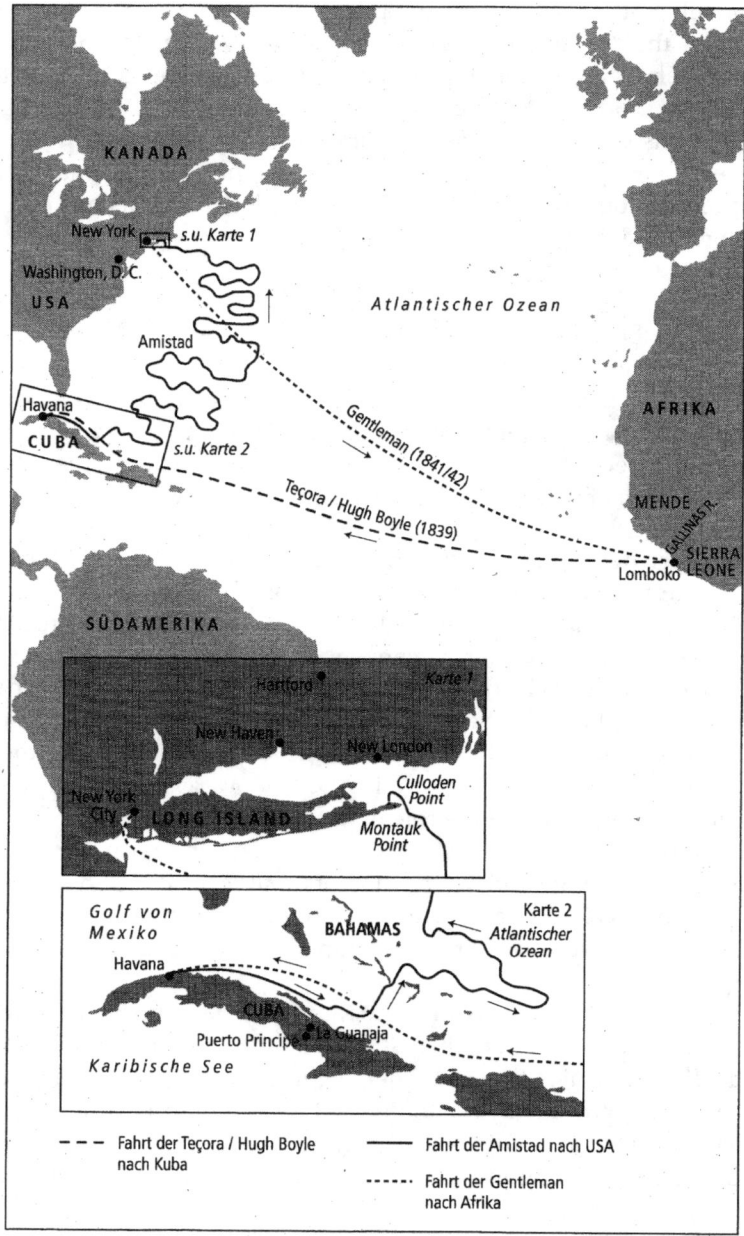

Karte 5: Die Fahrtrouten der *Teçora/Amistad*

Map 8.1. Atlantic itinerary of the schooner *Amistad*. Source: Davis, *Inhuman Bondage,* 25; Jones, *Mutiny on the Amistad,* ii.

papers those captured in Africa were inscribed as negros ladinos—that is to say, born in Cuba (or another colony of Spain, like Puerto Rico), or what today would be denominated *criollo*. The false papers described them as slaves brought from the interior of the island. The captives themselves knew otherwise, describing the cruel transatlantic passage lasting "three moons," and ten more days in the outskirts of Havana.[46]

The processes of corruption and the creation of false papers were later reconstructed in the research of the anthropologist Fernando Ortiz. Ortiz emphasizes the key concession that made possible the manipulation of the system by smugglers: "The ships carrying Africans acquired the privilege, denied to other boats, of entering the port at night."[47] Meanwhile, by the mid 1830s the system of bribery known as *cohecho* was well developed, provoking a serious conflict between the British judges of the Mixed Commission and the Captain General, Miguel Tacón. Ortiz detailed the evasive logical maneuvers in which the bureaucratic networks of the captains general were complicit.

In the case of the *Teçora,* however, there was no intervening capture by the British, and the captives could be landed near Havana without incident. The captives' journey across the Atlantic from Lomboko aboard the *Teçora*—a Portuguese flagship that may actually have been Brazilian (perhaps from Salvador, Bahia), or a Portuguese from Praia (Cape Verde Islands or from Luanda, Angola) or Cuban/Spanish—was thus followed by a coastal passage aboard the *Amistad,* under the control of those who had paid for them in Havana. And it was during this coastal voyage that the famous rebellion occurred.

By early October, with the *Amistad* now in custody in the United States, news of the details of the rebellion reached Cuba via New York, published in an article of the *Noticioso de Ambos Mundos*.[48] The schooner carried two crew members—Jacinto Verdague, from Catalonia, and Manuel Padilla, from Santo Domingo. Celestino was the cook. Also on board was a sixteen-year-old slave of Ferrer, described as a "negrito." The schooner carried two passengers, Don José Ruiz, known as Pepe, from Rodenzo in Old Castille, twenty-four years old, and Don Pedro Montes, born in Tortosa in Catalonia, fifty-eight years old, both residents of Puerto Príncipe, Cuba. The cargo: fifty-three Black men, women, and children, of whom forty-nine (including Cinqué, whose original name was Sengbe Pie)[49] had been bought by Ruiz, and four, including three girls and one boy, had been bought by Montes.[50] On the third day of the journey, after a storm, the only ones awake were the helmsman and the captives, of whom some were in the hold and some in the underdeck. There was a noise, and everyone awakened. Pedro Montes saw that the captives were in the process of killing the cook.[51] We do not know quite what had transpired between the

Figure 8.1. Death of Capt. Ferrer

cook and the captives, but an exchange between them seems to have been the trigger for the uprising.

Neither the testimony nor the film gives us much sense of the solidarities—and tensions—that existed between captives and shipboard crewmembers, some of whom were slaves. The testimony does make clear, however, that questions of food and of eating—both real and imagined—were at the heart of the episode. Ferrer had ordered that the captives be put on half rations of both food and water. Cinqué's testimony links the real atrocities of the captain to a malicious taunt uttered by the cook.[52]

Follow the Money: The Cuban *Amistad* and its Atlantic Networks

From the point of view of the Spanish authorities, the death of the cook Celestino was of little consequence, and the archives thus show few traces of his passage. The death of Captain Ferrer, by contrast, unleashed accusations by his fellow smugglers, and a more or less forced investigation by the *fiscal* (district attorney) of the Comandancia de la Marina (Naval Command) in Havana, followed by a trial concerning the "declaration of inheritance" made by his widow.

The context was contradictory. The normal trading economy in Cuba was built on written texts and legal processes, framed by a system of international treaties concerning the slave trade that had been signed by Spain, more or less to keep up appearances and extract concessions from Britain.[53] As a result, the participants in Ramón Ferrer's contraband network needed to create legal texts and processes of their own to secure their rights, but without calling attention to the conflict between their activities and Spain's treaty commitments. They and their fellow smugglers thus helped draw a veil over the archive of connections between the contraband slave trade and what is generally seen as the technological modernity of the Atlantic world. They could not, of course, keep all of their secrets. But they created a record that contains, in effect, two stories—one avowed, one disavowed.

The most important documentary traces of the investigation carried out by the attorney of the Naval High Command in Havana are two bundles of papers, now held by the Cuban National Archives, one titled "El C.S. Comandante Gral. de Marina sobre la sublevacion ejecutada por los negros que conducia la Goleta costera nombrada la Amistad" and the second a bundle on intestate successions held in the *fondo* Escribanía de Marina under the title "Ferrer, Ramón. Intestado de D. Ramon Ferrer."[54]

The district attorney began his investigations in Guanaja. An assistant port official noted that there was no official notary in Guanaja, so the document was improvised in front of two witnesses. On September 30, 1839, they recorded some basic information. The news of the death of Ferrer had arrived with the passengers of the steamer *Principeño*. Because Ferrer had strong interests in Guanaja, the authorities had called for the opening of an inquiry to determine what those interests might be. They took testimony from Pedro and Agustín Comas and others, as well as from the owners of warehouses in whose care Ferrer might have left merchandise or money.[55]

On that same day, D. Pedro Comas, caulker, from Barcelona, and a resident of Guanaja, declared that Ferrer had left two launches and a new skiff in his care. Agustín Comas confirmed this, and Juan Batista Gutiérrez explained that Ferrer used the launches to unload his larger boats. After Ferrer's death, the two launches—*Criolla* and *Catalana*—were auctioned off, yielding three hundred and thirty pesos, respectively. Such craft, of course, were ideal for unloading captives. The document included a list of services for which Ferrer still owed payment and a declaration by one of Ferrer's associates that he, too, held unpaid debts from Ferrer that the captain had promised to pay upon his return.[56]

Taken together, the evidence in the deposition suggested two key features of Ferrer's business. First, the port of Guanaja was a base of operations, and it was through Ferrer and others like him that the principal merchants of the region established links with traders operating through the port. After Ferrer's death, the cast of characters became clear: the warehouse owners José Antonio de Hecheverría and Juan Ricas, who transported goods to Puerto Príncipe and other zones in the interior; the Catalan brothers Pedro and Agustín Comas, the first a caulker and the second an administrator; the chief registrar Isidro Romero, himself involved in the merchandising of wood and tortoiseshell; the shopkeepers Leandro

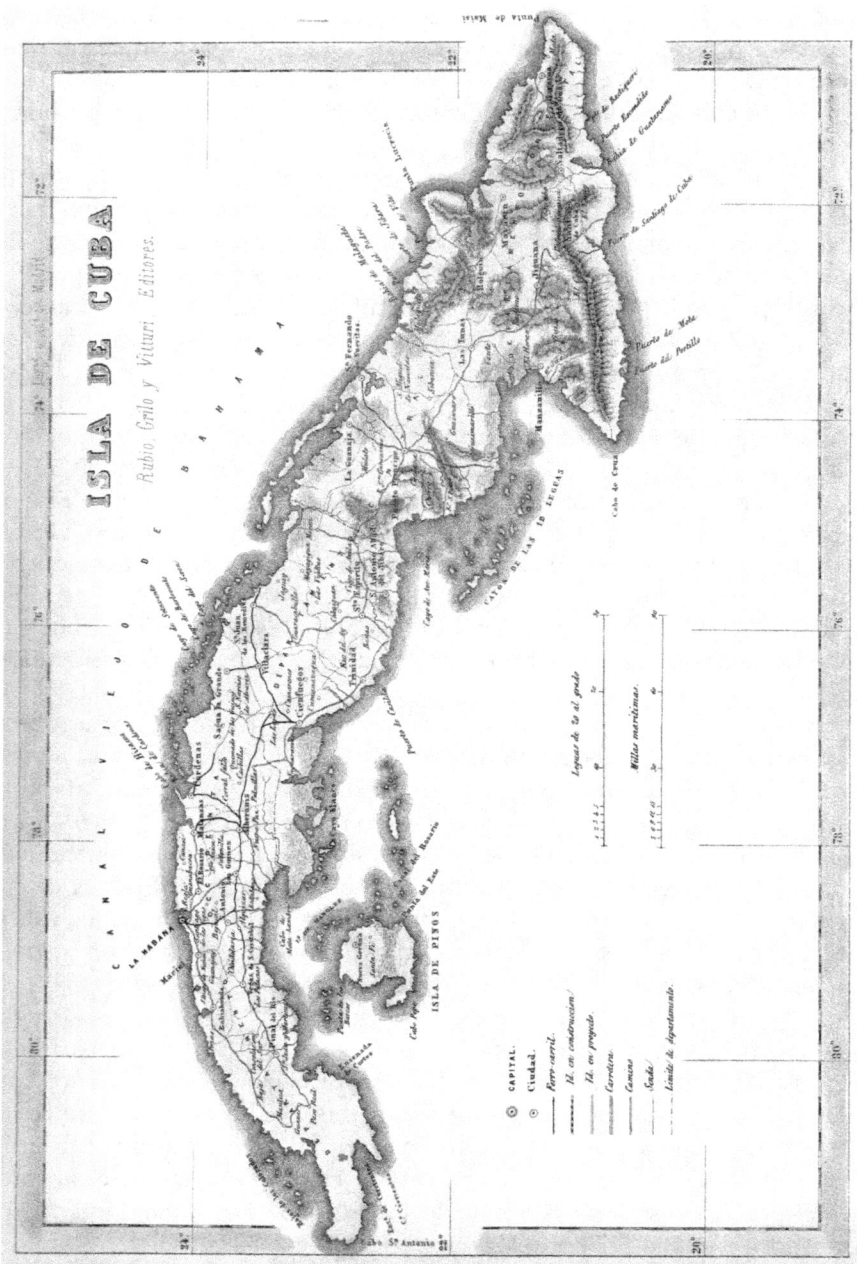

Map 8.2. Map of Cuba showing Guanaja ("Cuba in 1850"). Source: Justo G. Cantero, Los ingenios: colección de vistas de los principales ingenios de la Isla de Cuba. Eds. Luis Miguel García Mora and Antonio Santamaría García. Madrid: Editorial Doce Calles/Fundación MAPFRE, 2005.

Barrueta and Juan Bautista Gutiérrez; and the workman Manuel Braulio and the sailor Jacinto Verdague, who along with Manuel Padilla had survived the uprising aboard the *Amistad*.[57]

Second, we see the veil being brought down over the illegal activities of this network. If we think in terms of legal storytelling, to use the phrase suggested by Carol Rose, we find two stories within these multifaceted narratives. The first story is perfectly empirical and speaks of boats, accounts received, of launches and labors, often expressed in sums of money. The second story is unspoken. We cannot read it in the documents, but everyone involved in the investigation knew it well. This was the story of contraband slaving, of Atlantic Creoles, and of the hidden worlds of Atlantic slavery.[58]

Many of these men were very likely complicit in the activities that had already been denounced in a report issued eighteen years earlier on the occasion of the construction of a fort in Guanaja. That report noted that every day privateers came in and out of the port, bringing goods to the residents of the city and exporting the produce of the region. Guanaja was the point of intersection between the cattle-raising region of Puerto Príncipe (Camagüey)—a huge plain in the center of Cuba, filled with horses and cattle—and the Northern sea, as they called the Gulf of Mexico and the Atlantic. Camagüey in 1827 held 1,124 cattle-raising farms, 120 *hatos* (large grazing lands), 119 *potreros* (intensive stock-raising farms), 720 *sitios de labor* and *estancias* (smaller farms), 195 tobacco farms, and just 85 sugar plantations and 8 coffee plantations. With 61,990 residents, the population represented just 9 percent of the island's total. Slaves numbered 15,704, or 25 percent of the region's population. These slaves, however, were only a small fraction (5.5 percent) of the island's total slave population.

In their inquiry, the authorities sought out the widow of Ramón Ferrer and found her in Havana. First she declined to speak with them on the grounds of an unspecified illness. But she seemed to have been worried about the competing claims of Ferrer's associates, and by 1840 she was willing to collaborate—up to a point—with the colonial officials of the port of Havana. Things were complicated because Ramón Ferrer had died without leaving a will, and no one wanted to speak openly about where the trail of his money might lead. His widow, if she was to avoid losing out to his business associates, needed the support of the district attorney. Her difficult task was to present herself as the poor and humble widow of a humble captain of a boat in the coasting trade, while occluding the magnitude of her husband's contraband activities, even though the only explanation for the size of his estate was precisely the magnitude of those contraband activities. It was those revenues that had enabled him to invest heavily in steamship lines and in the development of the infrastructure of Guanaja. In a closed interrogation of the widow, the district attorney of the

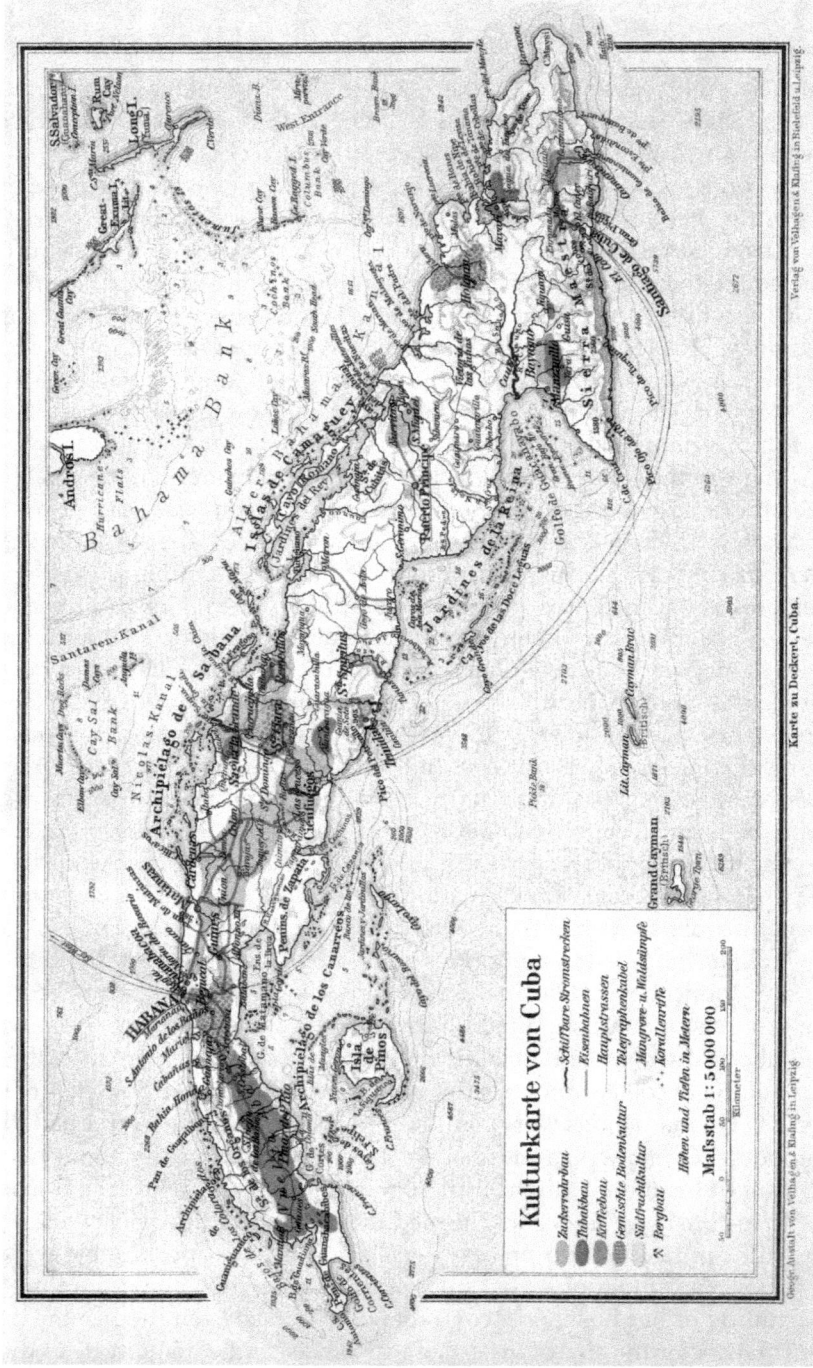

Map 8.3. Map of the Sugar Regions of Cuba. Source: Deckert, E., Cuba, Bitterfeld und Leipzig: Verlag von Velhagen & Klasing, 1899 (Land und Leute. Monographien zur Erdkunde; II), S. 11.

Apostadero de la Habana presented a list of questions to Juana González. The questions began with: "State whether it is true that your deceased spouse worked for many years in trade between this Port and those of Nuevitas and Guanaja"; and continued: "State whether he did so in ships of his own property, including most recently the *Amistad*"; and "State what other boats in addition to the one named were Ferrer's, and whether he had left them in the care of some companion or friend."

Assisted by a lawyer, González answered the first two questions in the affirmative and then replied to the third:

> [I]n addition to the schooner *Amistad* her spouse owned the *Bella Antonia*, which was captured by the English about three years ago, during a voyage to the coast of Africa, and that it was captained by a young man of the Portuguese nation, who as she recalls was named Alberto or Roberto, and that a man named Bascó [or Bassó] who is now in the hospital of San Juan de Dios was a sailor on that ship.[59]

We have already mentioned the *Bella Antonia* and the *Nueva Antonia*, but let us rethink this stunning detail. It is now becoming clear that Ferrer was not just a bit player in the coastal trade in slaves in which many Catalans were involved. He had also, according to his widow, tried his hand in 1836 or 1837 at the so-called big trade—the transatlantic trade—in a ship named after his daughter. This was the trade thought of as a specialty of the "Portuguese." The widow's formula for describing the voyage of the *Bella Antonia*—"la mandaba un joven de nación portuguesa" (it was captained by a young man of the Portuguese nation)—could refer to someone from Portugal, or from Bahia or Recife in Brazil, and even from the Cape Verde Islands or Luanda in Angola. Beside the scenarios already mentioned, other possibilities are that Ferrer organized the trip in Cuba and sent it out under the command of a "Portuguese" captain with experience in the African and transatlantic trade. It is also possible that Ruiz, the purchaser of the captives from the *Teçora*, had known this "Portuguese" captain as well.

The great difficulty here is that as we approach the veiled history, even what seems to be true testimony may be a mixture of truth and intentional falsehood. The empirical portions of Juana González's testimony may be real—as she presents herself as a poor widow and mentions the failure of the transatlantic enterprise. But what the captain's widow does not mention (and what she would have no interest in mentioning) are any possible other (successful and lucrative) transatlantic voyages of the *Bella Antonia* or even, as mentioned above, the *Nueva Antonia* before her shipwreck, or the steamer *Principeño*. As smugglers, of course, they could have changed flag and name with some frequency—a common occurrence after the signing of the 1835 treaty between Great Britain and Spain.

A short article in the *New York Journal of Commerce* from July 1839, immediately after the rebellion, opens even another possibility: "A Spanish schr. [schooner] that sailed hence a few days since for Neuvitas [Nuevitas, near La Guanaja] near Principe, had on board a valuable cargo, some passengers, and forty negro slaves. These latter rose upon passengers and crew,—two of the latter escaping in the boat to tell of the disaster. A schr. of war sailed immediately, but I am of opinion she will be too late, as it is probable the negroes have run the schr. ashore and fled to the woods. It is said that the Captain, owner of the schr., was warned, previous to sailing, to keep a look out for the negroes, as they had attempted to rise and take the vessel in which they were brought from Africa. He of course was careless, and has thereby lost life and property. The same captain lost his vessel in a squall some three years since, and narrowly escaped with his life at that time."[60] The author of this piece seems to have known quite a lot about Ferrer, including the shipwreck to which the *Diario de la Marina* had made reference. So we know that Ferrer had eventually lost the two ships with *Antonia* in their names—one in a squall (*La Nueva Antonia*) and the second (*La Bella Antonia*) on the shores of West Africa in 1837 or early 1837. This is another sensation. It is even remotely possible—though very difficult to determine—that the elusive *Teçora* was the *Bella Antonia* under another name. The *Teçora* had brought the *Amistad* captives from Lomboko near Río Gallinas, the region of operations in Africa of one of the very big *negreros* (slave dealers) from Havana named Pedro Blanco.

With this voyage (or possibly voyages) of the *Bella Antonia*, we touch on one of the most important—and intentionally hidden—aspects of interaction (or, to use Fernando Ortiz's word, *transculturation*) between Cuban culture and Brazilian-African culture. For the hidden Atlantic, including West Africa and parts of East Africa, as the base of emerging Western capitalism was the space of the complex culture of the Atlantic-African trade, of ships, captains, and traders from the Portuguese-Iberian world. Whereas the networks in Cuba were largely under the control of "Catalans," the transatlantic voyages were under the control of "Portuguese"—each term, of course, interpreted quite broadly to include Cubans of Spanish and Catalan descent, and Portuguese-speaking Brazilians. They, in turn, were surrounded by the even less visible Atlantic Creoles who worked as interpreters, guards, sailors, cooks, and even as musicians.[61]

What needs special emphasis here is that the flow of people and information did not just go in the east-west direction that is so familiar to us from the charts showing the slave trade to the Americas. It also went in the other direction, in voyages that carried captains and sailors, again and again, *from* the Americas to the Atlantic coast of Africa. Thus much of the transculturation brought the Atlantic Creoles—white and black—who were more or less intentional participants in the trade into contact on the coast of Africa with the black victims of the trade. For Ramón Ferrer, however, this all came to an abrupt end, first with the failure of the voyage of the *Bella Antonia* and then with his own death at the hands of the captives aboard the *Amistad*.

The magnitude of the "Portuguese" presence in the Cuba trade is striking. During the year 1837 there were forty-four ships that entered into the port of Havana flying the Portuguese flag: four frigates, sixteen schooners with a square-rigged foremast (*bergantines*), and twenty-four other schooners.[62] The role of the Portuguese ships becomes clearer in the press, particularly the *Diario de la Habana*. Phrases in the shipping news give clues of engagement in the contraband trade. For example, describing the activity in the port of Matanzas, the *Diario* described the arrival of the Portuguese ship *Ulises*, after a voyage of fifty days from Ayuda (Whydah), under captain Fernández, "en lastre" for D. Francisco Morell." The phrase *en lastre*—in ballast—was a kind of code, revealing to readers that this was a slaving voyage, because there would be little reason for a ship to sail with nothing but ballast in its hold from the coast of Africa to the port of Havana. The phrase appears again a few weeks later for a ship entering Havana: "From Matanzas ... the Portuguese schooner *Constitución*, captain Rodríguez, 80 tons, in ballast, for Martínez and Company." Then, the same month, on March 23: "From Matanzas, in a day, the Portuguese schooner *Victoria*, Captain Acuña, 97 tons, in ballast, for the captain."[63] The boldest use of the technical term *en lastre* appears in a rejection of a claim made by the British judges of the Mixed Court in Havana. The Captain General Miguel Tacón himself, after the obligatory inquiry in the case of such a denunciation, wrote to the British judges that he had no doubt of the goodwill of the Spanish captain and his officers, who assured everyone that after taking a cargo of rum to Cabinda they continued to Luanda to outfit the ship for a return voyage to Havana ... in ballast.[64]

The unwitting reader would imagine these Portuguese ships busily hauling loads of rock or bricks across the Atlantic; the reader in the know was well aware that cargos of captive Africans were aboard. The case is sealed when we note that Martínez and Co. of Havana and Francisco Morell of Matanzas, mentioned as consignees in the newspapers, were along with Pedro Blanco and Pedro José de Zulueta (and later his nephew Julián de Zulueta) perhaps the most important slave traders in the Northern Atlantic.[65]

Indeed, Pedro Martínez was the person to whom the captives later taken on board the *Amistad* had been consigned. And it was in this same period of the arrival of the Portuguese ship *Constitución* that we find the *Teçora* transporting captives to the *barracones* of Martínez and Company, where they would be purchased by José Ruiz Carrías. The document presented to the authorities in Havana by the Camagüeyan merchant Ruiz to board the schooner *Amistad* listed Martínez and Company as the legal seller of the captives. And the document was signed and certified by the captain general of the island, Joaquín de Ezpleta. In the document, of course, the African captives were presented as ladino slaves.[66] The slavers and smugglers were also using another term for hiding their cargos—*bulto* (bundle, sheaf). We do not know if by then Ramón Ferrer was in command of the *Principeño*. What we do know for certain is that by the end of 1838 and the beginning of 1839 Ramón Ferrer was again in command of the *Amistad,* making the Havana–La Guanaja run. And in this year of 1838 the contraband slave trade to Cuba reached such heights that Domingo del Monte wrote to his friend José Antonio Saco, the first great American historian of slavery, as follows: "From Havana there leave every year on average 36 ships, and from Matanzas various Catalans send another 15 or 20."[67]

At the beginning of 1838 the poet Felix Tanco Bosmenil wrote to Del Monte about the trade, "In these last days two ships from Africa landed happily, carrying about 800 [captives]." Then, on April 13, "Three expeditions are about to land on the coast with at least 1200 blacks: the schooners *La Gata, La Esperimenta,* and the *Feliz.*"[68] The merchants Francisco Morell, Jayme Padrines, Juan de la Cavana Fuentes, and Jaime Badia were among those who were implicated in the illegal trade in Matanzas, and through the so-called *ruta del tasajo* (cured meat route), to Catalonia, Spain, Cuba, South America (Angostura/Ciudad Bolívar, Buenos Aires, Montevideo), and Africa.[69]

The funds for trips like Ferrer's came from traffickers like José Ruiz Carrías of the *Amistad,* himself the nephew of the merchant Saturnino Carrías. Captives would then be sold with fully legal documents to propertied buyers in the rural and urban districts of Camagüey.

Conclusion: Cuba, Slaving, Technological Modernity, and the Hidden Atlantic

The commercial web revealed in the notarial and other documents involving Ramón Ferrer does more than change our image of the captain of *Amistad,* who is usually figured simply as the victim of a homicide. First of all, it brings back the Atlantic, the Atlantization, and especially the hidden Atlantic of the nineteenth century into American history. It also casts a bright and harsh light on the sources of capital for Cuba's infrastructural development—particularly railroads and steamship lines. It casts an equally bright light on the mobility that was necessary to produce that capital. At the same time, Ferrer's network of global mobility linked Cuba to Africa and to the industrial revolution in the West, providing another vantage point from which to look at the much-discussed thesis of Eric Williams on the role of slavery and slave trading in the European and American industrial revolution. In this case, it is the interwoven economies of Cuba, the United States, and Brazil and their African partners that are in the forefront of the hidden Atlantic, rather than England.[70] The Cuban, the Catalan, the Portuguese, and the Atlantic dimensions of the *Amistad* story, moreover, draw attention to two of the most important hidden dimensions of the transatlantic trade in this period: the networks of "Spanish" (Cuban, Catalan, etc.) and "Portuguese" (Brazilian, Angolan, Cape Verdian, etc.) slavers, negreros, *mongos, negreiros,* and smugglers, as well as the systematic financial structure of deceit required for the contraband trade and the multiple forms of resistance by captives themselves.[71]

What were the consequences for Cuba? Cuban slave society, fueled by the investments and hidden profits of the negreros, reached its peak between 1841 and 1861. After the crisis of 1857 and the Ten Years War (1868–1878), when the transatlantic slave trade was suppressed, many negreros took over the most modern sugar mills and converted them into ever more modern giant sugar factories. Some of the men behind Ferrer belonged to this group of the new extremely conservative Cuban-Spanish-Catalan elite.

None of the *Amistad* captives ever returned to Cuba. José "Pipi" Ruiz, the nephew of the big trader Saturnino Carrías, continued his nasty business. His networks let us discern that, despite the rebellion, the business of slaving was a going concern and brought good profits. His uncle and Pipi were investors in the Ferrocarril de Nuevitas (the railway from Puerto Príncipe to Nuevitas). Around its principal promoter, the famous "Lugareño" Gaspar Betancourt Cisneros, gathered the merchants Saturnino Carrías, Francisco de Iraola, Feliciano Carnesolta, Juan Auger, and others.[72] By this time, Pedro Montes (witness of the rebellion), Saturnino Carrías, José Ruiz Carrías, "Anglada, Rivas y Ca.," Ramón Bermejo, Tiburcio Sandoval, and Alejandro Bastian, all with branches at Puerto Príncipe, were signatories of the *Amistad*. It was a heterogeneous group of traders, in terms of economic strength, but able to pressure the city council. Some focused their activities on the renovation of the sugar plantations by lending money to planters. Others, such as Saturnino Carrias, diversified their business portfolios by supplying the planters of Nuevitas in exchange for their sugar and molasses.[73] Between 1836 and 1839 Carrías lent money for the building of estates; supplied flour; collected debts paid in *tabaco torcido* or *tabaco elaborado* at Yara; sold to grocery stores, warehouses, and other shops; lent money with interest; bought shares of Camagüey railways (Ferrocarril de Nuevitas); and expanded business, especially in Nuevitas and Santa Cruz del Sur.[74]

Very interesting are the connections established by the firm "Saturnino Carrías and Company" from 1837, both in the town of Trinidad and in its magnificent valley of sugar mills in the booming sugar-region of Cienfuegos.[75] All this seems to suggest the extension of the illegal slave trade to the southern coast of Cuba. He also conducted business with "Sres. Zulueta & Company" in 1839 to carry goods from Liverpool to the port of Santa Cruz del Sur.[76] Later in 1842, through traders Trinidad, "Apezteguía, Zaldo and Cia," he purchased the harvest of the sugar plantation *Santa Marta* in the vicinity of Cienfuegos, in those days owned by the Jiménez family from Matanzas.[77] In this transaction Julián Zulueta stands out as the main creditor, one of the most active negreros in the world by then. In 1840 Zulueta provided $18,884 to the brothers Acea at Cienfuegos for the conversion of a coffee mill into a sugar mill (ingenio).[78] Cienfuegos became the stage for three active players in the slave trade: Pedro Blanco, Julián Zulueta, and Saturnino Carrías, whose ties and networks were exposed by the rebellion of the schooner *Amistad*.

We do not have more information about the fate of Ferrer's widow, Juana González. One of the partners of Ferrer, Juan Martorell y Peña, occupied by the end of his career the lucrative position as investor and entrepreneur of a steamer fleet in Spain, like many other slavers and negreros who transferred their capitals to the *Madre Patria* after 1857 or 1868.[79]

We have found some direct traces of Pedro Montes. By the end of the judicial proceedings in the United States, the value of the so-called assets aboard the *Amistad* had been declared null and void, as the natural rights of the African captives superseded the imagined property rights of a smuggler. Montes nonetheless conveyed a power of attorney to one C. Cayetano Corvizón to defend his interests against both the naval district attorney (*Fiscalía de la Marina*) and against his creditors.[80]

These references are among the rare acknowledgments of the rebellion led by Cinqué that appear in the commercial documents in Cuba. Along with the deaths of Ramón Ferrer and the cook named Celestino (who mocked the captives rather than joining forces with them), the last will and testament of Pedro Montes suggests the ways in which the tumultuous risks, costs, and brutality of the slave trade came to be hidden.

Viewed from this angle, the *Amistad* case reminds us of some things that we already knew and suggests others that we may often overlook. The so-called modernity of the West directly involved not only the familiar North American, British, and European actors, but also the Creole cultures of the hidden Atlantic, West Africa, Brazil, and the island of Cuba, the hundreds of thousands of captives from Africa who reached its shores, and their captors in Africa—in sum, the whole Atlantic network of slaving. And Cuba, like other plantation societies, functioned simultaneously as a place of investment, secret accumulation, profit, and production, and as a space of intense transculturation between Africa and the Americas, operating through the vast machine of slaving.[81] At this stage of globalization in the nineteenth century, Cuba was not a secluded territory but, like many other plantation and slave societies, an enclave of Atlantization created through colonial slaving, creolization, diaspora, and migration.[82]

Notes

The authors thank Rebecca J. Scott for assistance with translation and editing, as well as Bárbara Danzie, *archivera por excelencia del Archivo Nacional de Cuba*.

1. An earlier version of this appeared in Spanish: Michael Zeuske and Orlando García Martínez, "La Amistad de Cuba. Ramón Ferrer, contrabando de esclavos, captividad y modernidad atlántica," *Caribbean Studies* 37 (January–June 2009): 119–187. The research and the travel for this essay were made possible by a research grant of DFG (Deutsche Forschungsgemeinschaft, 2007–2010: ZE 302/15-1 "Atlantischer Sklavenhandel als Schmuggel: Ramón Ferrer und die 'Amistad,' 1830-1840") and a research fellowship of the Gilder Lehrman Center for the Study of Slavery, Resistance, and Abolition, Yale University (2008). For recent treatments of the *Amistad*, see Michael Zeuske, *Die Geschichte der Amistad. Sklavenhandel und Menschenschmuggel auf dem Atlantik im 19. Jahrhundert* (Stuttgart, 2012); and Marcus Rediker, *The Amistad Rebellion: An Atlantic Odyssey of Slavery and Freedom* (New York, 2012).
2. José Antonio Saco quoted in Carmen Almodóvar Muñoz, ed., *Antología crítica de la historiografía cubana*, 2 vols. (Havana, 1986–1989), 1, 402.
3. The most complete book about the Amistad as part of U.S. national history is Howard Jones, *Mutiny on the "Amistad": The Saga of a Slave Revolt and Its Impact on American Abolition, Law, and Diplomacy* (New York, 1997); see also the well-researched piece about the African dimensions and the story of Cinqué and the *Amistad* captives in Africa after 1842 in Joseph Yannielli, "Cinqué the Slave Trader: Some New Evidence on an Old Controversy," *Common-Place* 10 (October 2009): http://common-place.org/vol-10/no-01/yannielli/.
4. Michael Zeuske, "Tres Amistades (o más)—varias películas en una," *Caribbean Studies* 36 (July–December 2008): 271–276.
5. David Brion Davis, "The Amistad Test of Law and Justice," in *Inhuman Bondage: The Rise and Fall of Slavery in the New World* (New York, 2006), 12–26.
6. The main corpus of the new archival material about the *Amistad* case belongs to Cuban archives: Archivo Nacional de Cuba (ANC), Gobierno Superior Civil (GSC), legajo (leg.). 1272, número (no.) 49909 (Julio de 1839): "El C.S. Comandante Gral. de Marina sobre la sublevacion ejecutada por los negros que conducia la Goleta costera nombrada la Amistad"; ANC, Escribanía de Marina, leg. 39, no. 385 (1839): "Ferrer, Ramón. Intestado de D. Ramon Ferrer"; ANC, Fondo Miscelanea (FM), leg. 2344, no. Aa (1836): "Entrada de la Goleta Española Cos.[ter]a Amistad su patron D.n Damian Ferrer procedente de la Habana con diez y seis permisos. Anclada en Guanaja el 18 de Feb.o"; ANC, FM, leg. 2462, no. F (1836): "Entrada de la Goleta Española Cos.tera Amistad. su

patron D. Ramon Ferrer; proced.te de la Habana con 24: permisos. Anclada en Guanaja el 8. de Diciembre"; Archivo Histórico Provincial de Camagüey (AHPCam), Protocolos Notariales Manuel Martínez Valdés, fondo 155, tomo 1834–1835; see also the documents from Madrid: Archivo Histórico Nacional (AHN) Madrid, Estado, Trata de negros, leg. 8024/30: "Negros, 1838. Buque de Vapor Principeño. Los comisarios Británicos dán parte del desembarco que ha efectuado de negros vozales en la costa de Tallapiedra"; see also: "Dec.on del testigo D. Ramon Ferrer [Declaración del testigo Don Ramón Ferrer]," in ibid., leg. 8024/30, no. 6: "Testimonio dela sumaria formada á conseq.a de queja producida p.r los Com.s de S.M.B contra el barco de vapor Principeño sobre haber introducido en este puerto negros bozales," La Habana, 22 May 1838, Juan B. Topete.
7. Different dates for the end of the transatlantic slave traffic are given, but 1866 and 1873 are the most usual. See David R. Murray, *Odious Commerce: Britain, Spain and the Abolition of the Cuban Slave Trade* (Cambridge, 1980). The Cuban historian José Luciano Franco, who had access to other forms of memory, wrote in a footnote at the end of the chapter about the slave-trading oligarchy in Cuba: "Conocí personalmente en 1907, en La Habana, a una africana que llamaban popularmente María la Conguita, residente en el cuarto 36 de la casa de vecindad 'Los Nichos,' Belascoaín 3; según nos contó, había sido traída a Cuba con otros africanos y vendida como esclava en 1878." See Franco, *Comercio clandestino de esclavos* (Havana, 1996), 178, n. 64. For further attempts by Cuban historians to analyze the "slavery bourgeoisie," see María del Carmen Barcia Zequeira, *Burguesía esclavista y abolición* (Havana, 1987); and Diana Iznaga, *La burguesía esclavista cubana* (Havana, 1987).
8. See also Lisa A. Lindsay, *Captives as Commodities: The Transatlantic Slave Trade* (New York, 2007), 5.
9. Javier Laviña and Michael Zeuske, "Failures of Atlantization: First Slaveries in Venezuela and Nueva Granada," *Review: A Journal of the Fernand Braudel Center* XXXI, no. 3 (2008): 297–343.
10. Archivo General de Indias (AGI) Sevilla, Spain, Ultramar, 358 (1830), "Licencias de embarque a la isla de Cuba"; AGI, Santo Domingo, leg. 2206, 1833–1834: "Registros y Expedientes sobre licencias de embarque: Cuba"; AGI, Santo Domingo, leg. 2203, 1821–1823: "Registros y Expedientes sobre licencias de embarque: Cuba"; AGI, Santo Domingo, leg. 2204, 1823–1829: "Registros y Expedientes sobre licencias de embarque: Cuba"; AGI, Santo Domingo, leg. 2205, 1830: "Registros y Expedientes sobre licencias de embarque: Cuba."
11. In a "Declaración de testigo" in 1838 Ramón Ferrer testified that he was forty years old, putting his birth date in 1797 or 1798. See: AHN, Estado, Trata de negros, leg. 8024/30: "Negros, 1838. Buque de Vapor Principeño. Los comisarios Británicos dán parte del desembarco que ha efectuado de negros vozales en la costa de Tallapiedra"; and "Dec.on del testigo D. Ramon Ferrer [Declaración del testigo Don Ramón Ferrer]," in ibid., leg. 8024/30, no. 6: "Testimonio dela sumaria formada á conseq.a de queja producida p.r los Com.s de S.M.B contra el barco de vapor Principeño sobre haber introducido en este puerto negros bozales," La Habana, 22 May 1838, Juan B. Topete. In the archive of Ibiza, colleagues and historians found in 2011 the following genealogical information about Ramon Ferrer in the Archivo de la parroquia de Sant Elm (San Telmo) from the Town of Eivissa (Ibiza): "Damià Ferrer, patrón de barco de profesión; casado en 1673 con Francesca Costa, tuvieron a su hijo: Damià Ferrer Costa, nacido en 1679, patrón de barco de profesión; casado en [?] con Caterina Martí Xareco, tuvieron a su hijo: Damià Ferrer Martí, nacido en 1713, patrón de barco de profesión; casado en 1736 con Joana Riusec Calbet, tuvieron a su hijo: [the fathers] Ramon Ferrer Riusec, nacido en 1758, no consta la profesión; casado en 1785 con Antònia Ferrer Ros, tuvieron a sus hijos: Francesc Ferrer Ferrer, nacido en 1789; Damià Ferrer Ferrer, nacido en 1794; Ramon Ferrer Ferrer, nacido en 1797 [this is our Ferrer]," in *Padrones parroquiales, Archivo de la parroquia de*

Sant Elm, Eivissa (Ibiza) (without pagination). We would like to thank the *canónigo* and *historiador* Joan Planells Ripoll (Ibiza) and historian Antoni Ferrer Abárzuza. See Joan Planells Ripoll, "Mariners i corsaris de les Pitiüses," *Revista Eivissa*, no. 39 (November 2002): 4–10.

12. For this scholarship, see Franco, *Comercio clandestino de esclavos*; Josep Maria Fradera, "La participacio catalana en el trafic d'esclaus, 1789–1845," *Recerques*, no. 16 (1984): 119–139; Enrique Sosa Rodríguez, *Negreros, catalanes y gaditanos en la trata cubana, 1827–1833* (Havana, 1998).
13. AGI Sevilla, Ultramar, 358 (1830), Licencias de embarque a la isla de Cuba, no. 69, "Ramón Ferrer y Xifra", f. 1r–9r, here f.1r.
14. Ibid., f. 9r.
15. Eduardo Marrero Cruz, "Traficantes de esclavos y chinos," in *Julián de Zulueta y Amondo. Promotor del capitalismo en Cuba* (Havana, 2006).
16. The document reads: "D.n. Ramon Ferrer, natural de Ibizá una de las Islas Valeares hijo legítimo de D. Ramon y D.a Antonia Ferrer, y a Juana Fomara Gonzalez natural del referido pueblo [Regla] hija legítima de D.n. Jose, y de D.a María de Regla Garcia"; see ANC, Escribanía de Marina, leg. 39, no. 385 (1839): "Ferrer, Ramón. Intestado de D. Ramon Ferrer," f. 2r. There are also copies of the certificates of baptism of the two daughters.
17. ANC, Fondo Miscelanea (FM), leg. 2344, no. Aa (1836): "Entrada de la Goleta Española Cos.[ter]ª Amistad su patron D.ⁿ Damian Ferrer procedente de la Habana con diez y seis permisos. Anclada en Guanaja el 18 de Feb.º"; ANC, FM, leg. 2462, no. F (1836): "Entrada de la Goleta Española Cos.tera Amistad. su patron D. Ramon Ferrer; proced.ᵗᵉ de la Habana con 24: permisos. Anclada en Guanaja el 8. de Diciembre."
18. Archivo Histórico Provincial de Camagüey (AHPCam), Protocolos Notariales Manuel Martínez Valdés, fondo 155, tomo 1834–1835, "Venta R.l [Real]," f. 123r., Puerto Príncipe, 26 September 1834.
19. Ibid., "Venta r.l," f. 125r–125v., Puerto Príncipe, 29 September 1834.
20. ANC, FM, leg. 2344, no. Aa (1836): "Entrada de la Goleta Española Cos.[ter]ª Amistad su patron D.ⁿ Damian Ferrer procedente de la Habana con diez y seis permisos. Anclada en Guanaja el 18 de Feb.º."
21. Ibid., leg. 2462, no. F (1836): "Entrada de la Goleta Española Cos.tera Amistad. su patron D. Ramon Ferrer; proced.ᵗᵉ de la Habana con 24: permisos. Anclada en Guanaja el 8. de Diciembre."
22. For another discussion of the *Amistad* and the coastal traffic, see Rediker, *The Amistad Rebellion*, 65–71.
23. ANC, FM, leg. 2462, no. F (1836): "Entrada de la Goleta Española Cos.tera Amistad. su patron D. Ramon Ferrer; proced.ᵗᵉ de la Habana con 24: permisos. Anclada en Guanaja el 8. de Diciembre."
24. ANC, Gobierno Superior Civil (GSC), leg. 1272, no. 49909 (Julio de 1839): "El C.S. Comandante Gral. de Marina sobre la sublevacion ejecutada por los negros que conducia la Goleta costera nombrada la Amistad."
25. ANC, FM, leg. 2462, no. F (1836): "Entrada de la Goleta Española Cos.tera Amistad. su patron D. Ramon Ferrer; proced.ᵗᵉ de la Habana con 24: permisos. Anclada en Guanaja el 8. de Diciembre."
26. ANC, Escribania de Marina, leg. 40, no. 400 (1840). Ferrer, Ramón, Incidente al intestado de D. Ramón Ferrer—formado para tratar del pago hecho á D. Francisco Rediés (Fotos "Ramón Ferrer." no. 3574).
27. "Habana. Extracto de una carta particular, Ingenio Jesús María de la Siguapa y junio 2 de 1836," *Diario de la Habana*, Havana, June 10, 1836, 2. The article is unsigned, but we have been able to deduce that the owner of the ingenio wrote it.
28. See John W. Barber, ed., *A History of the Amistad Captives* (New Haven, 1840), reprinted in *Journal of the New Haven Colony Historical Society* 36 (Spring 1990): 6. Barber's original

work can be found in the Beinecke Rare Books and Manuscript Library, Yale University, New Haven, Cb 79110. See also Rediker, *The Amistad Rebellion*, chap. 2.

29. "Protection for Celestino Ferrer" [translation from the original in Spanish], in *Message from the President of the United States to the two Houses of Congress, at the Commencement of the First Session of the Twenty-Sixth Congress* (Washington, 1839), 49.
30. Ibid.; see also "Protection for Jacinto Verdagne [sic]," in ibid., p. 49–50.
31. This steamer *Principeño* appears twice in http://www.slavevoyages.org: first as voyage 46676 (with a former name, Yumurí) and under steamer *Principeño* under the number 46679.
32. AHN Madrid, Estado, Trata de negros, leg. 8024/30, no. 5: carta de Joaquin de Espeleta desde la Habana, 30 May 1838 al primer Secretario de Estado en Madrid: "Los comisarios de S.M.B.ca me oficiaron con fecha de 4. del corriente ... el desembarco verificado en estas Costas p.r un buque q.e se supone ser el bergantin Ruso Gollupe, de un numero de negros bozales, los q.e fueron conducidos á este puerto en el vapor Principeño, q.e en numero de mas de trescientos los desembarcó en un muelle cerca de la Factoria." See also "Dec.on del testigo D. Ramon Ferrer [Declaración del testigo Don Ramón Ferrer]," in ibid., leg. 8024/30, no. 6: "Testimonio dela sumaria formada á conseq.a de queja producida p.r los Com.s [Comisarios] de S.M.B [Su Majestad Británica] contra el barco de vapor Principeño sobre haber introducido en este puerto negros bozales," La Habana, 22 May 1838, Juan B. Topete.
33. AHN Madrid, Estado, Trata de negros, leg. 8024/30, no. 5.
34. Ferrer "construyó [la *Amistad*] en el puerto de Bajas, Nuevitas, con permiso de esta Comandancia General de Marina del Apostadero de la Habana y navegaba en ella de Patrón." [Ferrer "built [the *Amistad*] in the port of Bajas, in Nuevitas, with the permission of the General Commandant of the Navy of the Port of Havana, and he sailed her as owner."] Bajas was a harbor with naval construction facilities near Ferrer's home base, the port of La Guanaja, on the north coast of Puerto del Príncipe (Camagüey). See Letter from Manuel de Cañas, Comandancia General de la Marina del Apostadero de la Habana al Excmo. Sor. Gobernador y Capitan General, La Habana, 16 February 1841, in: Gobierno Superior Civil, leg. (caja) 1272, no. 49909: "Expediente relativo a sublevación ejecutada por negros conducidos en la Goleta Amistad (Julio 1839)" (without foliation). About the hypothesis of the port of construction, see Christopher Martin, *The Amistad Affair* (London, 1970), 30–33; Jones, "The Mutiny," in *Mutiny on the Amistad*, 14–30, 23: "built and fitted in Baltimore for coastal slave trade"; Hugh Thomas, *The Slave Trade: The History of the Atlantic Slave Trade 1440–1870* (London, 1997), 718; Quentin Snediker, "Searching for the Historic Amistad," *The Log of Mystic Seaport* 49 (Spring 1998): 107–108.
35. ANC, Escribanía de Marina, leg. 39, no. 385 (1839): "Ferrer, Ramón. Intestado de D. Ramon Ferrer," f. 25r/v: Declaración de Juan Bautista Gutierrez, Guanaja, 30. September 1839.
36. "Interrogatorio cerrado q.e produce el fiscal de guerra de Marina del Apostadero á consecuencia de los autos del intestado de D. Ramon Ferrer para q.e a su tenor sea examinada la viuda albacea D.a Juana Gonzalez," en: ANC, Escribanía de Marina, leg. 39, no. 385 (1839): "Ferrer, Ramón. Intestado de D. Ramon Ferrer," f. 92r–97v, La Habana, pueblo de Regla, 4 June 1840, en la morada de D.a Juana Gonzalez.
37. Here are the clues that link these ship names to the *Principeño*: In the AHN in Madrid under the documents mentioning all ship names beginning with the letter A and B can be found this notice: "1838 Bergantin Aguila Vengadora. Vide [See]Vapor Principeño" (in AHN, Estado, Trata de negros, leg. 8015/32). Under the file that contains the ships whose names begin with V is a whole bundle of documents in which the two ships *Principeño* and *Aguila Vengadora* are mentioned together. See AHN, Estado, Trata de negros, leg. 8024/30: "Negros, 1838. Buque de Vapor Principeño. Los comisarios Británicos dán

parte del desembarco que ha efectuado de negros vozales en la costa de Tallapiedra." The same happens under the documents under letter D, E, G, H, and I. Under 8018/27 can be found a notice: "Negros. 1838. Escuna—Eliza vide Vapor Principeño," under 8018/28: "Negros. 1838. Bergantin Esplorador. Capitan D. Blas Mariano Gorde. Los Comisarios B.cos denuncian como procedente de la Costa de Africa vide Vapor—Principeño," and under 8020/21: "Negros. 1838. Bergantin—Irene, Capitan Ageo vide Vapor Principeño." This seems to give us clues to Ferrer's networks and to his list of names for his ships. Also in 1838 under 8019/37 "Negros. 1838. Bergantin Gollup vide Vapor Principeño."
38. Ibid., leg. 8024/30, no. 24: letter from William Hervey, British Legation in Spain, Madrid, and September 11, 1838 to the Duke of Trias. There is a third, less likely, possible match: the slave ship *Antonia* was captured in 1837 on a middle passage voyage from Río Congo to Trinidad de Cuba with 185 captives (90 men, 62 boys, and 33 girls); the captain was an Augusto José Victorio, alias Geronimo Giscafre. "Esped.te [Expediente] de la detencion de la goleta Mercante Española Antonia con cargam.to [cargamento] de negros bozales p.r el bergantin de Grra. Yngles Rasser su comand.te Santiago Hope," La Habana, September 5, 1837, in the National Archives, Kew (TNA), Foreign Office (FO) 313 Archives of Havana Slave Trade Commission, Nr. 48 Captured Ships (1836–1839).
39. In one record, Milá was listed as being from Asturias. Archivo Histórico Provincial de Santiago de Cuba (AHPStA), Fondo Protocolos, Escribanía Heraclio García, Bd. 210 (1844), f. 128r/128v: "Venta de esclavos," Manuel Collazo a favor de D. Salvador Camps, Santiago de Cuba, 29 October 1844; ibid., Escribanía de Lasso, vol. 489 (1857), f. 9r/v: "Venta de esclavos," D.a Micaela Gonzalez á D.n Juan Barcelo, Santiago de Cuba, 19 January 1857; así como: ibid., f. 9v/10r: "Venta de esclavo," D.a Manuela Diaz á D.n Juan Barceló, Santiago de Cuba, 19 January 1857; ibid., f. 21v: "Venta de esclava," D.n Pablo Simon á D.n Ruperto Galan, Santiago de Cuba, 10 February 1857; ibid., f. 37r/v: "Venta de esclavos," D.a Dominga Acosta á D.n Juan Milá, Santiago de Cuba, 12 March1857; ibid., f. 51r/v: "Venta de esclavo," Lic. D. Lino Guerra á D. Juan Milá, Santiago de Cuba, 17 April 1857; ibid., f. 52v/53v: "Venta de esclavas," M.ma Juana Petit á D.n Majin Masó y Girar, Santiago de Cuba, 18 April 1857. Madama Petit es también "natural de Sto. Domingo en la parte francesa"; ibid., f. 91v/92r: "Venta de esclavas," D.n Eduardo Escudero á Pedro Vivó, Santiago de Cuba, 16 July 1857; ibid., f. 98r/v: "Venta de esclavo," D.n Gregorio Sta Ana á Pedro Vivó, Santiago de Cuba, 7 August 1857; ibid., f. 107v: "Venta de esclavo," D. Heraclio Garcia á D. Ramon Mascaro y D. Manuel Pascual, Santiago de Cuba, 16 July 1857; ibid., f. 110v/111r: "Venta de esclavo," D.a Ysabel Bell de Herrera á D. Ramon Mascaró y D. Manuel Pascual, Santiago de Cuba, 2 September 1857; ibid., f. 118v/119r: "Venta de esclava," D.a Juana Fran.ca Martinez á D. Juan Sarda, Santiago de Cuba, 30 September 1857; see also Michael Zeuske, *Die Monte Christos des verborgenen Atlantiks. Sklavenhändler im 19. Jahrhundert* [The Monte Christos of the Hidden Atlantic).
40. Stephanie Smallwood, *Saltwater Slavery: A Middle Passage from Africa to American Diaspora* (Cambridge, MA, 2007)
41. The records of the Mixed Commission for 1839 contain no information on the *Teçora*. The ships recorded as arriving from Africa in June 1839 include: "9th [June]Portug. Sch[oone]r Dos Amigos José Silva Master f.m Sn.Tomé after land.d 413 Africans; 14th D[it]o Josefina A.o Rodriguez d.o d.o 240 [Africans]; 20 d.o Astrea Sabino d.o. d.o 440 [Africans]," in TNA, FO 313/17 (1839–1840), 37–38, relación. 23/1839 de S. Kennedy y C.A. Dalrymple to Palmerston from Havana, July 15, 1839, 37.
42. "Introductory Narrative," in *The African Captives: Trial of the Prisoners of the Amistad on the Writ of Habeas Corpus, before the Circuit Court of the United States, for the District of Connecticut, at Hartford; Judges Thompson and Judson, September Term, 1839* (New York, 1839), i–vi. This work is also available at Yale: Beinecke, Cb 79110.

43. Ibid., 7.
44. Such solidarity was crucial for the Atlantic history of slavery. See Sidney Mintz and Richard Price, "The Beginnings of African-American Societies and Cultures," in *The Birth of African-American Culture: An Anthropological Perspective* (Boston, 1992), 42–51; Marcus Rediker, Cassandra Pybus, and Emma Christopher, "Introduction," in *Many Middle Passages: Forced Migration and the Making of the Modern World* (Berkeley, 2007), 4–5.
45. *The African Captives*, 29–30.
46. On the trials and testimonies in the United States, see Rediker, *The* Amistad *Rebellion*, chaps. 4 and 5. Generally, the enslaved and captive had totally different memories of the passage and their traumatic beginnings. Usually they could not give this memory in written form during the years of slavery like Cinqué, but only much later.
47. Fernando Ortiz, "El arribo a Cuba. Privilegios de los barcos negreros. El contrabando favorecido por el cohecho," *Hampa afro-cubana: Los negros esclavos. Estudio sociológico y de derecho public* (Havana, 1916) reprint Ortiz, *Los negros esclavos* (Havana, 1976), 163–176.
48. *Noticioso de Ambos Mundos. Dedicado á las Artes, Comercio, Agricultura, Política y Bellas Letras*, New York, September 28, 1839, available in ANC, GSC, leg. 1272, no. 49909 (July 1839): "El C.S. Comandante Gral. de Marina sobre la sublevacion ejecutada por los negros que conducia la Goleta costera nombrada la Amistad" (sin foliación general, pero hay sendos documentos foliados); Jones, *Mutiny on the Amistad*, 14–30, especially 23, n.24.
49. Iyonolu Folayan Osagie, "The Amistad Story in the American Context," in *The Amistad Revolt: Memory, Slavery, and the Politics of Identity in the United States and Sierra Leone* (Athens, GA and London, 2000), 4–23, 5, n. 11. For new evidence on the African life of Cinqué after Amistad (travelling to Jamaica in 1845), see Yannielli, "Cinqué the Slave Trader."
50. *Noticioso de Ambos Mundos*.
51. Ibid., 1.
52. See Rediker, *The* Amistad *Rebellion*, 70.
53. The best work about the Cuban slave trade remains Murray, *Odious Commerce*.
54. ANC, GSC, leg. 1272, no. 49909 (July 1839): "El C.S. Comandante Gral. de Marina sobre la sublevacion ejecutada por los negros que conducia la Goleta costera nombrada la Amistad"; ANC, Escribanía de Marina, leg. 39, no. 385 (1839): "Ferrer, Ramón. Intestado de D. Ramon Ferrer."
55. Ibid., f. 23r, 27 September 1839.
56. Ibid., f. 23v/24r.
57. Ibid., f. 25r/v–48r/v: Declaración de Juan Bautista Gutierrez, Guanaja, 30 September 1839; Declaración firmada por D. Antonio Rivas, Guanaja, 7 October 1839.
58. See Carol M. Rose, *Property and Persuasion: Essays on the History, Theory, and Rhetoric of Ownership* (Boulder, 1994); and Zeuske, *Monte Christos des verborgenen Atlantiks*, passim.
59. ANC, Escribanía de Marina, leg. 39, no. 385 (1839): "Ferrer, Ramón. Intestado de D. Ramón Ferrer," f. 93r–97v, La Habana, Regla, interrogatorio cerrado de D.a Juana González, en la morada de D. Juana González, 4 June 1840.
60. "Correspondence of the Journal of Commerce," (Havana, July 6, 1839), in *New York Journal of Commerce*, July 25, 1839, 2. We would like to thank Marcus Rediker, who shared this important document with us.
61. Geneviève Fabre, "The Slave Ship Dance," in Maria Diedrich, Henry Louis Gates Jr., and Carl Pedersen, eds., *Black Imagination and the Middle Passage* (Oxford, 1999), 33–46; Smallwood, *Saltwater Slavery*.
62. William Gervase Clarence-Smith, "The Portuguese Contribution to the Cuban Slave and Coolie Trades in the Nineteenth Century," *Slavery and Abolition* 5, no. 1 (1984): 24–33.

63. Biblioteca Nacional de Cuba (BNC), La Habana, *Diario de la Habana*, January 16, 1838, 4; ibid., March 4, 1839, 4; ibid., Mach 23, 1839, 4.
64. "Esponen haber salido de este puerto [Havana] para el de San Pablo de Loanda y Santomé del dia veinte y uno de Set.e del año ant.or con una carga de aguardiente y el diez y ocho de D.bre por averia arribaron á la rada de Cabinda, donde la remediaron, saliendo de allí el cinco de Enero del corriente y el siete fondearon en San Pablo de Loanda donde descargaron y habilitaron el buque p.a regresar saliendo de aquel Puerto en lastre el catorce de Abril y llegaron á este el siete de Jun.o del corr.te año sin novedad en su viage," AHN, Estado, Trata de negros, leg. 8015/28: 1835 Fragata—Alerta. Capitan D. Juan Allende. Los comisarios Britanicos denuncian la llegada á la Habana, como procedente de Africa de la fragata Alerta; ibid., no. 1: Miguel Tacón from Havana, June 26, 1835, to the Secretary of State, ibid., no. 2: Habana, 23 June 1835, Manuel de los Rios.
65. Marrero Cruz, "Traficante de esclavos y chinos," 46–79.
66. http://www.amistad.org: File://A:/Ezpeleta June 25 1839 (May 18, 2007).
67. José Antonio Saco, *Historia de la esclavitud de la raza africana en el Nuevo Mundo y en especial en los paises américo-hispanos por José Antonio Saco con documentos y juicios de F. Arango y Parreño, Félix Varela, Domingo del Monte, Felipe Poey, José de la Luz y Caballero, José Silverio Jorrin, Enrique José Varona y otros*, Fernando Ortiz intro. (Havana, 1938) 4, 334.
68. Domingo del Monte, *Centón epistolario de Domingo del Monte* Domingo Figarola-Caneda ed., 7 vols., (Havana, 1923–1957), 4, 131.
69. There is as yet no evidence to link Ferrer directly with these men, but his frequent trips to Matanzas suggest that it would be worthwhile looking for such documents. See ibid., 4, 120, 150, 156; and Marc J. Prohom Durán and Mariano Barriendos Vallvé, "Los diarios de navegación catalanes: una nueva fuente de datos climáticos sobre los océanos (siglos XVIII a XX)," in J. C. García Codrón et al., eds., *El clima, entre el mar y la montaña* (Santander, 2004), 525.
70. Barbara L. Solow, "Caribbean Slavery and British Growth: The Eric Williams Hypothesis," *Journal of Developmental Economics* 17 (January–February 1985): 99–115; Solow, "Capitalism and Slavery in the Exceedingly Long Run," in Solow and Stanley Engerman, eds., *British Capitalism and Caribbean Slavery: The Legacy of Eric Williams* (Cambridge, 1987), 51–78; Robin Blackburn, The *Making of New World Slavery: From the Baroque to the Modern 1492–1800* (London, 1997), 509–573. On the problem of accumulation of capitals in the Americas and Cuba, see David Eltis, Frank Lewis, and Kenneth Sokoloff, eds., *Slavery in the Development of the Americas* (Cambridge, 2004), passim.
71. Eric Robert Taylor, *If We Must Die: Shipboard Insurrections in the Era of the Atlantic Slave Trade* (Baton Rouge, 2006).
72. AHPCam, Protocolos Notariales José Rafael Castellanos, fondo 123, tomo 1838, "Poder esp.l," f. 111v-112r, Puerto Príncipe, 12 June 1839.
73. Ibid., fondo 123, tomo 1836–1837, "Venta Real," f. 189r, Puerto Principe, 26 September 1937.
74. Ibid., Protocolos Notariales Manuel Martínez Valdés, fondo 155, tomo 1834–1835, "Transacción," f. 265r, Puerto Príncipe, 4 June 1835; ibid., tomo 1838, "Traspaso," f. 102r, Puerto Príncipe, 31 May 1838; ibid., tomo 1839, "Compañia," f. 215v, Puerto Príncipe 5 September 1839; tomo 1840, "Recibo," f. 94r, Puerto Príncipe, 16 May 1840; ibid., Protocolos Notariales José Rafael Castellanos, f. 123, tomo 1836–1837, "Cancelación," f. 397v, Puerto Príncipe, 19 July 1837; ibid., tomo 1838, "Venta," f. 45v, Puerto Príncipe, 7 April 1838; ibid., "Cancelación," f. 75v, Puerto Príncipe, 19 June 1838; ibid., "Obligación," f. 94v, Puerto Principe, 6 July 1838; ibid., "Obligación," f. 121r, Puerto Príncipe, 17 August 1838; "Obligación," f. 150v, Puerto Príncipe, 12 September1838.
75. Ibid., tomo 1836–1837: "Poder Especial," f. 394r, Puerto Príncipe, 14 July 1837. On slavery in Cienfuegos, see Orlando García Martínez, *Esclavitud y colonización en Cienfuegos 1819–1879* (Cienfuegos, 2008).

76. AHPCam, Protocolos Notariales Manuel Martínez Valdés, tomo 1839, "Poder Especial," f. 314r, Puerto Príncipe, 9 December 1839.
77. Archivo Histórico Provincial de Cienfuegos (AHPC), Fondo Protocolos Notariales J. J. Verdaguer, tomo 1842: "Obligación Hipotecaria," folio 178r-179v, Cienfuegos 1 September1842.
78. Ibid., tomo 1840: "Obligación Hipotecaria," f. 210r-211v, Cienfuegos 21 September 1840.
79. "Interrogatorio cerrado de José Martorell y Peña": ANC, Escribanía de Marina, leg. 39, no. 385 (1839): "Ferrer, Ramón. Intestado de D. Ramon Ferrer," f. 86v-87v, La Habana, 19 May1840. On Spanish indianos and their investments in Spain, see Angel Bahamonde Magro and José G. Cayuela Fernández, *Hacer las Américas. Las élites coloniales españolas en el siglo XIX* (Madrid, 1992); Arturo Arnalte, "Cónsules, comerciantes y negreros (españoles en Sierra Leona en el siglo XIX)," *Estudios Africanos* X, nos. 18–19 (1996): 65–79; Martín Rodrigo y Alharilla, *Los Marqueses de Comillas 1817–1925. Antonio y Claudio López*, (Madrid, 2000); Rodrigo y Alharilla, "Los ingenios San Agustín y Lequeitio (Cienfuegos): un estudio de caso sobre la rentabilidad del negocio del azúcar en la transición de la esclavitud al trabajo asalariado (1870–1886)," in José Antonio Piqueras, ed., *Azúcar y esclavitud en el final del trabajo forzado. Homenaje a M. Moreno Fraginals* (Mexico City, 2002), 252–268; Rodrigo y Alharilla, "Con un pie en Catalunya y otro en Cuba: la familia Samá, de Vilanova," *Estudis Històrics i Documents dels Arxius de Protocols*, no. XVI (1998): 359–397; Rodrigo y Alharilla, "Los Goytisolo. De hacendados en Cienfuegos a inversores en Barcelona," *Revista de Historia Industrial*, no. 23 (2003): 11–37. On Martorell as a big entrepreneur of mass transportation by steamer ships, see Rodrigo y Alharilla, "Navieras y navieros catalanes en los primeros tiempos del vapor 1830–1870," *Transportes, Servicios y Telecomunicaciones*, no. 13 (December 2007): 62–92.
80. AHPCam, Protocolos Notariales Manuel Martínez Valdés, fondo 155, tomo 1842, "Poder gral," f. 95r, Puerto Príncipe, 21 May 1842.
81. Joseph C. Miller, "Slaving as Historical Process: Examples from the Ancient Mediterranean and the Modern Atlantic," in Enrico Dal Lago and Constantina Katsari, eds., *Slave Systems: Ancient and Modern* (Cambridge, 2008), 70–102.
82. Dale Tomich and Michael Zeuske, "The Second Slavery: Mass Slavery, World Economy and Comparative Microhistories," *Review: A Journal of the Fernand Braudel Center* XXXI, no. 3 (2008): 91–100.

– Chapter 9 –

ANTISLAVERY BEFORE ABOLITIONISM
Networks and Motives in Early Liberal Barcelona, 1833–1844

Albert Garcia Balañà

In January 1842, John Scoble of the British and Foreign Anti-Slavery Society (BFAS) wrote to François Isambert of the Société pour l'Abolition de l'Esclavage, accepting a formal invitation to attend an international antislavery convention in Paris, motivated by the BFAS convention held in London in 1840. The British society also recommended a short list of individuals from the continent for the French association to invite. Scoble proposed three names with Spanish connections: the Cuban "Antonio José Saco" (José Antonio Saco), "Santiago Sos y Río" (Santiago Usoz y Río) in Madrid, and "Antonio Bergne de Barcelone."[1] "Antonio Bergne" was Antonio Bergnes de las Casas (1801–1879), the same Barcelona publisher who appeared as "Antonio Bergues" in the proceedings of the General Anti-Slavery Convention held in London in June 1843.[2] Bergnes was by then known to members of the BFAS, as in the summer of 1841 he had published the Spanish version of *Address on Slavery in Cuba, Presented to the General Anti-Slavery Convention* (1840) by Richard Robert Madden (1798–1886), with a short introduction by BFAS treasurer George William Alexander (1802–1890), a version in which Bergnes had left no doubt as to his antislavery stance.[3]

Should we interpret Scoble's only reference to Barcelona and European Spain, the figure of Bergnes, in his letter to Isambert (Saco was Cuban, and

Usoz was born in Spanish Peru) or Bergnes' widely cited translation of Madden and Alexander as indicating a lack of an antislavery tradition in Spain at the beginning of the 1840s? Was the publisher Bergnes simply a front man for British abolitionism in Spain during the critical moments of 1841, when David Turnbull had just arrived in Havana as British consul following BFAS pressure on Palmerston?[4] The short history of the Spanish edition of Madden's work seems to support this historiographical view of a British mission in terra incognita. The key figure in this series of connections was the Quaker Benjamin B. Wiffen (1794–1867), who had accompanied George W. Alexander on his trip to Spain in 1840 (and attended the first General Anti-Slavery Convention).[5] Wiffen made contact with Bergnes through the Usoz y Río brothers, Luis and Santiago, born in Spanish Peru and with connections and experience in London. After making inquiries with various Madrid publishers, Santiago Usoz eventually approached Bergnes in Barcelona, and even after 1841, Wiffen's interest in Bergnes would continue.[6] In Barcelona, Bergnes published a handbill dated 6 January 1841, signed by Wiffen and Alexander and titled *Observaciones que sobre el comercio de esclavos y la esclavitud hacen los infrascritos a los Españoles amigos de la Humanidad*.[7] During the same period, Madden sent Wiffen new writings on Spain, including copies of the Spanish originals of poems and texts attributed to the freed slave Juan Francisco Manzano, whom Madden had brought from Cuba in 1839 (some of these writings were translated and published in London—and in Paris by Schoelcher—in 1840).[8]

The image of Santiago Usoz earnestly searching for a publisher in Spain for Wiffen (that is, for Alexander and Madden) fits well with historiographical narratives that date the advent of Spanish abolitionism to the end of the 1850s and the beginning of the 1860s. Prior to then, and particularly during the two long decades in which the Anglo-Spanish antislave trade treaties of 1817–1820 and 1835 came into effect, a veiled British influence appeared to lie behind all public criticism of slavery in Spain, compliant with networks and motives that had their roots in London.[9] The present article does not set out to modify the essence of this narrative, but simply to examine some of its nuances. It essentially attempts to uncover some of the local driving forces prior to 1843 that Josep M. Fradera has described as "weak Catalan abolitionism"[10] and re-examine that political and organizational weakness by considering the correlations between local and Spanish forces (and not only the diplomatic trial of strength between London and Madrid via Havana). The article therefore attempts to shed some light on one aspect of early Spanish abolitionism, on the genesis of the transatlantic as well as the continental mobilization meticulously explained by Christopher Schmidt-Nowara.[11] My contribution appears to confirm this dual model, even in its noninstitutional antecedents, although the article refers to a setting (Barcelona) and a time (the critical years of the Liberal Revolution in Spain) that have received scant attention in the historiography on the subject.

That the article turns on the figure of Antonio Bergnes de las Casas can be explained by two circumstances. First, because his singular public antislavery stance in Barcelona in the early 1840s is doubly symptomatic: of the existence of a local antislavery tradition and of the weakness of this tradition. By 1840 Bergnes had already published translations of antislavery and pro-abolitionist articles in his monthly magazine for the middle classes, *El Museo de Familias,* and at the same time had started his translation into Spanish of *The Slave, or Memoirs of Archy Moore* (1836/1852) by Richard Hildreth, which he would publish some years later.[12] A letter received by George W. Alexander in Madrid from Barcelona and dated April 1842 testifies to the publisher Bergnes' active antislavery commitment: "He [Bergnes] will have explained to you all his views and indeed, I think, no two subjects could be well better blended ... than the pure doctrine of the Holy Scriptures and the question of freedom to the unhappy slave."[13] Moreover, as I will show, in Barcelona Bergnes had published on and against slavery years before 1841 and his connections with the BFAS. Second, through his documentable publishing activity, Bergnes appears simultaneously in various intellectual and political networks that, from the 1820s onward, placed Barcelona on the map of debates about the liberal revolution, the imperial crisis (and colonial reconstitution) and slavery in the Spanish monarchy.[14] These networks—as I shall try to demonstrate—link Bergnes with London and Havana, Paris, and New York years before 1841 through intermediaries that were less visible than the liberal Barcelona publisher, but more representative of local sources of antislavery sentiment.

Why do I use *antislavery* before, and instead of, *abolitionism*? This is due to the plurality of criticisms of the slave trade and slavery that converge in Bergnes' public activities, not all of which were abolitionist. This separation of ideology and strategy in part explains the inability of this incipient tradition to become institutionalized and political, because of its extremely limited critical mass during those years (in contrast to the French experience over the long decade prior to 1848).[15] Why *networks*? Precisely because of the informal and polycentric dynamic, barely institutionalized or coordinated, with which this local tradition evolved in the 1820s and 1830s. Here I present this dynamic as the sum of individual experiences with a certain public influence that converged in Bergnes and in Barcelona during Spain's liberal revolution, as a result of the renewed economic and political centrality of the city and its region in post-1820 transatlantic Spain. The considerable instability created by the liberal revolution in Barcelona, unequaled in the other regions of the peninsula, also goes some way to explaining the obstacles to early politicization of the slavery problem and to the crystallization of abolitionist movements and goals (in the British way as documented by Seymour Drescher).[16]

And finally, why Barcelona? The main aim of the article is to answer this question. It should, however, be noted here that the formation of this modest local antislavery tradition constituted the discrete reversal of the very different scenario discussed in this collection by Martin Rodrigo y Alharilla, Michael Zeuske, and Orlando García Martínez: the involvement of Catalan capital in the then illegal slave trade and in the plantation and forced labor economy. We now know a great deal more about this thanks to research by Fradera, Arnalte Barrera, and Rodrigo.[17] But Madden, Wiffen, and the BFAS were already aware of this involvement in the early 1840s. During his time in Havana as superintendent of Liberated Africans (1836–1839) in the service of the Colonial Office, Richard R. Madden had firsthand knowledge of the Catalans' central role in illegal trading. One example of this involvement was their management of the clandestine slave market in La Misericordia, which he attested to during his declaration in the *Amistad* case trial, in Hartford, Connecticut (winter 1839–1840).[18] At its 1843 general meeting, the BFAS also presented evidence that ships based in the port of Barcelona were being fitted out for slave trafficking. Likewise, in his memoirs Wiffen refers to buildings in Barcelona erected with capital accrued through the slave trade.[19] Consequently, by publishing Spanish editions of Madden and Alexander in Barcelona, Bergnes was issuing a challenge to this other sector of local society (a challenge that was also noted in London). Did this lead to anything resembling a public debate in the city? Who spoke in favor and who against, and what arguments did they use?

William Allen in Barcelona, or Who Was D.M. Vila?

In March 1833, eight years before the turbulent summer of 1841, Antonio Bergnes de las Casas received two recently arrived visitors at his house in Barcelona, both on a mission to Spain sponsored by the Society of Friends. The two travellers were William Allen, from London, and Stephen Grellet, from Philadelphia. Important Quakers in their own communities, Allen and Grellet left written testimonies of their travels in Spain during the final days of Ferdinand VII and noted the renewed expectations that London might fuel among the liberal supporters of Queen Maria Cristina and the reformist cabinet of Francisco Zea Bermúdez.[20] The objectives they set for their time in Barcelona faithfully reflected the purposes of their visit to Spain during the first months of 1833. They visited the Real Casa de Caridad (Royal House of Mercy), the hospital, and the women's prison. They struck up a friendship with Fèlix Torres i Amat, a late figure of Spanish Jansenism and translator of the Scriptures into Spanish. In the words of Allen, they spoke to Bergnes about his recent translations "of our Useful Knowledges works on chemistry and natural philosophy" and of the Catalan publisher's interest in "my Abridgment of Rural Colonies and the other little piece on the means of preventing mendacity."[21] They dined with Bergnes and other guests in the house of Judge Joaquim Compte in the village of Sarrià outside the city: there, according to Allen, "we had a good deal of conversation on different topics, with much openness, and there was quite a debate about the emancipation of slaves."[22]

Indeed, the emancipation of slaves was high on Allen and Grellet's agenda. Their report to Ferdinand VII, dated 7 March 1833 included a final point on "Negro Slavery," a diplomatic balance between their lament for the continuing traffic to the Spanish Caribbean and the very forced celebration of free labor on the island of Puerto Rico, while at the same time stating clearly that "the British nation will now very soon abolish Slavery in all its Colonies."[23] It should be noted here that since the decade following 1807, William Allen had been—in the words of David Brion Davis—"a key figure in the British antislavery movement" and that his trip to Spain in 1833 should not be considered in isolation from the simultaneous Slave Emancipation Bill debate in Westminster, nor from the renewed British pressure on Madrid that would crystallize in the bilateral treaty signed in 1835.[24] Allen had played an equally important role in the abolitionist experiment in Sierra Leone following its reconversion to Crown Colony in 1808. As a Quaker activist, his endeavors to secure international prohibition of slave trading in the Atlantic had not gone unnoticed by the Concert of Europe, particularly at the Congress of Verona in 1822.[25] It is important to my argument to stress that the good relationship William Allen and Antonio Bergnes de las Casas enjoyed was also based on Allen's generically utilitarian virtues: on Allen the Quaker, chemist, and promoter of the Society for the Diffusion of Useful Knowledge. This is suggested by the fact the first works Bergnes published in Barcelona were Spanish translations of articles from the Society for the Diffusion of Useful Knowledge, many taken from the controversial English publication, the *Penny Cyclopaedia*.[26] It is also confirmed by their second encounter in London in March 1835 and a visit to Borough Road with Lord Henry P. Brougham, as noted by two entries in Allen's diary.[27]

The collaboration between William Allen and Antonio Bergnes lends itself to a somewhat more complex reading than the strictly instrumental, or Allen's simply resorting to Bergnes to further his own aims. This is partly due to a detail that both Allen and Grellet noted in their respective diaries: the identity of a man who, on their arrival in Madrid, made arrangements for their stay in Barcelona. Both of them refer to him as D.M. Vila. In the words of Allen, "[H]e is just returned from England, and is acquainted with Friends; he resides at Barcelona, is kindly disposed to assist us, and will give us letters for that place." Vila was as good as his word, according to Allen, whereas Grellet reports that Vila "suffered deeply under the late disturbances in this kingdom; he was imprisoned for several months at Barcelona."[28] It can be assumed with all certainty that D.M. Vila was Domingo Maria Vila, a Barcelona lawyer and jurist, one of the liberal leaders of the city who in November 1823 had surrendered Barcelona to the French troops, after which he was imprisoned and exiled by Ferdinand VII's government. More importantly, however, Domingo Maria Vila had gained significant American experience during the final Spanish imperial crisis of 1820–1823, an experience for which the problematic relationship between liberal constitutionalism and slavery would prove to be a central issue, both before and after 1833.[29]

Briefly and simply, Domingo Maria Vila was one of the few voices—and without doubt the strongest—that, during the preparation of the 1837 constitution in the Spanish Cortes, opposed the exclusion of Cuba and Puerto Rico from the new constitutional and representative order, and the use of slavery to justify this exceptionality in the Spanish Caribbean. Elected as deputy on the Progressive Party list for Barcelona in 1836, Vila was one of the five representatives (of a total 155) who in the historical session of the Cortes on 16 April 1837 refused to support the device of special laws for the "overseas provinces of America and Asia." Furthermore, Vila acted as parliamentary spokesman for the minority who opposed the expulsion of the deputies recently elected in Cuba and Puerto Rico, who were waiting in Madrid and who would never take possession of their seats.[30] What is significant here is the conviction and tenacity with which Vila rejected the arguments of Agustín Argüelles (the architect of the idea of the "special laws") on the grounds of the absolute incompatibility between the liberal institutions of representation and government and the existence of slavery and its racial characteristics. Vila considered that recent revolutionary events in Spanish and Portuguese continental America provided proof of the possible civil and political virtues of the free black populations in societies with a tradition of slavery (and now post-slavery) and even spoke of them as potential voters and parliamentary candidates. "In vain are my efforts to arouse any repugnance in myself at the thought that a man of color might sit at my side on these benches"—thus Vila addressed Argüelles on 10 March 1837—; "their primitive African origins do nothing to make me value any less the civic virtues and knowledge that some of them possess; where I have seen their virtues, I can do no other than respect them.... Intelligence is also found under skin less pale than ours." Rarely were statements such as these heard in the Spanish parliamentary debates of 1836–1837, when Captain General Miguel Tacón governed *manu militari* in Havana following the swift defeat of the constitutionalist General Manuel Lorenzo in Santiago de Cuba.[31] Needless to say, Vila's parliamentary arguments sought to legitimize the representation of certain white and Creole interests in the restored liberal Cortes and in the new constitution. But Vila knew perfectly, given his American experience of 1820–1823, that recognition of the free blacks' political rights would announce the beginning of the end of slavery. Hence, in 1837 Vila's implicit antislavery speech went beyond the anti–slave trade and representational—but clearly racialized—program of the Cuban representatives waiting at the doors of the Cortes; a program that the deputy for Cuba, José Antonio Saco (whom Scoble would recommend to Isambert in 1842), would deliver to the press, given the impossibility of defending it from his parliamentary seat.[32]

What sources fueled the modest parliamentary antislavery position of Domingo Maria Vila in the 1830s? One seems to be related to his American experience prior to 1823: in 1821 and 1822 Vila had traveled to Río de la Plata and Brazil as representative of the short-lived Spanish constitutional government formed in 1820. He had dealt personally with José Tomás Guido, one of San Martín's men in Buenos Aires and in the Chilean campaign, and in all likelihood was aware of the one thousand freed slaves who had fought in the Army of the Andes that crossed from the Río de la Plata region to the Pacific in 1817.[33] In the Cortes of 1836, Vila also recalled seeing free blacks in the independent Brazilian monarchy, an idealized image of their participation in the break from Lisbon without a black revolution (idealized in opposition to the enslaved African Muslims in the Bahía region who revolted in 1835).[34] These experiences gave Vila considerable insight into the potential uses—in the context of an imperial crisis—of rupture and continuity of the legal, racial, and cultural divisions engendered by the slavery of Africans in Spanish America. He gained a clear and critical understanding of the consequences that could arise from excluding the *castas pardas* from the citizenship rights established in the Spanish Constitution of 1812, namely the exacerbation of Creole separatism, and at times, inappropriate supervision during the ending of slavery.[35] In 1836 Vila was perfectly aware of the racial and social distance that separated the Cuba of those times from Río de la Plata three decades earlier. Precisely for that reason, to prevent "the setting in motion, by unforeseen agents, of masses [in Cuba] against whose magnitude their own forces would be rendered incapable," he adduced that the Cortes should attend to the new Creole generations' expectations of political representation; at the same time he paid a well-informed tribute to the pardos, or freed mulatto Cubans, whom Vila saw as the custodians of much political intelligence on the island.[36] If Agustín Argüelles considered that slavery and its racial characteristics excluded Cuba from all selective policies of liberal representation, for Domingo Maria Vila these policies were the only guarantee that the ecosystem of slavery would be ended prudently, that its weight and power in the Cuban landscape would be wound down gradually.

It is not easy to be more precise about the depth of Domingo Maria Vila's antislavery conviction, partly because of the political and rhetorical limitations that the long shadow of the Caribbean possessions cast over the parliamentary debates of 1836–1837. Neither do we know exactly what Allen meant when he said of Vila, "[H]e is acquainted with Friends." Despite this, it is significant that Vila raised the moral legitimacy of resistance to slavery in the Cortes, as when he spoke of "the 300,000 African slaves awaiting [in Cuba] the moment to break the chains of slavery that oppress them."[37] This leads us to the second motive behind Vila's rejection of slavery: his aversion to the political corruption and despotism harbored by Caribbean slavery, carefully observed by Vila, and to its undesirable consequences for politics in European Spain. Vila's was the first parliamentary voice to suggest that praetorianism under Captain General Tacón in 1830s Havana, protected by the exceptionality of slavery, might bode ill for the unfolding of the new constitution in peninsular Spain. His defense of "provincial deputations" separate from the "Supreme government of the Nation" in Cuba and Puerto Rico as well as in "the provinces of the Peninsula," sought to neutralize the military's "supreme command" (which was more likely to be invoked, in the absence of these deputations, in more complex and socially conflictive regional contexts, such as Cuba and Catalonia).[38] In December 1836, Vila spoke in the Cortes against the deportation of political prisoners from the peninsula to Tacón's Cuba, an argument against the mechanisms that favored military authority and its arbitrary operations in both Barcelona and Havana. Some significant individuals of exalted Barcelona liberalism had been exiled to Cuba before the Cortes were formed in the summer of 1836; other representatives of the same political tradition endured Tacón's hospitality from the autumn of 1837 onward due to the state of war, supposedly only against the Carlists, declared by the captain general of Catalonia. They would leave written testimonials about the transatlantic nature of this early Spanish liberal praetorianism.[39] In short, slavery in Caribbean Spain spurred militarization in the metropole and colonies alike. Against this process, Vila represented civil constitutionalism in the Cortes.

Slavery According to Charles Comte
(and According to Tomás Gener)

The network that facilitated the relationship between Antonio Bergnes de las Casas and William Allen in 1833, through the figure and experience of Domingo Maria Vila, was not the Barcelona publisher's only antislavery connection at that time. In the summer of 1834, only months after his first meeting with Allen, Bergnes was contacted from Havana by a certain "Sirven," "a young man of Catalan origin" who had settled in Cuba. The result of this contact would come to light in Barcelona two years later: Bergnes' publication of the Spanish translation of *Traité de Législation* by Charles Comte, and particularly, "of book V, which deals especially and extensively with slavery." In Barcelona and in Bergnes, Sirven found a publisher disposed to take on the task, an achievement that had eluded the man behind the project and the translation, the Cuban Creole Domingo del Monte, both in Cuba under the recently appointed Tacón, and in New York and New Orleans.[40]

Book V of Comte's writings is a social and political indictment of slavery and of the colonial aristocracies it engendered, an indictment, moreover, full of references to Spanish America. It is not, however, a confidently abolitionist text, nor one that invokes the moment for emancipation as the time for a "mighty experiment" (the influence of Jean-Baptiste Say is clear on this point). For Comte, the disappearance of slavery in Spanish America and in the British Caribbean (in the 1835 edition), and naturally the memory of Saint-Domingue, made "regular abolition" in the French Caribbean a matter of urgency; namely, the individual and therefore staggered liberation of slaves with payments to their owners set by law. Comte believed that the impact of abolition must be deferred, both in time and in terms of the social fabric, a view that would be shared by the young Victor Schoelcher (1804–1893) in 1830 on his return to Paris from his illuminating first journey to Cuba.[41] It is thus an emancipationist rather than an abolitionist text.[42]

Charles Comte's extremely prudent antislavery stance was well attuned to the positions of the Cuban Creole reformist circle that, at the beginning of the 1830s, was led by young men such as Domingo del Monte (1804–1853) and the slightly older José Antonio Saco (1797–1879), mentioned above. Too much has been written about the significance of and the reasons behind this group's criticisms of slavery to be dealt with adequately here. The most lucid of these writings are undoubtedly those inspired by the argument of Manuel Moreno Fraginals concerning the growing perception among the better informed and most far-sighted Creole elites that, sooner than later, "they should free themselves from slavery, not free the slaves, which was a different question."[43] However, two pieces of unquestionably documented evidence are relevant. First, the summer of 1834 was critical to the group's future strategies and transatlantic connections, following Saco's expulsion from the island as decreed by Tacón, which led to the Del Monte group's inevitable withdrawal from public life. Significantly, these events would strengthen their commitment to writers such as Juan Francisco Manzano, at that point still a slave, and to a body of literature that, in the words of Jerome Branche, "has been canonized as early Cuban 'antislavery' writing."[44] The second piece of evidence confirms both the ambivalence and tactical nature of this Creole antislavery, but also its greater potential, depending on whom it was used by and for what purpose. Thus, whereas some recent research has demonstrated that Del Monte's critical view of Cuban slavery harbored a strong racial and anti-African prejudice, other scholars have confirmed that for Richard Madden and soon for the British and Foreign Anti-Slavery Society, Del Monte and Saco would be their men in Cuba.[45]

Were the political problems facing the reformists Saco and Del Monte in the context of Tacón's despotism and the pro-slavery Spanish Party of Havana sufficient to explain why, in 1834, Domingo del Monte contacted Antonio Bergnes in Barcelona to publish a Spanish edition of Charles Comte's *Traité*? Yes and no. Without the mediation of one of his political advisers whom he consulted about the translation project, Del Monte would never have made contact with Bergnes (through the above-mentioned Sirven, "a young man of Catalan origin"). In a letter conjointly written at the beginning of September 1834, this adviser counseled against publishing Comte's work in Cuba, or even in the United States where he lived, in the following terms: "It is our opinion that not a single word must be spoken [published] of freedom, for it will alarm them [the Cuban authorities] and they will concede nothing. Endeavors must only be made to increase the white population and end the trading of blacks. These two measures will prepare the ground and bring forward the termination of black slavery." Barcelona, however, was a safer place to publish, and the book would be just as likely to reach the Havana market (and more discretely, perhaps too much so). One of the two signatories of this letter was Tomás Gener (1787–1835), who since 1823 had been living in exile in New York after fleeing absolutist persecution for his role in the short-lived liberal Cortes of 1822–1823, when he was one of the three deputies elected to represent the province of Havana. Gener, however, was an unusual Creole: born in Catalonia in 1787, he had studied in the Barcelona Board of Trade Marine School at the beginning of the century and had first visited Cuba at the age of almost twenty-two in the winter of 1808–1809.[46]

Thus, Tomás Gener was the connection between Domingo del Monte and Antonio Bergnes in 1834, just as in the previous year Domingo Maria Vila had been instrumental in bringing together William Allen and Bergnes. Paradigmatically and exceptionally, Gener represented a certain Cuban experience from Barcelona and Catalonia in the first third of the nineteenth century. Like Domingo Maria Vila, therefore, Gener epitomized an extremely clear idea of the double crisis, imperial and constitutional, of the 1820s and 1830s held by exalted peninsular liberalism, particularly strong in Barcelona.

In what ways was the experience of Tomás Gener, after landing in the port of Matanzas in 1809, a paradigm of the Cuban experience in Catalonia around 1834? Firstly, Gener was part of the incipient wave of Catalan emigrants to Cuba that, by 1835, would lead peninsular emigration to the Gran Antilla. A wave that would give them a position of leadership in the expatriate community and, due to the profusion of young professionally trained Catalans from an urban background and with transatlantic and community connections, would also provide an outstanding capacity for economic cooperation and social advancement.[47] Gener, a sea captain by profession, immediately began to manage with great success a general store (*pulpería*) in Matanzas, a Cuban jurisdiction that in 1817 still had more general stores than coffee and sugar plantations and a population of almost as many whites (9,411; 2,420 in the city of Matanzas itself) as slaves (10,773; 1,016 slaves in the city of Matanzas and 1,010 free blacks). Over the next two decades, however, the social landscape of the Matanzas district shifted toward a categorical hegemony of slave labor, as a result of the spectacular growth in the number and size of the sugar plantations. In 1841 the white population in the new district was five times that of 1817, whereas the slave population was nine times higher: ninety-five thousand slaves as compared with just over ten thousand in 1817.[48] The merchant Gener's criticisms of the continued and increasing slave traffic to Cuba beyond 1817–1820 were also typical of the misgivings held by a certain sector of the Catalan emigrant population, a sector that has attracted less research attention than active or tacitly pro-slavery emigration. In the decade leading up to 1834, Gener's was a good precedent of the antislavery position, without abolition, that the reformists would adopt: his furious criticisms of the continuing traffic and its political and social consequences ("so strongly sustained by the complicity or by the opinion of the majority on the island, perverted by suicidal greed and self-assured ignorance"); his insistence on "promoting the immigration and colonialization of whites"; and even the greater moral and political demands he imposed on himself, which prevented him from accepting some of the expeditious formulas explored—with no chance of success—in Matanzas to whiten the population.⁴⁹ It is of note that in the 1822–1823 Liberal Triennium Cortes, Gener chose to align himself with another Cuban deputy, Félix Varela, great critic of the pro-slavery advocate Juan Bernardo O'Gavan and under the protection of the then bishop of Havana, the enlightened advocate of antislavery Juan José D. de Espada.⁵⁰ It should also be noted that in his *Autobiography*, the slave poet Juan Francisco Manzano referred to Gener as the "protector" who took him away from an inevitable life on the Matanzas sugar plantations long before Manzano was adopted—and freed in 1836—by the Del Monte circle, probably around 1816 or 1817.⁵¹

The important political role Tomás Gener adopted from 1817 to 1823 was undoubtedly exceptional amongst the Catalan colonists in Cuba. Equally exceptional was his flight from Cadiz to New York (via Gibraltar) in autumn 1823 and the dogged royalist persecution that forced him into exile for over ten years in the United States.⁵² From New York, he continued to have an influence on what the Cuban historian González García calls "the Matanzas liberal group," partially formed of men born in Catalonia and protected by Gener. These men included the merchant Jaume Badia (1796–1863) and the tailor Magí Pers (1803–1888), both very active in Matanzas public life during the 1820s and 1830s and critical of the slave trade, in all certainty due to their prompt understanding of the connection between the Africanization of Cuba and the arbitrary rule of the island's authorities.⁵³ But the networks Gener created during his years in New York, between 1823 and 1834, were more exceptional than was customary among the Catalan emigrant population in the Caribbean. Gener soon ventured beyond his comfortable economic position in the Cuban and Mexican expatriate community and successfully joined certain northern reformist networks. He participated in the American Lyceum Society—as evidenced by the society's affectionate obituary on his death in Cuba in 1835—and had personal contact with men like Joseph Lancaster (1778–1838), an English educational reformer and Quaker, who had received financial support from William Allen for his monitorial school model.⁵⁴ Tomás Gener also appears in the more widely known and detailed account of the first northern Whigs: the diary of Philip Hone (1780–1851), mayor of New York in 1826–1827 who may have introduced Gener to men such as Daniel Webster or the elderly John Adams.⁵⁵

The Impossible Popular Antislavery Movement in Barcelona, 1842

On 1 January 1841, a few weeks after the abdication of María Cristina and the return of the Progressive Party to power under the regent Espartero, the first "banquet" of the "associated working classes" was held in Barcelona. The speech given by Joan Muns, president and representative of the cotton weavers' union, included sentiments such as the following: "We do not propose to reproduce the bloody scenes that have stained the pages of the history of Lyon and other cities in foreign parts; we only wish to be heard, to be able to live from our own work, to be no longer treated as abject slaves, who with the sweat of their brow, must maintain the opulence of a handful of wretches who call themselves lords."[56] In this context of political liberalization and revolutionary pressure in peninsular Spain, and particularly in Catalonia, the incipient Barcelona trade union movement frequently employed the legitimizing language of "free men rather than slaves," the discourse of "the emancipation of the poor classes, slaves of the rich."[57] These formulas likewise contributed to the language of the first political republicanism, addressed to a public of all social classes, republicanism that in Barcelona in February 1841 proclaimed that "without civil and religious liberty we can only be compared to the Russian serfs or the black Africans who in America bow down to the humiliating oppression of their tyrant masters."[58] The summer of 1843 marked the height of prominence and power for the most radical Progressivism in Barcelona with a significant working class participation. Calls grew for a struggle against "the slave system, the system that turns the virtuous proletariat into slaves, and makes lords of those who become rich from the sweat of the workers."[59] The unions' condemnation of workers' slavery was in all certainty fueled by the rapid transformation of the city's main industry (cotton), by the political liberalization begun in 1840 (with a comprehensive review of the electoral laws), and by the ideological and sociological radicalization that remade Barcelona Progressivism from 1840 to 1843 (expressed in what Genís Barnosell has defined as "languages of citizenship and personal dignity" in the public speeches of the time).[60]

Was there any relation between this language of free men and slaves and the criticisms of Atlantic and Spanish slavery published by Bergnes in 1841? Was there at least an instrumental or rhetorical relationship, such as that documented by Kirsten McKenzie during the 1806 and 1807 electoral campaigns in Yorkshire?[61] An initial examination of the main—and without doubt the best—newspaper of Barcelona Progressivism during the Espartero Triennium (1840–1843), *El Constitucional*, reveals that this was not the case in the key moment of the summer of 1841. Or more precisely, it uncovers a collection of very forceful criticisms of David Turnbull in Havana, frequently invoking the risks of abolitionist activism in the context of the Cuban racial balance (at the same time blamed on "the lack of foresight in other times and by other legislators, who rest in their graves"). In other words, it invoked the shadow of Haiti.[62] Madden and Alexander's

Spanish edition was rebuffed in the pages of *El Constitucional* (although it was advertised) for opportunistically justifying Turnbull's policy to call into question, on behalf of London, the legality of the entire Cuban slave system with the new and challenging figure of the *emancipado* slave. This local anti-abolitionism was heavily based on Catalan economic fear of London (and not only in the Caribbean), and on anxiety over the recent transformation of Cuban society, of which much was known in Barcelona, "for the simple reason that experiments on these human societies should not be undertaken as though in a physics laboratory."[63] It was founded on a very direct knowledge of the Cuban situation in 1841 (and on the numerous Spanish warnings about Turnbull and his actions that spread "by word of mouth like wildfire"), and, above all, on the interests of Catalan commerce to conserve the island as a dual purpose colonial market; namely, as a final destination for exports and imports and as an asset for the accumulation of capital. It was thus a patrician anti-abolitionism, and a tacit defense of the status quo, that served interests such as those represented by the Junta de Comercio de Cataluña (Catalonian Board of Trade).[64]

However, the discourse on Caribbean slavery and abolition in the Barcelona *El Constitucional* would change over the months, particularly after the summer of 1842 (when Turnbull left Cuba, but remained in Jamaica). The timing of this change also coincided with the broadening out of the social base of local Progressivism to include the workers and the simultaneous emergence of a class rhetoric in the pages of *El Constitucional*, both of which are documented by Barnosell.[65] This shift can be dated to the period during which preparations were underway for two key episodes in the radicalization of the Progressive political circle of 1840–1843, both occurring in Barcelona: the popular-republican insurrection in the autumn of 1842 and the centralist (or Jamancia) revolt in the summer of 1843, finally suppressed by the army's bombardment of the city. The central facet of this shift in discourse was the critical emphasis on the supposed double morality of British abolitionism, for opposing the defense of sovereignty and property rights in Cuba (including slaves) in the articles it published during 1841. In September 1842, following a report of the arrival in Jamaica of "178 Africans, in the main sons of Sierra-Leone," *El Constitucional* continued, "English barbarity is no justification for Spanish cruelty, but is it appropriate for those who infringe it to speak so energetically in favor of a treaty?" Condemnations of the new contracted emigration to the West Indies (and of the final years of the apprenticeship system) then proliferated in the pages of the newspaper, which also alluded to the debate that divided antislavery opinion in Great Britain.[66] But if this first rejection of abolitionist self-interested double morality may be interpreted as a late introduction of the criticisms already formulated in France and in the United States, the second is more particular. In two editions at the end of the summer of 1842, following reports on work and mortality in Lancashire and Yorkshire, and comparing them unfavorably with allegedly parallel cases among the United States slave population, *El Constitucional* recommended: "Transfer [of the information] to the factories of Manchester and the English abolitionist philanthropists." It returned to this subject in later editions, ironically condemning living conditions in working-class England: "[T]hese English people who proclaim themselves such philanthropists, who in these times make the greatest efforts to extinguish the slave trade across the globe." In the same October 1842 edition (and in the same column) in which it reported new shipments of what were known as "free African immigrants," transported by "the English government to its possessions in the West Indies," it informed of new detentions (in Ashton, Manchester) of Chartist leaders and lamented the way "the magistrates separate the workers' causes from those of the Chartists, whom they present as culprits of a political assault."[67]

Did the radicalized editors of *El Constitucional*, on the eve of the Barcelona insurrection of 1842, know that barely a year before, Chartist agitators had interrupted and boycotted the BFAS national convention?[68] Of that we cannot be sure, but all the evidence suggests that they did. But we do know that the radicalization of politics in Barcelona during 1842 opened up new rifts in the local Progressive tradition and broke up some of the cross-class alliances that had been forged during the 1830s. A good example of this process is described in the public biography of Josep Melcior Prat i Colom (1779–1855), friend and protector of Antonio Bergnes de las Casas and his third link with antislavery presented in this article.

Like Vila and Gener, Josep M. Prat had participated in the Cortes of 1822–1823 and had been exiled during the subsequent absolutist restoration, in his case, in London. We know significantly more of Prat's years in England, before his return to Barcelona in 1832, than of Vila's exile.[69] Evidence exists of his contacts with the British and Foreign Bible Society, for which he translated the New Testament into Catalan. It was published in London and then in Barcelona by Bergnes, in 1836.[70] We know of the role he played in introducing the Lancasterian schools to Barcelona, projects for popular education with utilitarian origins, which undoubtedly contributed to the continued collaboration between Bergnes and William Allen after 1833.[71] And above all we know that these merits propelled him toward positions of power and representation in the Barcelona of the liberal revolution from 1835 onward. From these positions of power he would unleash particular confrontations with (and against) the community of small craftsmen and cotton workers in the city, a community in rapid and turbulent transformation during the period 1835–1844. One example is sufficient to illustrate this: following his term as governor of Barcelona during an exceptional episode of Luddite violence and popular revolt, in 1840–1841 Prat used his presidency of the Sociedad Económica de Amigos del País (Economic Society of Friends of the Country) to launch a furious campaign against bullfighting in the city. He considered that the immorality of the bullfight lay in the fact that "hundreds of people from varied trades ... abandon their workshops and lose at least half a day's work," because many of these "events take place on working day afternoons," frequently during "Sant Dilluns," the English Saint Monday. In 1850 the elderly Prat was still working for the Provincial Council in search of a solution to the "agglomeration of factories in Barcelona" and recommended locating the workers (in other words, the factories) "in a village with no Ramblas, bulls, cafes nor theaters" because "their demands—including their wage demands—must of necessity diminish."[72]

What was the relationship between Prat the utilitarian and the Atlantic slavery question? What was the link between Prat and Bergnes on this issue? According to detailed reports by the historian of science, Agustí Camós, Prat may have had an influence on one of Bergnes' most important publishing enterprises in Barcelona in the 1830s: the introduction into Spain of Lamarckian evolutionism. On the suggestion of Prat, a pharmacist by profession, in 1835 Bergnes translated and published Georges de Cuvier and Julien-Joseph Virey, followers of Lamarck and Buffon, and examples of the tension between monogenism and polygenism in France after the Revolution and Haiti.[73] Camós notes that Prat and Bergnes may have come across this evolutionist tradition through the latter's years in the London of the so-called radical doctors studied by Adrian J. Desmond, an environment highly receptive to Lamarckism (as was Robert Owen's circle, a further connection with William Allen).[74] This would perhaps explain some details in Bergnes' translation of the 1824 edition of *Histoire Naturelle du Genre Humain* by Julien-Joseph Virey, an unquestionable representative of the anthropological tradition that proclaimed African racial distance and intellectual inferiority. It would explain the translator's notes that Bergnes contributed—for further emphasis—to the subchapter "On the Traffic of Negroes and its Abolition," which celebrated Quaker abolitionism in 1835 and the break up of Spanish absolutism (in reference to 1824, the year of the French edition). It also explains the attention Bergnes paid to the scarce passages on the education and moralization of those who "are not our equals," his "let us extend a protective hand to the down-trodden and help him reach an honorable step on the stairway to perfection" (note the similarity in Drescher's findings on the English translations of Cuvier).[75]

Conclusion

The renewed tension embedded in the political and social landscape of Barcelona during the years 1842 and 1843 was a further hurdle to bridging the doctrinal and strategic distance that separated the well-informed antislavery position of Bergnes and Prat from the rhetoric against all slavery fanned by the discourse of incipient trade unionism and early worker republicanism. If some found it ironic, to say the least, to be concerned for Caribbean slaves and former slaves while Chartist leaders were being arrested in Lancashire, it seemed no less so in Barcelona, which had been bombed twice at a moment when class barriers had been crossed and the city was at its democratic height. That the man behind the bombing of Barcelona in 1843 was General Juan Prim, soon to be appointed captain general in Puerto Rico, was far from ironic, however. Neither was there any irony in the fact that 1843 was the year in which the supposed Escalera conspiracy, stirred up by David Turnbull, was hatched in Cuba and that the fierce repression against slaves and free blacks in 1844 was led by Captain General Leopoldo O'Donnell, another liberal general who would suppress working-class Barcelona by force.[76] Against this transatlantic backdrop it comes as no surprise that men such as Bergnes, Prat, or Vila felt as a political and personal defeat the division and collapse of local Progressivism in 1842–1843 and the return to power of the conservative Moderate Party in 1844 (and the drafting of a new, highly restrictive constitution in 1845).[77] Nor is it remarkable that, with the breakup of Progressivism and the simultaneous anti-African hysteria in Cuba in 1843 (particularly in Matanzas), antislavery publishing in the form that Bergnes had been involved since 1833–1834 would disappear from public life in Barcelona; and it would disappear for a long time beginning in 1844, when at least two apologies for the (illegal) trading of Africans were published in the city.[78]

What occurred after the summer of 1842 does not justify our ignoring the history of the previous decade discussed in this article. We cannot ignore the connection between Bergnes and William Allen through Domingo Maria Vila nor, especially, Vila's lucidity in linking the future of the "small Spanish empire," in the liberal era, to the prudent but gradual dismantling of an intensely pro-slavery Cuba. The arguments Vila put forward during the 1830s would reemerge among the metropolitan reformers of the 1860s in what was clearly a very different international context for Caribbean slavery (thus confirming Vila as an early Spanish interpreter of the highly contradictory relationships between liberal imperialism and slavery noted by Christopher L. Brown and Josep M. Fradera).[79] Nor can we ignore the connection between Bergnes, Domingo del Monte, and Tomás Gener, nor, particularly, the personal and sociopolitical experience Gener gained from his dual status as a peninsular in Matanzas and an American in Barcelona. Although noting that he was not a typical representative of the expatriate colonists in Cuba prior to 1835 (and in anticipation of discovering more on this), Gener demonstrates that autochthonous realities and mechanisms facilitated transatlantic criticisms of slavery in the Spanish Caribbean significantly earlier than the founding of the Spanish Abolitionist Society in 1865.

Finally, acknowledging the connection between Bergnes, Josep M. Prat, and the politics of popular Barcelona during the early 1840s allows us to put forward a partial hypothesis as to why no Spanish Abolitionist Society was formed until 1865, or why its cross-class repercussion was so limited, as described by Schmidt-Nowara, and why an abolitionist movement could not put down roots in Barcelona. Although the answers to this last question must essentially be sought in the strengthened connections between the Catalan and Cuban economies during the middle decades of the nineteenth century, perhaps we should highlight here a fact that is usually forgotten. Namely, that men like Laureà Figuerola (1816–1903), Joaquim M. Sanromà (1828–1895), or Fèlix de Bona (1822–1889), all of whom were decisive in founding the Spanish Abolitionist Society, were Catalans, young men born into the public and political life of Progressive Barcelona in the 1835–1843 period and who would have to move to Madrid in the years after 1844.[80]

Notes

This paper has benefited greatly from generous observations made by participants attending the conference "Slavery, Empire and Abolition: The Case of Spain Understood from a Comparative Perspective" held in Barcelona, 4–5 June 2009. I am grateful for all the comments received, together with decisive encouragement from Christopher Schmidt-Nowara to extend my work on these subjects, and the kind support of Josep M. Fradera, Rebecca J. Scott and Seymour Drescher to continue with this research. Last but not least, I wish to thank Mary Savage for her careful and professional translation of the original Spanish text, and Stephen Jacobson and Teresa Segura for their organizational help at every stage of the process.

1. All the information and literal quotations are taken from Nelly Schmidt, *Abolitionnistes de l'esclavage et réformateurs des colonies, 1820–1851. Analyse et documents* (Paris, 2000), 156–158 and note 66.
2. *Proceedings of the General Anti-Slavery Convention, London, 1843* (London, 1977), 186–187, 351.
3. The Spanish version: *Observaciones sobre la Esclavitud y Comercio de Esclavos por J.G. Alexander; é Informe del Dr. Madden sobre la Esclavitud en la Isla de Cuba* (Barcelona, 1841); Bergnes' significant end note ("Los Editores al Lector"), 63–67. Madden's original ver-

sion: Richard R. Madden, *Address on Slavery in Cuba, Presented to the General Anti-Slavery Convention* (London, 1840). On George W. Alexander (confused with the abolitionist Joseph Gundry Alexander [1848–1918] in many bibliographical references to the Spanish versión), see, in reference to Spain and Cuba: George W. Alexander, *Letters on the Slave-Trade, Slavery, and Emancipation: With a Reply to Objections Made to the Liberation of the Slaves in the Spanish Colonies* (London, 1842). On Antonio Bergnes de las Casas, liberal publisher and writer in Barcelona between 1829 and 1843 and professor of Greek at the Universidad de Barcelona from 1847, see Santiago Olives Canals, *Bergnes de las Casas, helenista y editor (1801–1879)* (Barcelona, 1947); and Josep Antoni Clua Serena, *El Humanismo en Cataluña en el siglo XIX: A. Bergnes de las Casas, 1801–1879* (Madrid, 1995).
4. David R. Murray, *Odious Commerce. Britain, Spain and the Abolition of the Cuban Slave Trade* (Cambridge, 1980), 133–147.
5. On Benjamin Barron Wiffen, brother of the poet and translator Jeremiah H. Wiffen, I have drawn on the extensive obituary published in *The Annual Monitor for 1868, or Obituary of the Members of the Society of Friends in Great Britain and Ireland for the year 1867* (London, 1867), 236–245; and Samuel Rowles Pattison, *The Brothers Wiffen: Memoirs and Miscellanies* (London, 1880), who confirms that Wiffen in all certainty visited Barcelona during his first trip to Spain (100–102 and 166), and would return with Alexander in 1843.
6. See Mar Vilar, "La lengua y civilización inglesas en sus relaciones con España a mediados del siglo XIX. Siete cartas de Santiago Usoz y Río al hispanista Benjamin B. Wiffen (1841–1850)," *Boletín de la Real Academia de la Historia*, CXCIII/1 (January–April 1996): 137–174; and in particular, the letter from Santiago Usoz to Benjamin B. Wiffen dated 9 January 1841 concerning the translation project (160–163) and the letter of 18 March 1843 with news for Wiffen about Bergnes in Barcelona (165–166).
7. Oxford University, Balliol College Library, Wiffen Papers: *Observaciones que sobre el comercio de esclavos y la esclavitud hacen los infrascritos* [J.G. Alexander & B. Wiffen] *a los Españoles amigos de la Humanidad* (Barcelona, 1841). I am indebted to the kindness of Christopher Schmidt-Nowara for my consultation of this source.
8. These copies of Manzano's Spanish original texts came into the hands of Luis Usoz y Río through Wiffen, with the consent of Madden, in 1842; they were discovered in the Biblioteca Nacional (Madrid) by Adriana Lewis Galanes, "Luis Usoz y Río, bibliófilo español del siglo XIX: no conocido custodio de textos literarios cubanos," published in A. David Kossof, ed., *Actas del VIII Congreso de la Asociación Internacional de Hispanistas* (Madrid, 1986), II, 151–160. The English edition of part of the works attributed to Manzano: *Poems by a Slave in the Island of Cuba, Recently Liberated, Translated from the Spanish by R.R. Madden, M.D., with the History of the Early Life of the Negro Poet, Written by Himself* (London, Thomas Ward and Co., 1840); the French translation of Manzano's poems, in Victor Schoelcher, *Abolition de l'esclavage, examen critique des préjugés contra la coleur des africains et des sang-mêlé* (Paris, 1840), 89–92. See section "Slavery according to Charles Comte (and according to Tomás Gener)" in this paper on the biography and autobiography of Juan Francisco Manzano.
9. Examples of this narrative are found in the collection edited by Francisco de Solano and Agustín Guimerá, eds., *Esclavitud y derechos humanos. La lucha por la libertad del negro en el siglo XIX* (Madrid, 1990). On the Anglo-Spanish treaties of 1817 (abolition of slave trading to Spanish colonies, in force from 1817 or 1820, depending on latitude) and of 1835 (on the persecution of illegal Spanish trading by London) Murray, *Odious Commerce*, 50–71 and 92–113.
10. Josep M. Fradera, "Limitaciones históricas del abolicionismo catalán," in *Esclavitud y derechos humanos*, 125–133, 128 (which avoids the chronological frame mentioned in the previous note).

11. Christopher Schmidt-Nowara, *Empire and Antislavery: Spain, Cuba, and Puerto Rico, 1833–1874* (Pittsburgh, 1999); a short presentation of the continental variation of the abolitionist movement, Seymour Drescher, "British Way, French Way: Opinion Building and Revolution in the Second French Slave Emancipation," *The American Historical Review* 96 (June 1991): 709–734, 713–715.
12. See, for example, "Los abolicionistas en Estados Unidos," *El Museo de Familias* IV (1840), 120–126; "De la esclavitud, su origen y resultados entre pueblos antiguos y modernos," *El Museo de Familias* V (1841), 56–70 (both articles translated from the *Edinburgh Review*, founded in 1802 by Henry Brougham, whom Bergnes had met in London in 1835). The translation of antislavery fiction by the North American Richard Hildreth and the publication of the extended version (*The White Slave, or Memoirs of a Fugitive*): Richard Hildreth, *El Esclavo Blanco: El compañero del Tío Tom, por Hildreth; traducido del inglés por Antonio Bergnes de las Casas* (Barcelona, 1853).
13. Oxford University, Balliol College Library, Wiffen Papers: letter from (Lord) Delamere to George W. Alexander "at Madrid" (Barcelona, 2 April 1842) (I am indebted to the kindness of Joan-Lluís Marfany for the identification of Delamere); Alexander's correspondent also writes in the same letter: "By last pack Mr. Bergnes wrote to you some account of what had occurred since you left us and mention to you some views of his to establish some public organ for the diffusion of matter bearing principally on this subject [the freeing from their cruel bondage so many thousands of Human souls], but at the same time touching on other matters which might at present be take up with more avidity by the Spanish people." I am indebted to the kindness of Christopher Schmidt-Nowara for my consultation of this source.
14. The most thorough, recent presentation and interpretation of the general process of the imperial crisis, colonial reconstruction in a metropolitan context of liberal revolution, and of the place of slavery and its racial features is to be found in Josep M. Fradera, *Colonias para después de un imperio* (Barcelona, 2005).
15. Lawrence C. Jennings, *French Anti-Slavery: The Movement for the Abolition of Slavery in France, 1802–1848* (Cambridge, 2000); Drescher, "British Way, French Way."
16. See Seymour Drescher, *Capitalism and Antislavery* (New York, 1987), particularly chapters 5 to 7.
17. Josep M. Fradera, *Indústria i mercat. Les bases comercials de la indústria catalana moderna (1814-1845)* (Barcelona, 1987), 54–78; L. Arturo Arnalte Barrera, *El Tribunal Mixto Anglo-Español de Sierra Leona, 1819–1873*, Ph.D. dissertation, Universidad Complutense de Madrid, 1992, I, 121–193, and II, Appendix III; Martín Rodrigo y Alharilla, *Indians a Catalunya: capitals cubans en l'economia catalana* (Barcelona, 2007).
18. During his declaration Madden referred to his visit to the said Bozal market in Havana ("called La Misericordia, or 'mercy'"), a place "kept by a man named 'Riera' ... and the factor or major domo of the master, in the absence of the latter, said to me that the negroes of the Amistad had been purchased there" (in "The Deposition of Richard Madden, British Superintendent of Liberated Africans," http://www.law.umkc.edu/faculty/projects/ftrials/amistad/AMI_TMAD.HTM). Madden recalled the *Amistad* case, the Catalan captain of *La Amistad*, Ramon Ferrer, and the "keeper named Riera" of La Misericordia, in R.R. Madden, *The Island of Cuba: its Resources, Progress, and Prospects, Considered in Relation Especially to the Influence of its Prosperity on the Interests of the British West Indies* (London, 1849), 234, 228–242.
19. *The Fourth Annual Report of the British and Foreign Anti-Slavery Society, for the abolition ...* (London, 1843), 41 ("At the port of Barcelona slavers are fitted out for the traffic. ..."); Samuel Rowles Pattison, *The Brothers Wiffen*, 166 ("When I was at Barcelona, I saw a splendid pile of buildings erected by a man who got his gains by Slavery in Cuba ...").
20. See *Life of William Allen with Selections from his Correspondence* (London, 1847), III, 112–143; *Memoirs of the Life and Gospel Labours of Stephen Grellet*, edited by Benjamin Seebohm (Philadelphia, 1860), II, 389–410.

21. *Life of William Allen*, III, 133–143 (139–140 on Bergnes); *Memoirs of the Life and Gospel*, II, 405–410.
22. *Life of William Allen*, III, 140.
23. *Life of William Allen*, III, 119–125 (literal quotation on 125). The other points in the report referred to "Mendicity," "Peasantry," and "Prisons."
24. David Brion Davis, *The Problem of Slavery in the Age of Revolution, 1770–1823* (Ithaca, 1975), 242 (and 242–249 on his presentation of William Allen); 1833 in Westminster: Seymour Drescher, *The Mighty Experiment: Free Labour versus Slavery in British Emancipation* (Oxford and New York, 2002), 121–143; the route to the Anglo-Spanish treaty of June 1835, Murray, *Odious Commerce*, 92–113.
25. Allen and Sierra Leone, see Drescher, *The Mighty Experiment*, 94–95; Allen and the delegations in Verona in 1822 (and his international activism after 1814): Betty Fladeland, "Abolitionist Pressures on the Concert of Europe, 1814–1822," *The Journal of Modern History* 38 (December 1966): 355–373, 358. and 370–373.
26. See *Biblioteca de Conocimientos Humanos, traducida del inglés. Filosofía natural* (Barcelona, 1831–1832, 2 tomes); details about a second edition in 1834 (with writings by Henry P. Brougham) in Olives Canal, *Bergnes de las Casas*, 126–128. William Allen, the *Society for the Diffusion* and on the subject of labor in the England of the Industrial Revolution: Davis, *The Problem of Slavery*, 242–249.
27. *Life of William Allen*, III, 198 ("Called upon Antonio Bergnese, the intelligent printer whom Stephen Grellet and I saw at Barcelona, and appointed him to meet me at the British and Foreign School.... Lord Brougham and Antonio Bergnese dined with us to-day; a satisfactory visit."). Bergnes makes only one imprecise allusion to his personal encounters with Allen (and Brougham), in a university speech in 1870: see Olives Canal, *Bergnes de las Casas*, 22–23 (and note 38).
28. *Life of William Allen*, III, 119 and 126–127 ("D.M. Vila called, and gave us much useful and interesting information. He mentioned to us some persons about Valencia and Barcelona, who meet to read tracts."); *Memoirs of the Life and Gospel*, II, 390–391.
29. My first presentation of Domingo Maria Vila appears in Albert Garcia Balañà, "Tradició liberal i política colonial a Catalunya. Mig segle de temptatives i limitacions, 1822–1872," in Josep M. Fradera et al., *Catalunya i Ultramar. Poder i negoci a les colònies espanyoles (1750–1914)* (Barcelona, 1995), 77–106, particularly 80–83. Vila's own testimony of his imprisonment in 1823–1824 and his subsequent exile from Spain, in *Diario de Sesiones de las Cortes* (henceforth DSC), 1841 Legislature, Session of 21 March 1841, 12–13.
30. See *Diario de Sesiones de las Cortes Constituyentes* (henceforth DSCC), 1836–1837 Legislature, Session of 16 April 1837, 2800–2802; also Session of 10 March 1837, 2036–2044, and Session of 11 March 1837, 2058–2063 (interventions by Domingo Maria Vila).
31. The words of Vila in DSCC, 1836–1837 Legislature, Session of 10 March 1837, 2037. On the political and colonial significance in 1836–1837 of the unfulfilled promise of special laws for Cuba and Puerto Rico, see Fradera, *Colonias para después*, 120–169; on the unequal confrontation between Tacón and Lorenzo (and their different social supporters) in the Cuba of 1836, see Jesús Raúl Navarro García, *Entre esclavos y constituciones (El colonialismo liberal de 1837 en Cuba)* (Sevilla, 1991).
32. On Saco, his condemnation of the continuing slave trade and the defense of civil, but not political, rights for free blacks in the pamphlets he published in Madrid in 1837, see Fradera, *Colonias para después*, 165–170.
33. Vila and Guido, DSCC, 1836–1837 Legislature, Session of 2 December 1836, 454–455 (intervention by Domingo Maria Vila). Freed slaves in the Army of the Andes (approximately fifteen hundred of the total of just over five thousand men) led by San Martín and Guido ("[W]e will make soldiers out of any creature," Guido wrote to San Martín): Beatriz Bragoni and Sara Mata de López, "Militarización e identidades políticas en la revolución rioplatense," *Anuario de Estudios Americanos*, 64 (January–June 2007): 221–256, 230–233.

34. DSCC, 1836–1837 Legislature, Session of 10 March 1837, 2037 ("Nearby was a free negro in Brazil, while the child Emperor, by the side of his brother, watched the Army parade in his honour ..." intervention by Domingo Maria Vila).
35. On the debate in the Cortes of Cadiz (1809–1812) concerning the castas pardas and the political representation of Spanish America and the role of Agustín Argüelles in this electoral exclusion, see Josep M. Fradera, "Raza y ciudadanía. El factor racial en la delimitación de los derechos políticos de los Americanos," in *Gobernar colonias* (Barcelona, 1999): 51–69.
36. In the session of 9 March 1837 Vila argued, "The seed of separation, a desire for independence, stirs a small number of young spirits born on the island [Cuba], with European origins, ...; and these young men, opposing even their own fathers, let themselves be guided without heed to intelligence, which lies mostly in the hands of a third class of inhabitants who, despite their freedom, with difficulty attain honors. I refer to the pardos, whose fathers at times tend to procure for them a good education in return for the legitimacy denied to them; and intelligence, gentlemen, is a power against which, sooner or later, coiled force always cedes." DSCC, 1836–1837 Legislature, Session of 9 March 1837, 2022, and 2021–2025 for other arguments attributed to Vila, including his command of demographic and racial information about Cuba in 1830.
37. DSCC, 1836–1837 Legislature, Session of 9 March 1837, 2022, and 2021–2022 on the general argument put forward by Domingo Maria Vila, specifically concerning how to avoid a slave revolt.
38. DSCC, 1836–1837 Legislature, Session of 10 March 1837, 2036–2038 (intervention by Domingo Maria Vila); further details in Garcia Balañà, "Tradició liberal i política colonial," 82–83. On Vila's questions to the government about Tacón's actions and powers in Havana: DSCC, 1836–1837 Legislature, Session of 11 March 1837, 2058–2063 (particularly 2060–2061 and 2063). On Tacón and the construction of the supreme command policy in Cuba, see Fradera, *Colonias para después*, 146–155.
39. See DSCC, 1836–1837 Legislature, Session of 7 December, 1836, 520–524 (interventions by Domingo Maria Vila). For accounts by "exalted" Barcelona liberals deported in 1837 by Captain General of Catalonia Baron De Meer to Tacón's Cuba, see Rafael Degollada, *Memoria del abogado Don Rafael Degollada en defensa de su honor ultrajado. Con las cuatro persecuciones sufridas por sus opiniones políticas, del mes de enero de 1836 hasta el de octubre de 1837 en que fué deportado a La Habana y de allí a Pinos* (Marseille, 1839); *Justificación de los deportados de Barcelona a Canarias y Pinos y relación de las vicisitudes de los fugados hasta su arribo a Barcelona* (Barcelona, 1839).
40. The short history of Del Monte's translation project and the final edition published by Bergnes is reported by Lourdes Arencibia Rodríguez, "La traducción en las tertulias literarias del siglo XIX en Cuba," *Hieronymus Complutensis* 4–5 (1996–1997), 27–40, 34–37, based chiefly on the correspondence of Domingo del Monte (from whence are taken the literal quotations on Sirven and book V). On the final publication by Bergnes in Barcelona: Carlos Comte, *Tratado de Lejislación, o Esposición de las Leyes Jenerales con arreglo a las cuales prosperan, decaen o se estancan los pueblos* (Barcelona, 1836–1837), from the original *Traité de Législation ou Exposition des Lois Générales suivant lesquelles les peuples prospèrent, dépérissent ou restent stationnaires* (Paris, 1826–1827), with contributions from the second French edition (Paris, 1835).
41. Carlos Comte, *Tratado de Lejislación*, V, 5–24 (references to Spanish America), 241–251, and 253–264 (motives and methods for abolition). On moral reasons in Comte's antislavery position and the influence of Jean-Baptiste Say in his defense of free labor, see Schmidt, *Abolitionnistes de l'esclavage*, 210–211; moral antislavery position in Jean-Baptiste Say, and "his deep pessimism about large-scale projects of manumission and emancipation" (which clearly influenced Comte), Drescher, *The Mighty Experiment*, 63–70 (literal quotation, 70). The young Schoelcher, his trip to Cuba in 1829 and the

arguments in his early article "Des Noirs" in the *Revue de Paris*, 1830 in Alain Yacou, "El impacto incierto del abolicionismo inglés y francés en la isla de Cuba (1830–1850)," in *Esclavitud y derechos humanos*, 455–475, 461.
42. I am grateful to Luiz Felipe de Alencastro for his suggestion on this semantic distinction.
43. See Manuel Moreno Fraginals, *Cuba/España España/Cuba. Historia común* (Barcelona, 1995), 190–201 for full details of the argument (literal quotation, 196).
44. Jerome Branche, "'*Mulato entre negros*' (*y blancos*): Writing, Race, the Antislavery Question, and Juan Francisco Manzano's *Autobiografía*," *Bulletin of Latin American Research*, 20, no. 1 (2001): 63–87, 63.
45. A magnificent example of the potent racial prejudice in Domingo del Monte in 1834, from his correspondence, in Luz Mena, "Stretching the Limits of Gendered Spaces: Black and Mulatto Women in 1830s Havana," *Cuban Studies* 36 (2005): 87–104, 98 (and note 37). On the collaboration between Madden and Del Monte during the second half of the 1830s, with different motives, see Murray, *Odious Commerce*, 128–132 and 148–150; on Madden, Del Monte and Manzano, Lewis Galanes, "Luis Usoz y Río, bibliófilo." On the BFAS and José Antonio Saco, see Schmidt, *Abolitionnistes de l'esclavage*, 158.
46. The lengthy letter from Tomás Gener and Félix Varela to Del Monte and Manuel González del Valle (12 September 1834) is reproduced in full in Arencibia Rodríguez, "La traducción en las tertulias," 35–37, and includes a "Nota" by Del Monte on contacts made with Bergnes and the poor sales of Comte's work in Cuba ("The students of law were the only ones to read it"). Biographical information on Tomás Gener (born in 1787 in Calella, on the north coast of Catalonia) comes from José Conangla Fontanilles, *Tomás Gener. Del hispanismo ingenuo a la cubanía práctica* (Havana, 1950), 9–10, 17–19, and 45–46.
47. On the emigration of Catalans to Cuba in 1830–1835, almost 60 percent of all emigration from Spain during those years, and the sociological profile of Catalan emigrants, see César Yáñez Gallardo, *Saltar con red. La temprana emigración catalana a América, ca. 1830–1870* (Madrid, 1996), 52–66; Raimon Soler, *Emigrar per negociar. L'emigració a Amèrica des de la Comarca de Garraf* (Vilanova i la Geltrú, 2003), 29–49.
48. All the demographic data on the jurisdiction and district of Matanzas (together with the number of pulperías and coffee and sugar plantations in 1817 and the number and size of the sugar plantations in 1841) are taken from Laird W. Bergad, *Cuban Rural Society in the Nineteenth Century: The Social and Economic History of Monoculture in Matanzas* (Princeton, 1990), 29–30 (for 1817) and 32–34 (for 1841). Tomás Gener and the early pulpería business (retail store selling foodstuff and other products) shared with his brother Josep, Conangla Fontanilles, *Tomás Gener*, 10–11.
49. All quotations are taken from Tomás Gener's letter to Domingo del Monte (New York, 11 May 1832) reproduced in Conangla Fontanilles, *Tomás Gener*, 62–64, which I previously discussed in Garcia Balañà, "Tradició liberal i política colonial," 79–80. The same letter sets out Gener's moral and political arguments against a project "to raise by means of subscription a considerable fund to exonerate the freed slaves of that island [Cuba]."
50. It should be remembered that Félix Varela cosigned, with Gener, the letter to Del Monte on the translation and publication of Comte's work in September 1834. On agreements and disagreements between Gener and Varela in the Cortes of 1822–1823, see Garcia Balañà, "Tradició liberal i política colonial," 78–79. On Espada and Varela against the large plantation owners in the Cuba of 1820–1823, see Moreno Fraginals, *Cuba/España España/Cuba*, 161–166. On the political and social weakness of the world represented by Varela (and in part by Gener) during the years 1820–1823, see Fradera, *Colonias para después*, 117–124, 131–132, and 142–145; the confrontation between O'Gavan and Varela in favor and against continuing slave trading and slavery itself, Fradera, "Imperial Adjustments: Inclusion and Exclusion in the Spanish Imperial Liberalism" (unpublished paper, 2009, cited by permission of the author).

51. See Juan F. Manzano/Ivan A. Schulman, *Autobiography of a Slave/Autobiografía de un esclavo (A Bilingual Edition)* (Detroit, 1996), 110–111. The date of the first meeting between Manzano and Gener I deduce from Manzano's own account (110–111) and the highly likely date of his birth, 1797, noted in Schulman's introduction (13–14). Although Manzano certainly wrote the first draft of his *Autobiografía* at the request of his liberator Del Monte (between 1835 and 1839), friend and protégé of Gener, it does not seem probable that the reference to Gener would have been a simple suggestion from Del Monte to Manzano because of the details Manzano provides about his years in Matanzas and the chronology of that first contact, 1816 or 1817, which coincides with Gener's entry into public life in Matanzas and his dedication to institutionalized "popular instruction" (see José Conangla Fontanilles, *Tomás Gener*, 11–15).
52. Gener, president elect of the Cortes in Seville that would approve the temporary incapacitation of Ferdinand VII (June 1823) with the advance of the French troops, was tried and sentenced *in absentia*; see, for example: Archivo General de Indias (AGI), Ultramar, 40, Nº 26: "Sobre el cumplimiento de la sentencia de la Audiencia de Sevilla contra Tomás Gener y José Santos Suárez, ex diputados en Cortes por la isla de Cuba" (1827).
53. Juan Francisco González y García, *Los catalanes y el grupo liberal de Matanzas* (Matanzas, 1994?), 47–57 (Gener in Matanzas), 59–76 (Jaume Badia in Matanzas). On Badia and the political consequences of the slave trade (in his correspondence with Domingo del Monte), see Albert Garcia Balañà, "Tradició liberal i política colonial," 83–84; on Badia in Cuba and the United States before his return to Catalonia in 1840, see Yolanda Blasco Martel, "'Retornos' de América, banca y capital humano. El caso de Jaime Badía," *Historia Social* 59 (2007): 125–149. On Magí Pers, Garcia Balañà, "Tradició liberal i política colonial," 86.
54. Gener and the American Lyceum: "Report Of the Corresponding Secretary on Lyceums at the Sixth Annual Meeting of the American Lyceum, New-York, May 5, 1836," *The American Monthly Magazine. New Series. Vol. I* (Boston/New York, 1836), 612–618, 615 ("[W]e had to regret the departure of one of the most ardent friends of the Lyceum, Don Tomas Gener"). Gener and Lancaster in 1824–1825: Conangla Fontanilles, *Tomás Gener*, 50–51. Lancaster and William Allen: James Walvin, *The Quakers: Money and Morals* (London, 1997), 104 and 129.
55. See Philip Hone and Bayard Tuckerman, *The Diary of Philip Hone, 1828–1851* (New York, 1889), II, 54–55 (meeting between Hone, Gener, and General Santander). Epistolary news of Gener to his wife on his meetings with Daniel Webster and John Adams, Conangla Fontanilles, *Tomás Gener*, 50–51.
56. "Banquete de trabajadores," *El Constitucional*, 11 January 1841 (nº 642), 6.
57. "Barceloneses, soldados del ejército," *El Constitucional*, 1 October 1843 (nº 1.601), 1 ("[W]e shall be free men, rather than the slaves we have been for so long"); "Barcelona, 11 de Mayo," *El Constitucional*, 12 May 1841 (nº 772), 4.
58. "Libertad y República," *El Constitucional*, 19 February 1841 (nº 681), 2.
59. *El Constitucional*, 21 September 1843 (nº 1.591), 3.
60. See Albert Garcia Balañà, *La fabricació de la fàbrica. Treball i política a la Catalunya cotonera (1784–1874)* (Barcelona, 2004), 247–352; Genís Barnosell, *Orígens del sindicalisme català* (Vic, 1999), 117–159; Genís Barsonell, "Ideologia, política i llenguatge de classes en el primer sindicalisme, 1840–1870," *Barcelona Quaderns d'Història* 6 (2002): 35–49, 35–39, and 43–45.
61. Kirsten McKenzie, "'My Voice is sold, & I must be a Slave': Abolition Rhetoric, British Liberty and the Yorkshire Elections of 1806 and 1807," *History Workshop Journal* 64 (2007): 48–73; Seymour Drescher, "Whose Abolition? Popular Pressure and the Ending of the British Slave Trade," *Past and Present* 143 (May 1994): 136–166.
62. Examples: "Colonias. Quien siembra tiranía cojerá libertad … (I)," *El Constitucional*, 17 February 1841 (nº 679), 3; "Colonias. Quien siembra tiranía cojerá libertad … (II)," *El*

Constitucional, 18 February 1841 (nº 680), 2 ("[B]y which we recall the terrible uprising of Santo Domingo where owner and slave drenched in a river of human blood, the former the remains of despotism, the latter the primacy of freedom"); "Folletín. Colección de puñales" (Fray Gerundio), *El Constitucional*, 22 July 1841 (nº 863), 1–2 ("[W]ord has come that our friends [original in italics; perhaps an ironic reference to Quaker abolitionism?] have disembarked in La Habana together with some estampitas [small holy cards] in which, rather than depicting the resurrection of our Lord or the beheading of St John the Baptist, it took their fancy to illustrate scenes of the negro rebellion in Santo Domingo; what difference?"). On the racial balance (more than the slavery itself) as a key factor of the shadow of Haiti in Cuba, see Ada Ferrer, "Cuba en la sombra de Haití: noticias, sociedad y esclavitud," in Mª Dolores González-Ripoll et al., *El rumor de Haití en Cuba: temor, raza y rebeldía, 1789–1844* (Madrid, 2004), 179–231, particularly 204–209.

63. The literal quotation and the reply to Madden and Alexander published by Bergnes ("Our endeavor through this announcement comes because in Barcelona we have seen an invitation printed and signed by two Englishmen with the ostensible objective of sowing seeds of grave compromises and discord amongst us"): "Sobre la esclavitud en las colonial españolas," *El Constitucional*, 2 June 1841 (nº 793), 2–3. Publicity for Bergnes' "edición española," which could be obtained from the Barcelona bookshop owned by Serafí Veguer: *El Constitucional*, 2 September 1841 (nº 906), 4. On Turnbull in Havana and his attempts to make political and legal use of the figure of the *emancipado* established by the 1835 Anglo-Spanish Treaty, Murray, *Odious commerce*, 120–124 and 141–148. On Anglophobia and tariff policy in the Barcelona of 1841, see Barsonell, *Orígens del sindicalisme*, 193 and 201–202.
64. Alarm over Turnbull and the policy of London: "Crónica interior," *El Constitucional*, 13 January 1841 (nº 644), 1–2 (source of the literal quotation); "Habana, 14 de Abril," *El Constitucional*, 30 May 1841 (nº 790), 2. Information and opinion from a Catalan, a "sensible progressive," who had lived for years in Cuba (the above-cited Jaume Badia, who significantly modified his positions on Matanzas on his return to Catalonia in 1843): "Comunicados (Jaime Badia)," *El Constitucional*, 18 February 1841 (nº 680), 3. The defense of the status quo (not of slave trading) by the Junta de Comercio: *Representaciones de la Junta de Comercio de Cataluña é Informes que acompañó relativamente al proyecto que ha propuesto el gobierno inglés de emancipación de esclavos de las Colonias Españolas* (Barcelona, 1841); Garcia Balañà, "Tradició liberal i política," 84.
65. Barsonell, *Orígens del sindicalisme*, 211–218 and 226–229.
66. The literal quotations and other examples: "Crónica Extranjera (London …)," *El Constitucional*, 22 September 1842 (nº 1,241); "Crónica Extranjera," *El Constitucional*, 19 August 1842 (nº 1,207), 1 ("In this word 'apprenticeship,' states El Correo of the United States, lies the whole secret of English negrophilism"); "Inglaterra," *El Constitucional*, 20 October 1842 (nº 1,268), 1 ("[T]he *Anti Slavery Reporter* criticizes this slave trade under the disguise of a new name"). Divisions in Great Britain over the question, at the juncture of the controversy over the Expedition to Niger and emancipatory failures are treated in Drescher, *The Mighty Experiment*, 166–169.
67. Examples and quotations in: "En Oldham, ¿quién lo creyera? a los cuatro años se oblige," *El Constitucional*, 19 August 1842 (nº 1.207), 1; "Horrores de la Esclavitud," *El Constitucional*, 22 August 1842 (nº 1.210), 1; "Costumbres inglesas (Leemos en el *Blackburn Journal*)," *El Constitucional*, 23 October 1842 (nº 1.271); "Inglaterra (En *The Post* …)," *El Constitucional*, 14 February 1843 (nº 1.369), 1; "Inglaterra (Londres, 8 de Octubre)," *El Constitucional*, 20 October 1842 (nº 1,268), 1.
68. Howard Temperley, *British Antislavery, 1833–1870* (London, 1972), 149; Drescher, *The Mighty Experiment*, 161 (for an explanation of Chartist hostility to the BFAS and the so-called upper-class abolitionists).

69. See Manuel Enrique de Casanova, *Elogio fúnebre del ilustre señor D. José Melchor Prat, director hasta su fallecimiento de la Sociedad Económica Barcelonesa de Amigos del País* (Barcelona, 1856); Vicente Llorens, *Liberales y románticos. Una emigración española en Inglaterra (1823–1834)* (Valencia, 1979), 49 and 161–162.
70. I consulted George Browne, *The History of the British and Foreign Bible Society, from its Institution in 1804 to the Close of its Jubilee in 1854* (London, 1859), II, 5–8 (Prat and Barcelona). The edition by Bergnes: *Lo Nou Testament de Nostre Senyor, Jesu-Christ; traduhit de la Vulgata Llatina en Llengua Catalana, ab presencia del text original* (Barcelona, 1836).
71. "Escuelas Lancasterianas" in Barcelona, see *El Constitucional*, 3 January 1841 (n° 634), 2–3; José Melchor Prat et al., *Reglamento de la Sociedad para mejorar la Educación del Pueblo* (Barcelona, 1845); Bergnes in Borough Road with William Allen, in 1835: see the second section of this paper.
72. On Josep Melcior Prat and the two initiatives, in 1840–1841 and 1850, with literal quotations, see Albert Garcia Balañà, "Ordre industrial i transformació cultural a la Catalunya de mitjan segle XIX: a propòsit de Josep Anselm Clavé i l'associacionisme coral," *Recerques*, 33 (1996), 103–134, particularly 106–107 and 114–-115; a shorter version in Spanish, in Albert Garcia Balañà, "Clase, Pueblo y Patria en la España liberal: comunidades polisémicas y experiencias plebeyas en la Cataluña urbana, 1840–1870," in Fernando Molina, ed., *Extranjeros en el pasado. Nuevos historiadores de la España contemporánea* (Bilbao, 2009), 97–128, particularly 107–110. Prat, civil governor of Barcelona during the turbulent summer of 1835, and during the Luddite attacks at that time. See Anna M. Garcia Rovira, *La revolució liberal a Espanya i les classes populars* (Vic, 1989), 337 and passim.
73. See G. Cuvier, "Historia de los progresos de las Ciencias Naturales desde 1789 hasta el día, por el Sr. barón G. Cuvier," in *Obras completas de Buffon, aumentadas con artículos suplementarios sobre diversos animales no conocidos de Buffon, por Cuvier (traducidas al castellano por Antonio Bergnes de las Casas)* (Barcelona, 1835), Tome II ("Suplemento de Cuvier"); J. J. Virey, *Historia Natural del Jénero Humano (aumentada y enteramente refundida)* (Barcelona, 1835). On Bergnes, Prat, and the spread of Lamarckism in Barcelona, see Agustí Camós, "Antoni Bergnes de las Casas (1801–1879), difusor de la cultura científica y del transformismo lamarckista," *Llull*, 21 (1998), 633–651; Olives Canals, *Bergnes de las Casas*, 180 (Prat, Bergnes and the Virey translation) and 21–23 (origins of the relationship between Prat and Bergnes). On polygenism and racial anthropology in post-1800 France, Drescher, *The Mighty Experiment*, 77–79.
74. Agustí Camós, *La concepció evolucionista de la natura en el programa de difusió científica d'Antoni Bergnes de las Casas (1801–1879)* (Bellaterra, 1994), 36–37; Adrian J. Desmond, *The Politics of Evolution: Morphology, Medicine and Reform in Radical London* (Chicago, 1989); Adrian J. Desmond and James Moore, *Darwin's Sacred Cause: How a Hatred of Slavery Shaped Darwin's Views on Human Evolution* (Boston, 2009). On William Allen, patron and promoter of Robert Owen's New Lanark enterprise, Davis, *The Problem of Slavery*, 248–249.
75. Virey, *Historia Natural del Jénero*, II, 85–86 ("The men most recommendable for their love of humanity have at all times proclaimed the horror with which they regard the slavery of the negro and the barbarity of the slave trade …") and 87–88 ("Although regrettably these observations are true, we do not lose hope for the future of these men. … However they are not our equals …"); I compared this with J. J. Virey, *Histoire Naturelle du Genre Humain (Nouvelle Édition)* (Paris, 1824), II, 104 and 106–107. On Virey and his racial anthropology, see Michael Adas, *Machines as the Measure of Men: Science, Technology, and Ideologies of Western Dominance* (Ithaca, 1989), 298–299, 140–141, and 213–214. On Virey and Cuvier's English translation, Drescher, *The Mighty Experiment*, 78–79.
76. On Prim, captain general of Puerto Rico in 1847, and his promulgation of the "Código Negro" in 1848, see Fradera, *Colonias para después*, 292–299. The organization of what

became known as "La Escalera conspiracy" and O'Donnell in Havana (together with a description of how very limited the antislavery stance of Domingo del Monte was) are the subjects of Robert L. Paquette, *Sugar is Made With Blood: The Conspiracy of La Escalera and the Conflict between Empires over Slavery in Cuba* (Middletown, 1988). On O'Donnell's clash with the radical workers of Barcelona in 1855–1856, see Garcia Balañà, "Patria, plebe y política en la España isabelina: la Guerra de África en Cataluña (1859–1863)," in Eloy Martín Corrales, *Marruecos y el colonialismo español (1859–1912). De la Guerra de África a la "penetración pacífica"* (Barcelona, 2002), 13–77, 45–48.

77. On Bergnes after 1843, Olives Canals, *Bergnes de las Casas*, 29–30. Vila after 1844, see Domingo María Vila, *Voto particular que presentó en 23 de Diciembre de 1845 Don Domingo María Vila sobre el Código Penal* (Madrid, 1847) (Vila in favor of religious freedom and against the death penalty for political crimes).
78. *El Tráfico de Negros, considerado como medio de emancipación inmediata y civilización universal. Por un piloto español* (Barcelona, 1844); *Vida Marítima del Día. Original de D. B. V.* (Barcelona, 1844).
79. Christopher Leslie Brown *Moral Capital: Foundations of British Abolitionism* (Chapel Hill, 2006); Josep M. Fradera, "L'esclavage et la logique constitutionnelle des empires," *Annales HSS* 63 (May–June 2008): 533–560.
80. On Figuerola, Sanromà and Bona, and the creation of the Sociedad Abolicionista Española, see Schmidt-Nowara, *Empire and Antislavery*, 94 and 100–122. On the young Sanromà in Barcelona during the 1840s and his Progressive political formation, also with Antonio Bergnes de las Casas, see Joaquín M. Sanromá, *Mis Memorias. I: 1828–1852* (Madrid, 1887).

– Chapter 10 –

MOMENTS IN A POSTPONED ABOLITION

Josep M. Fradera

These pages have no ambition other than attempting to impose some order on an issue that has concerned us for years, namely, the social links existing between imperial and colonial Spain and slavery as an institution. As we all know, the enlightened attitude of the British set the standard for abolition—firstly, of the slave trade, and then, twenty-five years later, of slavery itself. Most historians will agree, however, that slavery in the Spanish context needs to be analyzed in some isolation from the British experience. British abolition was imposed from above against the background of imperial changes unfolding at the close of the eighteenth century.[1] It came to be a moral position adopted by an entire nation, as the movement could not have prospered without the pressure and involvement of broad swathes of the population—this despite erosion of the movement through the increasingly sarcastic depiction of the Exeter Hall philanthropists by the British political and intellectual establishment from the middle of the nineteenth century.[2] Discussing the evident differences between the Spanish case and the pioneering example of the British in regard to what a contemporary called the "Mighty Experiment" sometimes requires us to shift our viewpoint away from the European stage where pro- and anti-abolitionists were playing out a cultural and political battle. Indeed, the battle was also fought on another front, and understanding the struggle requires us to examine the Spanish perspective as part of a broader horizon that takes account of relations between European metropolises and their colonial dominions, with slavery constituting a key pillar of economic development but also representing a patent contradiction in terms of value systems that were at some point theoretically hegemonic. Considering both the European and transatlantic stages involves greater complexity but also reveals the true dimensions of abolition.

In view of these observations, I would like to examine briefly certain aspects of slavery in the twilight years of the Spanish Empire and in terms of propositions that aim to deepen our understanding of the subject. I will also suggest new approaches that will enable a comparative discussion with regard to other empires.

Slavery and the Atlantic Empires

The first outstanding difference between the British and Spanish Empires in the eighteenth century was the lesser importance of slavery in the latter. Adopting Christopher Brown's perspective, reforming the British Empire necessarily implied extirpating slavery from the social body.[3] Thus, from 1783 onward, the British political establishment very overtly co-opted the message of the abolitionists, who had previously been perceived as something akin to a sect. By 1803–1804, abolitionism was yet another card being played in the game of British imperial politics—to the great surprise of rival European powers, who could hardly have expected a shift in that direction from a country so greatly involved in the slave trade in previous decades. It is worth remembering that Napoleonic France was, at this time, struggling to reconcile the idea of political unity inherited from the republican perspective with the incorporation of colonies that had not abolished slavery (the Mascarene Islands, for instance) and colonies that had reintroduced slavery (the Antilles).[4] Against this background, the attempt to reimpose control over Saint-Domingue by means of an expedition of nearly twenty thousand soldiers under the command of Leclerc ended in spectacular failure.[5]

Nonetheless, the abolition movement's significance needs to be set against the specific importance of slavery in each empire. The British Empire's economy depended greatly on the institution of slavery, despite the economic dynamism of colonies with few or no slaves, such as New England and the Middle Colonies, whose prosperity depended to a large degree on exports of food and maritime services to the slave-based economies of the South, the West Indies, and the colonies with slavery of other European countries.[6] In these conditions, reform of the empire and the purity of the new Republic of 1783 depended on the capacity to reform an institution that was the absolute antithesis of the notion of freedom that underpinned liberalism in the northwest Atlantic. The failure that led to the demarcation of a border between slave and non-slave states in the Republic needs to be considered from this perspective. Recent studies—for example, that by Robin Einhorn—demonstrate how this division largely conditioned the nature of the institutions forged in the early years of the new Republic.[7]

Slavery under the Spanish Empire never acquired the centrality it held in the Atlantic empires of the British, the French, the Dutch, and the Danes or of the Portuguese in Brazil. The reasons are so obvious that it is hardly necessary to state them; suffice it to say that although slave labor was used in the Spanish Empire, it was organized according to a different social principle, namely, regulated forced labor by the Indians. Although such a statement—rather like referring to the discovery of the Mediterranean in Barcelona—is never likely to be committed to posterity in the history books, it is worth reiterating, as an overall perspective is sometimes lost or distorted in local or regional studies of slavery and abolition. My particular focus—in the context of the relationship between slavery and imperial structures—is the perception, by Spaniards and other keen observers of contemporary events, of the place of slavery in their world. This perception has to be understood through particular cases and particular events.

I would like to illustrate how contemporaries perceived colonial slavery with two examples, quite different in their intentions and scope. The first refers to a text that was highly critical of both the workings of the Spanish Empire and of the most oppressive aspects of social life in the Americas in the eighteenth century. This was *Noticias Secretas de América* (1744)—the title chosen by the publisher of the work in England in 1826— written by the Spanish naval officers Jorge Juan and Antonio de Ulloa. Their criticisms of corruption in the viceroyalty of Peru's administration led to the authors' prosecution by the church, which prevented the manuscript's publication.[8] The two writers felt no qualms about criticizing the repeated oppression and extortion of the Indians; few mentions were made, however, of enslaved Africans or their descendants. When they referred, in passing, to the *libres de color* (free people of color), rather than highlight the oppression in which they lived, Jorge Juan and Antonio de Ulloa focused on their capacity to climb the social ladder. I will return to this topic later, as this line of reformist thought is generally credited with less importance than it merits.

Going forward fifty years to the time of the Prussian intellectual, Alexander von Humboldt, we can observe how matters had acquired a certain complexity by the close of the eighteenth century. His magnificent monograph on New Spain is a classic interpretation of what the empire represented; for example, he was highly perceptive of the poisoned logic of what has been called the *sociedad de castas* (society of castes). Yet, when von

Humboldt traveled around South America and New Spain, he showed little interest in slavery.[9] It was only during his second stay in Cuba, in 1804, that he would come to understand the innovation represented by the slave plantation and what it meant to the late Spanish Empire. When he subsequently wrote about the island, although very influenced by the biased information provided by the colony's leading planter, Francisco Arango y Parreño, he was capable of stating clearly the innovation involved in the genesis of a plantation-based society that functioned according to a set of rules that were significantly different from the Spanish Empire's traditional rules—and also exceptional in the context of an empire in its declining years.[10]

An important issue that has not been handled well by historians is the debate regarding ethnicity in the empire during the second half of the eighteenth century—and not so much with regard to slavery's conditions as to the ubiquitous *castas pardas* (the brown castes, those with some African blood). This is rather paradoxical, given that for every slave there were many more descendants of slaves, and the subject therefore needs to be discussed in terms of status, distribution, and permanence. From this viewpoint, it is not overly ambitious—nor is it an excuse for slavery prior to the nineteenth century—to claim that although the Spanish Empire tolerated slavery and slavery was crucial in several parts of it, it was not a slave-based empire. Many issues prevented replication of the prosperous plantation colonies in the Caribbean basin, the most important one being the narrow avenues through which Africans arrived into the Spanish American markets. The deregulation of slave imports in 1789 and subsequent legislative amendments led to the introduction of the plantation system that was yielding great economic rewards for the French and the British in the Caribbean.[11] This shift to a slave-based agriculture essentially benefited the imperial periphery of the Antilles, the Greater Caribbean (including the whole Viceroyalty of New Granada—roughly present-day Colombia) and the River Plate territories. However, the transformation was tardy and brought no appreciable results until the new century dawned, when both the beached whale of the West Indian planters and abolitionism once again came into the sights of the British and the politics of a new empire in ascendance.[12]

The overall significance of these factors points to a key difference in the Spanish Empire as compared with other empires, postulated as follows: it was unlikely that abolition would become a central political and moral issue when slavery as such was not the backbone of Spain's largest American colonies. However, the question remains: how can this aspect of the empire's political and social attitudes be explained, measured, and documented other than by indirect routes? The primary and most acute concern of the Spanish colonial authorities was the social advancement of the castas pardas, namely, the *pardos libres* (free, light-skinned persons), the *morenos libres* (free, dark-skinned persons), and the libres de color, to use the erratic but fluid classificatory terminology of the empire.[13] Their dilemma was, in itself, highly contradictory: on the one hand, there was an interest in removing the restrictions that prevented the castas pardas from obtaining access to specific positions in the empire's institutions (including high positions within the church or matriculation in universities) or in certain privately owned enterprises (for example, artisan guilds); on the other hand, these marginalized social groups kept up constant pressure to obtain access to enclaves from which they were legally excluded. As is well known, the castas pardas were socially mobile in a very able manner where and when this was feasible. This social drift allowed individuals, in some cases, to avoid paying the tribute (or poll tax) that all Indians and free blacks had to pay.[14] For example, a well-known vehicle for social promotion was the Bourbon militia of the late eighteenth century, without altering the rules and censuses that were constantly reshaping the different ethnic and social group denominations.[15] Thus, although their free status prevented them from being segregated, this status was the source of many problems and great distress in practice.

I would like, in passing, to cite an illuminating example. In 1795 the *cabildo* of Caracas asked the city to abolish the *gracias al sacar* system that permitted the descendants of slaves to purchase the right to eliminate all traces of their ancestors, thereby enabling them, in conditions of strict equality, to participate in the marriage market and take up government positions or posts in corporations.[16] As demonstrated by Verena Stolcke, the infamous Pragmatic Sanction on Unequal Marriages (applied to the metropole in 1776 and extended to the entire empire two years later) responded to a perceived need to preserve or raise barriers.[17] This preoccupation with classifications and the political dimension of the castas' exclusions arose again with renewed strength at the time of the first liberal experiment in Spain.[18]

Yet, the desire for social stability essentially arose from within the social body itself rather than from within the Bourbon state, although the latter gave reassurance of its growing capacity for control through that measure. Nonetheless, in colonial territories, those barriers applied more to marriages between whites and blacks and mulattos than between people of European origin and Indians.[19] Meanwhile, there were many reasons why the imperial state created possibilities for social advancement in its militias of pardos libres and morenos libres—it is likely that undermining the position of the elite social category of *españoles americanos* or *criollos* (criollos referring to persons of unmixed European ancestry born in the

Americas, though they rarely used it to describe themselves) was not the least important.[20] The social foundations of the empire were classificatory and paternalistic, with rules establishing hierarchies according to dimensions such as *peninsulares* (Spaniards) versus *americanos;* Europeans versus castas (descendants of Indians and slaves); free versus unfree. However, those rules needed to be rewritten constantly—and the metropole's real world knowledge of the Americas left much to be desired in this respect.[21] The enormous efforts to confront this reality made by the liberal Cortes of 1810–1812 are telling; they provoked the longest and toughest discussions ever heard in the chamber when drawing up and approving the monarchy's first liberal constitution, revealing the malleability of these distinctions and boundaries.[22] This inherent ambiguity was probably a decisive factor in the empire's extraordinary stability and lengthy survival.

The position of slavery, so ubiquitous yet of secondary importance within the broader social system, reveals all its contradictions in very classical developments at the end of the eighteenth century. The regulatory patterns of the Spanish Empire—a society with slaves but not a slave-based society—continued as before. Except for some regions, in this society with a unique legal tradition, masters and slaves lived and worked in close proximity to each other and the rhythms and intensity of the work performed by slaves were not very different from those of the work—often institutionally sanctioned—performed by free laborers and Indians. Assessing the importance of slavery in quantitative terms is perhaps less revealing but still of importance. In this light, the data compiled by Herbert Klein a number of years ago continue to be valid in general terms, even if revised for particular contexts. At the end of the eighteenth century, there were a total of 351,000 slaves in the Spanish Empire, with 80,000 in its Caribbean possessions and 271,000 slaves elsewhere. Peru, with important sugarcane plantations on the coast and an impressive community in Lima, had almost 90,000 slaves, nearly a quarter of the total, followed by Venezuela and New Granada.[23] As for emancipated slaves and slaves' descendants, these were estimated to number around 820,000 (650,000 on the Spanish mainland and 169,000 in the Spanish Caribbean), taking into account the tricky categories in the censuses. The weight of the free blacks and mulattos was therefore significant. Moreover, what was really crucial was the growth of the so-called castas (between about 2 million and 2.5 million people), including the whole range of origins and mixtures. Obviously the importance of slavery was unequal throughout the imperial geography, occupying a ladder of descending importance depending mainly on the availability of Indian and casta labor.

In this respect, the case of New Spain is striking. By the end of the eighteenth century, the number of slaves was stable, having decreased to very modest figures (no more than ten thousand individuals), although they had been of crucial importance in the workforce of Northern silver mining.[24] At the same time, impressive population growth had raised the numbers of the native Indian population to 2.3 million; meanwhile the *mestizo* group, which had been about 177,000 in the middle of the seventeenth century rose, to 1.1 million and the free colored population counted some 360,000 individuals.[25] In Peru, the number of slaves also declined, both in absolute numbers and as a percentage of total population.[26] All in all, the ubiquitous and unequal distribution of castas prevented the idea of slavery from being the central issue to tackle in any hypothetical reform of the empire and, on the contrary, forced the authorities to find local and sometimes disparate solutions for classificatory variations amongst castas.[27] To conclude: Spaniards were confronted with a society with more nuanced social relationships than the ones in the French and British Caribbean or in Portuguese Brazil. Let us compare, for a moment, the aforementioned figures for Spanish America with the ones provided by Dauril Alden for Brazil. There, in the late colonial period, the distribution among groups was as follows: whites amounted to 29.4 percent; blacks and mulattos to 65.9 percent (with 31.4 percent being free and 34.5 percent slaves—the latter approximately a million people); and Indians 4.6 percent.[28] During the same period, the population of the whole of Spanish America, including the continental mainland and the Caribbean islands, was approximately 12,577,000 people. The enslaved population amounted to only a modest 2.79 percent of this total, and 6.51 percent of the population was of African ancestry (this second figure being a rough estimate).[29]

Moreover, compared with slavery's fixity and invisibility from outside, castas were both socially fluid and highly visible, as they benefited from a legal tradition that made this mobility possible, although free blacks and mulattos had to face discriminations in terms of marriages, posts, and occupations that were unknown to descendants of mixed couples of whites and Indians. The enormous amount of legal work protecting Indian communities, tied closely as it was to land ownership and head taxes (*tributo*), was considerably less in the case of slaves and their descendants. However, even in this case, the many protective laws and statutes protected slaves and guaranteed, sometimes, their access to the courts. Also evident was the great degree of dispersion in terms of concentrations of slaves, whose regional and local importance needs, nonetheless, to be acknowledged. The relative proportions of people of African origin across the empire, whether free persons or slaves, essentially explains why there was no genuinely negative perception of African slavery—either in terms of deprivation of liberty or shameful subjugation of the kind exemplified by the endless violence and lack of human rights on the plantations—until the British example awoke dormant consciences. The failure to develop a Spanish version of the French Code Noir (Black Code) is very illuminating in this regard.[30] While Frank Tannenbaum's emphasis on the importance of the Spanish legal tradition is still efficacious, there is no point in returning to the scholarly perspectives of the 1940s. Subsequent decades of research show us that differences among imperial regimes can be explained in terms of forms of slavery and their interplay with the social and legal structure. Although forms of slavery have been widely studied, how they interact with social and legal structures has attracted much less interest, and studies that have been conducted are possibly inaccurate. Alejandro de la Fuente's chapter in this book indicates just how important it is to pursue this topic further. To sum up, the nature of forced labor systems was governed by the type of economic activity but also by local circumstances.

In the Spanish Empire—a society in which slavery had been an element in the established order almost since its inception but which was not a slave-based society—very specific rules imbued the institution with an unusual flexibility.[31] These rules were not the result of any benevolence on the part of property holders or the political establishment; rather, they derived from a legal tradition—with both ancient and more recently developed norms—that shaped a social model that was not based on the dichotomous concept of free versus enslaved. Take, for example, the *coartación* system that enabled slaves to negotiate their own manumission and even impose it legally, plus voluntary manumission by the owner due to the slave's age, as a way of expressing gratitude or to encourage good behavior among the still enslaved.[32] Or take the gracias al sacar procedure (previously referred to), which allowed emancipated slaves and the descendants of slaves to have the ignominious mark of slavery removed.[33] The savings of the libres de color, who were very active throughout the empire and formed the backbone of many professions (other than those from which they were excluded), were thus pocketed (whatever its limited use) by the state, as the savings of the slave population were pocketed by masters through coartación. The gracias al sacar cleansing was necessary to study at universities and join some guilds until the Cortes of Cadiz abolished the measure.[34] In short, those institutions could serve either slaves' strategies for acquiring greater freedom or masters' and the state's need for a stable society.

An evident aggravation of tensions in the Spanish Caribbean and the surrounding coasts of Venezuela and New Granada in the second half of the eighteenth century led to unforeseen consequences for the Spanish empire. The greatest changes occurred as a result of the development of an international slave market that palliated the narrowness of the previous system of *asiento de negros* (contracts between the Spanish crown and slave-trading companies).[35] The emergence of the mining and rudimentary plantation economies in tropical agriculture, as well as of concentrations of newly arrived slaves, would lead to a transformation in the manner slavery was perceived.[36] Nonetheless, leaving aside the responses that were only to be expected in the enclaves where this transformation was most advanced, the extent of cultural change and policy implementation remains unclear.[37] Local studies suggest that the old protective culture and legal system suffered a great strain and often gave way, bringing about a harsher condition for the slave. The same can be said of what happened some decades before with the slaves owned by the Jesuits, after their expulsion from the King's dominions in both the Americas and the Iberian Peninsula.[38] But even amid the rapid transformation of slavery in Cuba, slaves kept going to the courts and exerting pressure upon the Spanish legal system as a whole, as Alejandro de la Fuente's chapter in this collection demonstrates. However, isolated experiences need to be assessed in the context of an enormous empire beset by other problems that were given priority by the authorities. This probably goes some way toward explaining the aforementioned long delay in the creation of Spain's first slave code and its ultimate failure. The origin of the initiative was the Spanish part of Santo Domingo—which says a great deal about its nature and the influence of developments in the French part of the island. It was, essentially, an attempt to modernize the empire's repressive apparatus in a scandalous imitation of what had happened in the neighboring Antilles. The same happened in nineteenth-century Cuba, when plantation owners and the military apparatus of the new Spanish colonialism (which I discuss below) were unable to agree when it came time to decide what kind of slave code they needed.[39]

I would like to conclude this section with a statement that may be perceived as controversial, but that links to my earlier comments. Abolitionism in Spain was never likely to unfold along similar lines to British abolitionism, given the differences in social conditions. Abolitionism made little sense in a context very different from the most general defining features of the Anglo-American pattern of social development: a crucial dichotomy between free and enslaved, a society in which free people of color were relatively few in number, and in which the native population had been largely displaced from the social body. Is there any point in speculating on why Spaniards would imitate a philanthropic phenomenon that originated in a very different context?

Early Liberalism and Abolition

Penetration in the Hispanic world of the humanitarian ideas spreading throughout Europe in the eighteenth century should not be underestimated and influenced attitudes toward indigenous peoples and slaves in the Americas and even in Africa.[40] There is not much sense, however, in expecting the kind of condemnations of slavery that originated in French society, for example, where the position was close to that of the British until around 1814.[41] In the neighboring country, the colonial imagination was almost entirely focused on the sugar islands, especially after Nouvelle France was handed over to Britain under the terms of the Treaty of Paris of 1763. Two issues in particular were of special concern to Spanish reformers, which became apparent during the discussions that took place in 1810 in the Cortes of Cadiz. The first was the condition of the so-called Indians, especially with regard to forced labor systems such as the *mita* in mining fields and the system of *repartos forzosos* (labor obligations in return for the forced distribution and sale of goods)—both very typical from the outset of conquest and fully regulated by the eighteenth century. A recent book by David Weber eloquently explores the humanitarianism that fostered the exercise of authority and imperial tutelage over the indigenous peoples in Spain's colonial dominions in the late eighteenth century.[42] This attitude, with undoubted advantages and drawbacks representing the two sides of the same coin, reflected an ambiguous culture of domination by the first and largest of the European empires of the modern period, built as it was upon the American continent's indigenous populations.

The second issue concerning reformers was the challenge represented by the mobility of the castas pardas, for fairly obvious reasons. The Spanish Empire was a vast hierarchical and paternalistic system, organized not only in terms of officialdom but also according to a meticulous legalistic perspective—a subject that has been studied in depth by James Lockhart and Susan Kellogg for the Indians in seventeenth-century New Spain.[43] In this context, with legislative order and an institutionalized hierarchy holding sway, excessive mobility by the libres de color represented an ongoing dilemma for the imperial authorities. The pardos and morenos libres demonstrated a great capacity for social advancement against which it was very difficult to raise barriers. Documented time and again in texts of the period, this problem greatly preoccupied the Spanish administrators who wished to uphold the rights of emancipated slaves and the descendants of slaves while ensuring that they did not move too far up the social ladder. This protective yet precautionary attitude, highlighted by Antonio de Ulloa in his *Noticias Americanas*, was central to the earliest Spanish expressions of abolition.[44] Irrespective of it being right or not, slavery was perceived not as a permanent condition but as a transitional stage toward the category of casta parda, and in such circumstances, society could not be viewed in terms of a strict division between free and enslaved peoples. Reinforcing those assumptions, many Spanish high administrators in America saw, in line with Juan and Ulloa, the condition of Indians subjected to the mining mita or to restrictions of movement outside Spanish-owned estates as being closer to slavery than the condition of the castas pardas.[45] There are many unknowns in both these attitudes and in the overall logic of the system that remain to be explored in depth, yet this is the background in which turn-of-the-century responses need to be analyzed, for this was the time when early liberalism was forced to draw its own conclusions as part of a far-reaching reform of the empire.

It was in the closing years of Charles IV's reign that the abolition of slavery first came to the fore as a pressing political issue. By 1803–1804, British support for the French military effort to recover their colonies in the Antilles—with the overt purpose of reestablishing slavery—came to an end. At this point, Whitehall articulated a strategy for the separate abolition of slave trading and of slavery and then began exerting constant pressure on its European neighbors with the intention that they implement similar measures.[46] Spain and Portugal were particularly in Britain's sights for very obvious reasons: their political weakness, combined with the extent of slavery in their American dominions.[47] From this point onward, the question of abolition consistently featured on the government's agenda and positions on slavery began to be openly adopted in Spain. The first public speech on the subject was given in 1802 by Isidoro de Antillón at the Real Academia Matritense de Derecho Español y Público. The Academia de Santa Bárbara, as it was popularly known, was founded in 1730 in Madrid and awarded the category of royal academy in 1763 by the Count of Floridablanca.[48] Although the text of Antillón's speech was not published until 1811, during the Peninsular War—by which time the issue was being openly discussed in the Cadiz Cortes—the author's abolitionist stance is likely to have had a wide impact. [49]

The information available to us makes it difficult to ascertain the origins of Antillón's interest in the fate of slaves.[50] To my understanding, the only reasonable conjecture is that it arose in the milieu of the Real Seminario de Nobles of Madrid, where this geographer from Aragon was appointed as an instructor in 1799. The Seminario was one of Spain's foremost teaching centers in the last third of the eighteenth century. The establishment was founded to educate the sons of nobles; the Jesuits ran it until their expulsion in 1767. At that point Jorge Juan, a native of Alicante and a high state official, was appointed to ensure its transformation. Jorge Juan—who had previously suffered ostracism in the Spanish navy because of his joint authorship, with Antonio de Ulloa, of the *Noticias Secretas*—directed the institution for three years until his death in 1770. Although it is not possible to establish a clear intellectual genealogy regarding abolitionism, it is hardly wild conjecture to suggest that there was a link between Jorge Juan's critical spirit and the humanitarian stance of Antillón. Antillón's text, in fact, explicitly refers to Antonio de Ulloa at a key point, as we shall see below, in particular to his *Noticias Americanas*, which attracted great interest.

Ulloa was a well-known writer even referred to by Thomas Jefferson, who in his *Notes on the State of Virginia*, called him a "judicious" author and used him extensively as a principle source of information on the Indians in the Spanish Empire.[51] Careful reading of Antillón's text of 1802 and the amendments of 1811—by which time the issue of abolition of the slave trade and of slavery was being considered by the Cortes—reveals that his stance should not be considered as merely a distillation of British or French arguments.[52] He defended an abolition that was not simply abstract or merely humanitarian. Rather, his abolitionism responded to the conviction—very much in line with that of his precursors—that the first obligation with regard to the multiethnic empire inherited by the generation of 1808 (as the historian Manuel Moreno Alonso has described it) was to reform its governing institutions and in particular those that permitted or upheld extortion of the Indians.[53] This model of reform advised against the introduction of the British model of slavery, which, in appearance at least, was what was being pursued by slave trade liberalization measures adopted in 1789. Citing Antillón: "It is irrefutable that the Indians could supplant in our Americas the work of the Negroes … should they be treated with less harshness and arbitrariness than has been the case until now; if only the excellent laws that have been decreed in their favor by our sovereigns, although presently of no worth, were enforced … the agents of the authority have supplanted them by unjust and oppressive practices."[54]

Between 1799 and 1808 the director of the Real Seminario de Nobles was Andrés López de Sagastizábal, army brigadier and military governor of Cadiz during the Peninsular War, a committed reformer, and the person who had appointed Antillón in 1799. He commissioned Antillón—whose previous dedication to canon law had evolved into an interest in geography—with the translation and writing of textbooks for the college. Another teacher at the Real Seminario de Nobles would also play a prominent role in the history of Spanish abolition, namely, the future bishop Felix Torres Amat, nephew and protégé of Felix Amat, confessor to Charles IV and an eminent Francophile and a collaborator of the British Society of Friends.[55]

A number of other events occurred between the period that these two gentlemen spent in Madrid and the year 1811, when the issue of abolition was discussed for the first time in the Cortes. Against the background of the war against the French, for example, Antillón established contact with a group of liberals who would become core contributors to the *Semanario Patriótico*, an unapologetically liberal periodical that gave free expression to the voices most vehemently raised against slavery and the liberal constitution's refusal to grant full citizenship rights to the castas pardas.[56] This group, which very vociferously supported abolition during the Cadiz Cortes' reforming period, included Manuel José Quintana—writer of some of the *Junta Suprema Central*'s famous decrees promising political equality to the Americans—and the great radical writer, José María Blanco White. Blanco, who left Spain for London in 1810, published a newspaper while in the employ of the British Foreign Office; called *El Español*, it contained explicit propaganda against slavery, the slave trade and constitutional discrimination against full citizenship for the castas pardas.[57] His proposals and those of Americans who supported abolition would, however, collide head-on as a consequence of powerful but opposing interests.[58]

It is appropriate to locate these issues in their context. It was not the Spanish political establishment, to which all these politicians and writers belonged, that caused a change in attitudes toward slavery. Rather, it was the perseverance and insistence of the British with regard to forcing abolition upon other countries, in particular, Spain and Portugal, Britain's allies during the Peninsular War when the French occupied Spanish territory.[59] Portugal had no choice but to accept the conditions imposed by British trading and abolitionist interests—both of which were at the service of British naval hegemony in the Atlantic. The treaty of friendship signed between the two countries in 1810 thus included, in its Article 10, the terms for gradually dismantling the slave trade. A similar solution was also augured for Spain given its position of dependence on the British as far as resisting the French was concerned.[60] The man who took on board this delicate task was the British Ambassador, Henry Wellesley—brother to both the Foreign Secretary and the Duke of Wellington, commander of the British forces in Spain. The Spanish leaders responded to the British pressures because many were as sensitive to the abolitionist message as to the need to satisfy their powerful ally's ambitions. It is therefore undeniable that the tentative Spanish abolitionism of this period responded basically to the vision of an empire in crisis held by the intellectual and governing elite, in particular its most decidedly liberal fringes. It was perhaps these origins from above that, from the outset, condemned Spanish abolitionism to humiliating failure—a failure that was also the failure of British diplomacy.

The shortcomings of Wellesley's mission are very relevant to understanding what was to happen during a large part of the nineteenth century until abolition became definitive very late in the nineteenth century. It was José Miguel Guridi Alcocer, the New Spain deputy for Tlaxcala, who first renewed the debate on the convenience of abolition in the 26 March 1811 session of the Cortes. It was not the first time the question of abolition had been broached in the Spanish Empire; earlier experiments had occurred on the margins of Spanish sovereignty. In 1806, Francisco de Miranda, in his ill-fated attempt to gain independence for Spain's American possessions, had promised abolition in Coro in Venezuela. Coro was a very conflictive context, characteristic of the consequences of the rapid expansion of slavery in the twilight years of the empire and also of the broad and unstoppable impact of the events in Saint-Domingue/Haiti.[61] This initiative perhaps inspired Esteban Fernández de León, an official quite familiar with Venezuela. A former provincial governor there (not to mention a signatory to the famous proclamation by the mayor of Móstoles calling for an uprising against the French army in 1808), he drew up a very critical report on the slave trade and slavery for the *Junta Suprema Central* that called for the suppression of the traffic and a form of slavery based on natural reproduction that was also limited in duration, rather than hereditary and perpetual.[62] Father Hidalgo promised abolition at the onset of the Mexican insurgency against Spain in 1810, a decision that makes Guridi Alcocer's proposal in the Cortes all the more understandable.

The abolitionist proposal of Guridi Alcocer in Cadiz was aimed directly at slavery as an institution. Spanish deputies, with Argüelles at their head, and including other leading figures such as the jurist and deputy for Soria, Manuel García Herreros, readily took up the gauntlet, although they circumscribed the proposal to abolish the slave trade. Nonetheless, the immediate reaction of the Cubans completely altered the course of events. What seemed to be a debate among humanitarian liberals regarding the scope of the measures to be taken became a serious conflict, in which the Antilleans used all the means at their disposal to torpedo the initiative.[63] The pressure exercised by the pro-slavery faction was such that discussion of the abolitionist proposals was relegated to a secret commission, presided over by the deputy for Cordova, the radical Muñoz Torrero, who was entrusted with drawing up a report on the subject. The commission was composed of six members, two from the Antilles (one of these from Cuba). On 27 May, during a night and almost secret session of the Cortes, a letter from the captain general of Cuba, the Marquis of Someruelos, was read aloud; it warned of the disaster that could overtake the island if the abolitionist measure were to succeed. In the end the commission was dissolved without even producing a report: its work had been fully blocked by the obstacles placed before it by the Cuban deputies and the insistent pressure of the main Cuban institutions and the island's supreme authority. The same would occur when Isidoro de Antillón brought up the subject of abolition again, without warning, in the 23 November 1813 session of the Cortes.[64]

A similar scenario would unfold a few years later, during the period known as the liberal triennium (1820–1823), with a similar cast (although not all committed to defending slavery) that included Wellesley as the British Ambassador; the Count of Toreno, Álvaro Flórez Estrada; and the Cuban deputies who were a constant presence in the Cortes. The slavery commission created in 1821 to comply with the aspirations of the British came to naught in circumstances similar to those surrounding the 1811 commission. In view of the spectacular and repeated successes of the pro-slavery faction, some of the Cuban representatives and institutions that supported them gave serious thought to breaking with the abolitionist treaty signed with the British government by Ferdinand VII in 1817. Hindsight confirms that this treaty was hardly worth the paper it was written on. It merely forced the trade in Africans, whether by Spain, Cuba or other countries, to go underground, with all that this implied. The only tangible achievement of the liberal triennium with regard to abolitionism was the approval of a Penal Code, in 1822, which set out severe penalties for the trade in or purchase of slaves in the section referring to *derecho de gentes* (jus gentium). The gesture was pointless, as this provision was never enforced.

The foregoing is a brief summary of the facts known to historians, although further and in-depth research into the subject is required. Likewise, the reasons why the Spanish Catholic Church was so reluctant to intervene—with some few notable exceptions on the margins, some of them already mentioned—need further examination. It was the liberal conscience that led to the issue of abolition being raised in Spain, although within narrow limits and with little success.

The Political Economy of Colonial Survival

A number of key events occurred between 1811 and 1821, a decade in which the question of abolition was taken up by the Spanish legislature.[65] For the liberals, in power again by 1820, many of the issues discussed in the Cadiz Cortes no longer made sense. There were no further attempts to reform the empire, the fate of the Indians was no longer referred to, discrimination against the castas pardas continued and was aggravated by exclusion from citizenship. No major changes to the empire's economic and social institutions were planned. The explanation for such shifting interest is quite simple. On the one hand, the empire was coming apart at the seams in the Americas, and, in the parts that remained under Spanish sovereignty it was the final struggle between the americanos and peninsulares that brought political and institutional questions to the fore. On the other hand, the idea of a general reform of the empire—which had been the broad ambition of the Cortes of Cadiz—was abandoned in favor of a less ambitious project adapted to more immediate needs and possibilities.

Economic circumstances in Spain in the 1820s were such that the liberals set the Spanish economy as the horizon for their reforming zeal. Although the main targets were the landholding and church tithe systems, a broader project aimed at revitalizing the domestic market by linking up the wheat and flour producers of the interior (primarily Castile and Andalusia) with manufacturers located on the periphery (primarily the burgeoning textile industry in Catalonia) was also undertaken. This economic pact between the center and the periphery included parts of America still under Spanish control.

A key element in this new system was the tariff introduced on 5 October 1820, conceived as a means to consolidate economic linkages, develop economic interdependence between the different parts of the monarchy and tackle the deflation that was negatively affecting Spanish trade with its European neighbors. This implied, in turn, another radical change that involved promoting Spanish exports (wines and raisins, flour, paper) to the Americas and partly displacing the flow of manufactured goods from other parts of Europe. This eminently reasonable project can be interpreted as a last-ditch attempt to rebuild and reshape the economies of Spain and its American possessions.[66] It can also be interpreted as a desperate effort to unify a territorially smaller empire and ensure its survival. In brief, the idea was to give life to an axis connecting Spain, Havana, New Orleans (in Spanish hands until 1802, then sold to the Americans by the French in 1803, but with a huge Spanish community) and Veracruz, the economic fulcrums of an empire in decline. We should not overlook the fact that in the past the Spanish Empire was in fact built as an economic unit on axes linked by the circulation of precious metals rather than by the exploitation of territorially demarcated areas. However, by 1820 a new reality was configured by goods, maritime services, emigrants, and the slave trade.[67] In other words, the colonial system of the nineteenth century was beginning to take shape. The active participation of Havana and Cuba in the circuit was absolutely crucial. Consequently, the acceptance of slavery (and the illicit slave trade) was an indispensable condition for developing this new colonial system's political economy. As well as forming the basis for the Cuban economy, with its capacity for absorbing imports of wine and flour from Spain, it was also the basis for a strategic tradeoff with the Havana elite.

This was the genesis of the political and economic model that took shape in the aftermath of the imperial crisis and that was aimed at colonial survival. The question of abolition arose but now the debate was transformed. During the Cadiz Cortes the Spanish had been prepared to accept the terms, along Portuguese lines, proposed by Great Britain. During the liberal triennium, Spanish liberals did not raise the subject of slavery in Cuba, for the reasons described. This change in position was astonishing, particularly as the years 1820 to 1823 were the only time when key figures in Cuban politics advocated the abolition of slavery. These included the Catalan-born Tomás Gener, a leading figure of the Matanzas liberal milieu, and above all, the group headed by Félix Varela, protégé of Bishop Espada and an avowed abolitionist.[68] The two groups' different perspectives, on this issue and others, should not be confused, but their relevance is undeniable. For Gener, abolition was part of necessary statutory reforms that should not, however, lead to independence (as had happened in Venezuela). For Varela, however, abolition was a key factor in internal Cuban reform, political and moral, and the most salient element in the confrontation between two views of how the island's future should unfold. Varela's stance met with silence in Spain; in Cuba, trading interests prevailed above political interests, with Varela himself referring to questions of state all being resolved "on the docks and in the warehouses."[69] Both of them, Gener and Varela, were eventually forced into exile, never to return to Cuba. The silence in Spain was thus matched by the euphoria of major Cuban economic interests. This euphoria explains, for example, how the Cuban deputy Juan Bernardo O'Gavan—elected to the Spanish Cortes on two occasions—could publish an openly pro-slavery pamphlet in Madrid, aimed at shielding slave-trading interests against possible philanthropic inroads by the peninsulares; the only person in Spain to take him to task for his aggressive pro-slavery stance was a young English traveler, John Bowring, a tireless student of foreign languages and a future diplomat in Asia.[70] Isolated groups of abolitionists did exist, including sympathizers in Barcelona who translated and published Thomas Clarkson's tract *The Cries of Africa* in 1825 and disseminated humanitarian ideology. But they failed to make any legislative impact or to raise discernible popular support. It was not until the political changes of 1868 that a new departure was heralded.

Cuban political influence in Spain increased decisively, and this, in practice, meant the postponement sine die of any abolitionist proposals. In fact, the overall situation can help us to understand the dénouement of the most crucial point: in short, why those first liberal shoots of Spanish humanitarian attitudes failed to lead to a grassroots movement. Noteworthy during the brief liberal rule of 1820 to 1823 was systematic noncompliance with the abolition treaty already referred to, a situation that obviously continued after the second liberal experiment's failure and the restoration of the neoabsolutist Ferdinand VII. Clear evidence of the Spanish governments' position between the 1820s and the critical period (1854–1855) when Juan de la Pezuela was in charge in Cuba, was noncompliance with the treaty for prosecuting dealing in slaves. This abandonment of principles was relieved only by some moments of vacillation, for example, in 1835, when it was agreed to make the terms of the treaty harsher (regarding the equipment carried by suspected slave traders on the high seas) or when coastal patrols to control the entry of African slaves were intensified during the period 1841 to 1843 when Gerónimo Valdés was Governor of Cuba.[71] In general, however, passiveness and complicity were the dominant notes.

Although historians are familiar with these facts, it is appropriate to examine their significance in terms of how they hampered abolitionism in Spain. In the period 1820 to 1840, no doubt remained as to the viability of the Cuban development model and the pressing need to permit the entry of slave labor. This unwritten golden rule of Spanish politics in the first half of the nineteenth century condemned the weak and divided Spanish abolition movement to the margins of political and intellectual life. This occurred in paradoxical circumstances, as slavery was being abolished through successive waves everywhere (with the exception of Brazil, where the slave trade was not abolished until 1851 and slavery in 1888) and being replaced by laborers often employed in conditions very close to those of the slaves. For this reason, Spain, which, unlike the former Portuguese possession, did not have a diplomatic statute of protection and subordination, was several times on the verge of being declared and treated as a rogue state.

Spain's motives for adopting this increasingly untenable position need to be examined in greater depth. This examination needs to take into account both the circumstances surrounding the abolition movement and the deeper meanings underlying arguments in favor of abolition. Circumstances dictated several changes in direction that shifted the debate's focus on numerous occasions. As we have seen, from the 1820s until 1837, the greatest arguments in favor of tolerating slavery in Cuba were unquestionably economic. Cuba was a guarantee, from the late 1820s, of remittances of surplus money that contributed greatly to Spain's coffers.[72] The great deal of 1822 to 1825 between the Cuban plantation owners and the authorities defined this do ut des: tolerance of slave trading and defense of slavery in exchange for fiscal remittances to Spain. The lucrative trade of private individuals, whether as ship-owners, sailors, merchants, manufacturers or investors in different sectors of the buoyant Antillean economy, not to mention migration flows, relied upon that tradeoff between the metropolitan power and the Cuban planter elites. It is still difficult to measure the importance of all of those elements involved in the colonial relationship, with the opacity of slave trade earnings and the colonial tax system's obscure operations being the most but not the only tricky business in this story; but it seems difficult to underestimate them.[73] The economic potential of the Cuban plantation system, which was extended to Puerto Rico from the 1830s, guaranteed a strong connection with the Atlantic world and also led to the above-mentioned revival of the liberal project of the twenties. In practice—even despite the political folly represented by the imperial restoration of Ferdinand VII, which closed the door fully on Spanish trade with the rebellious American continent—the 1820s witnessed the establishment of trading relations between the Spanish periphery (Santander, Cadiz, Malaga, Alicante, and Barcelona) and Havana and, via the Cuban entrepôt, with the cotton ports of northern Brazil and the southern United States, not to mention the development of a number of other complementary routes to the south and the Gulf of Mexico. However, all this depended in the end on the Cuban market, which, in turn, depended on the plantation system of agriculture that was expanding rapidly during this time. It is no accident that this period witnessed Cuban slavery's significant expansion, despite the illegality of slave trading with the Antilles. In fewer than fifteen years—between 1827 and 1841 (problematic though the 1841 census was, given evident manipulation by the authorities)—the number of slaves in Cuba rose from 186,942 to 436,495, with slaves arriving from Africa at a rate of 17,000 per year in the 1830s. By 1846 the number was 323,759, with 5,000 Africans entering Cuba per year in the 1840s—numbers that reflect British actions under Palmerston's auspices to suppress the slave trade.[74] Given the very low level of slave reproduction, the growth in numbers employed in the *ingenios* (sugar plantations) and on the coffee plantations can only be accounted for by new arrivals—in other words, the illegal trade was taking place in contravention of international treaties. In these conditions, a broad-based social alliance between key economic interests in Spain and Cuba effectively banished abolitionism to the margins.

The liberal revolution and the political process that brought the liberals to power between 1835 and 1842 reopened the Cuban and colonial debate. With the entrenchment of the postimperial economic system, the debate shifted toward the question of how to ensure Spanish colonial survival in the Antilles and the Philippines. As I have explained elsewhere, three approaches were combined to address this problem: a) reinforcement of political and military authority in the island enclaves; b) political exclusion of colonials from representation (in particular, from the supreme legislative body) and prevention of the application of the liberal political framework (freedom of association, press and reunion, whatever restrictions they faced on metropolitan soil; loss of representation in the Spanish Cortes) in overseas provinces; and c) maintenance of ethnic distinctions in the three colonial enclaves—what the Cuban captain generals referred to eloquently as *equilibrio de razas* (racial balance).[75] The first two measures ensured a strong executive power, united in a policy based on force in prima ratio—that is, not on a consensus with the colonials, as was tried in the previous periods of 1810–1814 and 1820–1823. The third measure ensured that this policy would maintain and take advantage of a particular social structure in the enclaves under Spanish influence. Any proposal for the abolition of slavery clearly represented a real threat. For this reason, despite British abolitionists' campaigns in Spain and the fact that news of abolition in the British Empire in the period 1833–1838 and in the French and Danish colonies in 1848 circulated widely in Spain, the real impact on policy and on Spanish public opinion was minimal and incidental.

The Spanish government's position was reinforced by two central and overlapping arguments. First, there was no possibility of arriving at an understanding with the white elites in the overseas possessions. In this postimperial period, the notion of a liberal pact was totally absent from official Spanish thinking on how to preserve its remaining possessions.[76] This standpoint did not arise exclusively as a consequence of resentment toward criollos by the Spanish officials defeated in wars in the Americas (referred to as the *ayacuchos,* in reference to the decisive Battle of Ayacucho in Peru) who governed the overseas possessions. However, it is indeed true that a large proportion of the liberal high command who were leading colonial figures beginning in the 1830s—among them, Gerónimo Valdés, de la Camba, Anglona, Jacobo and Juan de la Pezuela (brothers), José and Manuel Gutiérrez de la Concha (brothers), and Leopoldo O'Donnell— not to mention many of their peers who were eminent public figures in Spain, inherited bitter personal memories of defeat from their predecessors. However, the fundamental issue was that some of these officials had witnessed firsthand what happened in Spain and its colonies each time a constitutional framework was reestablished. In other words, they had firsthand experience of the complexity of managing societies split along both political and ethnic lines. During the liberal triennium of 1820–1823 and when the Cadiz constitution was reestablished in 1836, senior functionaries, both civil and military, had witnessed how difficult it had been to maintain political stability in overseas possessions in the Americas and the Philippines, where severe confrontations on issues such as fair representation in the central and local institutions were taking place.[77] These confrontations, which threatened the continuity of Spanish sovereignty, occurred between both criollos and peninsulares and between criollos and castas pardas (or *indios* and mestizos, that is, individuals of Chinese descent in the Philippines) and other excluded groups. We should place events like the Aponte freedmen conspiracy in Havana in 1812 or the popular uprising against the Chinese and foreigners in Manila in 1821 in this broad framework of social distress and imperial transformation.[78] The dramatic change of the entire colonial policy in 1837 should therefore be understood as a response to this chronic instability and to the prolongation of a conflict that had sharpened in response to the unbridled expansion of plantation slavery and coerced labor.

The second argument underpinning the Spanish government's stance was an unexpected by-product of the interminable debate regarding the exclusion of castas pardas from Spanish citizenship, implicit in the arguments given above. The expansion of the plantation system in Cuba (which was a product of the nineteenth century) further fueled the conflicts of a multiethnic society.[79] Sugar plantations began to transform the social landscape of the western side of the island from the beginning of the nineteenth century, decisively shifting productive activities toward those relying on large contingents of slaves. Clearly manifested for the first time in Spanish imperial history were the demographic and social characteristics of a true plantation-based society—comparable to those of the southern United States, northern Brazil, and the British and French Antilles until 1833 and 1848. The Cuban plantation model was based on a moving frontier and was not valid by any means for the entire island. Nor was it valid for Puerto Rico, where, apart from the Ponce sugar plantations on the southern coast of the island, most slaves worked on small-scale peasant-style agricultural holdings. A significant change in the nature of Cuban slavery occurred between 1820 and 1840, a period in which conditions were extremely harsh for the many thousands of Africans and Asians involved in those international market-oriented agricultures. They improved slightly in 1843–1844, however, in response to the dramatic events surrounding the plot known as the Conspiración de la Escalera (literally, "the Ladder Conspiracy"), the most repressive event in the history of Cuban slavery. The definitive change in that direction occurred as a result of a steady increase in slave prices in the decades of the 1850s and 1860s.[80]

Abolition and the Transformation of Slavery

Abolition movements were pluralistic by definition, and studies by Roger Anstey, David Brion Davis, Seymour Drescher, and David Eltis have focused on many different aspects of British and European abolitionism.[81]

Christopher Brown's work throws light on certain questions of interest to us here; for example, what led high imperial officials to pay attention to a movement for abolition that originated on the fringes of society and—apart from the exceptional case of Wilberforce—alien to their world? To many in England, abolition was an instrument for Christian purification, as in the hands of Granville Sharp and James Stephen (father of Sir James Stephen, under-secretary of State for the Colonies from 1836 to 1847, who played a key role in effectively abolishing slavery).[82] Against the background of the turbulence of the industrial revolution and social upheaval, abolition was for others a possibility for simultaneous moral and political reform (an argument that Alexis de Tocqueville would import into French politics prior to the events of February 1848).[83] We also know that abolition fit well into classical political economics paradigms, the Utilitarian School and the lay sermons of the *Edinburgh Review,* which viewed free labor as a formula for progress and which preached the advantages of waged labor and free trade to the world.[84] These issues lead again to our central question: what exactly was the Spanish experience of abolitionism? More precisely, what was the real significance of the Spanish abolitionism of the 1850s and 1860s after some decades of silence and conformity? I refer to the abolitionism that managed to make its gospel heard after the revolution of September 1868, when the issue of abolition was included in the large basket of reforms demanded for the country by the *Juntas Revolucionarias* created in Spain's most important cities.[85]

Attempting to draw parallels between the British and Spanish experiences is, I repeat, an endeavor doomed to fail. Nonetheless, links can be identified, such as those forged between intellectual and social groups, which—to a greater or lesser degree—shared opinions and a similar worldview or, to be more precise, of certain aspects of the world. From this perspective, two distinct currents of thinking with different chronologies can be identified. Although both movements had lain dormant for a long time, the political changes of 1868—when the dismantling of slavery became identified with a desire for political reform—enabled them to impose their perspective. Furthermore, a very favorable opportunity for colonial reform and the dismantling of slavery (the illegal slave trade had ended in the mid-1860s) was presented by the Civil War in North America, with the victory of the northern states sounding the death knell of slavery. The first current was represented by a local liberal reforming tradition in which the flame of abolition had continued to burn throughout all the years of mid-century tension; the best-known example was the tenacious Catalan-Barcelona movement. This abolitionism, which acted in the context of a city experiencing great turmoil, was characterized by underground Protestantism, open admiration for the British example, and sensitivity to events in Cuba, based on observation and concern for an island with many links to the city and region in those crucial years. This group garnered influence and achieved public visibility in the liberal debates of 1820–1823 and also in the debates that took place in 1836–1837 and in 1842–1843, when, given its inherent contradictions and the pressures of the British consul in Cuba, David Turnbull, the Cuban slavery system seemed to be on the point of imploding.[86] Even so, these abolitionist circles failed to impose themselves or win sufficient social influence to seriously pose a challenge to official policy. Because this issue has been dealt with in depth elsewhere, there is no need for me to discuss it further here.[87] Still, the problem remains: why were those discreet circles in Barcelona so obviously isolated both in their own city and from the rest of the country?

The second current is associated with discourses on labor and has been examined in depth by Christopher Schmidt-Nowara.[88] Mid-nineteenth-century labor discourses developed—in relation to our topic—along two parallel lines.[89] One of these legitimized slavery and coerced labor on the basis of numerous arguments (disease, discipline, work in tropical agriculture), few of them explicitly racial. The other line exalted the supremacy of free waged labor, given its economic potential and greater dignity. Both discourses, although they point in different directions, were typical of liberal economics. From the time of the Revolution of September 1868 and the Moret Law of 4 July 1870—which granted *libertad de vientres* (free wombs) and the manumission of elderly slaves—abolition was gradually and partially introduced in Cuba, conditioned by the first separatist war and the emancipation policies taken by the insurgent command.[90] Once abolition was definitively approved in Puerto Rico in March 1873, the two discourses' general lines of development became clear.[91] Gathered on one side were those in favor of maintaining the colonial status quo, continuing with slavery in Cuba and maintaining the tariff protection of Spanish trading and ship-owning interests. On the other side there were those who, convinced of the impossibility of maintaining a servile labor system and conceding the impossibility of forging a protectionist economy under pressure from the international economy, supported political reforms in the Antilles and the lowering of tariffs. Joaquín Sanromá—a Catalan who fled to Madrid to escape the asphyxiating atmosphere of support for the status quo in the Antilles among the upper classes—exemplifies the disjunctions that were so typical of the period. He was so removed from his origins, in fact, that he entered the Cortes as a deputy for Puerto Rico, with an agenda that included the immediate abolition of slavery. The future of a process that required fifteen years to reach its logical and legitimate conclusion in Spain and in Cuba depended, above all, on the relative strengths of the two coalitions and their interface with political maneuvering. When a window on reform opened in the 1870s, attempts to impose an ambitious project for immediate abolition—with compensation for slave owners—failed in Cuba in the face of lobbying by pro–status quo groups, which included the pro-slavery faction.[92] One of the more ambitious proposals was tabled by some of the most reputable figures backing abolitionism in this period, namely, Julio Vizcarrondo (from Puerto Rico and founder of the Spanish Abolition Society in 1865), Rafael María de Labra, Francisco Pi y Margall, Nicolás Salmerón, and Francisco Giner de los Ríos.

The core problem was that both those labor discourses already mentioned unfolded against the background of the fundamental changes occurring in colonial Spain in the interim years between the two episodes of greatest public visibility for abolitionism: the first decades of the century and the 1860s and 1870s. Abolitionism was a reactive discourse that swam against the tides of change that were covering the Spanish colonial world in this crucial period. Among the many pieces of that current, the notion that waged labor by Europeans and locals could not underpin an agricultural system geared toward tropical agricultural exports was perhaps at the center.[93] In some sense this assumption was the flip side of free-soil ideologies in areas of settler-capitalism in other countries, the United States being the prime example.[94] Behind the defense of slavery and forced labor as the norm for the entire Spanish colonial world from the 1820s until the late nineteenth century (and fully applied still in the twentieth century in the Spanish colonies in the Gulf of Guinea) was the idea that agricultural work and certain kinds of craft and factory work could not be performed in colonial settings by free labor.[95] Thus, forms of independent peasant labor typical of these colonies during the eighteenth century were gradually displaced by more intensive forms of labor—with the slave plantation representing the most developed of these labor systems. Whereas the peasant family unit did not rule out the aid of slave labor on a small scale (compared with what would come later), the plantation directly precluded the use of free labor.[96] Unfree labor was almost always imposed in sectors associated with the international market, a very competitive one. Of all the agricultural enterprises based on unfree forms of labor, the slave-based plantation system was best positioned to take advantage of the extraordinary elasticity in demand for food products and raw materials from the most developed economies of Europe and North America.[97] In this regard, events in Cuba between 1810 and 1870 were a clear demonstration of the economic potential of the plantation and the slave labor associated with it.[98] Nonetheless, the emergence of the plantation system in the Greater Antilles should not be viewed in isolation from the expansion of slavery and other forms of coerced labor elsewhere—for example, in Puerto Rico, which had small-scale sugar plantations in several coastal zones and peasant-based coffee production in the mountains, or in the Philippine tobacco monopoly, which was based on the coerced labor of family-based households and the expansion of regulated capitation systems based on labor and affecting all the peasants in the archipelago.[99] What linked the sugar plantations of Cuba and the tobacco plantations of the Cagayan valley on the island of Luzon was the authorities' growing awareness of the unavoidable need for unfree labor in the colonies—whether slave, contracted, forced, or passbook-controlled. This was not merely economic reasoning; there was also the issue of perpetuation of and accentuating ethnic divisions in labor systems inherited from the empire and adapted to the colonies of the nineteenth century. Furthermore, a perverse division of labor allowed sharing of free-labor values on metropolitan soil while embracing the blessings of coerced labor in its colonial possessions.

Nonetheless, the perception of the appropriateness of coerced labor in tropical agricultural economies was largely shared by other colonial countries—including those that abolished slavery between 1833 and 1848—and also by the many thousands of emigrants from Spain and Europe, who, escaping the jaws of harsh labor systems in their own countries, now stood to benefit from their status as colonial whites abroad. There were few antidotes to this logic, which imbued Cuban and Puerto Rican slavery with an air of colonial normality until very late. In Spain, neither humanitarian abolitionism nor free-labor discourse was capable of producing and imposing an alternative to this dark vision of labor in the tropics. The failure, in the 1840s and 1850s, of concerted attempts to whiten Cuba by contracting Spanish peasants for agricultural work on the island merely contributed to extending and confirming the notion that drawing on a pool of free European labor for the island colonies was not a viable option. Instead, the success of incorporating Chinese coolies and enslaved Indians from Yucatan reinforced the dreadful appreciation of a world constituted by a correspondence between degrees of servitude and degrees of color.[100] Again, in the context of the mid-nineteenth-century Caribbean, nothing seemed extraordinary about this appreciation for the advantages of a combination of slave and indentured work.[101]

We need somehow to establish how full-scale slavery and nineteenth-century regulations modified and threatened the social stability and more paternalistic and fluid norms inherited from the old world of slavery and servitude. The literature is conclusive in stating that the capacity of slaves acting autonomously in earlier phases of the empire was severely limited although never entirely eliminated. Furthermore, although the plantation certainly was the "cause of all distress," to cite James Walvin's apt phrase, we also have to remember that the plantation was the key social institution in only one part of Cuba and some coastal areas in Puerto Rico.[102] The island as a whole formed part of a greater colonial system, and it was in that colonial system as a whole that the age-old social and cultural norms held sway, despite their eventual erosion and limitation in both scope and in practice by the plantation system and the imbalance in the proportion of slaves and free persons.[103] The brutality of the plantation system has indeed been depicted, but using broad brushstrokes. What is still lacking, perhaps, is a more in-depth analysis of mobility, the formation of slave families and conditions both in and outside the ingenio for this period, when the largely disruptive model of large scale plantations—even for societies in which slavery dated back to the sixteenth century—was ascendant.

Nineteenth-century Cuban history seems to indicate that reduced possibilities for social advancement and oppressive practices within the plantation world motivated the open revolts against slavery that occurred in the 1840s, leading to harsher repressive violence against slaves in both Cuba and Puerto Rico.[104] The most exceptional case of violence being unleashed was the Conspiración de la Escalera of 1843–1844, referred to earlier, which undoubtedly hastened changes in attitudes.[105] Under the pretext of a plot by the British consul to raise slaves employed in the ingenios, the colonial authorities neutralized the criollo followers of the reformer Domingo del Monte, the pardos libres and the morenos libres, and harshly repressed the slaves in the ingenios.[106] These events led to a mobilization of major pro-slave-trading and ship-owning interests in Spain's main cities in a massive campaign of support for the Spanish authorities in Cuba. Nonetheless, such dynamics should not distract us from studying the real conditions of slaves and also their lives outside the plantation, in economic and social settings that lent themselves to legal claims, buying freedom through coartación, the formation of families and interracial unions, and, indeed, the construction of important enclaves of socialization and mobility.[107] The linearity and humanitarian compassion of abolitionist discourse lent itself poorly to registering the transformations and nuances of a very complex system. Abolition, the product of the liberal conscience, had as its aim the liberation of slaves; consequently, more practical issues such as improvements to the slaves' living conditions or access to the courts and protection of state officials did not penetrate the logic of the abolitionist project. Given this context, it is easy to understand that discussions on crucially important issues concerning living and working conditions—referred to as "amelioration" in the British West Indies during the period subsequent to the abolition of slave trading in 1833—hardly caused a ripple in the Spanish-speaking Caribbean.[108]

An essential factor in determining the scope of abolitionism was the achievement of a broad consensus regarding the need to expand slave and coerced labor so as to ensure the survival of the Spanish colony—reflecting the political convenience of permitting servile forms of labor in Spain's overseas possessions. As mentioned previously, in the aftermath of the imperial crisis, two key pillars supported the Spanish colonial system: the political exclusion of the criollo elite and the notion of equilibrio de razas. Political exclusion was the outcome of the radical tack of 1837 away from the inclusive program of the liberals of 1810. If the liberal program had initially intended to include the Americans in a politically unified system—a proposal whose contradictions are beyond the scope of this text—from 1837 it very pointedly and deliberately excluded representatives from the overseas' possessions. Following colonial disintegration, Spain did not build a separate political system for the colonies along the lines of the many political statutes implemented by the British and French, the latter, for example, drawing a clear distinction between old and new colonies after 1848. Rather, it simply excluded the colonies from the liberal framework, dangling before them a vague promise of future special legislation that would never be enacted.[109] The social heterogeneity of the colonies was the excuse used to justify this policy of the criollo upper classes' political exclusion. The other side of the coin of exclusion was authoritarian government, as personified in the hypertrophied figure of the captain general–governor. His unconditional authority in colonial affairs, both political and military, was underpinned by a policy of deliberately maintaining the equilibrio de razas by skillfully manipulating racial differences and ethnic distrust and conflict in the Spanish dominions.[110] In this context, what remains to be studied in depth by historians is how the new reality of the plantation—with its undercurrent of violence and radical alteration of the conditions in which slaves lived and worked—modified the traditional paternalism of an empire functioning according to a legal tradition (the vaunted *Leyes de Indias*) that was still theoretically valid. What remains clear, for the reasons given above, is that defense of the colonial status quo was increasingly identified with a defense of slavery. Doubts remain regarding the extent to which the military, civil and judicial administration complied and colluded with the owners of the ingenios in their defense of slavery in their everyday circumstances. Furthermore, we have not been able to determine whether the rules were different for slaves living within plantations as opposed to slaves living outside their confines, or, being more precise, the degree to which they were. It is difficult to address these questions given how research stands at present, and, I reiterate, comparisons between contexts need to be appropriate. They need to be made, for example, for locations (it should be a relatively easy matter to list them) where plantation slavery was juxtaposed with slavery on a smaller scale and with concentrations of ex-slaves and the descendants of slaves.

In conclusion, the comments above need to be assessed with a view to posing the right questions and advancing our understanding of the complexity of slavery in different contexts. One such inquiry is why—in a country dealing with major internal upheaval but with liberal institutions in place since the 1830s—the abolition movement failed to make headway until reformers on all sides realized, following the civil war in North America, that slavery was in its death throes.[111] Indeed, the new departure and change in perception heralded by the political events of September 1868 led to a confrontation in Spain between those who wished to prolong the status quo of colonial subordination and slavery, and those who perceived the system to be simply unsustainable as well as unjust and cruel. The abolitionism of the period 1865 to 1874 was essentially represented by a coalition that included in its ranks free-trade economists (Laureano Figuerola, Joaquín Sanromá, and Luis María Pastor), colonial reformers (Julio Vizcarrondo and Rafael María de Labra), leading figures in the republican movement who felt that the liberty they invoked as a principle could not deny a free status to their fellow human beings (Francisco Pi y Margall, Nicolás Salmerón, and Estanislao Figueras), and liberal politicians with long careers such as Salustiano Olózaga, who had participated in the debates of 1837. Popular backing for abolition in Spain—over and above, for example, the massive campaigns of 1868 motivated by the prospect of political change—requires further study and assessment. Nonetheless, casting a glance back over the nineteenth century, we need to explain the lengthy hiatus in open and effective abolitionist activity between the earliest calls for abolition in 1811, inspired by the British example, and abolition with tangible results following the implementation of the Moret Law of 1870 and the social pressures caused by war in Cuba, in which enslaved men and women took an active part. To contribute to a better answer to all these questions (which is not the purpose of these pages) and to improve our knowledge about the past, it is clearly not enough to observe just one of the stages on which the drama unfolded. Rather, events in the metropolitan arena as well as in the remotest colonial societies need to be assessed, especially in view of the fact that slavery was an institution so ancient that it appeared, to the view of too many and for such a long time, to be perfectly coherent with the ruling social order.

Notes

1. A complete discussion in comparative terms in Robin Blackburn, *The Overthrow of Colonial Slavery, 1776–1848* (London, 1988).

2. Regarding the change in attitudes with regard to these matters, still irreplaceable is the old work by Douglas Lorimer, *Colour, Class, and the Victorians: English Attitudes to the Negro in the Mid-nineteenth Century* (Leicester, 1978).
3. Christopher Leslie Brown, *Moral Capital: Foundations of British Abolitionism* (Chapel Hill, 2006).
4. Yves Bénot and Marcel Dorigny, eds., *1802: Rétablissement de l'esclavage dans les colonis françaises. Ruptures et continuités de la politique coloniale française (1800-1830)*. Aux origines d'Haiti (Paris, 2002); Claude Wanquet, *La France et la première abolition de l'esclavage 1794–1802: les cas des colonies orientales* (Paris, 1998); Miranda Frances Spieler, *Empire and Underworld: Captivity in French Guiana* (Cambridge, MA, 2012).
5. Laurent Dubois, *Avengers of the New World. The Story of the Haitian Revolution* (Cambridge, MA, 2004); Carolyn Fick, *Making of Haiti: The Saint Domingue Revolution from Below* (Knoxville, 1990).
6. A vigorous defense of the southern colonies' greater dynamism can be found in Jack Greene, *Pursuits of Happiness: The Social Development of Early Modern British Colonies and the Formation of American Cultures* (Chapel Hill, 1988).
7. Robin L. Einhorn, *American Taxation, American Slavery* (Chicago, 2006).
8. The famous text's title should be the following: *Discurso y reflexiones políticas sobre el estado presente de los reinos del Perú*. The best introduction to the text's creation is in Luís Javier Ramos Gómez, *Las "Noticias secretas de América." de Jorge Juan y Antonio de Ulloa (1735–1745)* (Madrid, 1985).
9. An excellent approach to the learned Prussian's viewpoint can be found in Michael Zeuske, "Cuba, la esclavitud atlántica y Alexander von Humboldt: ¿de mal ejemplo a globalización eficaz?" in Imilcy Balboa and José A. Piqueras, eds., *La excepción americana. Cuba en el ocaso del imperio continental* (Valencia, 2006), 21–35.
10. *Ensayo político sobre la isla de Cuba* Miguel Angel Puig-Samper, Consuelo Naranjo Orovio, and Armando García González, eds. (Madrid, 1998); see also, Dale Tomich, "The Wealth of Empire: Francisco de Arango y Parreño, Political Economy, and the Second Slavery in Cuba," Christopher Schmidt-Nowara and John Nieto-Phillips, eds., *Interpreting Spanish Colonialism: Empires, Nations, and Legends* (Albuquerque, 2005), 55–85.
11. I dealt with this in "La participació catalana en el tràfic d'esclaus (1789–1845)," *Recerques* 16 (1984): 119–140.
12. On this point, see David Murray, *Odious Commerce: Britain, Spain and the Abolition of the Cuban Slave Trade* (Cambridge, 1980), 27.
13. James Lockhart and Stuart Schwartz, *Early Latin America: A History of Colonial Spanish America* (Cambridge, 1983), 315–321; on the tricky subject of castas classifications, see María Elena Martínez, *Genealogical Fictions: Limpieza de Sangre, Religión, and Gender in Colonial Mexico* (Stanford, 2008); Andrew B. Fisher and Matthew D. O'Hara, eds., *Imperial Subjects: Race and Identity in Colonial America* (Durham, 2009); Tamar Herzog, *Defining Nations: Immigrants and Citizens in Early Modern Spain and Spanish America* (New Haven, 2003).
14. Gonzalo Aguirre Beltrán, "The Integration of the Negro into the National Society of Mexico," in Magnus Mörner, ed., *Race and Class in Latin America* (New York, 1970), 17.
15. An interesting argument regarding the censuses and their meaning is in John K. Chance and William B. Taylor, "Estate and Class in a Colonial Oaxaca City: Oaxaca in 1972," *Comparative Studies in Society and History* 19 (1997): 454–487; Robert McCaa, Stuart Schwartz, and Arturo Grubessich, "Race and Class in Colonial Latin America: A Critique," *The Hispanic American Historical Review* 64 (1984): 477–501.
16. Cited by Marixa Lasso in "Race and War in Caribbean Colombia, Cartagena, 1810–1822," *American Historical Review* 111 (2006): 342. These matters are dealt with more extensively in her book: *Myths of Harmony: Race and Republicanism during the Age of Revolution, Colombia 1795–1831* (Pittsburgh, 2007), 19–33. Also, Jorge Conde Calderón,

"Castas y conflicto en la provincial de Cartagena del Reino de Nueva Granada a finales del siglo XVIII," *Revista de Historia y Sociedad* 3 (1969): 83–101.
17. Verena Stolcke, *Marriage, Class and Colour in Nineteenth-Century Cuba: A Study of Racial Attitudes and Sexual Values in a Slave Society* (Cambridge, 1974). An excellent case study for late colonial and independent Peru is Chistine Hünefeldt, *Paying the Price of Freedom: Family and Labor among Lima's Slaves, 1800–1854* (Berkeley, 1994).
18. See, for instance, the central government's instructions on statistics given to the functionaires in America, in Francisco Castillo Meléndez, Luisa J. Figallo Pérez, Ramón Serrera Contreras, *Las Cortes de Cádiz y la imagen de América. La visión etnográfica y geográfica del Nuevo Mundo* (Cadiz, 1994), 75–78.
19. Magnus Mörner, *Race Mixture in the History of Latin America* (Boston, 1967), 39.
20. Regarding the matter of colored militias, there is a very extensive bibliography. For that reason, I will mention only some of the most important works, including Allan J. Kuethe, *Military Reform and Society in New Granada, 1773–1808* (Gainesville, 1978); Juan Marchena Fernández, *Ejército y milicias en el mundo colonial americano* (Madrid,1992); Ben Vinson III, *Bearing Arms for His Majesty: The Free-Colored Militia in Colonial Mexico* (Stanford, 2001).
21. The metropolitan authorities' efforts to map the social and ethnic reality of the late empire during the Cadiz period are of great interest. See Castillo Meléndez et al., *Las Cortes de Cádiz y la imagen de América*.
22. Josep M. Fradera, "Raza y ciudadanía. El factor racial en la delimitación de los derechos de los americanos," in *Gobernar colonias* (Barcelona, 1999), 51–70.
23. *La esclavitud africana en América Latina y el Caribe* (Madrid, 1986), 173; reprinted in Herbert S. Klein and Ben Vinson III, *African Slavery in Latin America and the Caribbean* 2nd ed. (Oxford, 2007). See also the more recent but not very different account by Laird Bergad, *The Comparative Histories of Slavery in Brazil, Cuba, and the United States* (Cambridge, 2007), 63.
24. Peter J. Bakewell, *Silver Mining and Society in Colonial Mexico. Zacatecas, 1546–1700* (Cambridge, 1971).
25. *African Slavery in Latin America and the Caribbean*, 76–77.
26. Carlos Aguirre, *Agentes de su propia libertad. Los esclavos de Lima y la desintegración de la esclavitud, 1821–1854* (Lima, 1993), 45–48. Aguirre's figures for the whole of Peru are lower than those given by Klein in *African Slavery in Latin America and the Caribbean*.
27. A good example of periods of variation in terminology and classificatory procedures in R. Douglas Cope, *The Limits of Racial Domination: Plebeian Society in Colonial Mexico City, 1660–1720* (Madison, 1994).
28. Dauril Alden, "Late Colonial Brazil, 1750–1808," Leslie Bethell, ed., *Colonial Brazil* (Cambridge, 1987), 290; also, Herbert S. Klein and Francisco Vidal Luna, *Slavery in Brazil* (Cambridge, 2010) (figures by groups and provinces from 1819 to 1872 in 181–187).
29. I use the figures provided by Lockhart and Schwartz in *Early Latin America*, 338.
30. On this matter, consult Manuel Lucena Salmoral, *La esclavitud en la América española* (Warsaw, 2002), 221–270.
31. For the origins of American slavery, the following is still very useful: Charles Verlinden, "Medieval Slavery and Colonial Slavery in America," *The Beginnings of Modern Colonization. Eleven Essays with an Introduction* (Ithaca, 1970), 79–97.
32. Robin Blackburn, "Introduction," in Rosemary Brana-Shute and Randy J. Sparks, eds., *Paths to Freedom: Manumission in the Atlantic World* (Columbia, 2009), 3–4.
33. The importance of coartación leads us once again to Frank Tannenbaum's theses and their intellectual foundation, the observations of Humboldt in Havana. A case study for the same location but at an earlier period, is in Evelyn Jennings, "Paths to Freedom: Imperial Defense and Manumission in Havana," *Paths to Freedom*, 121–143.

34. John T. Lanning, *The Royal Protomedicato: The Regulation of the Medical Professions in the Spanish Empire* (Durham, 1985), 175–200.
35. This institutional transformation and its effects are treated in Josep M. Delgado, *Dinámicas imperiales (1650–1796): España, América y Europa en el cambio institucional del sistema colonial español* (Barcelona, 2007), 560 ff.; and Herbert S. Klein, *The Middle Passage: Comparative Studies in the Atlantic Slave Trade* (Princeton, 1978), 209–227. See also Delgado's chapter in this collection.
36. Regarding the plantation areas given over to the products of tropical agriculture, there is a fair amount of bibliographical information in the text. For the case of mining in New Granada, very relevant is the work by William F. Sharp, *Slavery on the Spanish Frontier: The Colombian Choco, 1680–1810* (Norman, 1980). See also German Colmenares, *Historia económica y social de Colombia. Tomo II: Popayán, una sociedad esclavista, 1680–1800* (Bogota, 1979).
37. The best approach to the response by the leading groups in the new slave societies is still that by Manuel Moreno Fraginals in *El Ingenio: complejo económico social cubano del azúcar* 3 vols. (Havana, 1978), 1, 105–136. Also Tomich, "The Wealth of Empire."
38. This is clearly demonstrated in the study by Jean-Pierre Tardieu, *Noirs et Nouveaux Maitres dans les "vallées sanglantes" de l'Equateur, 1778–1820* (Saint-Denis, 1997).
39. Rafael de Bivar Marquese, *Feitores do corpo, missionários da mente. Senhores, letrados e o controle dos escravos nas Américas, 1660–1860* (São Paulo, 2004), 305–330.
40. Martin Daunton and Rick Halpern, eds., *Empire and Others: British Encounters with Indigenous Peoples, 1600–1850* (London, 1999).
41. An exhaustive overview in the most recent book by Seymour Drescher: *Abolition: A History of Slavery and Antislavery* (Cambridge, 2009).
42. David J. Weber, *Bárbaros: Spaniards and Their Savages in the Age of Enlightenment* (New Haven, 2005).
43. James Lockhart, *The Nahuas after the Conquest: A Social and Cultural History of the Indians of Central Mexico, Sixteenth through Eighteenth Centuries* (Stanford, 1992); and Susan Kellogg, *Law and the Transformation of the Aztec Culture, 1500–1700* (Norman, 1995).
44. *Noticias Americanas*, ed. Miguel Molina Martínez (Granada, 1992), 323.
45. A well-known example of this attitude in the late moments of the empire (1788) is expressed in Francisco de Viedma, *Descripción geografica y estadística de la provincia de Santa Cruz de la Sierra* (Cochabamba, 1969).
46. Murray, *Odious Commerce*, 24 ff.
47. Leslie Bethell, *The Abolition of the Brazilian Slave Trade: Britain, Brazil and the Slave Trade Question, 1807–1869* (Cambridge, 1970); Beatriz Gallotti Mamigonian, "A proibição do tráfico atlântico e a manutenção da escravidão", Keila Grinberg and Ricardo Salles, eds., *O Brasil Imperial. Vol I: 1808–1831* (Rio de Janeiro, 2009), 209–233.
48. There are few studies of Antillón, but see Christine Benavides, "Isidoro de Antillón y la abolición de la esclavitud," paper presented to the conference "Las élites y la Revolución de España (1808–1814)," Madrid, Casa de Velásquez, June 2007, pending publication.
49. *Disertación sobre el origen de la esclavitud de los negros, motivos que la han perpetuado, ventajas que se le atribuyen y medios que podrían adoptarse para hacer prosperar nuestras colonias sin la esclavitud de los negros* (Palma de Mallorca, 1811).
50. A biographical approach in Eloy Fernández Clemente, "Isidoro de Antillón: política y economía en un diputado liberal," in *Josep Fontana: Història i projecte social. Reconeixement d'una trajectòria* (Barcelona, 2004), 999–1022.
51. *Noticias Americanas*.
52. Despite the fact that one of Antillón's most frequent references is the well-known text on abolition by Jacques Pierre Brissot (1754–1793), one of the founders of the *Société des amis des Noirs*.

53. Manuel Moreno Alonso, *La generación española de 1808* (Madrid, 1989). Jefferson's comments on Ulloa are in "Notes on the State of Virginia," *Writings* (New York, 1984), 184–185.
54. *Disertación sobre el origen de la esclavitud de los negros*, 66–67.
55. Ramón Corts i Blay, *L'arquebisbe Fèlix Amat (1750–1824) i l'última il·lustració espanyola* (Barcelona,1992).
56. A selection from this, with an introduction by the editors Antonio Garnica and Raquel Rico Linaje is in *José María Blanco White, Semanario Patriótico* (Granada, 2005).
57. Among other fundamental texts is his *Bosquejo del comercio en esclavos* Manuel Moreno Alonso, ed. (Seville, 1999). Regarding the link between Blanco and British foreign policy interests, Martin Murphy, *Blanco White: Self-banished Spaniard* (New Haven, 1989), 84–85.
58. Roberto Breña, "José Maria Blanco White y la independencia de América: ¿una postura proamericana?" *Historia Consitucional*, 3, June 2002; http://www.seminariomartinezmarina.com/ojs/index.php/historiaconstitucional
59. Gabriel Paquette, ed., *Enlightened Reforms in Southern Europe and its Atlantic Colonies, c. 1750–1830* (Burlington, 2009).
60. Jeremy Adelman, *Sovereignity and Revolution in the Iberian Atlantic* (Princeton, 2006).
61. Ada Ferrer, "Speaking of Haiti; Slavery, Revolution, and Freedom in Cuban Slave Testimony," in David Patrick Geggus and Norman Fiering, eds., *The World of the Haitian Revolution* (Bloomington, 2009), 223–248; and Jeremy D. Popkin, *Facing Racial Revolution. Eyewitness Accounts of the Haitian Revolution* (Chicago, 2007).
62. Juan Andrea García, *La intendencia de Venezuela: Don Esteban Fernández de León, Intendente de Caracas, 1791–1803* (Murcia, 1991).
63. José Antonio Piqueras, "Leales en época de insurrección. La elite criolla cubana entre 1810 y 1814," *Visiones y revisiones de la independencia americana* (Salamanca, 2003), 183–206. See also Arthur Corwin, in a work that continues to be an important source regarding Spanish abolitionism, *Spain and the Abolition of Slavery in Cuba, 1817–1836* (Austin, 1967), 22–25.
64. Corwin, *Spain and the Abolition of Slavery in Cuba, 1817–1886*, 25.
65. See the standard work by Josep Fontana, *La quiebra de la monarquía absoluta (1814–1820). La crisis del antiguo Régimen en España* (Barcelona, 1970).
66. Josep M. Fradera, *Indústria i mercat. Les bases comercials de la indústria catalana moderna, 1814–1845* (Barcelona, 1987).
67. On the migratory factor, essential in this new stage that begins in the years 1810–1820, see Jordi Maluquer de Motes, *Nación e inmigración: los españoles en Cuba (ss. XIX y XX)* (Oviedo, 1992); César Yáñez Gallardo, *Saltar con red. La temprana emigración catalana a América, ca. 1830–1870* (Madrid, 1996).
68. See Albert Garcia Balanyà, "Tradició liberal i política colonial a Catalunya. Mig segle de temptatives i limitacions," Josep M. Fradera and César Yáñez, eds., *Catalunya i Ultramar. Poder i negoci a les colònies espanyoles* (Barcelona, 1995), 77–106; on Varela, Eduardo Torres-Cuevas, *Félix Varela. Los orígenes de la ciencia y con-ciencia cubanas* (Havana, 1997).
69. The famous sentence in which Varela refers to the strength of the plantation complex in Cuban politics is found in the "Consideraciones sobre el estado actual de la isla de Cuba," in *Félix Varela. Obras* Eduardo Torres-Cuevas, Jorge Ibarra Cuesta and Mercedes García Rodríguez, eds. (Havana, 1997), 2, 152–155.
70. Juan Bernardo O'Gavan, *Observaciones sobre la suerte de los negros en África, considerados en su propia patria y trasplantación a las Antillas españolas, y reclamación contra el tratado celebrado con los ingleses en 1817* (Madrid, 1821).
71. Murray, *Odious Commerce*, 92–113.

72. Candelaria Sáiz Pastor, "Las finanzas públicas en Cuba: la etapa de las desviaciones de fondos a la península, 1823–1866," in Inés Roldán de Montaud, ed., *Las Haciendas públicas en el Caribe hispano durante el siglo XIX* (Madrid, 2008), 69–108.
73. See Martin Rodrigo y Alharilla's article included in this volume; see also, the important but not conclusive effort by Angel Bahamonde Magro and José-Gregorio Cayuela Fernández, *Hacer las Américas. Las elites coloniales españolas en el siglo XIX* (Madrid, 1992).
74. I take this information from the following works: Franklin W. Knight, *Slave Society in Cuba during the Nineteenth Century* (Madison, 1970), 22; Rebecca J. Scott, *Slave Emancipation in Cuba: The Transition to Free Labor, 1860–1899* (Princeton, 1985), 7; Laird W. Bergad, Fe Iglesias García, María del Carmen Barcia, *The Cuban Slave Market, 1790–1880* (Cambridge, 1995), 30–31.
75. The connection among the different aspects is set out in the second chapter of my *Colonias para después de un imperio* (Barcelona, 2005), 183–326.
76. Michael P. Costeloe, *Response to Revolution: Imperial Spain and the Spanish American Revolutions, 1810–1840* (Cambridge, 1986).
77. Josep M. Fradera, "Divide to Rule: Inclusion and Exclusion in Spanish Imperial Liberalism," Matthew Brown and Gabriel Paquette, eds., *Connections after Colonialism: Europe and Latin America in the 1820s* (Tuscaloosa, 2013), 64–86
78. Regarding the Aponte rebellion, a crucial work is the monograph by Matt Childs, *The 1812 Aponte Rebellion in Cuba and the Struggle against Atlantic Slavery* (Chapel Hill, 2006); see also, Ferrer, "Speaking of Haiti."
79. Regarding precedents in the eighteenth century, Mercedes García, *Entre haciendas y plantaciones. Orígenes de la manufactura azucarera en La Habana* (Havana, 2007).
80. On the prices of slaves, see Manuel Moreno Fraginals, Herbert S. Klein, and Stanley L. Engerman, "The Level and Structure of Slave Prices on Cuban Plantations in the Mid-Nineteenth Century: Some Comparative Perspectives," *The American Historical Review* 88 (1983): 1201–1218. See also, *The Cuban Slave Market*, 38–78; and Laird Bergad, *The Comparative Histories of Slavery in Brazil, Cuba, and the United States*, 158–159; idem., *Slavery and the Demographic and Economic History of Minas Gerais, Brazil, 1720–1888* (Cambridge, 1999), 169.
81. Roger Anstey, *Atlantic Slave Trade and British Abolition, 1760–1810* (Cambridge, 1975); also, Christine Bolt and Seymour Drescher, eds., *Anti-Slavery, Religion and Reform: Essays in Memory of Roger Anstey* (Folkestone, 1980); David Brion Davis, *Slavery and Human Progress* (Oxford, 1984); Seymour Drescher, *Capitalism and Antislavery: British Mobilization in Comparative Perspective* (Houndmills, 1986); and *The Mighty Experiment: Free Labor versus Slavery in British Emancipation* (Oxford, 2002); and David Eltis, *Economic Growth and the Ending of the Transatlantic Slave Trade* (New York, 1987).
82. Adam Hochschild, *Bury the Chains: Prophets and Rebels in the Fight to Free an Empire's Slaves* (Boston, 2005).
83. See Alexis de Tocqueville, *Writings on Empire and Slavery*, ed. Jennifer Pitts (Baltimore, 2001).
84. The *Edinburgh Review*'s position in the economic debate, but without any mention of these matters, is discussed in Biancamaria Fontana, *Rethinking the Politics of Commercial Society: The Edinburgh Review, 1802–1832*, (Cambridge, 1985).
85. Jordi Maluquer de Motes, "El problema de la esclavitud y la revolución de 1868," *Hispania*, no. 117 (1971): 55–75; Consuelo Férnandez Canales, "Exposiciones en la opinión pública ante la abolición de la esclavitud en Puerto Rico," in Francisco de Solano and Agustín Guimerá, eds., *Esclavitud y derechos humanos. La lucha por la libertad del negro en el siglo XIX* (Madrid, 1990), 279–292.
86. See Márcia Berbel, Rafael Marquese, and Tâmis Parron, *Escravidão e política. Brasil e Cuba, 1790–1850* (São Paulo, 2010), chap. 4.

87. The best analysis of the crisis provoked by David Turnbull's action is found in Murray, *Odious Commerce*, chaps. 8 and 9.
88. Christopher Schmidt-Nowara, *Empire and Antislavery: Spain, Cuba, and Puerto Rico, 1833–1874* (Pittsburgh, 1999).
89. Regarding the labor discourses, referring to their internal, European aspect, see the excellent reconstruction by Fernando Díez in *El trabajo transfigurado. Los discursos del trabajo en la primera mitad del siglo XIX* (Valencia, 2006).
90. Ada Ferrer, *Insurgent Cuba. Race, Nation, and Revolution, 1868–1898* (Chapel Hill, 1999).
91. Miquel Izard, *Manufactureros, industriales y revolucionarios* (Barcelona, 1979).
92. Scott, *Slave Emancipation in Cuba*, 63–83.
93. A nuanced interpretation of those discourses and policies can be found in Thomas C. Holt, *The Problem of Freedom: Race, Labor, and Politics in Jamaica and Britain, 1832–1938* (Baltimore, 1992).
94. Robin Blackburn, *The American Crucible: Slavery, Emancipation and Human Rights* (New York, 2011), 344–351.
95. María Dolores García Cantús, *Fernando Poo: una aventura colonial española. I: Las islas en Litigio: entre la esclavitud y el abolicionismo, 1777–1846* (Vic, 2006); Ibrahim K. Sundiata, *From Slaving to Neoslavery. The Bight of Biafra and Fernando Po in the Era of Abolition, 1827–1930* (Madison, 1996).
96. Philip D. Curtin, *The Rise and Fall of the Plantation Complex: Essays in Atlantic History* (Cambridge, 1990).
97. On the intersection between the different labor discourses in the United States before the Civil War, see Eric Foner, *Free Soil, Free Labor, Free Men: The Ideology of the Republican Party before the Civil War* (New York, 1970).
98. In this I follow very closely arguments that were set out very eloquently by Stanley L. Engerman in several studies. I refer the reader to the exhaustive bibliography compiled in David Eltis, Frank W. Lewis, and Kenneth L. Sokoloff, eds., *Slavery in the Development of the Americas* (Cambridge, 2004), 353–362.
99. On Puerto Rico, see Francisco A. Scarano, *Sugar and Slavery in Puerto Rico: The Plantation Economy of Ponce, 1800–1850* (Madison, 1984); Luis Figueroa, *Sugar, Slavery, and Freedom in Nineteenth-Century Puerto Rico* (Chapel Hill, 2005); and Astrid Cubano-Iguina, *El hilo en el laberinto: claves de la lucha política en Puerto Rico (siglo XIX)* (Río Piedras, 1990); idem, "Freedom in the Making: The Slaves of Hacienda La Esperanza, Manatí, Puerto Rico, on the Eve of Abolition, 1868–1876," *Social History* 36 (August 2011): 280–293. On the tobacco industry and the obligations weighing on the peasants, see Ed. de Jesús, *The Tobacco Monopoly in the Philippines: Bureaucratic Enterprise and Social Change, 1766–1880* (Quezon City, 1980); and Josep M. Fradera, *Filipinas, la colonia más peculiar. La hacienda pública en la determinación de la política colonial, 1762–1868* (Madrid,1999).
100. Juan Pérez de la Riva, "Demografía de los culíes chinos en Cuba (1853–1874)," *El barracón y otros ensayos* (Barcelona, 1978), 55–87.
101. Denise Helly, *Ideologie et Ethnicité: les Chinois Macao à Cuba, 1847–1886* (Montreal, 1979); Juan Jiménez Pastrana, *Los chinos en la historia de Cuba, 1847–1930* (Havana, 1983). For a recent contribution on the British Caribbean, see Walton Look Lai, *Indentured Labor, Caribbean Sugar: Chinese and Indian Migrants to the British West Indies, 1838–1918* (Baltimore, 1993).
102. James Walvin, *Fruits of Empire: Exotic Produce and British Taste, 1660–1800* (New York, 1997), 132–154.
103. This was the approach taken by Franklin W. Knight, "Slavery, Race, and Social Structure in Cuba During the Nineteenth Century," in Robert Brent Toplin, ed., *Slavery and Race Relations in Latin America* (Westport, 1974), 204–227.
104. Manuel Barcia, *Seeds of Insurrection: Domination and Resistance in Western Cuban Plantations, 1808–1848* (Baton Rouge, 2008).

105. Robert L. Paquette, *Sugar is Made with Blood: The Conspiracy of La Escalera and the Conflict between Empires over Slavery in Cuba* (Middletown, 1988).
106. For the context in which this repressive operation by O'Donnell occurred, see Fradera, *Colonias para después de un imperio*, 270–298.
107. See Alejandro de la Fuente's chapter in this volume.
108. J.R. Ward, *British West Indian Slavery, 1750–1834: The Process of Amelioration* (Oxford, 1988); Jack Hayward, ed., *Out of Slavery: Abolition and After* (London, 1985).
109. Josep M. Fradera, "Why were Spain's Overseas Laws Never Enacted?" in Richard L. Kagan and Geoffrey Parker, eds., *Spain, Europe and the Atlantic World. Essays in Honour of John H. Elliott* (Cambridge, 1995), 333–349.
110. Josep M. Fradera, "Quiebra imperial y reorganización del poder imperial en las Antillas españolas y Filipinas," *Gobernar colonias*, 95–125.
111. Kate Ferris, "Modelos de abolición: Estados Unidos en la política cultural española y la abolición de la esclavitud en Cuba," in Alda Blanco and Guy Thomson, eds., *Visiones del Liberalismo: Política, identidad y cultura en la España del siglo XIX* (Valencia, 2008), 195–218.

– *Chapter 11* –

FROM EMPIRES OF SLAVERY TO EMPIRES OF ANTISLAVERY

Seymour Drescher

For half a millennium the empires of the Atlantic World were linked to slavery. For more than three of those five centuries it was axiomatic for European powers that the transatlantic slave trade and the institution it fed were major contributors to the wealth and well-being of their nations. In world historical perspective Western slavery was merely another phase in the evolution of a perennial institution. Even at the very end of the eighteenth century, when the African slave trade and New-World slavery were both coming under sustained assault, a member of the British House of Lords dismissed slavery's challengers as quixotic imperialists. Who, he asked, did these "emperors of the world" think they were, who were suddenly measuring a new empire of liberty by "degrees and lines of the globe?"[1] For Lord Westmoreland, an inveterate opponent of abolitionism, the whole of human history could be offered as evidence of the persistence of the institution in its many forms.

Just fifteen years later the British government was pressing all of Europe's great powers to halt the flow of captives that formed the lifeblood of their slaveholding empires. Now it was the turn of Continental European diplomats to ask, with astonishment, "Do you English mean to bind the world?"[2] Within three more generations this once global institution had been entirely outlawed in the New World by the descendants of the Europeans who had expended so much blood and treasure to maximize their shares of the system of slavery.

Studying the different trajectories of Europe's empires, first toward and then away from slavery has become a rapidly growing field of scholarly inquiry. How should we assess the results of this expansion of historiographic interest? One can begin with the general findings of economic historians and historical demographers. Fifty years ago it was widely accepted that New-World plantations based upon slavery were fundamentally inefficient enterprises. At best, they were hothouse systems, yielding short-term profits and long-term decline. British slavery across the Atlantic, like British industry in the metropole, was the pioneer example. In his classic, *The Problem of Slavery in Western Culture,* David Brion Davis could casually point to Eric Williams demonstration of "the simple fact that no country thought of abolishing the slave trade until its economic value had considerably declined." Two decades later, in a new edition of his work, Davis noted that the once self-evident linkage of slavery's economic decline to abolition had been convincingly challenged and undermined.[3] It now seems fairly clear that, in comparative Atlantic perspective, historians of abolition must begin with a paradox. In every major transatlantic empire the political attack against the slave trade and slavery began when the systems institutions were economically viable and expanding. Nowhere was there a so-called natural economic ending.[4]

In the 1780s all of the participants in the Atlantic system, both actual and potential, assumed that slavery was and would continue be a significant component of imperial wealth and power. The transatlantic slave trade reached its all-time peak in the decade after 1783. Expansion of the system was not confined to the century's big three plantation empires — the British, the French, and the Portuguese. Merchants from the Habsburg Netherlands to Italy sought to shift capital into the booming slave or sugar trades. The king of Sweden chartered a new merchant company to operate out of his new island colony of St. Bartholomew, acquired from France. The Spanish monarchy began to abandon its centuries-old policy of contracting monopoly rights to deliver controlled cohorts of Africans to American colonies. The British Caribbean colonies rapidly regained the momentum interrupted by the war of the American Revolution. The British slave trade reached an all-time peak in 1792. By the end of the 1790s more Africans were also arriving in the Ibero-American colonies than ever before. Of all the jostling participants in the slave sectors of the Americas in the 1780s the French became the frontrunners. Between 1785 and 1790 more slaves were brought into the French orbit than into those of any other empire. The fifty-five thousand slaves unloaded there in 1790 outpaced the volume ever sailing before under any national flag.[5]

Dreams of tropical empire continued to spread during the most violent revolutionary generation of what we call the age of revolution (1789–

1815). Watching the first great metropolitan debate on British abolition in 1792 the Dutch excitedly speculated on the market that might open up to their ships by the ending of the British trade. German slavers, who had carried almost no slaves across the Atlantic for nearly three generations, returned to Africa in the 1790s.[6] Even when German rulers lacked tropical settlements, a professor could dream of filling new sugar colonies with deported Jewish laborers. As late as 1806–1807, the emperor of Russia, hitherto the only major European ruler not directly involved in Atlantic colonial imperialism, enquired about the possibility of acquiring a colony in the Caribbean. Slavery was very far from being viewed as a declining economic asset by any imperial power before the abolition of the British slave trade.[7]

Throughout the century after 1789 slavery remained economically viable in every major colonial economy in which it was permitted to continue. After the emergence of political abolitionism, Brazil, Cuba, and the United States, the last major New-World slave empires, remained robust slave systems, producing coffee, sugar, and cotton. In global perspective they were dynamic centers of innovation. In 1838 Cuba inaugurated the Caribbean's first railroad line. A decade later, its railway network, the most "sophisticated in all of Latin America, was constructed almost exclusively to serve the sugar economy." Railroad construction began later in Brazil, but the network was first developed in the most dynamic slave zone. The first railroad in the United States was also constructed in a slave state, just a few years after Europe's pioneer commercial railroad from Liverpool to Manchester. On the eve of Southern Secession the region's ninety-five hundred miles of track, was greater than those of France, Germany, or Great Britain, Europe's industrial leaders. Nor can we ignore the fact that the postemancipation British Empire remained a principal source of capital and technology in the development of Cuba and Brazil. In the late 1840s the British metropole became a major source of demand for Cuban and Brazilian sugar. American cotton, of course, fed Britain's major export industry.[8]

The demographics of slavery also rightly play a large role in accounts of its demise. Statesmen, slaveholders, and abolitionists of the Western world always recognized the reliance of most slave systems on a continuous stream of recruitment for the maintenance and growth of their enslaved populations. Only in the United States did the institution grow primarily through natural reproduction. Between 1790 and 1860 its slave population rose from seven hundred thousand to four million, by far the largest cohort in the New World. Elsewhere, ending the transatlantic trade offered abolitionists an opportunity to hasten the precipitous decline of plantation slave systems. For decades an ever-eroding supply of slave labor could be concentrated in the most productive plantation sectors. Without further political action, slavery would have lasted far longer.[9]

An interregional comparison of proportions of slaves within each slaveholding society also casts light on the timing and means of emancipation. Once abolition became a political possibility in a given area, the proportion of slaves would often be an indicator of how quickly a society could legislate the end of the slave trade or slavery. In Spanish America—as in Anglo-America—recruitment into insurgent or imperial military forces often provided a path to slaves under arms.[10]

In many parts of the New World the racial composition of the population could also provide an incentive to legislate against further slave imports. It is now well established that within the French Caribbean the relatively numerous population of wealthy *gens de couleur libres* played a key role in the Saint-Domingue slave revolution. By 1790 they outnumbered the whites in two of the three provinces and formed the backbone of the colonial militia. As well-to-do slaveholders, men of color were initially inclined to support the institution. They were ultimately driven by intransigent white hostility to support the slave revolution.[11]

The same racial fears in societies with large proportions of blacks could act as political hurdles to emancipation. The formation of the American Colonization Society, designed to encourage the simultaneous emancipation and exportation of black slaves, was merely the most extreme form of the fear of Africanization—and the corresponding hope of ultimately whitening a slaveholding society. To a degree this was the same fear haunting many anti–slave trade Cuban intellectuals for half a century before slave emancipation. In Cuba, one could be simultaneously vehemently in favor of slave trade abolition, of U.S. annexation, and deeply opposed to the liberation of African-born *emancipados*, unless they were immediately repatriated. By contrast, in 1870 Puerto Rican slaveholders, living on an island with a slave population lower than that of New York's seventy years earlier, could much more easily reconcile themselves to slave emancipation.[12]

With Saint-Domingue as its emblematic event, the past half-century has also produced a cascade of scholarship on the role of slave resistance in the process of emancipation. For some historians the Haitian Revolution marks the ideological and catalytic turning point in the history of emancipation, sending unending vibrations through much of the Atlantic world. For Robin Blackburn the events in Haiti "instilled a sort of permanent panic in the minds of slave owners."[13] Nevertheless, David Geggus cautions against exaggerating the impact of the Haitian Revolution and of reading into every plot and rebellion in these years the influence of Haiti. Viewed in comparative imperial perspective one might make two significant observations. In the period between the outbreak of the Saint-Domingue Revolution in 1791 and Haitian independence in 1804 the two Caribbean areas that most massively increased their importations of African slaves and their output of sugar were Jamaica and Cuba, the two islands closest to the revolution's epicenter.[14] Three out of the four major imperial governments (Portugal, Spain, and France) affirmed or reaffirmed their desire to expand the slave trade and expand slavery during the generation after the Haitian Revolution. In the fourth, Britain, the Franco-Caribbean revolutions initially served to postpone rather than to accelerate the abolition of the slave trade. As I will discuss later, it was the slave uprisings in the British colonies that had the greatest impact in furthering British slave emancipation in 1833.

There is another aspect of the abolition process that has begun to be reexamined more carefully in the past two decades. It may well prove to offer a comparative perspective that most clearly explains the timing and sequence of Atlantic emancipations. I refer to the political dimension of the destruction process. Comparative analysis requires attention to both the intra-and interimperial aspects of the politics of emancipation. Intraimperial factors include the balance of forces within each area's civil society and the condition of the public sphere in each empire. The interimperial political sphere includes the complex of diplomatic, economic organizational, and ideological relations.

In an earlier overview I developed the idea of two variants of European antislavery, the Anglo-American and the Continental.[15] In the Anglo-American variant antislavery took on the characteristics of a broad social movement. It had and seized the opportunity to massively enter the public sphere. It could and did bring massive pressure to bear on hostile economic and political vested interests. It could use traditional and new tools of mass mobilization: public meetings, petitions, and elections. Its membership was broadly based and its leaders aimed at maximizing the role of participants who were otherwise excluded from the political sphere by reason of gender, religion, race, or class. From the 1780s Britain became both the pioneer and representative of a new mode of mobilization. As with metropolitan industrialization, the British achievement formed a potential model for antislavery elsewhere.[16]

Half a century later on the other side of the Atlantic, U.S. antislavery consciously imitated British abolitionism between the 1830s and 1860s. This variant of popular mobilization by no means guaranteed an orderly political process leading to abolition. Large-scale mobilizations might be met with large-scale political countermobilizations. So it unfolded in the northern and southern sections of the United States. Indeed, if one counts the bodies left along the way, Anglo-American mass mobilizations may have produced both the least and the most violent transitions from slavery to emancipation.¹⁷

The other variant of metropolitan antislavery I termed continental abolitionism. It was characteristic of most mainland organizations for most of century between the 1780s and the 1880s. It was usually confined to a small political and cultural elite, unable and often reluctant to seek mass recruitment and mobilization in the public sphere. It was embedded in political systems with relatively small electorates that rarely allowed room for mass organizations. It rarely succeeded in making abolition of either the slave trade or of slavery a high-priority political issue. Consequently, abolitionist initiatives were either the work of a small elite associations or revolutionary committees, usually without public accountability (Denmark, the Netherlands, Sweden, and Portugal) or were imposed ad hoc during revolutions or coups d'etat (France and Spain). In such societies revolutionary and counterrevolutionary coups were endemic. Each lurch might witness the extension, suspension, or reversal of abolitionist initiatives. France, of course, offers the classic example, in which hundreds of thousands slaves were freed by the French revolutionary republic and then tens of thousands reenslaved. Characteristically, France's second period of slavery (1802–1848) was followed by secondary postrevolutionary abolitions and emancipation (in 1815, 1831, and 1848).¹⁸

British abolitionism, on the contrary, emerged as a national movement in 1787–1788. It lasted, with interruptions, for half a century. This dramatic change was, in turn, embedded within a far longer Anglo-American transformation. Eighteenth-century Britons and British North American colonists shared one of the most highly developed civil societies in the Atlantic world. In the metropole, the thickening network of newspapers nationalized an evolving dialogue between people and legislators. Parliamentary debates and governmental initiatives were the daily grist of provincial readers. Letters, advertisements for public gatherings, political pamphlets, and news items about activities of political debaters in London provided fare for ongoing public conversations. Newspapers linked provincial readers not only with the center in London, but with interested actors from all parts of the island.

Within this broader process abolitionism came to occupy a distinctively innovative position. Between its emergence as a national social movement in 1787 and the internationalization of slave trade abolition a generation later, abolitionism became a pioneering organization in the mobilization of hitherto untapped groups as political actors. The British public sphere rapidly expanded in many directions. From the outset organized religious dissenters rallied to the movement. Unitarians, Congregationalists, Baptists, Methodists, and evangelical Anglicans quickly added their support to the crucial Quaker cadres.[19]

As British abolitionists moved toward advocating the emancipation of colonial slaves in the early 1820s the mobilization process continued and expanded. More than five thousand petitions reached Parliament in 1831 and again in 1833. Women increasingly inserted themselves as legitimate organizers and petitioners. By 1830 dissenters recognized women as a decisive abolitionist presence. At the climax of the campaign for emancipation, in 1833, the largest single antislavery petition in British history arrived by carriage at the doors of Parliament. "A huge featherbed of a petition," it bore 187,000 signatures in "one vast and universal expression of feeling from all the females in the United Kingdom." Four years later, in the last great mobilization against "Negro apprenticeship" in 1837–1838 the number of women's signatures to petitions to Parliament and addresses to the sovereign may have exceeded that of men.[20]

Even colonial slaves, legally excluded from the public sphere, began a series of extra-legal uprisings. Slaves, now attuned to events in the metropole, began to frame their demands in terms used by free laborers. They were treated as such by abolitionists in the metropole. The transformation was behavioral as well as ideological. The number of white people who died in all of the massive revolts of tens of thousands slaves in the British colonies (Barbados, 1816; Demerara, 1823; and Jamaica, 1831–1832) did not equal one third of the sixty men, women, and children killed in the brief Virginia slave revolt led by Nat Turner in August 1831. The contrast with Saint-Domingue with its widely publicized atrocities and its hundreds of thousands dead could not have been starker.[21]

The British campaigns against the transatlantic slave trade also proceeded in careful stages. By the last stage of the Napoleonic wars the ending of the trade had become a British imperial priority. Already in 1813 the Portuguese ambassador in London observed that the British government refused to regard the slave trade as subject to the principles of modern political economy. Britons now viewed that trade "with a blindness and ardour which equals other times of Religious Fanaticism whether sincere or affected."[22] In 1815 the British government, under abolitionist pressure, induced the Vienna peace conference to adopt an article directed toward the world beyond Europe. The great powers condemned the slave trade as contrary to natural and religious law and pledged themselves to work for its termination. The British then launched an international campaign to shut down the Atlantic to slavers. During the next fifty years all of Europe's transatlantic imperial rulers and most of the emergent American nations restricted or prohibited slave traders from sailing under their flag.

Britain secured treaties allowing its navy to search the ships of most nations and to try offenders in unprecedented international tribunals.[23]

The result was the creation of a new world system. By the end of the 1830s British popular abolitionism stood at the height of its political power. It successfully induced its government to expand the attack against the slave trade and slavery to truly global proportions. Abolitionists held two World Antislavery Conventions in London in 1840 and 1843. British diplomatic initiatives and treaty negotiators reached a peak of activity. The British government extended abolitionist initiatives to India, to the Muslim world and to Sub-Saharan Africa. It intensified pressure on slaving to the Americas.[24]

By 1840, the British abolitionists who organized the first world's international antislavery convention were hardly emperors of the world. Nevertheless, they had managed to convert the world's leading industrial, commercial, and naval power into a powerful agent against the slave trade and slavery. Every diplomatic request or demand issuing from the British Foreign Office was now presented as an initiative of both the British monarch and the British people. No previous empire in world history had ever adopted anything remotely like the abolitionist perspective that affected slave trading from the Atlantic to the Indian Ocean, and slaveholders' behavior from Texas to Brazil to India. Of course, slavers and ruling elites experienced this British bid for a reordering of the moral boundaries of legitimate trade and labor as a form of economic, legal and cultural imperialism that was rarely interrupted over the course of the century between.[25]

The only periods when abolitionism was suspended was during moments of great internal or external threat: at the height of the revolutionary wars in the 1790s, during the post-Napoleonic popular agitation in Britain in the late 1810s, and in the constitutional and political crisis preceding the passage of parliamentary reform in 1831–1832. In British imperial terms the overwhelming supremacy of the metropolitan parliament over its Caribbean elites was never in doubt. It is equally important to note that during the entire generation between the emergence of British political abolitionism in 1787 and its internationalization by the end of the Napoleonic wars slaves did not rise anywhere in the British West Indies demanding an end to the institution. Leading the government's case for ending the slave trade, Lord Howick boasted of the notoriety of the fact that slave revolts had been less frequent during twenty years of open debate throughout the metropole.[26]

The fact that both British slave trade abolition and colonial slave emancipation were implemented without any major upheaval or loss of life made the deepest impression on foreign abolitionists as an alternative to the Haitian example. For abolitionists abroad, like Alexis de Tocqueville in France, the great surprise of the British process was the fact that the slave trade and slavery were both legislated after a long nonviolent people's movement. In 1834 nearly eight hundred thousand slaves had been called from "death to life" in a single day without the shedding of a drop of blood. For Americans like William Lloyd Garrison it was "the moral great miracle of the age," and for the ex-slave Frederick Douglass, it demonstrated that "England's passage to freedom is not through rivers of blood" but through "the House of Commons."[27]

Internationally, the two decades between 1787 and 1807 were also a watershed in the history of imperial slavery. Ideologically the crucial paradigmatic shift to viewing the African slave trade as something more than a question of economics was accepted by members of the British government itself as early as 1788. The Anglo-American transatlantic slave trades were legally abolished and virtually ended by 1808. During the Napoleonic wars, French, Dutch, and Danish participation in the transatlantic trade was suspended, first by British naval action and then by conquest of their colonies themselves. For the Iberian empires however, the result of the long conflict between the French and British Empires was initially the obverse of those in the Northern European orbits. In the wake of the Saint-Domingue uprising and the war-induced interruptions of trade beginning in the 1790s, Iberian American merchant capitalism set off at fever pitch to increase their colonial slave-grown staples. Slaving became virtually a free trade and the Iberian Atlantic's increasingly valuable means of production. After 1808 the combination of British war gains and Anglo-American legal prohibitions gave Iberian-American ports overwhelming dominance in the transatlantic slave trade. Between 1809 and the fall of Napoleon 97 percent of the African captives who crossed the Atlantic were landed in Spanish and Portuguese ports. Rio de Janeiro became the largest receiving port in the New World.[28]

The return of peace increased the demand for slaves. For four decades thereafter the slave trade was repeatedly affirmed to be a crucial element of their economic prosperity and the mainstay of their Iberian Atlantic imperial revenues. This remained especially true on both sides of the former Portuguese empire after Brazilian independence, and on both sides of the remaining Spanish American empire. As late as 1855, in a rare discussion of slavery, the Spanish Cortes unanimously approved a resolution supporting its government's "innermost conviction that slavery is a necessity and an indispensable condition for the maintenance of landed property in the Island of Cuba." The Cortes vowed never "to meddle with the system in any manner whatsoever."[29]

With the reduction of abolitionist popular mobilization after the early 1840's, British policy began to present mixed signals to the remaining slave empires. Official policy remained as firm as ever. However, with the triumph of free trade in Britain in 1846, the doors were thrown open to Cuban and Brazilian exports. The output and value of those major exports rose dramatically. Despite continuous British pressure on the Spanish-Caribbean and Luso-Brazilian transatlantic slaving, the trade in Africans peaked in Rio de Janeiro during the last three years before the British naval blockade of Brazil in 1850. The trade to Cuba continued unabated until the United States Civil War.[30]

Ideologically, there was a generational gap between Anglo-French and Iberian perspectives. Before 1807 Iberian diplomatic observers did not regard British abolitionism as a serious threat. Encouraged by abolitionist failures for nearly twenty years they doubted whether humanity could ever triumph over commercial greed. The Portuguese ambassador tended to regard failed British abolitionist initiatives as nothing more than "a kind of stage-play," with the same actors, roles, and outcomes. As the Latin-American colonies became ever more dependent upon slave labor during the two decades after 1790, abolitionism remained "a non-starter" both in the Spanish and Portuguese empires: of one thing both the elites and rulers of the Iberian empires were sure — the South Atlantic system and colonial political economies did depend upon the survival of slavery. There was no sustained moral attack on the institution that was not balanced by the acknowledgement that slavery was at least a necessary evil. As with North American contemporaries in the Chesapeake, slavery was seen as too deeply embedded in the fabric of society to be constrained except over a long and indefinite time period — what João Pedro Marques refers to as "Tolerationism." The most significant element of discourse on the slave trade was indeed the "Sounds of Silence."[31]

Whatever the ideological anxieties and musings on the dangers of internal slave revolts from below or of revolutionary inspiration from the French Caribbean, we must beware of assigning to the violent struggles over slavery a uniquely bloody place in the West during the age of revolution. The mutual infliction of horrible atrocities in the slave Caribbean had their European parallels in the guerilla struggles in the Vendée, Calabria, and Spain. What most decisively opened up paths to antislavery in Spanish America after 1808 were events in Europe. Napoleon, the great restorer of slavery in the French colonies, unintentionally initiated the attack on slavery in the Portuguese and Spanish empires.[32]

The empire most heavily invested in the slave trade after 1808, was also the one most dependent upon British protection. Thereafter, Portugal's imperial, economic, and mercantile vulnerability made it the prime target for both British abolitionism and British governments both before and after the Portuguese-Brazilian split. In a succession of diplomatic and military demarches over nearly half a century the Luso-Brazilian-African transatlantic slave trade was brought to an end. At the peak of abolitionist political influence in 1839 the British government obtained from Parliament a virtual declaration of war against its oldest ally and succeeded in coercing Portugal to assent to withdrawing the protection of the Portuguese flag from the slave trade within three years.[33] Eight years later, on the other side of the Atlantic, the British navy initiated its strongest single naval action against any Western empire to ensure the ending of the transatlantic slave trade to Brazil. In this case the escalation was an indirect result of the shift to British free trade after 1846. In the next three years the Brazilian slave trade reached its all-time peak. Some free traders urged the British government to disband its antislave trade patrol on grounds of its ineffectiveness. With public support ebbing, the British government escalated its pursuit of slavers into Brazilian territorial waters.[34]

In the Spanish segment of the Iberian Atlantic Napoleon's dethronement of the Bourbon dynasty resulted in fragmentation of the empire. A war for Spanish national liberation from France was matched by wars for independence from Spain in South America. On both sides of the Atlantic a devastating mixture of formal military and guerilla warfare became the defining characteristic of the conflict. It left in its wake a legacy of militarized politics, civil suppression, and further civil war. As the Spanish-American empire fragmented, the creole elites who had begun the mobilization for independence found themselves caught in an escalation of social insubordination. The hierarchies of law and labor became ever harder to control. For slaves the conflict offered unanticipated opportunities to escape both their existential coercion and their legal condition.[35]

As in revolutionary North America, armies on both sides were major recruiters of slaves, with consequent possibilities for personal liberation. In Spanish America, however, the conflict was deeper, longer, and more disruptive to postrevolutionary authority and civil society. The Spanish Caribbean, which more closely resembled Brazil in its large proportions of slaves and dependency upon staple production, weathered the crisis of the monarchy far more easily than its less slave-dependent counterparts on the continental mainland. Situational opportunity, not demographic destiny, motivated slaves in Spanish America to compel both patriots and loyalists to convert de facto gains into de jure liberations. Revolutionary elites may also have been influenced by the desire to halt the further Africanization of their regions, a prospect exacerbated by the expansion of the slave trade during the previous two decades.

The external situation was also important. After 1810, the combatants bidding for British supplies and diplomatic support legislated an end to slave imports. Beginning with Argentina in 1812, most independent countries entered easily into the British bilateral network of anti–slave trade treaties. Whatever induced the Creole revolutionaries to enact prohibitions against fresh imports, most insurgent regimes also definitively acted to place an endpoint on their slave systems well before the British abolitionists themselves agitated for a gradual end to slavery in their own colonies. The overwhelming majority of newly independent republics enacted "free womb" laws on the Pennsylvania model by 1825.[36]

In the Caribbean and metropolitan sectors of the Spanish empire progress toward abolition was miniscule. Far more enslaved Africans were brought into the Spanish empire than were liberated by the combined military mobilizations and legal liberations of the mainland areas in between 1790 and 1820. Almost as many additional Africans were landed in the Spanish empire in the four following decades. Both during the period of Caribbean revolutionary warfare (1791–1804) and of maximum British abolitionist pressure on the slave trade (1817–1845), few in the Spanish Atlantic empire seriously demanded preparations for an end to the institution.

The British government was also confronted in the Caribbean by growing United States' power and ambition. Many Americans regarded Cuba as their nation's special sphere of influence and possible annexation. The potential impact of British antislavery on Cuba deeply concerned United States. As early as 1824 the special U.S. agent in Cuba advised his government against supporting any British pressure on Cuban authorities in favor of abolition. The United States, he noted, was too interested in Cuba's future to "identify itself with a Convention [the Anglo-Spanish abolition treaty of 1817] so odious to all Spaniards that they make a merit of violating it."[37] Almost immediately thereafter the British government, under abolitionist pressure, resolved to prepare its colonial slaves for emancipation. The United States Senate refused to ratify an already negotiated right-of-search treaty with Britain.[38]

The impact of the growing Anglo-American divergence over Cuba sharpened in the wake of Britain's successful blockade of the slave trade to Brazil in 1850. Cuba remained the last transatlantic market for enslaved Africans in the Americas. As with Brazil, Britain's adoption of free trade in 1846 served to stimulate economic growth in Cuba. The island's imports of African slaves more than quadrupled in the four years between 1846 and 1849. The per capita output of Cuba probably placed it among the top half dozen of the world's nations.[39]

Moreover, by the early 1850s British abolitionists were no longer capable of mobilizing mass petition campaigns in favor of aggressive British action. British governmental pressure on the Spanish empire actually diminished in the 1850s. In part this was in response to the peak of American

Southern agitation for annexation of Cuba to the United States. The British government was faced with the incompatible policies of simultaneously threatening Spain over the continuation of the slave trade, opening its metropolitan market to slave-grown sugar, and offering Spain diplomatic and even naval assistance against imperializing expeditions launched from American soil. Meanwhile, the American flag, exempt from a British naval search for slaves, now protected the rapidly expanding Cuban slave trade. The situation reached a crisis point in 1858. British warships attempted to search vessels of all nations sailing into Cuban waters. Northern and Southern U.S. politicians united in denouncing the searches and called for the seizure of British warships in retaliation. The British government backed away from armed confrontation. The following year Cuban slave imports reached their highest level in a generation. If the ending of slavery in Spanish mainland America had been accelerated by a long military stalemate during the wars of independence, it was deferred by a great power diplomatic stalemate in the Caribbean.[40]

The American Civil War broke the stalemate. In April 1862 the United States Senate approved an Anglo-American right of search treaty without dissent. As the tide of the Civil War turned against the Confederacy, the Madrid government allowed its military governor to implement a thorough prohibition. By 1865 the sugar planters themselves were suddenly petitioning for slave trade abolition. There was overwhelming agreement in all parts of the empire on the need to abolish the transatlantic trade and to plan for an orderly ending to the institution itself.[41] As the U.S. Civil War drew to a close, the Madrid government inaugurated a planning commission (Junta de Información de Ultramar) to formulate an exit strategy from colonial slavery. In Brazil, the emperor saw the handwriting on the wall as early as 1863. In January 1864 he directed his prime minister to note that American events now forced them to think about the means of abolition, "so that what occurred in respect to the slave trade [in 1850] does not happen to us again."[42]

The various components of the Iberian Atlantic empires aligned themselves with Northwestern European abolition at various moments between the 1850s and the 1880s. Portugal began the process of gradually abolishing the institution in its African colonies in the 1850s. The state provided for a transition period of twenty years to allow for the emergence of a free labor force. In 1878 all slaves became *libertos*, a large lingering cohort of forced labor. Spain's free womb gradual abolition act of 1870 (the Moret law) was supplemented by legislation for immediate abolition in Puerto Rico in 1873. In 1886 final abolition was legislated for Cuba. Brazil enacted its own free womb legislation in 1871 and full abolition in 1888.

Internal Pressures

Most interesting, in comparative perspective, is the internal context within each empire. Domestic pressures were crucial in determining the modes of transformation in the Spanish and Brazilian empires. As with other plantation empires, the endings of their transatlantic slave trades and of their slave systems shared one important characteristic. In every major zone of the plantation Americas American rulers had to cope with slaveholders' perceptions that slave labor was more competitive than any other variety of bound or free labor immediately available to them. As noted above, the century of abolitionism began with an upward infusion of slaves in both the Spanish and Portuguese empires. For both that dependency did not decrease thereafter. For half a century after the 1780s, in both segments of the Portuguese Empire and in the Caribbean remnant of the Spanish Empire, slave imports reached their all-time peak. More slaves lived within the boundaries of the shrunken Spanish empire in 1825 than had resided there before the outbreak of the Spanish American wars of independence.

For Spain, of course, Cuba became more significant to its economic growth than ever before. Eric Williams's emphasis on the role of slavery in the development of capitalism is probably more applicable to nineteenth-century Spanish economic development than it was to eighteenth-century British industrialization. In any event, Spanish industrialists, in the 1860s and 1870s, were to be the last in a long line of Continental economic interests who bitterly opposed the ending of Atlantic slavery.[43]

At the level of high politics new revolutionary regimes or constituent assemblies always created potential windows of opportunity for discussing the future of slavery. The American convention of 1787, the French National Assembly of 1789, the Spanish imperial Cortes of 1811, the conventions of new nations in Spanish America, the Brazilian convention of 1823, and the Portuguese imperial Cortes of 1821–1822 all opened public space for challenges to slavery.[44] Nineteenth-century governments, on the contrary, usually tried to avoid discussions of slavery in Ibero-American legislatures. Silence or evasion was characteristic of most civil societies between internal upheavals. This encapsulates the relation of abolition to the state of civil society. All imperial polities (except the British) suffered from a long deficit in the capacity of antislavery voices to mobilize the public sphere in favor of decisive action. Apart from the Haitian example, all supporters of antislavery movements on both sides of the Atlantic had before them the British model of an aroused and sustained public opinion inciting a series of legal steps from curtailing the slave trade to providing for postemancipation transitions.

Crucially, nowhere during the first half century after the British abolitionist breakthrough in 1788 did any other mass metropolitan national abolitionist movement emerge.[45] Fifty years after the end of American War of Independence there was still no formal national abolitionist society anywhere on the mainland of Europe. Even in the United States, only regional abolition societies existed. Antislavery spokesmen kept a rhetorical distance from discussions of the radical modes of collective action. The French abolitionist society of 1834, formed within a few months of the implementation of British emancipation in 1834, never harked back to the *Amis des Noirs* let alone to the insurgents of Saint-Domingue or the French radical emancipation of 1794.[46]

The Franco-Caribbean revolutions resulted in a polarized split between unqualified emancipation in Haiti and unqualified reenslavement in every other French tropical colony. Long after Haiti was given up as irrevocably lost the French Antislavery Society remained the preserve of a small elite until the eve of the Revolution of 1848. In the metropole of other Northern European slaveholding empires slave emancipation was even less salient as a public issue. In the Dutch, Danish, and Swedish cases one can hardly speak of an aroused public consciousness of slavery as a moral issue, much less as a significant political issue.

It would be interesting to know whether European proponents or opponents of the status quo on slavery more frequently evoked the Franco-Caribbean upheavals after Haitian independence. Europe's religious organizations rarely initiated or mobilized their followers for antislavery initiatives. This was as true for protestant organizations in the Netherlands, Denmark, Sweden, and Switzerland as it was for overwhelmingly Roman Catholic societies. Their ecclesiastical establishments gave very little encouragement to antislavery mobilizations until late in the nineteenth century. When Britain managed to convince the Vatican to issue a formal condemnation of the slave trade in 1839, it had to seem untainted by a prior British initiative.[47]

When a continental civil society did become antislavery, it was almost always secular radicals who took the place earlier filled by noncomformists in Anglo-America. For many foreigners the connection of antislavery with nonconformity in Britain led to the rhetorical conflations of abolitionism with conspiratorial, alien, or racial threats. At the height of British popular mobilization in the 1830s and early 1840s, Spanish and Cuban officials informed Madrid that they were dealing with abolitionist Methodists and Baptist agents intent on proselytizing revolutionary doctrines among slaves, free blacks, and white dissidents. Evidence of communication between white dissidents and free blacks became woven into the most extensive and brutal repression of slaves in Cuban history—the Escalera conspiracy.[48]

Another potential source of civil society recruitment for antislavery was also relatively scarce in the Catholic empires. In the 1840s Victor Schoelcher, one of France's most outspoken antislavery campaigners, regretted the reluctance of French women to rival their British sisters in petitioning or organizing for antislavery. In the Spanish Empire the launching of the nation's first abolitionist society in 1865 was paralleled by the formation of a women's chapter. At least as significant as its founding, however, was the fact that the women's organization was ephemeral after its founding. In Brazil, too, at least into the 1880s, the rank and file formally integrated into the structure of the new abolitionist societies were almost all men.[49]

The recruitment of workers into abolitionist civil societies also apparently differed from the pattern of British popular mobilization. During the fifty years between the late 1780s and the late 1830s, one of the remarkable features of British antislavery was its ability to attract massive support from the lower echelons of the social structure. Before emancipation British radical dissidents who denounced abolitionism as a distraction from metropolitan labor problems were unable to dissuade workers from participation in abolitionist activities. Only after final emancipation did the British movement lose much of its cross-class and mass appeal. On the continent, only in France did a small portion of the working class offer substantial support to emancipation. Workers in Paris and Lyon launched the first modest working-class petition for emancipation in 1844. In Spain abolitionists seem to have mobilized large groups of workers on some occasions but failed to do so on others.[50]

In assessing the impact of popular mobilizations on antislavery legislation, it is important to bear in mind the political context. In some cases countermobilizations in civil society were able to match abolitionist mobilizations. In the British case anti-abolitionists were confined to a relatively miniscule portion of the society. Even at their greatest strength opponents of emancipation accumulated less than four tenths of 1 percent of the total number of signatures on petitions to Parliament. Overseas, of course, slaves outnumbered their owners by a margin of ten to one. On the other hand, at the beginning of the French Revolution an anti-abolitionist mobilization was able to deter the National Constituent Assembly from taking any action against slavery. It was primarily the unprecedented uprising of the slaves of Saint-Domingue that drove the legislature to proclaim universal freedom for all France's slaves.[51]

This violent mobilization and militarization of societies accelerated abolition in Spanish mainland America. There, the ebb and flow of military victories created a contest for gradual emancipations. From that experience, of course, the Spanish rulers drew the lesson that an autonomous civil society was a perennial threat both to the empire and its overseas economy. Cuba's slaves, the most dynamic wealth-producing labor force in the empire, were therefore sustained within a colony with maximum inhibition of civil and political institutions, lacking any formal representation in the metropolitan legislature. When the disparate regions of the empire finally reassembled in a second united imperial Cortes the stage was set for another explosive stalemate and another violent fragmentation over the issues of independence and slavery.[52]

While civil war exploded in the Cuban segment of the empire in 1868, civil society mobilized in the metropole and Puerto Rico as well. In Cuba a decade-long stalemated revolutionary military conflict provided avenues to liberation and an incremental extension of ambivalent expansion of freedom. As in the South American wars of liberation, "the disrupted conditions of the countryside and the changes in expectations brought about by insurrection" led to a disruption of the plantation order.[53] Meanwhile, Spain seemed to echo divisions over slavery in the antebellum United States a decade earlier. Abolitionist mobilizations in some areas were countered by metropolitan mobilizations that were as deeply wedded to the protectionist political economy as the abolitionists were to the political economy of wage labor. The Moret law, enacting gradual emancipation in 1870, reflected the balance of power in each sector of the empire.[54]

The accelerated emancipation of all of Puerto Rican slaves in 1873 occurred amidst the interplay of countervailing tensions in the metropolitan and Cuban conflicts. At one point Cuban slaveholders aligned with industrial protectionists to produce a wave of petitions that outnumbered those favoring abolition. The abolitionists countered with a wave of demonstrations. The outcome was again determined only by yet another revolutionary coup and another regime change. As a result, empire-wide slave emancipation had to await the conclusion of the war in Cuba in 1878. The final act of 1886, terminating the remnant of the *patronato*, was probably the least contested action in the seventy-five-year process of Spanish imperial emancipation.[55]

Brazil was the last remnant of the Atlantic slaveholding empires to abandon the institution. Of all the great transatlantic empires, the Luso-Brazilian separation between colony and metropole occurred with the least military or revolutionary violence. Despite high levels of slave flight, conspiracy, and revolt in the first third of the nineteenth century, the Brazilian empire was established with an overwhelming elite consensus on the maintenance of slavery as an institution. Neither the passage of slave trade abolition in 1850 nor of gradual (free womb) emancipation in 1871 was the outcome of a major political split within the dominant planter-merchant class. They were not preceded by major popular mobilizations by either freemen or slaves. As yet there was no major sectional split in the Brazilian empire between a free-soil zone and defenders of the status quo.[56]

The final stage of Brazilian abolition, however, occurred within the context of one of the most remarkable civil mobilizations in the history of imperial slavery. In formal terms, Brazilian slavery was peacefully brought to an end by formal legislation in 1888. Two elements of the Brazilian political and civic structure stand out in comparative perspective. In its national legislature, political power remained constitutionally concentrated in the hands of the empire's slaveholders and their mercantile allies from beginning to end. Within Brazil's political culture, the fundamental distinction among its free inhabitants remained the one between the small cohort of well-off citizens and the far larger so-called class of those less favored by fortune. The empire was constitutionally designed to be a regime of notables. The system maximized both elite representation and legal and social stability. Fixed elections regularly produced orderly working majorities. Civil liberties for free subjects were generally respected. The system appeared sufficiently unthreatened that newspapers, the principal avenues for public opinion, had remarkable latitude for criticism of the government and even of the political and social system.[57]

Long before the emergence of any popular antislavery movement, urban newspapers occasionally condemned slavery in Brazil in a manner that would have elicited swift official reprisal in Cuba or popular violence in the antebellum U.S. South. In part, newspapers were tainted by well-deserved reputations for subsidized corruption by domestic or foreign pressure groups. As late as the gradual emancipation debates of 1871, journalists seemed to have had little impact on national legislators. The most striking manifestation of public mobilization during the passage of the free womb law in 1871 actually came from those who fiercely registered their opposition with a record number of petitions to the legislature.[58]

Although slaves never ceased attempting to gain individual liberation through manumission or flight, there was no measureable surge in collective resistance through conspiracy or insurgency during the generation after slave trade abolition in 1850. Nor did the slaveholding class encounter large-scale opposition to the institution from the free population before 1880. Whatever the earlier manifestations of popular antislavery sentiment, there is broad agreement among historians of Brazil that only the 1880s opened the period of sustained mass mobilization.[59] Just before this mobilization, however, another involuntary movement of slaves occurred. In the wake of shifting economic prospects there was an expanded slave trade from the northeastern and extreme southern provinces into the central south coffee region. As in the antebellum American South, planters in the booming importing zone began to fear that the rapid redistribution of slaves might erode support for the institution from the exporting areas. They moved to stem tide "to preserve the uniformity of the country."[60]

It was too late. In 1880 the national legislature still refused to reopen the issue of slavery. It was an issue that the majority regarded as resolved by the free womb law of 1871. Initially the public response was muted. Slowly newspapers, some edited by foreigners, began to support the formation of abolitionist societies. Strikingly, neither the national nor the provincial governments attempted to suppress the new manifestations of popular antislavery. This early phase of popular abolitionism drew on some British recipes: newspaper publicity, mass rallies, and creation of provincial and local societies. Opponents of the new movement also mobilized in the guise of agricultural clubs to sustain the status quo. Almost immediately, however, Brazilians also gave these traditional modes of action new twists that simply bypassed the still solid consensus against abolition in the national legislature. Societies were formed to create emancipation funds to accelerate the operation of the 1871 legislation. They initiated discussions of emancipation in provincial legislatures.[61]

The mobilization process also involved the launching of abolitionist events, designed, like those of their Anglo-American predecessors, to create popular abolitionist identities through functions like bazaars and theatrical functions. Unlike their Anglo-American predecessors their models were not Anglo-American formal meetings, with their parliamentary procedures and petitions, but popular spectacles. They injected abolitionist floats into carnival celebrations, taking advantage of the increasing presence of the free Afro-Brazilian population in popular spectacles. They staged theatrical performances. They organized fairs (*kermeses*) to accumulate emancipation funds. Rather than stressing the moral linkage of protest created by abstention they stressed a consumer link by consumption, wrapping cigars with portraits of abolitionists. They reinscribed traditional slave-grown products as freedom symbols.[62]

Successive piecemeal emancipations at the local level became the hallmark of Brazilian emancipation. The most dramatic instance was the creation of Brazil's first free soil province, Ceará. The liberation began as a mobilization against the exportation of its slaves to the prosperous provinces to its south. By the spring of 1884 the city telegraphed the message, "Ceará is free" to the world and dubbed itself the "second Canada." For the first time in Brazilian history, a free soil zone was established in a whole province. The southern Brazilian provincial capital of Porto Alegre acted next, declaring itself a free city at a bazaar in September 1884.[63]

Significantly, the one major Anglo-American abolitionist technique not emphasized by the Brazilian movement was a nationwide petition campaign to the national legislature. Did this reflect the fact that the Brazilian national legislature and Brazilian civil society appeared to be moving along divergent trajectories during the 1880s? As de facto zones of freedom were established province by province, city by city, and block by block, the national legislature moved to constrict the national public sphere sharply. In 1881 an electoral law combined a minimal property qualification with a rigorous requirement of documentary proof of income. The great majority of the previously eligible population was reduced to less than 2 percent of the adult male population of Brazil.

The results were dramatically apparent by the mid 1880s. Reacting to the threatened disintegration of the slaveholders' authority, the rural slaveholding elite gave the conservatives an overwhelming parliamentary victory in 1885. In the provincial legislature abolitionism was also silenced. The governments suppressed abolitionist election rallies. Although the vast majority of abolitionist societies still adhered to a nonviolent approach to slave liberation, "a new, uncompromising abolitionist strategy took hold that trespassed all parameters of the law." A militant branch created an underground railroad that helped free tens of thousands of slaves. Fleeing slaves often boarded the Brazilian railway system itself to freedom. In collective flights whole plantations were simultaneously abandoned. Thus, the hemorrhage of slaves actually accelerated in the three years that followed the conservative electoral victory. By late 1887 the dynamics of Brazilian politics took an irrevocable turn. The military refused to track down runaway slaves. The hard-core coffee planters abandoned their last-ditch attempts to stem the accelerating erosion of their labor force. Planters decided to cut their losses and manumit their slaves. Newspapers began to emphasize the acceleration of planter emancipations. The slaveholders decided that an orderly and legislative transition of the remaining half of their slaves was preferable to the uncertainties of uncontrolled disintegration.[64]

Outside parliament popular mobilization was no longer contestation but celebration. As the final bill of emancipation in the Americas proceeded through its stages during the second week of May 1888, it was paralleled by a series of public processions. The abolitionists saw emancipation as a direct result of their extra-parliamentary efforts rather than as an action mediated through the national legislature. As Celso Castilho concludes, popular mobilization associated with the campaign had changed the dynamics of antislavery politics.[65]

We must be wary of reading too much into this climactic nonviolent victory over New-World slavery. The structure of legislative power yielded upon one issue, but remained intact. No American-style reconstruction alliance emerged from the Brazilian path to abolition. The triumph of the new Republican Party in 1889 foreclosed the possibility of further legislative involvement in assisting former slaves. The new government's efforts and revenues were directed toward ensuring a fresh European labor supply for the plantations and for their project of whitening Brazilian. Emancipation left no legacy of a more biracial citizenry like the one that emerged from the generation of common struggle for independence and abolition in Cuba.

Brazilian abolition did mark a major moment in the emergence of a new Western consensus linking the empire to antislavery. In February 1888, Pope Leo XIII issued an encyclical on Brazil's forthcoming abolition. He referred, in passing, to the "new roads" and new commercial enterprises undertaken in the lands of Africa, where "apostolic men" could now endeavor to find out how to "best secure the safety and liberty of slaves." The message from the Vatican coincided with a great shift of European imperial ambitions toward Africa. The Papal encouragement was followed within months by Cardinal Lavigerie's organization of another anti–slave trade crusade in Europe. For the first time a mass antislavery movement was launched by, and for, Catholic Europe. Organizations were founded in Belgium, France, Germany, Switzerland, Spain, Portugal, Austria, Italy, and in Haiti across the Atlantic.[66]

The outcome of Lavigerie's campaign was the convocation of an international anti–slave trade conference at Brussels in 1889. Just seventy-five years after the Congress of Vienna, the governments of the new colonial powers entered into the scramble for Africa. These new "emperors of the world" were nation-states—Germany, Italy, and Belgium. They joined the older imperial powers in linking abolition to their shares of Africa. The signatories to the Brussels Act of 1890 included more than the imperial European powers. The United States of America, the Netherlands, Russia, Austria, Sweden, Denmark, Zanzibar, the Ottoman Empire, and Persia all pledged to prohibit the further export, import or mutilation of slaves.[67]

Antislavery was clearly an afterthought to empire. The new imperialism actually combined the suppression of the Muslim and Sub-Saharan slave trades with fresh sanctions for European-sponsored coerced labor for two more generations to come. Nevertheless, at the end of the nineteenth century at least one form of human bondage seemed to be destined for destruction at a pace that had been unimaginable to Adam Smith little more than a century before. As late as the 1780s, all European rulers had scrambled for whatever share they could get of Africa's enslaved captives and of America's slave-grown commodities. For the emperors of the world a century later antislavery was now an opportunity and slavery an embarrassment. Because the institution was a shrinking exception, confined to the still-uncivilized world, it seemed destined for rapid destruction in the early twentieth century.

For the signatories of the Brussels Act in 1890 it was simply unimaginable that there would soon be more slaves toiling in the heart of Europe itself than in all of the Americas in 1850 or that more Europeans would then be considered as enslavable by other Europeans than at any moment since before the beginnings of European overseas expansion; or that during the second third of the twentieth century, Eurasia, not Africa or America, would contain the world's largest cohorts of coerced labor. If nothing else, a comparative perspective teaches us that success is never final.

Notes

I take this opportunity to express my deep appreciation to Josep Fradera, Christopher Schmidt-Nowara, Stephen Jacobson, and all attendees at the conference on Slavery, Empire and Abolition for providing me with the opportunity to participate in analyzing the process of Spanish imperial abolition in comparative perspective.

1. Quotation in Debbrett's *Parliamentary Register* (London, 1799), 586. See also, Christopher L. Brown, "Empire Without Slaves: British Concepts of Emancipation in the Age of the American Revolution," *William and Mary Quarterly* 56, no. 2 (1999): 273–306; and Seymour Drescher, *Abolition: A History of Slavery and Antislavery* (New York, 2009), Part I. For a hypothesis about long-run determinants of abolition, see, David Eltis, "Abolition and Identity in the Very Long Run," in *Migration, Trade, and Slavery in an Expanding World: Essays in Honor of Pieter Emmer,* ed. Wim Klooster (Leiden/Boston, 2009), 227–258. For a world perspective on the slave trade, see Olivier Pétré Grenouilleaux, *Les Traites négrières: Essai d 'histoire globale* (Paris, 2004).
2. Quoted in Reginald Coupland, *Wilberforce: A Narrative* (New York, 1968), 396–397. Other foreigners regarded British abolitionism as a form of fanaticism, alternately akin to religious extremism or to the French revolution.
3. Compare Davis, *The Problem of Slavery in Western Culture* (Ithaca, 1966), 153 n. 56; and ibid. (rev. ed., 1988), 153–154, n. 56. See also Davis, *The Problem of Slavery in the Age of Revolution,* with a preface to the new edition (New York, 1999), 13; and Davis, "Foreword," *Econocide: British Slavery in the Era of Abolition* (Chapel Hill, 2010).
4. For a summary of recent research, see Laird W. Bergad, *The Comparative Histories of Slavery in Brazil, Cuba, and the United States* (New York, 2007), chap. 5; and Robert William Fogel, *Without Consent or Contract: The Rise and Fall of American Slavery* (New York, 1989), Part I; and the three companion volumes (New York, 1991–1992). On the transatlantic slave trade, see, above all, David Eltis, *Economic Growth and the Ending of the Transatlantic Slave Trade* (New York, 1987). For the most recent variant of the economic decline theory of the abolition of the British slave trade, see David Beck Ryden, *West Indian Slavery and British Abolition, 1783–1807* (New York, 2009), 8–11 and 175–176.
5. For an overview, see Drescher, *Abolition: A History of Slavery and Antislavery,* chap. 6. For transatlantic slave trade figures, see http://www.slavevoyages.org/tast/assessment/estimates.faces, ed. David Eltis et al.

6. Andrea Weindl, "The Slave Trade of Northern Germany from the Seventeenth to the Nineteenth Centuries," in *Extending the Frontiers: Essays on the New Transatlantic Slave Trade Database*, eds., David Eltis and David Richardson (New Haven, 2008), 250–274. On intraregional New-World trades, see the essays in *The Chattel Principle: Internal Slave Trades in the Americas*, ed., Walter Johnson (New Haven: Yale University Press, 2004).
7. Jonathan M. Hess, *Germans, Jews and the Claims of Modernity* (New Haven, 2002), chap. 2.
8. See Bergad, *Comparative Histories*, 10, 18, 145; and Fogel, *Without Consent or Contract*, 67.
9. The following illustrates the pattern. When the slave revolution broke out in Saint-Domingue in 1791 the colony was the world's most productive source of sugar and coffee. When the British abolished their slave trade in 1806–1807, no other system had ever held so dominant position in the tropics; the British Caribbean had succeeded the French West Indies as the world's premier producer of sugar and coffee. Even with access to enslaved Africans, it took Brazil and Cuba a full generation after slave trade abolition to overtake the British tropical production in sugar and coffee. As the last recipient of the slave trade, Cuba, by the 1850s, had become the last "pearl of the Antilles." At that point the island ranked just below the U.S. South in per capita income: "Cuba must have ranked among the top half dozen of the world's nations." See David Eltis, "The Slave Economies of the Caribbean: Structure, Performance, Evolution and Significance," in *The Slave Societies of the Caribbean*, ed., Franklin W. Knight (UNESCO, 1997) chap. 3, 123. See also, Eltis, *Economic Growth*, 6, figure 1, and 294, n. 6.
10. On Spanish South America see George Reid Andrews, *Afro-Latin America, 1800–2000* (New York, 2004), chap. 1; and Peter Blanchard, *Under the Flags of Freedom: Slave Soldiers and the Wars of Independence in Spanish South America* (Pittsburgh, 2008).
11. See David Patrick Geggus, *Haitian Revolutionary Studies* (Bloomington, 2002), chaps. 1 and 10.
12. Don E. Fehrenbacher, *The Slaveholding Republic: An Account of the United States Government's Relations to Slavery*, ed., Ward M. McAfee, (New York, 2001), 141–142. On Puerto Rico, see Christopher Schmidt-Nowara, *Empire and Antislavery: Spain: Cuba, and Puerto Rico* (Pittsburgh, 1999), chaps. 2 and 7.
13. Robin Blackburn, "Haiti, Slavery, and the Age of the Democratic Revolution," *William and Mary Quarterly* 63, no. 4 (2006): 643–674, quotation on 654. See also Blackburn, *The American Crucible: Slavery, Emancipation and Human Rights* (London, 2011), 171–210. For other recent assessments of the Haitian Revolution and its impact, see *The World of the Haitian Revolution*, eds., David Patrick Geggus and Norman Fiëring (Bloomington, 2009); Ada Ferrer, "Haiti, Free Soil, and Antislavery in the Revolutionary Atlantic," *American Historical Review* 117, no. 1 (2012): 40–66; and Laurent Dubois, *Haiti: The Aftershocks of History* (New York, 2012). David Patrick Geggus's assessments may be found in Geggus, "Slavery, War, and Revolution in the Greater Caribbean, 1789–1815," in *A Turbulent Time: The French Revolution and the Greater Caribbean*, eds., David Barry Gaspar and David Patrick Geggus (Bloomington, 1997), 1–50; and his preface to *The Impact of the Haitian Revolution in the Atlantic World*, ed., David Geggus (Columbia, 2003), ix–xiv.
14. Seymour Drescher, "Econocide, Capitalism and Slavery: A Commentary," *Boletin de Estudios Latinoamericanos y del Caribe* 36 (June 1984): 49–67, esp. 57, Table 5: Average increase in Muscavado production (Cuba on Jamaica) 1786–1790 to 1801–1805.
15. For the initial formulation, see Seymour Drescher, "Two Variants of Anti-Slavery: Religious Organization and Social Mobilization in Britain and France, 1780–1870," in *Anti-Slavery, Religion and Reform*, eds., Christine Bolt and Seymour Drescher (Hamden, 1980), 43–63; rept. in Drescher, *From Slavery to Freedom* (New York, 1999), 35–56.
16. Seymour Drescher, *Capitalism and Antislavery: British Mobilization in Comparative Perspective* (New York, 1987). For an update, see Drescher, "Public Opinion and Parliament

in the Abolition of the British Slave Trade," in *The British Slave Trade: Abolition, Parliament and People*, eds., Stephen Farrell, Melanie Uniwin, and James Walvin (Edinburgh, 2007), 42–65.
17. Drescher, *Abolition*, chaps. 8, 9, and 11.
18. See, inter alia, Lawrence C. Jennings, *French Anti-Slavery: The Movement for the Abolition of Slavery in France, 1802–1848* (Cambridge, 2000); *The Abolitions of Slavery From Léger Felicité Sonthonax to Victor Schoelcher: 1793, 1794, 1848*, ed., Marcel Dorigny (New York, 2003); Jeremy Adelman, *Sovereignty and Revolution in the Iberian Atlantic* (Princeton, 2006); Schmidt-Nowara, *Empire and Antislavery*; *Abolir l'esclavage: Un réformisme à l'epreuve (France, Portugal, Suisse, xviiie-xixe siècles)*, ed., Olivier Pétré-Grenouilleau (Rennes, 2008); João Pedro Marques, *The Sounds of Silence: Nineteenth-Century Portugal and the Abolition of the Slave Trade* (New York, 2006); and David Brion Davis, *Inhuman Bondage: The Rise and Fall of the Slavery in the New World* (New York, 2006). For an estimate of the costs of alternative paths to emancipation, see Frédérique Beauvois, "Indemniser les planteurs pour abolir l'esclavage? Entre, etude o des débats parlementaires français et britanniques (1788–1848) dans une perspective comparée," Ph.D. dissertation, University of Lausanne (2011) esp. 452–467.
19. Drescher, *Capitalism and Antislavery*, chap. 2–4; J.R. Oldfield, *Popular Politics and British Anti-Slavery* (Manchester, 1995).
20. Clare Midgley, *Women Against Slavery: The British Campaigns, 1780–1870* (London, 1992).
21. Davis, *Inhuman Bondage*, chap. 11; Seymour Drescher, "Civilizing Insurgency: Two Variants of Slave Revolts in the Age of Revolution," in *Who Abolished Slavery? Slave Revolts and Abolitionism: A Debate with João Pedro Marques*, eds., Seymour Drescher and Pieter C. Emmer (New York, 2010), 120–132.
22. Adelman, *Sovereignty and Revolution*, 256.
23. Eltis, *Economic Growth*, esp. parts III–IV.
24. Drescher, *Abolition*, chap. 10.
25. Howard Temperley, *British Antislavery, 1833–1870* (London, 1972); and Temperley, "Anti-slavery as a Form of Cultural Imperialism," in Bolt and Dreshcer, *Anti-Slavery*, 335–350; Leslie Bethell, *The Abolition of the Brazilian Slave Trade: Britain, Brazil and the Slave Trade Question* (Cambridge, 1970). Marques, *Sounds of Silence*; David R. Murray, *Britain, Spain and the Abolition of the Cuban Slave Trade* (Cambridge, 1980); and Ehud R. Toledano, *The Ottoman Slave Trade and its Suppression: 1840–1890* (Princeton, 1982).
26. *Hansard's Parliamentary Debates*, vol. 8 (1806–1807), col. 952.
27. Seymour Drescher, *Capitalism and Antislavery*, 87; and Drescher, *Abolition*, 265–266.
28. See Voyages: The Transatlantic Slave Trade Database Website, http://www.slavevoyages.org/tast/assessment/estimates.faces (hereafter TSTD). For the Iberian Atlantic, see Adelman, *Sovereignty*, 73–100.
29. Arthur F. Corwin, *Spain and the Abolition of Slavery in Cuba, 1817–1886* (Austin, 1967), 125.
30. Eltis, *Economic Growth*, 284–286; Murray, *Odious Commerce*, chap. 11; and the estimates at www.slavevoyages.org.
31. Adelman, *Sovereignty*, 98–99; Marques, *Sounds of Silence*, 22–25.
32. See, David Bell, *The First Total War: Napoleon's Europe and the Birth of Warfare as We Know It* (Boston, 2007), chaps. 5 and 8; and Jeremy Adelman, "The Rites of Statehood: Violence and Sovereignty in Spanish America, 1789–1821," *Hispanic American Historical Review* 90, no. 3 (2010): 391–422.
33. Marques, *Sounds of Silence*, chap. 4.
34. Bethell, *Abolition*, chaps. 6 and 7; Eltis, *Economic Growth*, chap. 12; and Jeffrey D. Needell, "The Abolition of the Slave Trade in 1850: Historiography, Slave Agency and Statesmanship," *Journal of Latin American Studies* 33, no. 4 (2001): 681–711.

35. Adelman, *Sovereignty*, chaps. 5 and 7; and Blanchard, *Under the Flags of Freedom*.
36. Andrews, *Afro-Latin America*, chap. 1.
37. Quoted in Murray, *Odious Commerce*, 77.
38. Fehrenbacher, *Slaveholding Republic*, 77.
39. David Eltis, "Slave Economies of the Caribbean," 123.
40. Fehrenbacher, *Slaveholding Republic*.
41. Murray, *Odious Commerce*, 316.
42. See, Roderick Barman, *Citizen Emperor: Pedro II and the Making of Brazil, 1825–91* (Stanford, 1999), 195; and Jeffrey D. Needell, *The Party of Order: The Conservatives, the State, and Slavery in the Brazilian Monarchy, 1831–1871* (Stanford, 2006), 234.
43. See Luis Alonso, "Comercio exterior y formacion de capital financier: el trafico de negros hispano-Cubano, 1821–1868," *Anuario de Estudios Americanos* 51 (1994): 75–92; Robert Whitney, "The Political Economy of Abolition: The Hispano-Cuban Elite and Cuban Slavery, 1868–1873," *Slavery and Abolition* 13, no. 1) (1992): 20–36; and Schmidt-Nowara, *Empire and Antislavery*, 131–134 and 144–153.
44. For the Portuguese Imperial Cortes, see Marques, *Sounds of Silence*, passim. For the Spanish Imperial Cortes, see Marie Laure Rieu-Millan, *Los Disputados Americanos en las Cortes de Cadiz (igualidad o independencia)* (Madrid, 1990), 169–172.
45. On Dutch Abolition, see *Fifty Years Later: Antislavery, Capitalism and Modernity in the Dutch Orbit*, ed., Gert Oostindie (Leiden/Pittsburgh, 1995).
46. See Jennings, *French Anti-slavery*, 120–121.
47. Paul Michael Kielstra, *The Politics of Slave Trade Suppression in Britain and France, 1814–1848* (London, 2000), 198–199.
48. Robert L. Paquette, *Sugar is Made with Blood: The Conspiracy of La Escalera and the Conflict Between Empires over Slavery in Cuba* (Middletown, 1988), chaps. 5 and 6; Murray, *Odious Commerce*, 115–120.
49. Jennings, *French Antislavery*, 239. For Brazil, see Celso Thomas Castilho, "Abolitionism Matters: The Politics of Antislavery in Pernambuco, Brazil, 1869–1888," Ph.D. thesis, University of California at Berkeley, 2008, 155.
50. Schmidt-Nowara, *Empire and Antislavery*, 83–91.
51. Michael Craton, *Testing the Chains: Slave Rebellions in the British West Indies, 1629–1832* (Ithaca, 1982), 294–295; Robin Blackburn, *The Overthrow of Colonial Slavery 1776–1848*, (London, 1988), 169–177; Daniel P. Resnick, "The Société des Amis des Noirs and the Abolition of Slavery," *French Historical Studies* 7 (1972): 558–569; Yves Benot, *La Revolution Française et la fin des colonies* (Paris, 1989); and Jeremy D. Popkin, *You are all Free: The Haitian Revolution and the Abolition of Slavery* (New York, 2010) chap. 8.
52. Schmidt-Nowara, *Empire and Antislavery*, chaps. 5 and 6.
53. Rebecca Scott, *Slave Emancipation in Cuba: The Transition to Free Labor, 1860–1899* (Princeton, 1985), 55.
54. Ibid., chap. 3.
55. Ibid., chaps. 6 and 7, Schmidt-Nowara, *Empire and Antislavery*, chap. 7.
56. Needell, *Party of Order*, chap. 7.
57. Ibid., chap. 4; Richard Graham, *Patronage and Politics in Nineteenth-Century Brazil* (Stanford, 1990).
58. Needell, *Party of Order*, 289.
59. See, inter alia, Robert Conrad, *The Destruction of Brazilian Slavery, 1850–1888* (Berkeley, 1972); Castilho, "Abolitionism," chap. 2; Roger A. Kittleson, *The Practice of Politics in Postcolonial Brazil: Porto Alegre, 1845–1895* (Pittsburgh, 2005), chaps. 4 and 5; Dale Torston Graden, *From Slavery to Freedom in Brazil, Bahia, 1835–1900* (Albuquerque, 2006), chap. 7; and Emilia Viotti da Costa, *The Brazilian Empire: Myths and Histories* (Chicago, 1985), 193.

60. Robert W. Slenes, "The Brazilian Internal Slave Trade, 1850–1888: Regional Economies, Slave Experience, and the Politics of a Peculiar Market," in *The Chattel Principle*, 325–370; and Conrad, *Destruction*, 172.
61. Castilho, "Abolitionism," 84.
62. Ibid., 102–103.
63. Conrad, *Destruction*, 179–192; Graden, *From Slavery*, 164; and Castilho, "Abolitionism," 107–109.
64. Graham, *Patronage and Politics*, Maria Helena Machado, *O Plano e o Pânico: Os Movimentos Sociais na Década da Abolição* (Rio de Janeiro and São Paulo, 1994), chap. 4; Slenes, "Brazilian Internal Slave Trade," 360; Castilho, "Abolitionism," 246.
65. Castilho, "Abolitionism," 176–190.
66. Drescher, *Abolition*, 370–371 and 385–386.
67. Suzanne Miers, *Britain and the Ending of the Slave Trade* (London, 1975), 201–206; and François Renault, *Lavigerie, L'esclavage Africain, et l'Europe, 1868–1892*, 2 vols. (Paris, 1971), II, 72.194; and Daniel Laqua, "The Tensions of Internationalism: Transnational Anti-Slavery in the 1880s and 1890s," *International History Review* 33, no. 4 (2011): 705–726.

Selected Bibliography

Adelman, Jeremy. *Sovereignty and Revolution in the Iberian Atlantic.* Princeton, 2006.
Adorno, Rolena. *The Polemics of Possession in Spanish American Narrative.* New Haven, 2007.
Alencastro, Luiz Felipe de. *O trato dos viventes: formacão do Brasil no Atlântico Sul, séculos XVI e XVII.* São Paulo, 2000.
Andrews, George Reid. *Afro-Latin America, 1800–2000.* New York, 2004.
Barrett, Ward J. *The Sugar Hacienda of the Marqueses del Valle.* Minneapolis, 1970.
Berbel, Márcia, Rafael Marquese, and Tâmis Parron. *Escravidão e política: Brasil e Cuba, 1790–1850.* São Paulo, 2010.
Bergad, Laird. *The Comparative Histories of Slavery in Brazil, Cuba, and the United States.* Cambridge, 2007.
———. *Cuban Rural Society in the Nineteenth Century: The Social and Economic History of Monoculture in Matanzas.* Princeton, 1990.
Bergad, Laird, Fe Iglesias García, and María del Carmen Barcia. *The Cuban Slave Market, 1790–1880.* Cambridge, 1995.
Berlin, Ira. *Many Thousands Gone: The First Two Centuries of Slavery in North America.* Cambridge, MA, 1998.
Bernard, Carmen. *Negros esclavos y libres en las ciudades hispanoamericanas.* Madrid, 2001.
Blackburn, Robin. *American Crucible: Slavery, Emancipation, and Human Rights.* London, 2011.
———. *The Making of New World Slavery: From the Baroque to the Modern, 1492–1800.* London, 1997.
———. *The Overthrow of Colonial Slavery, 1776–1848.* London, 1988.
Blanchard, Peter. *Under the Flags of Freedom: Slave Soldiers and the Wars of Independence in Spanish South America.* Pittsburgh, 2008.
Bowser, Frederick. *The African Slave in Colonial Peru, 1524–1650.* Stanford, 1974.
Brown, Christopher Leslie. *Moral Capital: Foundations of British Abolitionism.* Chapel Hill, 2006.
Childs, Matt. *The 1812 Aponte Rebellion and the Struggle against Atlantic Slavery.* Chapel Hill, 2006.
Corwin, Arthur S. *Spain and the Abolition of Cuban Slavery, 1817-1886.* Austin, 1967.
Cowling, Camillia. "'As a Slave and as a Mother': Women and the Abolition of Slavery in Havana and Rio de Janeiro." *Social History* 36 (August 2011): 294–311.

Cubano Iguina, Astrid. "Freedom in the Making: The Slaves of Hacienda La Esperanza, Manatí, Puerto Rico, on the Eve of Abolition, 1868–1876." *Social History* 36 (August 2011): 280–293.
Curtin, Philip D. *The Atlantic Slave Trade: A Census.* Madison, 1969.
———. *The Rise and Fall of the Plantation Complex: Essays in Atlantic History.* Cambridge, 1990.
Davis, David Brion. *The Problem of Slavery in the Age of Revolution, 1770–1823.* Ithaca, 1975.
———. *The Problem of Slavery in Western Culture.* New York, 1966.
De la Fuente, Alejandro, ed. "Su 'único derecho': los esclavos y la ley." Special issue of *Debate y perspectivas: cuadernos de historia y ciencias sociales* no. 4 (2004).
De la Fuente, Alejandro, with César García del Pino, and Bernardo Iglesias Delgado. *Havana and the Atlantic in the Sixteenth Century.* Chapel Hill, 2008.
Delgado i Ribas, Josep M. *Dinámicas imperiales: España, América y Europa en el cambio institucional del sistema colonial español, 1650–1796.* Barcelona, 2007.
Díaz, María Elena. *The Virgin, the King, and the Royal Slaves of El Cobre: Negotiating Freedom in Colonial Cuba, 1670–1780.* Stanford, 2000.
Domínguez Ortiz, Antonio. "La esclavitud en Castilla en la Edad Moderna." *Estudios de historia social de España* II (1952): 369–428.
Drescher, Seymour. *Abolition: A History of Slavery and Antislavery.* Cambridge, 2009.
———. *Capitalism and Antislavery: British Mobilization in Comparative Perspective.* New York, 1987.
Drescher, Seymour, and Christine Bolt, eds. *Anti-slavery, Religion, and Reform: Essays in Memory of Roger Anstey.* Folkestone, 1980.
Dubois, Laurent. *Avengers of the New World: The Story of the Haitian Revolution.* Cambridge, MA, 2004.
Dunn, Richard. *Sugar and Slaves: The Rise of the Planter Class in the English West Indies, 1624-1713.* Foreword Gary Nash. Chapel Hill, 2000.
Eltis, David. *Economic Growth and the Ending of the Transatlantic Slave Trade.* New York, 1987.
Eltis, David, and David Richardson, eds. *Atlas of the Transatlantic Slave Trade.* New Haven, 2010.
———. *Extending the Frontiers: Essays on the New Transatlantic Slave Trade Database.* New Haven, 2008.
Fernández-Armesto, Felipe. *Before Columbus: Exploration and Colonization from the Mediterranean to the Atlantic, 1229–1492.* Philadelphia, 1987.
Ferrer, Ada. *Insurgent Cuba: Race, Nation, and Revolution, 1868–1898.* Chapel Hill, 1999.
Fisher, John Robert, Allan J. Kuethe, and Anthony MacFarlane, eds. *Reform and Insurrection in Bourbon New Granada and Peru.* Baton Rouge, 1990.
Fradera, Josep M. *Colonias para después de un imperio.* Barcelona, 2005.
———. *Gobernar colonias.* Barcelona, 1999.
———. "La participació catalana en el tràfic d'esclaus (1789–1845)." *Recerques* no. 16 (1984): 119–139.
Franco, José Luciano. *Comercio clandestino de esclavos.* Havana, 1980.

Garavaglia, Juan Carlos. *Les hommes de la Pampa: une histoire agraire de la campagne de Buenos Aires (1700–1830)*. Paris, 2000.
Garcia Balañà, Albert. *La fabriació de la fàbrica: treball i política a la Catalunya cotonera, 1784–1874*. Barcelona, 2004.
García Martínez, Orlando. *Esclavitud y colonización en Cienfuegos, 1819–1879*. Cienfuegos, Cuba, 2008.
Garrigus, John D. *Before Haiti: Race and Citizenship in French Saint-Domingue*. New York, 2006.
Geggus, David Patrick, ed. *The Impact of the Haitian Revolution in the Atlantic World*. Columbia, 2001.
Geggus, David Patrick, and Norman Fiering, eds. *The World of the Haitian Revolution*. Bloomington, 2009.
González-Ripoll, Ma. Dolores, and Izaskun Álvarez Cuartero, eds. *Francisco Arango y la invención de la Cuba azucarera*. Salamanca, 2010.
González-Ripoll, Ma. Dolores, Consuelo Naranjo, Ada Ferrer, Gloria García, and Josef Opartny. *El rumor de Haití en Cuba: Temor, raza y rebeldía, 1789–1844*. Madrid, 2004.
Inikori, Joseph E., and Stanley L. Engerman, eds. *The Atlantic Slave Trade: Effects on Economies, Societies, and Peoples in Africa, the Americas, and Europe*. Durham, 1992.
Izard, Miquel. *El miedo a la revolución: la lucha por la libertad en Venezuela (1777–1830)*. Madrid, 1979.
Johnson, Lyman. "Manumission in Colonial Buenos Aires, 1776–1810." *Hispanic American Historical Review* 59 (May 1979): 258–279.
King, James Ferguson. "The Latin-American Republics and the Suppression of the Slave Trade." *Hispanic American Historical Review* 24 (August 1944): 387–411.
Klein, Herbert S. *The Atlantic Slave Trade*. 2nd ed. Cambridge, 2010.
Klein, Herbert S., and Ben Vinson III. *African Slavery in Latin America and the Caribbean*. 2nd ed. New York, 2007.
Knight, Franklin. *Slave Society in Cuba during the Nineteenth Century*. Madison, 1970.
Landers, Jane. *Black Society in Spanish Florida*. Urbana, 1999.
Lane, Kris. *Quito 1599: City and Country in Transition*. Albuquerque, 2002.
Maluquer de Motes, Jordi. "La burgesia catalana i l'esclavitud colonial: modes de producció i pràctica política." *Recerques* no. 3 (1974): 83–136.
Marques, João Pedro. *The Sounds of Silence: Nineteenth-Century Portugal and the Abolition of the Slave Trade*. Trans., Richard Wall. New York, 2006.
Marquese, Rafael de Bivar. *Feitores do corpo, missionários da mente: senhores, letrados e o controle dos escravos nas Américas, 1660–1860*. São Paulo, 2004.
Moreno Fraginals, Manuel. *El ingenio: complejo económico social cubano del azúcar*. 3 vols. Havana, 1978.
Murray, David R. *Odious Commerce: Britain, Spain and the Abolition of the Cuban Slave Trade*. Cambridge, 1980.
Newsom, Linda A., and Susie Minchin. *From Capture to Slavery: The Portuguese Slave Trade to Spanish South America in the Early Seventeenth Century*. Leiden, 2007.

Pagden, Anthony. *The Fall of Natural Man: The American Indian and the Origins of Comparative Ethnography*. Cambridge, 1982.

Palmer, Colin. *Human Cargoes: The British Slave Trade to Spanish America, 1700–1739*. Urbana, 1981.

———. *Slaves of the White God: Blacks in Mexico, 1570–1650*. Cambridge, MA, 1976.

Phillips, William D. *Slavery from Roman Times to the Early Transatlantic Trade*. Minneapolis, 1985.

Price, Richard, ed. *Maroon Societies: Rebel Slave Communities in the Americas*. 3rd ed. Baltimore, 1996.

Rodrigo y Alharilla, Martín. *Indians a Catalunya: capitals cubans en l'economia catalana*. Barcelona, 2007.

Rout, Leslie B. *The African Experience in Spanish America, 1502 to the Present Day*. Cambridge, 1976.

Russell-Wood, A. J. R. "Iberian Expansion and the Issue of Black Slavery: Changing Portuguese Attitudes, 1440–1770." *American Historical Review* 83 (February 1978): 16–42.

Saunders, A. C. de C. M. *A Social History of Black Slaves and Freedmen in Portugal, 1441–1555*. Cambridge, 1982.

Scarano, Francisco. *Sugar and Slavery in Puerto Rico: The Plantation Economy of Ponce, 1800–1850*. Madison, 1984.

Schmidt-Nowara, Christopher. *Empire and Antislavery: Spain, Cuba, and Puerto Rico, 1833–1874*. Pittsburgh, 1999.

———. *Slavery, Freedom, and Abolition in Latin America and the Atlantic World*. Albuquerque, 2011.

Schwartz, Stuart B. *Sugar Plantations in the Formation of Brazilian Society: Bahia, 1550–1835*. Cambridge, 1985.

Schwartz, Stuart B., ed. *Tropical Babylons: Sugar and the Making of the Atlantic World, 1450–1680*. Chapel Hill, 2004.

Scott, Rebecca J. *Degrees of Freedom: Louisiana and Cuba after Slavery*. Cambridge, MA, 2005.

———. *Slave Emancipation in Cuba: The Transition to Free Labor, 1860–1899*. Princeton, 1985.

Scott, Rebecca J., and Jean Hébrard. *Freedom Papers: An Atlantic Odyssey in the Age of Emancipation*. Cambridge, MA, 2012.

Spieler, Miranda Frances. *Empire and Underworld: Captivity in French Guiana*. Cambridge, MA, 2012.

Stein, Stanley J., and Barbara H. Stein. *Apogee of Empire: Spain and New Spain in the Age of Charles III, 1759–1789*. Baltimore, 2003.

———. *Edge of Crisis: War and Trade in the Spanish Atlantic, 1789–1808*. Baltimore, 2009.

———. *Silver, Trade, and War: Spain and America in the Making of Early Modern Europe*. Baltimore, 2000.

Temperley, Howard. *British Antislavery, 1833–1870*. Columbia, 1972.

Thomas, Hugh. *The Slave Trade: The Story of the Atlantic Slave Trade, 1440–1870*. New York, 1997.

Thornton, John K. *Africa and Africans in the Making of the Atlantic World, 1400–1800*. 2nd ed. Cambridge, 1998.

Tomich, Dale. *Through the Prism of Slavery: Capital, Labor, and World Economy.* Lanham, MD, 2004.

———. "The Wealth of Empire: Francisco Arango y Parreño, Political Economy, and the Second Slavery in Cuba." In Christopher Schmidt-Nowara and John Nieto-Phillips, eds. *Interpreting Spanish Colonialism: Empires, Nations, and Legends.* Albuquerque, 2005, 55–85.

Tomich, Dale, and Michael Zeuske, eds. "The Second Slavery: Mass Slavery, World-Economy, and Comparative Micro-Histories." Special issues of *Review: A Journal of the Fernand Braudel Center* XXXI, nos. 2 and 3 (2008).

Verlinden, Charles. *The Beginnings of Modern Colonization: Eleven Essays with an Introduction.* Trans., Yvonne Freccero. Ithaca, 1970.

Vila Vilar, Enriqueta. *Hispanoamérica y el comercio de esclavos.* Seville, 1977.

Walvin, James. *The Zong: A Massacre, the Law and the End of Slavery.* New Haven, 2011.

Weber, David. *Bárbaros: Spaniards and Their Savages in the Age of Enlightenment.* New Haven, 2005.

Zeuske, Michael. *Sklavereien, Emanzipationen und atlantische Weltgeschichte: Essays über Mikrogeschichten, Sklaven, Globalisierungen und Rassismus.* Leipzig, 2002.

Contributors

Luiz Felipe de Alencastro is professor of Brazilian and South Atlantic History at Université de Paris Sorbonne. He is the author of *O trato dos viventes. Formação do Brasil no Atlântico Sul, séculos XVI e XVII* (2000).

Alejandro de la Fuente is the Robert Woods Bliss Professor of Latin American History and Economics as well as professor of African and African American studies at Harvard University. He is the author of *Havana and the Atlantic in the Sixteenth Century* (2008) and of *A Nation for All: Race, Inequality, and Politics in Twentieth-Century Cuba* (2001).

Josep M. Delgado Ribas is professor of history at the Universitat Pompeu Fabra (Barcelona). He is the author of *Dinámicas imperiales (1650–1796). España, América y Europa en el cambio instituticonal del sistema colonial español* (2007).

Seymour Drescher is Distinguished University Professor of history at the University of Pittsburgh. He is the author of *Abolition: A History of Slavery and Antislavery* (2009); republished as *Abolição: uma história da escravidão e do antiescravismo* (2011).

Ada Ferrer is professor of history and Latin American and Caribbean studies at New York University. She is the author of *Insurgent Cuba: Race, Nation, and Revolution, 1868–1898*, which won the 2000 Berkshire Book Prize and appeared in French and Spanish translation in 2010 and 2011, respectively.

Josep M. Fradera is professor of history at the Universitat Pompeu Fabra and an Institució Catalana de Recerca i Estudis Avançats (ICREA) researcher. He is the author of *Colonias para después de un imperio* (2005) and co-editor of *Endless Empire: Spain's Retreat, Europe's Eclipse, America's Decline* (2012).

Juan Carlos Garavaglia is research professor of history at the Universitat Pompeu Fabra and the Institució Catalana de Recerca i Estudis Avançats (ICREA). He is the author of *San Antonio de Areco (1680–1880). Un pueblo de la campaña del Antiguo Régimen a la modernidad argentina* (2009).

Albert Garcia Balañà is professor of history at the Universitat Pompeu Fabra. He is the author of *The Making of the Factory: Work & Politics in Cotton-Making Catalonia (1784–1874)* (2004, in Catalan).

Orlando García Martínez is a historian and the president of UNEAC (Unión Nacional de Escritores y Artistas de Cuba) of the province of Cienfuegos. For many years he was the director of the Archivo Provincial Histórico de Cienfuegos.

Martín Rodrigo y Alharilla is professor of contemporary history at the Universitat Pompeu Fabra. He is the author of *Indians a Catalunya. Capitals Cubans en l'economia catalana* (2007).

Christopher Schmidt-Nowara is professor of history and Prince of Asturias Chair in Spanish Culture & Civilization at Tufts Univeristy. He is the author of *Slavery, Freedom, and Abolition in Latin America and the Atlantic World* (2011).

Michael Zeuske is a historian and senior professor at the University of Cologne (Universität zu Köln). He is the coeditor of *The End of Slavery in Africa and the Americas: A Comparative Approach* (2011).

INDEX

A
abolition
  in British Empire, 147–153, 160–161, 294–300
  in Brazil, 47, 303, 308–311
  in independent Spanish America, 93–98, 301–302
  in Saint-Domingue, 137–147
  in Spanish colonies, 9, 193–196, 276–280, 301, 303, 307–308
abolitionism, 1–12, 134–157, 158–175, 229–255, 276–283, 291–316
  compared, 158–175, 276–279, 291–316
African Institution, 160, 170
Albornoz, Bartolomé de, 4
Alcáçovas, Treaty of, 14, 167
Alexander, George William, 229, 230, 231, 232, 241
Allen, William, 232–234, 236, 237, 239, 240, 243, 244, 245
Anchieta, José de, 45, 53, 54, 57, 62
Angola, 4, 7, 18, 20, 21, 43–67, 209, 215
Aponte rebellion (Cuba), 12n19, 152–153, 276
Antillón, Isidoro de, 168–169, 171, 266–268, 270
Arango y Parreño, Francisco, 8, 137–139, 140, 141, 142, 145, 147, 164–167, 169, 259
Argüelles, Agustín de, 165, 234, 236, 269
asiento, 3–4, 6, 16–35, 53, 60, 264
Azcárate, Nicolás, 123

B
Bachiller y Morales, Antonio, 120, 122–123, 126
Badia, Jaume (or Jaime), 186, 218, 240

Barcelona, 2, 9, 179–188, 193, 194, 195, 201, 211, 229–246, 258, 272, 274, 277, 278
  abolitionism in, 229–246
  and resistance to abolitionism, 193–196
  and slave trade, 176–199
Barreira, Baltazar, 53–62
Bergnes de las Casas, Antonio, 229–233, 237–239, 241, 244–246
Blackburn, Robin, 294
Blanco, Pedro, 188, 198n48, 216, 217, 220
Blanco White, Fernando, 160, 161, 162–164
Blanco White, Joseph, 158–175, 268
Bowring, John, 272
Brandão, Pedro (Bishop), 51–53, 59
Brazil
  abolitionism in, 303–304, 306–311
  independence, 235, 299
  slave trade to, 21, 26, 43–73, 293, 299–300, 301, 302
  and Spanish American slavery, 33, 76, 86, 87, 93, 216, 219
British and Foreign Anti-Slavery Society (BFAS), 229, 230, 231, 232, 243
British and Foreign Bible Society, 243
Brown, Christopher Leslie, 245, 257, 277
Buenos Aires, 76–88, 93–95

C
Cadiz, 8, 14, 20, 22, 23, 25, 28, 31, 159, 165, 166, 182, 183, 188, 191, 206, 240, 263, 265, 266, 267, 268, 269, 270, 271, 272, 274, 275
Canary Islands, 2, 14, 18, 26
Cape Verde, 14, 18, 19, 20, 31, 43, 48, 51, 52, 54, 56, 59, 60, 70n53, 201, 209, 215
Cartagena de Indias, 19, 20, 24, 25, 28, 60

Casa de Contratación, 15, 16, 18, 19, 21
castas, 235, 258–262, 265, 266, 268, 270, 276
Catalonia
    and migration to Cuba, 183–188,
        201–202, 238–240
    and slave trade, 176–199, 206–207, 218,
        219
Charles V (King of Spain), 14, 16, 169
Christophe, Henri (Emperor of Haiti), 145,
    153, 157n41, 161
Cienfuegos, 150–151, 180, 188, 189, 220,
Cinqué, 200, 207, 209, 210, 220
Círculos Hispano Ultramarinos
    Barcelona, 193–195
    Madrid, 194
citizenship, 235, 241, 268, 270, 276, 311
Clarkson, Thomas, 4, 34, 157n41, 173n7, 272
Code noir, 263
Compañía de Filipinas, 32–33
Compañía Gaditana de Negros, 31–32
Comte, Charles, 237–238
Congo, 21, 43–46, 54
Consejo de Administración, 124–126
Constitucional, El (Barcelona newspaper),
    241–243
Constitution of Cadiz (1812), 159, 165, 261,
    268, 275
Coro, 269
Cortes of Cadiz, 8, 162, 165, 261, 263,
    265–270, 271, 272, 304
Council of the Indies (Consejo de Indias),
    6, 19, 21, 22, 37n18, 116, 117, 120, 138,
    169
Cuba
    French refugees in, 137–147
    influence of planter class, 8, 34, 119,
        137–139, 164–169, 258–259, 269–270,
        272–273, 299
    plantation revolution in, 7–9, 134–175,
        259, 270–276, 293
    praetorian rule in, 236, 274–276, 282
    rebellions, 9, 119, 144–145, 152–153, 193,
        276, 281, 307
    slave laws in, 101–133, 166
Curaçao, 21–25

D
Davis, David Brion, 44, 233, 276, 292
Del Monte, Domingo, 186, 218, 237–239,
    240, 241, 281

E
El Español, 159–160, 162, 165
Eltis, David, 3, 14, 149, 177, 276
Espada, Juan José D. De, 240, 272
Espartero, Baldomero, 240–241

F
Ferdinand VII (King of Spain), 159, 169, 232,
    233, 234, 252n52, 270, 273, 274
Fernando Po, 31–32
Ferrer, Celestino, 200, 203, 204, 209, 210, 220
Figueras, Estanislao, 283
Figuerola, Laureano, 246, 283
Flórez Estrada, Álvaro, 270
Floridablanca, Count of, 31–33, 266

G
García, Miguel, 49–53
Garrido, Fernando, 179
Geggus, David, 294
Gener, Tomás, 237–240, 243, 245, 246, 272
Giner de los Ríos, Francisco, 279
gracias al sacar, 260, 263
Grellet, Stephen, 232–234
Guridi Alcocer, José Miguel, 269–270

H
Haitian Revolution, 7, 8, 135, 136, 137–147,
    149, 151, 152, 153, 154, 168, 257, 269,
    294–295
Havana
    Mixed Commission in, 182, 192, 207,
        209, 217
    slave laws in, 104, 112, 113, 114, 116, 118,
        120, 121, 122, 123, 124
    and slave trade, 8, 32, 34, 35, 136–153,
        165, 168, 170, 176, 177, 180, 182,
        183–188, 191, 192, 194, 201–211, 213,
        216–218, 230, 231, 232, 235, 236–238,
        241, 271, 274, 276,
Humboldt, Alexander von, 176, 258–259,
    285n33

I
indentured labor, 280
Indians
    as source of labor in Spanish colonies,
        2–5, 168–169, 258, 261–262, 265–267
    enslaved in Cuba, 280
    in Brazil, 62–67

in Mendoza, 89
Isambert, François, 229, 235

J
Jamaica, 25, 28, 30, 35, 152, 242, 295, 297
Jefferson, Thomas, 267
Juan, Jorge, 258, 266–267

K
Klein, Herbert S., 176, 261

L
La Escalera, Conspiracy of, 119, 245, 276, 281, 305–306
Labra, Rafael María de, 279, 283
Las Casas, Bartolomé de, 2, 4, 160, 166, 167, 171, 174n35
Las Casas, Luis de, 35, 141, 142
Leyes de Indias (Laws of the Indies), 109, 169, 282
Lisbon, 19, 43, 46, 49, 50, 51, 53, 54, 60, 66, 70n53, 201, 235
London, 29, 66, 159, 161, 163, 165, 201, 229–233, 242, 243, 244, 268, 296, 297, 298
López y López, Antonio (Marquis of Comillas), 179–182, 188–190, 192, 193, 194, 195,
Louverture, Toussaint, 135, 143, 144, 145, 153, 164, 168
Luanda, 43, 44, 48, 49, 53, 54, 55, 57, 58, 60, 62, 209, 215

M
Madden, Richard Robert, 229, 230, 232, 238, 241
Madeira, 43
Madrid, 25, 27, 28, 29, 54, 60, 142, 159, 160, 162, 163, 190, 231, 233, 234, 305
  abolitionism in, 8, 168, 229–230, 266–268, 278, 303
  proslavery lobbying in, 137–139, 165, 170, 194–195, 272
manumission, 52, 103, 105, 107, 108, 115, 116, 121, 123, 125, 129n18, 250n41, 263, 278, 308
marronage, 4, 108, 169
Manzanedo, Juan Manuel de (Marquis of Manzanedo, Duke of Santoña), 190, 192, 193,194
Manzano, Juan Francisco, 113, 230, 238, 240, 247n8

Matanzas, 111, 126, 181, 182, 184, 186, 188, 203, 206, 217, 218, 220, 239–240, 245, 246, 272
Mendoza, 88–93, 95–97
Mercado, Tomás de, 4, 167
Mexico/New Spain, 4, 18–19, 22, 26, 165, 258–259, 261–262, 269
Miranda, Francisco de, 269
Moret Law, 278, 283, 303, 307
Moret y Prendergast, Segismundo, 194

N
New Granada, 7, 19, 37n17, 259, 261, 263
New Orleans, 237, 271
New York City, 186, 187, 207, 209, 231, 237, 238, 240
Nóbrega, Manuel da, 45–48

O
O'Donnell, Leopoldo, 245, 275
O'Gavan, Juan Bernardo, 240, 272
Olózaga, Salustiano, 283

P
Palmerston (Lord), 230, 274
Park, Mungo, 161, 162, 164
Pastor, Luis María, 283
Patterson, Orlando, 47, 51
Peru, 3, 25, 26, 28, 33, 37n18, 95, 96, 230, 258, 261, 262, 275
Pezuela, Juan de, 273, 275
Philip II (King of Spain), 16, 17, 19, 54, 58, 59, 69n28
Philippines, 274–276
Pi y Margall, Francisco, 279, 283
plantations, 3–8, 17, 32, 62, 136, 139–142, 144,150–151, 165, 169, 186, 187, 193, 194, 203, 213, 219, 220, 221, 232, 239, 240, 259–264, 274, 276, 279–282, 292, 293, 294, 310, 311
Portobelo, 24, 28
Portugal, 2, 4, 14, 15, 17, 32, 43, 48, 49, 56, 57, 58, 60, 63, 158, 167, 170, 266, 268, 295, 296, 301
  abolition in African colonies, 303, 311
  African slavery in, 51–53, 55
  and early slave trade to Spanish America, 15–22
  and "Portuguese" slave traders, 205, 207, 209, 215–217, 219

Pragmatic Sanction, 260
Prim, Juan, 245
Progressive Party (*Partido Progresista*), 234, 240, 242, 243, 246,
Puerto Rico, 7, 9, 34, 116, 150, 177, 193, 194, 195, 196, 203, 209, 233, 234, 236, 245, 274, 276, 278, 279, 280, 281, 303, 307

Q
Quintana, Manuel José, 268

R
Real Seminario de Nobles, 266–268
Reglamento de Esclavos (1842), 102, 103–104, 118–127
Richardson, David, 13
Río Gallinas, 198n48, 216

S
Saco, José Antonio, 176, 218, 229, 235, 237, 238
Saint-Domingue, 34, 135–147, 154, 168, 237, 257, 269, 294, 295, 297, 299, 305, 306
Salmerón, Nicolás, 279, 283
San Martín, José de, 95–96, 235
Sandoval, Alonso de, 60
São Tomé, 20, 43, 47, 56, 60, 71n61, 201
Sanromá, Joaquin, 246, 278, 283
Schoelcher, Victor, 230, 237, 306
Scoble, John, 229, 235
second slavery (Dale Tomich), 7, 136, 154
September Revolution (Spain), 193–196, 277–278
Seville, 3, 14, 15, 16, 18, 19, 20, 23, 25, 46, 68n16, 159, 160, 162, 201, 252n52
Sierra Leone, 54, 60, 61, 166, 185, 200, 233, 242
Siete Partidas, 109, 110, 112, 114, 116, 120, 131n48
Síndico procurador, 101–102, 105–106, 112–118, 120–126
slave trade (to Spanish colonies)
    abolished, 301–303
    British participation in, 26–31
    coastal trade in Cuba, 202–204, 213, 215
    debated, 13–42, 164–169, 266–270
    Dutch participation in, 21–26
    illegal, 147–153, 176–199, 200–228
    impact of Bourbon reforms on, 30–36
    Portuguese participation in, 15–22, 25–26, 52–53, 207, 217, 219
    profits from, 177–179
    regulation and deregulation of, 13–42, 137–139
    Spanish and Cuban participation in, 31–36, 134–157, 158–175, 176–199, 200–228, 229–255
    transatlantic, 13–42, 147–153, 158–175, 215, 216–217, 218, 220–221
slavery
    beyond the plantation, 1–6, 74–100, 101–133, 261–264
    Catholic Church and, 4, 9, 43–73, 159–161, 171–172, 240, 270, 272, 305, 306, 311
    compared, 1–12, 164–169, 257–264, 292–294
    criticisms of, 4, 8–9, 46, 49–53, 144–146, 152–153, 161–169, 171, 234–236, 239–240, 245–246, 266–269, 276–279
    defended, 53–66, 137–139, 165–166, 193–195, 240–244, 270–276, 279–282
    historiography, 1–12
    and the law, 4, 9, 55, 60, 61, 65, 101–133, 166, 262
    in relation to other forms of labor, 1–12, 74–100, 278–280
Sociedad Abolicionista Española, 246
Société pour l'Abolition de l'Esclavage, 229
Society for the Diffusion of Useful Knowledge, 233
Society of Friends/Quakers, 34, 230, 232, 233, 240, 244, 297
Society of Jesus/Jesuits, 43–73, 91, 99n29, 264, 266
Someruelos, Marquis of, 269

T
Tacón, Miguel, 209, 217, 235, 236, 237, 238
Tannenbaum, Frank, 6, 263, 285n33
Torres i Amat, Fèlix, 233, 267
Trans-Atlantic Slave Trade Database (www.slavevoyages.org), 13–14, 177, 201
Turnbull, David, 119, 230, 241, 242, 245, 278

U
Ulloa, Antonio de, 258, 265–267
Usoz y Río, Luis, 230
Usoz y Río, Santiago, 229, 230

V

Valdés, Gerónimo, 118–119, 123, 273, 275
Varela, Félix, 240, 272
Venezuela, 7, 23, 24, 165, 203, 261, 263, 269
Veracruz, 20, 22, 24, 26, 271
Vieira, Antonio, 54, 59, 63–66, 68n24, 73n97, 73n98, 73n103
Vila, Domingo Maria, 232–237, 239, 243, 245
Vizcarrondo, Julio, 279, 283

W

Wellesley, Henry, 268–270
Wellesley, Richard, 158–160
Wellington, Duke of, 268
Wiffen, Benjamin B., 230, 232
Wilberforce, William, 4, 34, 153, 158–164, 170, 171, 172, 277

Y

Ybarra, José Antonio de, 191–192

Z

Zulueta, Julián (Duke of Álava), 192, 194, 202, 217, 220